ARKANSAS
IN MODERN
AMERICA
SINCE 1930

T0289534

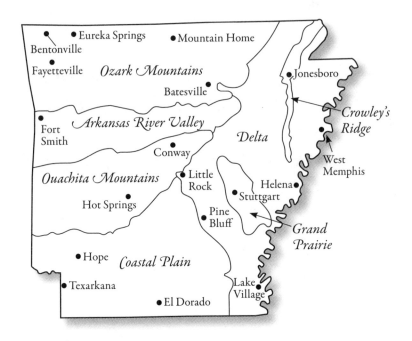

Eureka Springs
Bentonville
Mountain Home
Fayetteville
Ozark Mountains
Batesville
Jonesboro
Crowley's Ridge
Fort Smith
Arkansas River Valley
Delta
West Memphis
Conway
Ouachita Mountains
Little Rock
Helena
Stuttgart
Hot Springs
Pine Bluff
Grand Prairie
Hope
Coastal Plain
Texarkana
Lake Village
El Dorado

ARKANSAS IN MODERN AMERICA SINCE 1930

2nd Edition

Ben F. Johnson III

The University of Arkansas Press | Fayetteville | 2019

Copyright © 2019 by The University of Arkansas Press

All rights reserved

Manufactured in the United States of America

ISBN: 978–1-68226–102–6
eISBN: 978–1-61075–672–3

23 22 21 20 19   5 4 3 2 1

Designer: April Leidig

∞ The paper used in this publication meets the minimum requirements
of the American National Standard for Permanence of Paper for Printed
Library Materials z39.48–1984.

Library of Congress Cataloging-in-Publication Data
Names: Johnson, Ben F., 1953– author.
Title: Arkansas in modern America since 1930 / Ben F. Johnson III.
Description: 2nd edition. | Fayetteville : The University of Arkansas Press,
    [2019] | Includes index. |
Identifiers: LCCN 2019000981 (print) | LCCN 2019002838 (ebook) |
    ISBN 9781610756723 (electronic) | ISBN 9781682261026 |
    ISBN 9781682261026 (pbk. : alk. paper) | ISBN 9781610756723 (eBook)
Subjects: LCSH: Arkansas—History—1865–
Classification: LCC F411 (ebook) | LCC F411 .J64 2019 (print) |
    DDC 976.7/05—dc23
LC record available at https://lccn.loc.gov/2019000981

For Sherrel

In Memory of
Stayton Wood II
Jodie Mahony

Contents

Acknowledgments

Neither the first nor the second editions of this book would have been completed without the generous help and advice from friends and colleagues.

Bettie H. Mahony skillfully edited the initial drafts of the manuscript for both the first and second editions.

Those who offered critical revisions and insightful suggestions for the first edition include Elliott West, Ernest Dumas, Willard Gatewood, Roy Reed, Martha Rimmer, Bill R. Wilson, and Bill Worthen. Robert Brown and Rex Nelson kindly took time to answer my questions about recent developments in the course of preparing this edition.

Those who provided invaluable advice and suggested revisions for the final section of the second edition include Fred Harrison, Uvalde Lindsey, Emon Mahony, Joe David Rice, Bobby Roberts, and Bill R. Wilson. I am also grateful for the comments from the University of Arkansas Press's anonymous reviewers.

These readers deserve credit for the book's strengths, but I must answer for its faults.

I am also in the debt to those who provided suggestions, documents, and favors in the course of my research for either the first or second editions: Charles Bolton, Michael Dabrishus, Holly Hope, Alan Hughes, Steve Jones, Greg Kiser, Carl Moneyhon, Michael Pierce, Linda Pine, Travis Ratermann, Stephen Recken, Wendy Richter, Scott Simon, Keith Sutton, Ed Swaim, Curtis Sykes, Donald Tatman, Becky Thompson, Charles Venus, Ralph Wilcox, Patrick Williams, Steve Wilson, Susan Young, Lee Zachery.

I am profoundly grateful for the assistance of the staff at Special Collections, University of Arkansas, Fayetteville, the staff at Archives and Special Collections, University of Arkansas at Little Rock, and the staff of the Butler Center for Arkansas Studies. At the Magale Library, Southern Arkansas University, Margo Pierson navigated me to relevant sources while Donna McCloy patiently responded to my requests for interlibrary loan materials. I also owe considerable thanks to my former colleagues at the South Arkansas Community College Library: Phillip Arndt, Joyce Adams, and Ellen McGowan.

My current colleagues in the Department of History, Political Science, and Geography at Southern Arkansas University have my deepest appreciation for their collegiality and friendship.

The editors and staff of the University of Arkansas Press have been patient beyond all reasonable measure over the prolonged life of this project.

I received support from the Southern Arkansas University Research Fund, and I am indebted to the generosity of John G. Ragsdale Jr., who has contributed in countless ways to the study and awareness of Arkansas history.

Over the course of many years, Jodie Mahony explained to me how things were done in Arkansas, and his influence permeates this book. Out of my family of long-standing Texans, my cousin Ethel Johnson Wood and I had the good fortune to marry Arkansans. Beyond offering gracious encouragement, Sherrel kept the book on track through incisive editing and ideas that cleared narrative roadblocks.

ARKANSAS
IN MODERN
AMERICA
SINCE 1930

INTRODUCTION

RKANSAS BETWEEN THE grim years of the Great Depression and the advent of a new century moved by fits and starts to become a modern American state. The state's traditional economy and society gave way slowly, and vestiges remained even with the state's integration into the nation.

This edition, like the first published in 2000, is a narrative overview of recent Arkansas history incorporating a range of topics rather than offering a focused argument underpinned by footnotes. A number of themes developed in the previous edition persist in this volume. State politicians, federal officials, and business leaders formed shifting, sometimes uneasy coalitions centered on the assumption that economic modernization required expanded government services untainted by favoritism and graft. The outflow of population from rural sections eroded political localism and gave reformers the opening to build upon federal policies to uproot voter disfranchisement and fraud. The long struggle for racial justice continued after the downfall of official and overt segregation to confront less conspicuous but formidable barriers to opportunity and equity. Observances of the 1957 Little Rock Central High desegregation crisis increasingly became civic debates over whether reconciliation masked enduring burdens weighing on African Americans in the new century.

Even as the daily experiences of Arkansans more closely resembled those of other Americans, writers and promoters of regional folkways cultivated a distinct state identity that echoed a rustic past. Premodern customs that Arkansas boosters and defenders had once derided as backward and stereotypical were respectfully studied and slated for preservation. The Ozark region became the seedbed of Arkansas cultural attributes as well as the location for a line of urban centers that challenged Little Rock's traditional preeminence in the state. Corporations with a global reach underwrote the prosperity of the northwest corner and sharpened the contrast between struggling rural communities and expanding cities.

The Arkansas that Bill Clinton left to begin his presidency in 1993 was far different than the post–World War II state into which he was born. He likely would not have reached the White House if governing a state in which the corrupt politics and narrow economy of that older era had endured. Yet agricultural interests and natural-resource industries retained a greater influence and more economic heft than elsewhere. Small communities withered, sometimes leaving behind only a name on a roadside sign at the edge of a pine plantation. Neighbors were more likely to see one another on weekends at a favorite catfish buffet or barbecue joint than a town square or local hardware store. Arkansas, however, still ranked as one of the most rural in the nation and trailed only Mississippi among the former Confederate states in percentage of residents not living in towns.

The essay on sources at the end of this volume demonstrates the substantial and worthwhile scholarship that has been published since the original edition. The contributions of these works allowed me to fill in gaps and reconsider conclusions. Few historians have a second chance to set matters straight and clear up mistakes. Not wishing to squander the privilege, I set out to rewrite the volume rather than merely update the material. While all sections have been substantially revised, the final one here bears little resemblance to its counterpart in the earlier book. I remain hopeful that the shortcomings and omissions in this edition will inspire others to correct and elaborate.

The "Introduction" in my first attempt to grasp and explain modern Arkansas closed with this observation: "A state is a political entity, but its citizens also come to see themselves as part of a community. The history of Arkansas breathes through the lives of its people." I see no reason to alter that judgment.

DEPRESSION ARKANSAS

A Season Without Rain

ARA WHITE RAGSDALE recalled a childhood in which hard times were traced by burrowing cracks in the dry earth. "Swirling dust boils up from the gravel roadbed, enveloping the trees and hollyhocks. Everything is the same monochromatic tan: people, trees, flowers, and dogs. The choking, gasping heat of South Arkansas fills your throat. Why do I only remember the summertime? Later years and better years have winter, spring, and fall. But for me the summer and Depression are synonymous."

In 1930 the collapse of the international industrial and financial system was a distant echo for Arkansans who grappled with the familiar nemesis of bad weather. That year's prolonged drought shriveled livelihoods, and famine haunted farm homes. Eight out of ten Arkansans lived outside towns with at least 2,500 people, and most rural dwellers worked the land. The rains returned, but falling crop prices thwarted recovery. Already among the poorest states in America, Arkansas hit bottom. Overstrained charities and an empty state treasury left families dependent upon local generosity or their own diminishing resources. Stout loyalty to the Democratic Party had not served Arkansas well during years of Republican ascendency, but the 1932 election of Franklin Delano Roosevelt raised hopes for federal favor.

In 1935 Ragsdale's mother, Mrs. J. Courtney White, worked for a federal relief agency in northern Arkansas. She and her children soon planned to leave the state to join her husband, who had a good job with the Tennessee Valley Authority. Surveying clients who had requested commodity aid, Mrs. White found "people living under bridges, in shacks, crannies and cracks of the White River Valley."

At certain times and places during the Depression, loss and displacement provoked challenges to entrenched interests. Yet political and economic elites quelled, suppressed, and turned aside the demands for fair distribution of federal aid, the unionization of farm tenants, and restoration of voting rights for African Americans. The insurgents' hope for allies in federal agencies turned into disillusionment over the limited reform aspirations of the New Deal. The state government remained insular and corrupt. Not all campaigns to shape the future stirred battles over elections and opportunity. Writers, artists, and academic scholars strove to preserve traditional practices and cultural expressions from corrosive consumerism and entertainment. Folklore collectors and tourism proponents initiated the formation of an Arkansas cultural identity rooted in a richly imagined Ozarks upland.

Daily and persistently, Arkansans bravely grappled with gale-strength forces upending their lives within a system dominated by those intent on riding out the storm.

I. Before the Flood

No single event introduced the Depression to Arkansas. Instead, a series of interlocking crises swept over the state before the 1929 Wall Street crash: cataclysmic natural disasters, plummeting commodity prices, and mounting public debt. These crises battered an economy that had been steadily developing since 1900 on a comparable track with those of other industrializing Southern states. A sprawling web of railroad lines connected growing Arkansas towns. New manufacturing and processing plants raised the hopes of urban business promoters that the state had finally embarked upon economic diversification and market integration. But in the midst of the apparent national prosperity of the 1920s, Arkansas began a long decline that prevented its people from sharing fully in the American abundance.

The state's geographic diversity forged regional specialization within the dominant agricultural economy.

Cotton plantations worked by tenants had become the common arrangement in the Delta, the familiar name for the state's Mississippi River alluvial plain. Between 1880 and 1930, volatile cotton prices, along with the expensive land clearance projects, had doubled the percentage of Arkansas tenants. By the Depression most farmers did not own the land they cultivated. As cotton dropped to nineteen cents a pound by 1929, Arkansas planters ignored the pleas of University of Arkansas agricultural agents and continued to open new tracts for cultivation. A new cotton belt emerged in Oklahoma and Texas, insuring continued oversupply of the commodity.

The university agronomists had promoted rice cultivation in the clay subsoil of the Grand Prairie along the western edge of the Delta. But few cotton farmers were willing or able to invest in the expensive machinery needed for rice operations.

Since the turn of the century, the Springfield Plain at the northwest edge of the Arkansas Ozarks supported a thriving apple and peach agricultural economy that in turn sustained cannery and vinegar plants as well as an apple brandy distillery. By the 1930s, the rise of large commercial fruit farms in parts of the United States with more suitable climates, as well as the codling moth infestation of the Ozark apple trees, made abandoned orchards a more common sight. Cattle and poultry raising had also gained a toehold in Washington and Benton Counties, but extension agents met frustration when attempting to extend this production into the Ozark interior regions.

Distance from markets, thin soil, and inhospitable topography left hill farmers with few options, particularly as the logging jobs that supplemented their incomes dwindled. Many families simply left in the first phase of a general migration from Arkansas that would crest in the 1940s.

The first Arkansas industrial revolution unfolded in the opening decades of the twentieth century, when the number of manufacturing firms grew from 547 to 1,167. Late nineteenth-century industries such as sawmills, coal mines, cottonseed processing, and railroad shops were complemented by new enterprises such as bauxite and zinc mining, automobile manufacturing, and oil refining. But manufacturing employment peaked in 1919 and would not regain the same levels until the World War II era. By the end of the 1920s, only a fifth of the American workforce toiled on farms, but in Arkansas half the workers depended on agriculture.

State leaders did not lose their appetite for new factories. On behalf of the Arkansas Advancement Association, former governor Charles Brough extolled the treasures and productivity of Arkansas on tours throughout the nation during the 1920s. The Arkansas State Chamber of Commerce, founded in 1928, built a network of local chambers dedicated to what became known as economic development; the affiliated Associated Industries of Arkansas was also formed that year to serve as a trade group representing business and manufacturers. The marketing of Arkansas extracted selected data to refute stereotypes of the state as backward, underdeveloped, and risky.

The disfranchisement of African Americans in the 1890s had reduced the Republican Party in the state to irrelevancy and centered political competition within a Democratic Party splintered by local bosses and personal rivalries. The general election contests between Republicans and Democrats were the anti-climaxes to the outcomes of the Democratic primary balloting. Nevertheless, a stagnant one-party system did not shield the state from the new attitudes toward government that were shaping national politics. A rising generation of leaders in Arkansas after 1900 took for granted that the unfolding twentieth-century economy required effective public services, particularly modern schools and good roads. In both cases, the likelihood for significant improvement was unpromising.

One-room schoolhouses survived across the state in thousands of school districts that operated six or fewer months each year. Aspiring schoolteachers gained entry into the profession by passing a county examination rather than completing college or even high school. Tiny districts teetered on a fragile local property base with bare-bones support from the state. Local and state revenue was largely withheld from African American schools that kept the doors open with dollars from northern philanthropic foundations. The Julius Rosenwald Fund, likely responsible for the most extensive school construction program in the Southern states, underwrote the building of nearly four hundred schools for black students throughout Arkansas.

The push for better roads intensified as the first automobiles arrived in Arkansas towns with great fanfare. In 1912 the Carlisle town leaders demonstrated their town's progress to former president William Howard Taft by giving him a car tour of rice fields and modern creameries. Rather than devote state resources to an interconnected transportation system, the Arkansas General Assembly enacted in 1915 a measure that permitted local road improvement districts to issue bonds for highway projects within their own boundaries. Numbering over five hundred by the early 1920s, the overextended road districts fell short of establishing a network of well-maintained, paved roads and were rife with fraud.

The link between reform and economic development was embraced by the small but influential urban business and professional class in the state. This outlook aligned the Arkansas reformers with the Progressive movements that evolved throughout the nation in the decades before the Great Depression. Those who touted consolidation of the multitude of school districts as necessary to achieve an equitable and efficient education system crashed against the engrained tradition of local autonomy.

The good roads movement was more successful. A 1927 law liquidated the woebegone road districts and assumed the $70.5 million in debt they had amassed. The legislature pledged new taxes on gasoline purchases to meet payments on the districts' obligations as well as on new state bonds for future state

highway construction. Elated reformers scarcely emphasized the fiscal consequences. The new debt payments amounted to over half of the annual revenue
of the state.

Rather than adding paved miles, the new road funds were channeled to
reconstruct existing highways and bridges swept away by the Lower Mississippi
Valley flood of 1927. The high waters that covered thirteen percent of the state
cost 127 people their lives. Under the supervision of U.S. commerce secretary
Herbert Hoover, the national government relied upon Red Cross volunteers
to feed and provide tents for refugees. Rather than distribute federal subsidies, Hoover enlisted private businesses to rehabilitate and rebuild devastated
regions. In the aftermath of the flood, he encouraged the formation of credit
corporations that mingled local investment with capital from northern financial institutions to supply loans to farmers. The diminishing class of Arkansas
farm owners, save for the largest, found the new mortgages out of reach in the
face of continued crop price declines.

For Hoover, management of the Mississippi flood devastation confirmed
that federal officials best served the public by coordinating private efforts from
the sidelines. Taking office as president of the United States in 1929, he was confident he could manage future calamities in the same manner. The next natural
disaster to sweep over Arkansas proved him wrong.

II. The Old Politics Survives the New Deal

Many Arkansans who survived the Great Depression insisted in later years that
they barely noticed the hardships that appeared to catch the rest of the nation
by surprise. Evelyn Langley of Guy observed to an interviewer, "We didn't realize we was having it rough, because that was just the way of life." The gauge for
getting by was modest. Charles Whitfield, living outside Bismarck, insisted,
"We always had plenty to eat. We had butter, molasses, bacon."

Nevertheless, things did become worse as the steady descent of commodity
prices throughout the 1920s became an avalanche. The 70 percent drop between
1929 and 1931 sent cotton prices to depths not seen since the 1890s. The collapse
of the cotton market was overshadowed in the memories of Arkansans by the
more familiar and chronic burden of bad weather. Floods and droughts regularly took a toll on the state without garnering national headlines. The Flood of
1927 had been an exception. So was the Drought of 1930.

While dry conditions took hold in the summer of 1930 across Southern and
mid-Atlantic states, Arkansas suffered more than others, with weeks of no precipitation and temperatures steadily above 100. Autumn brought no relief, and

the reach of the catastrophe became not the drama of widespread destruction but the quiet terror of emptying pantries. The notes of a Red Cross worker visiting Delta tenants recorded laconically the minutia of despair: "barefoot and without decent clothes, no meal, no flour in the bin, ragged children crying from hunger . . . nothing but hunger and misery . . . far worse than the Mississippi flood." Another Red Cross agent visited thirty-seven cabins in St. Francis County and found none with coffee or butter and only two with milk.

The ravages of unemployment throughout the rest of the nation overextended the Red Cross, and the national office instructed its twenty-nine chapters in the state to expect no help in tending to their own communities. The local organizations could not feed the estimated two hundred thousand malnourished families but in October distributed turnip seeds, a reliable late-fall crop. Lard, cornbread, and turnips became the famine staples of rural Arkansans. In December the national Red Cross office began to funnel money into the state, but fewer than ten percent of the needy benefited. In early January 1931 the national leadership finally agreed to start large-scale aid after headlines in the *New York Times* gave news of a "food riot" in England, Arkansas.

The scattered seizure of supplies by small crowds in Conway, Fort Smith, and Pine Bluff had generated little notice but the decision by jittery businessmen to distribute free food from England grocery stores to the hundreds of farmers demanding relief struck some observers as a warning shot for future agitation. Governor Harvey Parnell refused to deploy the Arkansas national guard, counting on the Red Cross to ease the tumult with expedited allocation of supplies.

Before shutting down distribution in April 1931, the Red Cross continued to keep the wolf from the door of about one-third of the Arkansas population. Clearly, lives had been saved, but Arkansans discerned the scorn that came with assistance. R. L. Carter of Rich recalled in an interview: "Back in 1930 I remember the Red Cross giving us sacks of beans that had rocks in them. It was just like they had gone out there and piled upon along a rocky place and loaded the rocks, which were the same color as those beans." Evelyn Langley remembered when she and her grade-school classmates were given shoes by the Red Cross in Conway: "The shoes came from an old store that had been down there for no telling how many years. They was old and rotten and didn't last no time. They came all to pieces."

The Red Cross, fearing that charity would undermine self-reliance, linked aid to a work requirement. In eastern Arkansas, plantation owners dominated committees that determined supplies families received. Tenants cleared land

and made improvements on plantations in return for Red Cross staples or for warrants to be redeemed at the landlords' commissaries. In Lincoln County, John I. Smith, director of work projects in his county, used Red Cross funds to pay his tenants $1.50 a day to construct a road from his farm to a new state highway.

Out-of-state reporters sent to cover the England disturbance remained to shadow a national celebrity inspecting the blistered landscape. Will Rogers, a popular radio and movie comedian, had written in his national newspaper column before visiting Arkansas that "you let this country get hungry and they are going to eat, no matter what happens to budgets, income taxes or Wall Street values. Washington mustn't forget who rules when it comes to a showdown." Rogers launched a tour to raise funds for drought victims after President Hoover rebuffed his plea to supply direct government aid to families.

U.S. Senators Joseph T. Robinson and Thaddeus Caraway of Arkansas regarded the drought as a natural catastrophe, much like a flood or windstorm, and advocated limited and short-term federal aid. The president spied danger in even this conservative proposal. He was apprehensive that provisioning rural Arkansans would provoke similar demands from the urban unemployed. Consistent with his policies during the 1927 flood, Hoover offered credit to farmers in order to get crops in the ground rather than food in their stomachs. The senators were unappeased but eventually agreed to a compromise that included loans to landowners to purchase food. This arrangement meant once again that tenant families would only receive staples at the discretion of their landlords.

Drought-stricken Arkansas became a metaphor for anxieties spawned by the Depression. The consequences of Hoover's stand to distance the federal government from the ravages of the drought nourished, albeit unfairly, a popular perspective that he was callous. Readers were moved when Will Rogers wrote that an England, Arkansas, schoolboy explained that his lunch of a cooked turnip and square of cornbread meant his mother would not eat that day.

The plaintive stories from the scorched fields of Arkansas contributed to the 1932 defeat of Hoover by Franklin D. Roosevelt, who became the first Democrat to serve as president since the 1921 departure of Woodrow Wilson.

Hoover's staunch opposition to public aid for the needy was echoed in the speeches of Governor Harvey Parnell in the early days of the Great Depression. The Arkansas chief executive also tracked the Hoover policy by underwriting programs that boosted production and development. Parnell insisted more and better rural roads rather than income support for farmers alleviated market downturns and natural cataclysms. In its 1931 session, the General Assembly ratified the governor's request for another bond proposal for highways, compounding the state's already record-high debt.

Decrepit country schools in the governor's view stymied prosperity as decisively as muddy roads. In 1929 he had overcome urban business opposition to secure passage of an income tax designed to fund rural school consolidation. Parnell's initiatives on behalf of schools and roads were a continuation of the Progressive reform program from the turn of the century. He would be the last Arkansas Progressive. Roosevelt's policies in the 1930s reoriented the liberal agenda in America, and many once-brash reformers joined the ranks of conservative opposition.

Critics of the Parnell highway program emphasized that graft rather than inaction thwarted the extension of paved thoroughfares. They had a point. A 1932 state audit found that highway commissioners and contractors had benefited more from expenditures than had travelers. Most of the U.S. highway mileage in the state remained graveled, and numerous local roads were designated "impassable." At least 11.5 percent of appropriated highway funds since Parnell had taken office in 1928 had been skimmed, including $105,000 siphoned into the personal accounts of the chair of the state highway commission.

As the Arkansas economy nosedived in tandem with national markets, Parnell's reputation slid alongside that of President Hoover. While the governor did not have to look out at shantytowns bearing his name, blame for mounting ills fell on him. When A. B. Bank's American Exchange Trust tumbled, dragging sixty-six other banks in the state into receivership, many recalled how the financier had ladled money into Parnell's 1930 reelection campaign. In 1931 Carl Bailey, the ambitious Pulaski County prosecuting attorney, secured a conviction of Banks for continuing to accept deposits as his institution lurched toward failure. The banker avoided jail when Parnell pardoned him before leaving office.

Rewarding a political supporter was common and expected in Arkansas politics, but business as usual was less tolerable at a time when everything was falling apart.

THE WEAKNESS of state government in comparison to the power enjoyed by county leaders shaped Arkansas political culture. County judges exercised almost unchecked discretion over disbursement of funds, management of road projects, and awarding of contracts. The constitutional guarantee that provided each county, regardless of population, a member in the state House of Representatives meant the interests of growing towns were at the mercy of the rural majority in the Arkansas General Assembly. Local autonomy buttressed landed magnates.

The adoption in 1892 of the poll tax had not only advanced the exclusion of black voters and killed partisan competition but proved an effective tool for the sovereign Democratic Party to ward off unanticipated election results. The adoption by the Democrats in 1906 of rules allowing only whites to cast ballots in their primary elections had largely been greeted as unnecessary by prominent landowners in east Arkansas, the home of the majority of African American residents.

With nearly three-quarters of African American farmers mired in tenancy, local oligarchs perfected techniques of coercion and manipulation to subvert black political independence. County machine bosses and planters purchased stacks of poll taxes and either distributed the tax receipts to tenants to present at polling places or simply "voted" the receipts without going to the trouble of commandeering actual voters. Outside the Delta, local machines paid voters or altered and discarded ballots to assure an agreed upon outcome.

In a 1934 congressional primary contest, around eight hundred more ballots were cast in Yell County than the entire number of voters on the poll tax rolls. Brooks Hays, who lost that election, noted in his memoirs that he was puzzled by the sight of men milling around a polling site. A local supporter made it clear: "They are waiting for the courthouse crowd to send some more money out here for them. The amount passed out to them earlier in the day was less than expected for their votes, so they are waiting."

With rampant election fraud, voter participation through the 1940s fell to one of the lowest levels in the nation, and white Republicans contented themselves with angling for federal patronage jobs. The lack of competition from "post office" Republicans splintered the Democratic Party organization into local fiefdoms. A statewide political establishment did not exist in Arkansas. Ambitious white males could rise in the political ranks if they secured the backing of a sufficient number of key county elites and machines. The alliances of those who controlled the votes that led to candidate success in one election were unstable and could fall apart for reasons that bewildered anyone trying to make sense of the state's politics.

Even the adversity of the early Great Depression inspired no popular, grass-roots insurgency. Vitriolic denouncements of perceived enemies of honest folk were a mainstay in stump speeches, but few Arkansas politicians could bellow louder than the whirlwind that swept across the southern border in the summer of 1932.

U.S. senator Huey Long, whose political machine dominated Louisiana, thought well of the quiet woman from Arkansas who sat next to him in the Senate chamber. Harvey Parnell had appointed Hattie Caraway to the U.S. Senate to replace her husband Thaddeus upon his sudden death in November 1931. Parnell knew he would have alienated a swarm of political kingpins if he had chosen from among several prominent men who hungered for the post. Caraway became the first woman elected to the U.S. Senate following the called special election in January 1932 that attracted no other Democratic challengers. A bevy of contenders were unconcerned though surprised when Caraway filed for reelection in the scheduled August Democratic primary. Her rivals failed to appreciate that her record in the Senate reflected her husband's popular stands and that her years in the maelstrom of Arkansas politics honed her campaign dexterity. Caraway's unprecedented statewide tour with Long shortly before election day sealed her triumph.

Accompanied by two massive sound trucks leapfrogging from community to community, the two senators addressed around two hundred thousand in thirty-seven towns over the course of seven days. Long was the main attraction and ardent listeners urged him to "pour it on" as he excoriated banks and corporations. "We're out here to pull a lot of pot-bellied politicians off a little woman's neck. She voted with you people and your interests in spite of all the pressure Wall Street could bring to bear." He accomplished his aims of returning his friend to the Senate and rehearsing his script for his own anticipated presidential campaign.

Caraway herself credited the votes of women for the amassing of her majorities in sixty-eight of seventy-five counties. During the campaign, leading women in Russellville and Glenwood organized special welcoming ceremonies for Caraway and Long. All of the Mount Ida city officials were women, and they emphasized to Caraway that their recent reelection against an all-male slate signaled that she was correct when asserting that "the time has passed when a woman should be placed in a position and kept here only while someone else is being groomed for the job."

Caraway began her new term in the U.S. Senate as her party assumed majority status after a long hiatus, and as the new Democratic president launched the New Deal initiatives that sent unprecedented sums of federal dollars to states. If she introduced few bills, Caraway shrewdly leveraged her support for Franklin Roosevelt's measures into construction projects and programs for Arkansas communities. For their part, New Deal officials quickly grasped that the woeful conditions prevailing in the state made Arkansas an emergency case even within the ruins of Depression America.

———————————

THE FDR ADMINISTRATION resisted employing battalions of bureaucrats to allot relief to the needy. The New Deal formula was to supply funds to be distributed by state committees and agencies in line with federal regulations to insure accountability. This method required state officials willing to follow the rules and efficient government operations to carry out the relief programs. Arkansas fell short on both counts.

The new Arkansas governor who took office in January 1933 opposed the expanded government actions associated with the New Deal. If Harvey Parnell was the Arkansas Herbert Hoover, J. Marion Futrell was no Franklin Roosevelt. The new governor blamed the state's insolvency on his Progressive predecessors' campaigns for better schools and roads.

Arkansas, with nearly the lowest per capita income, had the highest per capita state government debt in the United States. Much of it was owed to those who had purchased the highway bonds. The crisis in state finances was replicated throughout Arkansas as institutions and organizations hovered at the fiscal brink. Bank failures had swallowed meager school funds, and nearly every district hurried the students out the doors before the school term was finished. Teachers were handed vouchers rather than paychecks.

By 1933 the Arkansas Baptist State Convention had already defaulted on payments to bondholders, and several members of the governing board proposed dissolving the Convention. In the end, the creditors accepted deeply discounted or reduced payments on the obligations, and Baptists flocked to chip in at pay-the-debt rallies across the state. A number of the creditors were individuals who wrote plaintive messages to Convention executives that the lower payments endangered their livelihoods. An elderly preacher explained that he and his blind wife had been counting on the meager bond income since they had become physically unable to tend their small livestock herd.

Those holding the state highway bonds refused to accept the refunding plan approved by the General Assembly in 1933 that lowered interest rates on the obligations from 4 and 6 percent to 3 percent. That rejection led Arkansas to default in August on its scheduled debt payment. The following year Governor Futrell concocted a new proposal that extended the maturity dates on some bonds without lowering interest rates. The state earned a respite from another fiscal embarrassment when creditors approved the scheme. Fitful negotiations did not produce a comprehensive settlement until 1941, when the state reissued a new set of lower-interest bonds. The federal Reconstruction Finance Corporation purchased this entire issue at interest rates that saved Arkansas almost $30 million. This bailout was among the last of a series of New Deal assistance programs that buffered the state during the Depression.

Throughout the debt wrangling, Futrell insisted state taxpayers were left holding the bag for extravagant borrowing that enriched a few without building highways. The governor cut the state budget in half in 1933 on the grounds that the move both freed funds for debt repayment and deprived officials of moneys to misallocate. He rebuffed a general tax increase to meet debt payments out of fear that new revenue only fed corruption. "Our problem," the governor instructed the legislature, "is not how to raise money, but how to get along with much less money." To hobble government over the long term, Futrell drafted two constitutional amendments that the voters overwhelmingly approved in the November 1934 general election. The measures were blunt instruments that failed to establish a budget process, institute oversight to check graft, or fulfill existing financial obligations.

Amendment 19 stipulated that existing taxes could be increased only by a majority of votes in a general referendum or by a three-fourths vote in both chambers of the legislature. The amendment also compelled the General Assembly to muster the same super-majority to pass most appropriation bills. The ability of a small bloc of legislators to defy the majority on taxing and spending set the Arkansas General Assembly apart from other legislatures in the United States.

Under Amendment 20, general obligation bonds required authorization by popular referendum before being issued. Not unexpectedly, state funding for highways languished, and voters did not ratify a bond issue for transportation needs until 1949. Roads were built in Arkansas during the 1930s, but the money came from Washington.

The New Deal in the gloom of 1933 concentrated on relieving hunger and misery for those unable to find work. The Federal Emergency Relief Administration (FERA), headed by Harry Hopkins, set up state organizations to distribute aid. Hopkins deferred to Futrell when the governor insisted upon the appointment of W. R. Dyess, a fellow landowner from Mississippi County, as state director of relief. With his man in charge, Futrell found it easier to tolerate the unprecedented federal presence and reach.

Dyess not only oversaw the distribution of commodities to needy families, often through plantation commissaries, but also decided which communities obtained funds for construction projects under the Civil Works Administration (CWA). By the time this first New Deal public works program closed operations in March 1934, wages and materials for newly built schools, court houses, hospitals, and roads soaked up most of the $11 million in CWA expenditures in Arkansas.

Hopkins shared President Roosevelt's strong preference for work relief initiatives rather than the "dole" or direct government payments to the impoverished. The FERA required that states take responsibility and provide support for the so-called "unemployables," or those unable to work because they were too young, infirm, or disabled. Futrell agreed these destitute individuals should not become wards of the national government, but pinched by the state debt, he diverted federal welfare funds to their aid rather than use state moneys. In addition, the governor placed public school teachers on the FERA rolls. This ploy lowered education spending by 40 percent, and enabled the state to meet its debt payments even as the legislature authorized the forgiveness of delinquent state property taxes. Hopkins gave Arkansas until the regular 1935 session of the General Assembly to stop the misuse of federal assistance.

The legislature in that session approved the formation of the Department of Public Welfare to aid clients not covered by federal payments. The lawmakers, however, could not muster the 75 percent majority to authorize appropriations to fund the program. Hopkins suspended relief funds to Arkansas, and Futrell wailed that food riots were inevitable. With the legislature still in session, the governor reluctantly acknowledged that new revenue offered the only solution. Lawmakers had already rebuffed his plan to save money by ending state support for high schools.

Futrell proposed to allow pari-mutuel betting on dog racing at West Memphis and horse racing at Hot Springs, as well as to repeal the general prohibition bill that the state had enacted twenty years earlier. With the end of national prohibition in 1933, the General Assembly moisturized the state by approving the sale of low-alcohol beer and wine. The 1935 measure made every county in the state wet and imposed an excise tax. Since these taxes on formerly illegal activities did not exist when Amendment 19 was ratified, only a bare majority of legislators needed to vote aye. Yet, even as the General Assembly passed the measures, state officials understood the new money fell short of meeting the requirements to open the FERA spigot.

Futrell detested taxes, but the state's thoroughgoing reliance upon federal subsidies compelled him to raise revenue on a scale not seen since Reconstruction (the income taxes enacted during the Parnell administration generated little return at this point). The governor knew that his Amendment 19 forced him to devise a new levy rather than boost existing taxes. Through furious effort, he steered through a recalcitrant legislature a 2 percent sales tax that exempted most but not all food and medicine. The sales tax provoked a widespread back-lash. Grocery store owners, unwilling to become tax collectors, threatened to ignore the law.

Even though Arkansas still did not fully meet FERA qualifications, Harry Hopkins believed the state was acting in good faith. Manna from Washington fell once more. Hopkins also understood that Arkansas did not have the insti-tutions and expert personnel to operate an efficient welfare system. Throughout the 1930s, the federal government continued to aid a large share of the "unem-ployables" in Arkansas even as it refused to extend the same lenience to other states.

In January 1936 W. R. Dyess was returning from a meeting in Washington with Harry Hopkins when his plane crashed with no survivors. Floyd Sharp, Dyess's deputy, became the new relief czar in the state and deviated little from his predecessor's approach, including solidifying a political affiliation with Futrell.

THE COMPARATIVE TIDAL WAVE of New Deal money and programs altered and expanded the traditional politics that rested on centers of local power. A widely acknowledged "federal faction" emerged, revolving around the powerful and volatile U.S. senator Joseph T. Robinson, who became the major-ity leader when the Democrats took control of the chamber. Robinson's man on the ground in Arkansas was Homer M. Adkins, a former Pulaski County sher-iff and Ku Klux Klan leader during the 1920s. Robinson arranged for Adkins to become the federal commissioner of internal revenue in the state, and Adkins in turn coordinated patronage to satisfy factional allies. A formidable polit-ical machine took shape when Adkins joined forces with Futrell, an alliance sparked by their shared distaste for Carl Bailey, an ambitious rival and reformer.

Bailey's career illustrated how a familiar patron-client system permitted even outsiders to ascend the Arkansas political ladder. As a young lawyer in Augusta, Bailey first attracted the attention of an officer in the Arkansas Cotton Growers Association, who brought him to Little Rock. Bailey then gained the confi-dence of the Pulaski County prosecuting attorney, whom he succeeded in the post. Bailey's prosecution of the widely loathed A. B. Banks earned him head-lines and abetted his 1934 election to the state attorney general's office. Robust and outgoing, Bailey had the essential personal skills required for success in the Arkansas political arena.

Bailey earned greater recognition when he refused a bribe to thwart the extradition to New York of mobster Lucky Luciano, who was on the lam in Hot

Springs. Futrell did not bid for a third term, and Bailey ran for governor in 1936 as a supporter of New Deal government programs. This stance insured fierce opposition from the leaders of the federal faction who oversaw the operation of the New Deal in the state and who were in league with the anti–New Deal incumbent governor. Ideological consistency counted for very little compared to personal connections and feuds in Arkansas political campaigns.

Bailey slipped into office when Futrell and his partners procrastinated until late in the campaign to settle upon a single candidate. The new governor waved aside any cloud over his narrow victory to advance a wide-ranging set of reforms in the 1937 legislative session. Arkansas became the first Southern state to establish a civil service system; the state welfare department was reorganized to distribute federal aid more effectively; a state workers' compensation amendment was submitted to the voters who approved it in 1938; and funds for local school districts were more than doubled with the reenactment of an expanded sales tax that now included levies on groceries and medicine. Clearly, the measure to replace patronage with a limited merit system had the potential to unknot the web of political favoritism.

Those who believed that the character of state politics had been altered by the birth of a little New Deal in Arkansas were soon disappointed. When Joseph T. Robinson's death in July 1937 presented the opportunity for advancement, Bailey displayed the instincts of a political warlord.

The governor leaned on the state party committee to install him as the Democratic nominee for the October special election. The raw grab for power by a politician who had only been elected to statewide office three years earlier cost Bailey the good-government mantle. Fighting for survival, Homer Adkins and the Futrell forces threw together a rump convention to nominate U.S. representative John Miller as an independent candidate. Miller's drubbing of Bailey in the special election embittered the governor, who vowed to adopt the methods of his adversaries. "I know now what we are going to do. We are going to drive a wedge; we are going to get our share of the factions," he confided to a supporter.

Bailey recovered to win reelection as governor in 1938, aided by the federal faction's preoccupation with senator Hattie Caraway's successful rebuff of U.S. representative John L. McClellan's challenge. Settling scores rather than building on accomplishments appeared to preoccupy Bailey during his second term. Bailey made little effort to stop the 1939 legislature from repealing his signature merit appointment law. The reversal of Bailey's earlier enthusiasm for the New Deal sprang from his clashes with adversaries who administered federal programs in Arkansas. He launched a hostile investigation of Floyd Sharp, the federal works project director, and condemned a proposed federal regulation to shield state welfare workers from political pressure. Bailey was unwilling to settle for the customary two terms afforded governors, and Adkins was unwilling to let him stay any longer.

Homer Adkins's easy triumph in the 1940 gubernatorial primary did not inaugurate a harmonious federal-state relationship. The outlook of the former U.S. tax official mirrored that of his predecessors; his enthusiasm for federal funds was matched by his disdain for federal direction on how those funds were to be spent. Adkins's complaints became shriller as Southern segregation became divisive and no longer a settled issue.

White business and political leaders had reached a consensus on the role of African Americans in Arkansas: conspicuous racist brutality and mass assaults threatened the agricultural economy and hampered industrial development. Planters understood their dependence on black sharecropper labor, and urban boosters were sensitive to the pall that lynchings and riots cast over the state's reputation for stability. These leaders also held that segregation preserved racial peace and that exclusion of African Americans from the polls stymied challenges to Democratic Party domination.

Many among the African American urban elite in Arkansas were apprehensive that disturbing the racial status quo risked igniting violence that would takes lives and destroy property. Dr. John Marshall Robinson, a Little Rock physician, shared this perspective, but a horrific lynching in the heart of the city in 1927 persuaded him that the safety of black citizens remained all too fragile. Unlike many of his class, he belonged to the National Association for the Advancement of Colored People (NAACP) and endorsed its judgment that influential whites would not acknowledge African American interests without African American voting rights. Robinson, having pragmatically concluded that black loyalty to the Republicans delivered few benefits in a state controlled by Democrats, formed in 1928 the Arkansas Negro Democratic Association (ANDA).

Shortly after its founding, ANDA filed suit in a Pulaski County chancery court to challenge the constitutionality of the whites-only Democratic primary. The ruling of state judges that the Democratic Party was a private organization that could establish its membership qualifications on any basis, including race, was allowed to stand by the U.S. Supreme Court.

Over a decade later Robinson and ANDA, heartened by favorable federal district court decisions outside of Arkansas, urged selective groups of African Americans to cast ballots in the 1942 Democratic Party primary. Robinson reassured Democratic leaders, "We make no effort for the mass voting of

negroes. . . . We want orderly, liberty loving, loyal negro Democrats to vote."
Governor Adkins was adamant, insisting that the Democrats had the "right to
make their own rules." Scores of black voters in a number of towns in addition
to Little Rock arrived at the polls, where they were turned away.

Other civil rights organizations emerging in the 1940s did not share
Robinson's fears that including working-class participation in a wider move-
ment stiffened white opposition. Nevertheless, Robinson had loosened a rail.
The ANDA-inspired turnout in the 1942 primary revealed that urban African
Americans, unencumbered by rural overlords, were prepared to reshape an exclu-
sionary political culture.

III. Land and Labor

As was true throughout the nation, the triumphs of organized labor in Arkansas
during the pre–World War I era were reversed in the face of 1920s antiunion
drives. By 1904 the United Mine Workers (UMW) organized or gained collective bargaining rights for Arkansas coal miners and extended its influence
by drawing other unions into the newly formed Arkansas State Federation
of Labor. The federation deviated from most other labor groups by enrolling
African American members. The UMW lost public support after a violent 1914
strike incapacitated mines. In 1925 miner owners voided union contracts in a
successful campaign to lower wages, prolong the work day, and impose open
shop practices that allowed mines to hire nonunion workers.

In 1933 national UMW president, John L. Lewis, seized the opening offered
by the passage of the National Industrial Recovery Act (NIRA). Under the act,
industry-wide committees curbed production to inflate prices for goods and
augment wages. A section of the law assured workers of the right to engage in
collective bargaining. In Arkansas, as in the Appalachian coal-mine fields, the
UMW reestablished the closed shop and secured wage increases.

In 1935 Lewis founded the Committee for Industrial Organization (CIO)
after the American Federation of Labor (AFL) failed to take advantage of the
National Labor Relations (Wagner) Act. The new measure outlawed long-
standing union-busting practices and permitted workers to vote on whether
to have their workplace organized. The CIO targeted major industries that had
resisted unionization.

Having regained the upper hand in the western Arkansas coal fields, the
CIO in 1937 moved to organize locals in the diversified manufacturing plants
of Fort Smith. Over five thousand workers were employed in 121 of the city's
factories, which included fourteen furniture plants; three glass works; three

zinc smelters; as well as apparel, cutlery, and cottonseed firms. Within a year, the United Furniture Workers negotiated contracts with a number of Fort Smith plants to emerge as a leading manufacturing union in the state. The CIO locals formed the Arkansas Industrial Council, publishing the *Labor Journal* from Fort Smith as an alternative to the AFL's Little Rock-based *Union Labor Bulletin*.

Before the 1930s, labor organizers had not breached the sawmill industry, which employed the greatest proportion of the state's manufacturing workers. Because sawmills were constructed in the heart of the virgin forests, owners erected company towns to house and supply the workers with provisions and services. Mill owners prodded employees to patronize the company commissary, an additional source of profit. Despite the dangerous jobs and company paternalism, refugees from tenancy as well as failed farmers saw sawmill communities as a promising alternative to the harsh plantation regime. The company's constant monitoring of activities in the town it owned and a largely immobile work force were formidable obstacles for unions.

The lumber industry plummeted along with construction projects sidelined by the Depression. State board feet production dropped 80 percent between 1925 and 1932 while sawmill employment fell by 60 percent. Long regarded with suspicion, the U.S. Forest Service saw its reputation soar with western and northern Arkansas residents. Money was the catalyst. The federal agency purchased swaths of cutover forest tracts as well as exhausted small farms to expand the Ozark and Ouachita National Forests. The Forest Service offered only $1.40 an acre but was swamped by offers from near-bankrupt lumber firms and landowners desperate to unload unprofitable assets.

The advent of the NIRA wage codes lifted mill laborers' incomes to unprecedented levels. The workers' flirtation with prosperity only deepened their resentment in 1935, when the Supreme Court declared the NIRA unconstitutional. Confronted with salary cuts, workers went on strike at West Helena, Warren, and Crossett. None of the actions salvaged former wage scales. In 1938 the Sawmill and Timber Workers Union successfully petitioned the National Labor Relations Board, which had been created by the Wagner Act, to reinstate striking workers dismissed during the Warren strike. By 1940 the union established locals at several sites, including Crossett, Warren, Sheridan, and Malvern, while the United Paperworkers International became the bargaining agent at the Camden and Crossett paper mills.

If New Deal policies opened the door for union organization in the lumber industry, the disruption of the market resulting from rising competition and the jolt of the Great Depression impeded labor activism. Arkansas sawmills were losing the struggle against the more efficient mechanized plants on the Pacific Coast, where forest reserves were abundant. Closed mills in the state deprived workers of bargaining clout. Labor leaders also navigated racial divisions with varying degrees of success. Company proprietors in the Ouachita Mountains timberlands invariably confronted hostility from the largely white communities when they recruited African American labor. In the southern Arkansas pine woods, the biracial mill workforce reflected the population of that region. By the end of the decade, some of the new timber union locals in the lowland piney areas included both black and white members.

In the summer of 1940, a local chapter of the United Brotherhood of Carpenters and Joiners of America failed after a nearly three-month strike at the Crossett Lumber company to win its demands for preferential hiring of union members. The Crossett operations included the paper mill and other smaller manufacturing plants that depended on wood processed by the company's lumber division. The company was the only employer in the town and owned all the property. When the union struck the lumber plant, hundreds of employees at the other operations found themselves involuntarily idled. Labor solidarity faltered when management cut off credit at the company commissary to the families of all workers. Financially anxious residents heeded a young Baptist minister who professed the entire community should not be endangered by the demands of a disgruntled minority.

With their own contract in hand, members of the separate paperworkers' union voted to resume work when nonunion haulers delivered wood to the paper mill. This action prodded a substantial number of lumber workers to cross picket lines to go back on the job. Both white and black workers entered the lumber mill, but whites at a public meeting of union sympathizers charged African Americans were responsible for the floundering strike. Internal strife drove labor leaders to settle the dispute. The new contract provided a small wage increase in lieu of a preferential hiring clause. Occupational and racial divisions had undercut the union and led others in the town to view it as a source of turmoil and instability.

New Deal favoritism and a revived national labor movement reinforced the confidence of state labor organizers that union expansion was the silver lining to the Depression. Yet union members were a fraction of the state's manufacturing labor force, and their occasional victories did not stem the overall drop in wages for factory workers. Even by World War II, the state's per capita income remained shy of the 1929 level. Race decisively configured the income data. Black Arkansans disproportionately labored on farms and earned much less than even the paltry Arkansas average wage.

NEW DEAL INITIATIVES had also buoyed hopes for a new day in the bleached fields of the Delta. But tenant farmers demanding redress met resistance more sweeping and violent than that faced by industrial workers.

The 1933 Agricultural Adjustment Act was the New Deal answer to the chronic overproduction of crops. Attempts by Southern states to organize on their own a general planting moratorium to arrest the sliding cotton market fizzled. The Agricultural Adjustment Administration (AAA) program of payments to withdraw acreage from production began memorably in the spring with the plowing up of about 26 percent of Delta cotton fields. In subsequent years, agreements were hammered out that specified payments for keeping land out of production. The AAA funds slowed the cycle of farm bankruptcies. A 1934 economic survey revealed planters lived well with an 8 percent return on investment and on an income more generous than that enjoyed by any member of the Arkansas professional class. In contrast, prospects darkened for bereft farmers who waited in vain for crop reduction checks that the AAA sent to planters for distribution to their tenants.

In each county, the local agricultural extension agent worked with a committee to adjust allotments and to settle disputes. Tenants knew that filing protests with these officials was both futile and dangerous. One sharecropper wrote AAA officials that tenants did not sit on the committees that considered whether landlords acted fairly: "We cannit get results by replying to thim for they ar crooked the Bunch." The AAA, in line with operations in other New Deal programs, relied upon those within a state to disburse funds to beneficiaries, and national administrators were reluctant to overrule local officials, even those clearly aligned with prominent landowners. In 1934 a survey by the AAA found that 346 of 477 complaints from Arkansas tenants were without merit. The findings were based upon investigations by county extension agents in cooperation with planters.

The endurance of the traditional Delta hierarchies under New Deal programs kindled the founding of the Southern Tenant Farmers' Union (STFU). In 1934 H. L. Mitchell, a dry-cleaning proprietor, and Clay East, a service station owner and town constable, were two young white socialists in Tyronza who formed a short-lived unemployment league to help those excluded from the Civil Works Administration jobs program. The two took steps to address tenant grievances more broadly after Hiram Norcross ousted twenty families from his nearby plantation in order to inflate his AAA payments. In July East and Mitchell joined seven black and eleven white tenants at Sunnyside schoolhouse, on the edge of the Norcross holdings, to form a union that would press for the fair distribution of federal payments and protections for tenants facing eviction.

Participants at this first meeting decided that a biracial union (rather than a segregated organization) would stall the inevitable attempts by planters to incite white hysteria over black activism. Yet, as STFU chapters developed throughout the region, the integration question depended largely on population balance and individual preferences. In Marked Tree, organizers formed separate locals, but the two groups met together in an African American fraternal hall, the largest available building in the community.

In developing their overall strategy, Mitchell and East concluded that white tenants often would pay attention only to white organizers and that black sharecroppers trusted only African American recruiters. A 1937 report documented that only eighteen of fifty-five STFU locals were biracial, and most of those had a clear preponderance of one race or the other. African American members throughout the era suffered more gravely from organized, fierce terrorism than did white unionists. Union branches exercised caution when crossing the color line. In 1934 armed plantation hirelings attacked an STFU meeting, cudgeling and then spiriting an African American union leader off to the Crittenden County jail. The union hired a well-regarded local attorney who advised that only white union members attend the court hearing. After the prisoner was released into the attorney's custody, his white STFU brethren escorted him to a rally on the town square. The union practice of integrated seating at annual conventions prompted its ejection in 1938 from a Little Rock auditorium.

From the outset, the union leadership represented a rich, often contentious, mixture of ideologies: democratic socialism, Christian social reform, communism, and Garveyite Black Nationalism. Yet, the STFU was also a product of its locale. During the organizational phase, sermon-like exhortations and movement songs adapted from familiar hymns roused local gatherings. By consciously appealing to farmers through familiar religious ritual and culture, the STFU also encouraged the involvement of rural women, the mainstays of country churches. Female members invariably managed the records and accounts for union locals.

Although Mitchell later argued that the STFU's interracial gatherings and shared leadership were a prelude to the civil rights campaigns, a 1936 STFU document emphasized class over race as instigating oppression: "Most of the trouble arising between the races is directly rooted in the problem of bread and jobs and economic security. It is not primarily a problem of color." Yet landless blacks did not believe exploitation was color-blind. In 1937 a New Deal agency asked Jefferson County tenants on a survey form to identify which "class of people" were on the bottom rung of the ladder. Most of the whites responded by listing renters or sharecroppers or common laborers. African American tenants replied with "colored" or "colored people."

Conservative opponents feared that union activism would go beyond claiming a fair share of AAA payments to challenging racial discrimination. During a February 1936 visit to a camp of evicted STFU members near Parkin, Governor Marion Futrell had his own suspicions confirmed when an African American farmer described pervasive inequality: "We feel that we are not getting our just dues. We are not getting sufficient schools, we pay taxes and do not get a chance to vote." Futrell in his subsequent address to the group responded with a paternalism rarely directed at poor whites: "You had better listen to the white folks who have always been your friends.... There are people who will get you in trouble if you listen to them."

The white STFU leaders, including Mitchell, Howard Kester, and J. R. Butler, mapped a moderate course of selective strikes, striving to keep at bay more radical left-wing adherents and anti-segregation advocates. E. B. McKinney, an African American preacher and farmer, served as vice president of the union, but his increasing criticism of Mitchell's caution and demands for additional black union officers led to his expulsion.

The union's strikes had mixed results. A September 1935 work stoppage by pickers to force a raise in compensation to one dollar per hundredweight was declared a victory when several landowners raised the rate to 75 cents. The following spring Mitchell announced that cotton choppers would not enter the fields for less than one dollar a day. Since 1934 Delta planters had directed riding bosses and law enforcement officers to attack and arrest union members, but violent assaults grew more numerous and brutal during the strike.

In Crittenden County thirteen black tenants were seized by authorities and imprisoned indefinitely. With a mob on his heels, Sam Bennett fled to Chicago from the same county after quietly greeting with a shotgun an armed planter who approached his cabin. Another black union official escaped to Memphis but his frustrated assailants pistol-whipped a woman who refused to help them. The beating severed her ear. Outsiders were not immune to the official terror. A Pulitzer Prize–winning reporter from St. Louis was held without charges or bail in St. Francis County until her newspaper arranged a release. Though the strike failed, planter reprisals publicized the union's cause.

Distressed by the violence and documentation of peonage in Arkansas, President Roosevelt became increasingly skeptical of the Department of Agriculture's deference to local elites. Governor Futrell was also shaken by the turmoil and by the attention fixed on what visiting journalists were describing as a benighted land almost without parallel in the world. Wary of a pending federal grand jury investigation into peonage and concluding that the tenant system was now a deadweight on the state's economy, Futrell appointed the nation's first tenancy commission.

At the initial commission meeting in Hot Springs on September 21, 1936, the STFU protested the absence of tenant representation and was rewarded with the seating of two of their members. In December the commission issued its final report that characterized tenancy as "a serious menace to American institutions." The report urged the federal government to purchase state lands and offer tenants long-term, low-interest financing to set up their own farms on the reserved parcels. The commission argued the rebirth of the small family farm would furnish "healthy and strong citizens."

———————————

THIS CONSERVATIVE VISION for a stable and traditional agricultural economy was also the ambition of the tenants throughout the Arkansas Delta. A 1936 STFU poll of its rank-and-file members revealed that most respondents aspired to be independent farmers, while only a small number preferred to join a cooperative farming operation. Delegates at subsequent union conventions continued to approve resolutions calling for a national homestead program. STFU leaders such as Mitchell understood the tenants' hope for independence but deemed individual homesteads to be nostalgic anachronisms.

Arkansas planters were beginning to purchase tractors and employ seasonal wage laborers to replace evicted tenant families. Mitchell argued that only cooperative agricultural communities gave small farmers a chance to compete against plantations. In the cooperative operations the former tenants could enjoy the advantages of mechanization, crop diversification, and group purchase contracts. They could also avail themselves of decent schools and medical care without depending upon planter benevolence.

Elements of both the STFU goals and the homestead concept appeared in the 1937 Bankhead-Jones Act, establishing the Farm Security Administration (FSA). Consolidating a number of earlier farm programs, the FSA oversaw rehabilitation loans to farmers, easy credit for better-off tenants to purchase farms, and construction of migratory labor camps. The centerpiece of the legislation in the eyes of the STFU was the community projects section.

In 1934 William Dyess established the first resettlement community in Arkansas, dividing 17,500 acres of cutover timberland in Mississippi County into family plots and platting a complete town. Subsequently, the FSA supervised sixteen resettlement projects throughout the state. The agency established in each project a cooperative association of resident representatives that leased the plots to the homesteaders and maintained the buildings. The associations selected families as "clients" to join the projects based upon a set of criteria that required farming experience and favored families with fewer than six children. Larger families would be cramped in the new, white, frame houses of three to five bedrooms that boasted electric lights and running water. After a five-year trial period, families could acquire their farms through a forty-year payment schedule. Three resettlement communities included only African American residents, while elsewhere white and black families lived in segregated sections of the same project.

While critics accused the FSA of setting up communist-style farm collectives, the agency's aim was to foster widespread farm ownership among the rural poor. Before hostile Congressional conservatives dismantled the agency in 1946, the resettlement communities sustained thousands of Southern farmers at a cost lower than that of direct relief. Yet the FSA did not tame rural poverty in Arkansas or elsewhere. While many of the 1,438 resettled families in Arkansas took possession of their parcels and repaid their government loans, they were a fraction of the tenant population.

Since its first clearing, the Arkansas Delta rewarded the comparatively few who, through initiative and ruthlessness, were able to produce a staple crop for the commercial market on a massive scale. The majority in the region were left poor and exploited. The attempt by the FSA to turn small tenancies into small independent farms went against the grain of history as well as the future trajectory of modern agriculture.

By the end of the 1930s, reforms within the AAA sped crop-reduction payments directly to tenants but landlords were already adjusting their handling of labor in a still-fragile economy. Increasingly, cotton was harvested by wage workers and the declining number of tenants were squeezed into smaller parcels that produced meager returns. Lack of opportunity in Depression-era America discouraged displaced tenants from hitting the road, but they shook off Arkansas dust with prosperity's revival in the following decade.

The STFU had amplified the cries from the cotton fields but did not dethrone the plantation economy. Instead, it was the union that collapsed. In 1937 the STFU entered an affiliation with a national CIO farm- and food-workers' union to steady its finances and gain organizers. The merger uncorked simmering ideological and racial tensions. With the blessing of the national union, the communists within the STFU in 1939 undertook to oust liberal socialists such as H. L. Mitchell and J. R. Butler, who countered by reclaiming the organization's independence. Most of the African American members stayed with the racially progressive CIO, and a rump STFU held on in two eastern Arkansas counties.

EVEN BEFORE 1939 white communists and black union leaders in the STFU cultivated allies and an institutional base at Commonwealth College. In 1925 its socialist founders moved Commonwealth from Louisiana to a lush valley near Mena, where the students built classrooms and vigorously discussed politics and economics. During the Depression, the students, or Commoners, left campus to aid strikes and campaign for Socialist Party candidates. In January 1935 the STFU gained reinforcements from Commonwealth to assist sharecroppers appealing AAA decisions. Commonwealth's role on behalf of the STFU caught the attention of the Arkansas legislature.

During February hearings by a House investigation committee, college opponents denounced Commonwealth's labor radicalism but ardently pursued rumors of atheism and free love. The final committee report in March 1935 concluded that even though the college did not espouse violent revolution, authorities should keep a "close check" on its endeavors. After 1936 the radicalism of new leaders at the school prodded Commoners such as Orval Faubus from Madison County to leave the institution while attracting Little Rock native Lee Hays, who directed the theater program and galvanized students with his rendering of familiar hymns into labor anthems. The burly Hays soon also left Commonwealth to advance the labor cause on a national stage with Pete Seeger in the Almanac Singers, a folk revival group that sang about a better world to come. The local prosecuting attorney believed Mena would be better off without Commonwealth College and in 1940 seized the buildings in lieu of a fine for anarchy and sedition. By that time, the STFU had broken with the college during the fracturing of the leftist movement in the state.

The profound agricultural crisis sweeping the land during the Great Depression sparked what proved to be the final agrarian insurgency in Arkansas. The Southern Tenant Farmers' Union pioneered interracial cooperation to aid impoverished black and white farmers. Future Arkansas biracial movements would be devoted primarily to securing citizenship equality and opportunity for African Americans, and these groups were often urban and middle-class. The STFU's notable achievement was to develop a model democratic movement shaped by ideological engagement and by the vital culture of the dispossessed tenants. A stream of memoirs and histories insured that the model remained an inspiration.

IV. The Quest for Tradition and Identity

In 1930 two professors of history, David Y. Thomas and J. H. Atkinson, attempted to revive the Arkansas Historical Association, which had been supplanted by the 1905 creation of the state history commission. Their eventual success in 1941 reveals that Arkansans in the 1930s began to develop the outlines of a state identity. A force for change in politics and the economy, the federal government was also a catalyst in the construction of an Arkansas culture. Through innovative public rituals and pageants the Roosevelt administration promoted a popular awareness of the past to counter the anxieties of an insecure present.

The Farm Security Administration's encouragement of the independent farm owners was only one example of New Deal romanticism for a lost world of self-sufficiency and plain living. In Arkansas, as elsewhere in the South, the agricultural extension service agents distributed "Live at Home" bulletins. These pamphlets advised that those who kept a dairy cow and hens while also planting a vegetable garden and orchard could survive the rise and fall of crop prices. The Civil Works Administration, Federal Emergency Relief Administration, and other agencies subsidized the construction of over a thousand canning centers in Arkansas to preserve the harvest of family gardens as well as to offer employment.

Taking for granted wives' control of household accounts and home production, the extension service often placed women as canning-center supervisors. Female Home Demonstration agents introduced rural wives to appliances and offered careful instruction on how to serve healthy meals from what foods were on hand. The Home Demonstration program had been established by the same 1912 federal act that created the Extension Service, and it, too, found its responsibilities widened during the Depression. Evelyn Langely recalled how these agents were seen almost as missionaries of modernization: "The first thing that came into the community that helped a lot was a woman who was kind of knowledgeable about all things. The county furnished her with a pressure cooker and she'd go from place to place and help the women can their stuff."

Just as gender governed the roles and the clients for the male extension agents and the home demonstration agents, segregation boundaries guided African American agents exclusively to black farm families. In 1936 an African American and a white home demonstration agent founded the State Council of Home Demonstration Clubs. This primarily black organization welcomed those not admitted to the all-white Arkansas Council of Home Demonstration Clubs, founded seven years earlier. The State Council assisted the demonstration clubs already in place in black communities and extended the network into new locales.

In some communities the encouragement of rural women to apply their domestic skills to entrepreneurial ends disrupted the consumer and labor market. In northwest Arkansas the public canning program competed with the commercial canning operations that employed young women to process local fruits and vegetables. Washington County canning-factory owners needed a ready supply of female workers willing to accept low wages. In 1933 these firms refused to pay more than two-thirds of the wage scale set by the National Recovery Administration on the grounds that their workers were not breadwinners for their families. By 1935 the commercial owners forced the closing of the local canning center. Thirty women produced clothing for welfare recipients at a federally supported sewing center in Fayetteville. It survived only until the arrival of commercial textile plants. The city of Fayetteville provided the building for the sewing operations but in 1940 evicted the women to offer the site rent-free to a private company.

A growing proportion of the fruit and vegetable production in the Ozarks originated in small, five-to-twenty-acre plots cultivated by new "back-to-the-land" farmers. Between 1929 and 1932 nearly 184,000 displaced and unemployed persons throughout the state returned to family parcels or rented sufficient acreage for subsistence. Some back-to-the-landers thought the breakdown of the industrial economy was an opportunity for utopian experiments. In 1931 a group of out-of-work professionals and technicians homesteaded a cooperative farm on public land south of Eureka Springs. The organizers established a forum to determine group policy, distributed family titles for ten-to-fifty-acre sections, and agreed to assume mutual responsibility for the ill and injured. The neo-homestead ventures faded as the New Deal began its own program to prop up small farms.

AS WERE MANY OTHERS, Charlie May and Howard Simon in 1934 were preparing to return to New York City, after spending three years at their cabin dubbed "Possum Trot." They had found that the beauty and silence in upland Perry County could not sustain a viable career for Howard as an artist and Charlie May as a writer. In May 1934 they entertained the state's best-known literary figure as one of their final visitors at the rustic cabin, which had rare amenities such as running water. John Gould Fletcher had fled Little Rock for London before World War I to seek recognition as a leader of the modern poetry vanguard in the company of fellow expatriates Ezra Pound and

T. S. Eliot. Suffering from intensifying bouts of depression and a declining literary reputation, Fletcher had only recently repatriated when he made the expedition to Possum Trot. As had the more romantic back-to-the-landers, the urbane Fletcher thought authenticity and meaning could be more readily found in the backwoods than among the madding crowds of cosmopolitan centers.

When Fletcher won the 1939 Pulitzer Prize for poetry, many Arkansans took pride that their state was reaching cultural parity with its neighbors. Privately, Fletcher was restless with the lack of publishing outlets and an energetic literary community. Yet he stayed because his new wife would not live elsewhere. Unhappy in New York with Howard, Charlie May Simon had continued to correspond with the fierce older poet whose visit had impressed her. Following her divorce, Charlie May in 1936 married Fletcher in Little Rock, where they would spend much of the rest of their lives. Throughout the following decade, Fletcher continued to set many of his most fully realized poems in rural Arkansas and eventually published the finest popular history of the state.

In 1935 the urbane Fletcher eagerly accepted an invitation to lecture at radical Commonwealth College, indulging his fascination with people much unlike himself. During the trip to Mena he visited a small cabin on the outskirts of the town to hear a blind singer who seemed to know all the forgotten songs. Others followed Fletcher, and the recordings of Emma Dusenbury's remarkable repertoire of folk ballads were eventually preserved in the Library of Congress. Fletcher was an earnest if diffident amateur collector, but he conferred frequently with Vance Randolph, whose books became the fountainhead of Ozark folklore studies.

Mountain folk culture had been almost exclusively associated with the slopes and valleys of Appalachia since the early twentieth century. Devoted to keeping the hill peoples as they were imagined to be, middle-class preservationists organized folk festivals, ballad-singing clubs, and handicraft guilds to counter the modern viruses of textile mill jobs, popular sheet music and records, and consumer goods. Even so, preservation altered actual traditions and retained aspects of folk culture compatible with the assumptions of the well-meaning conservators.

With the Depression, reformers no longer saw the fundamental Appalachia problem as modernization threatening a way of life but poverty blighting the lives of mountain folk. As it waned in Appalachia, the preservation campaign emerged in the Ozarks. Vance Randolph, seeking to call attention to a place absent from the mental maps of most Americans, presented the region in his groundbreaking 1931 volume, *The Ozarks: An American Survival of Primitive Society*, as the frontier cousin of the more familiar Appalachia.

Randolph was not an Ozark native, but his own experiences made him sensitive to the obscurity of his adopted home. He had left Columbia University before earning a doctorate, when famed anthropologist Franz Boas rebuffed his proposed study of the Ozarks. Randolph underwrote his folktale collecting through popular articles and genre writing before finally tapping into the New Deal's program of cultural revival. During the 1940s he toted recording equipment supplied by the Library of Congress to cabin porches. The 1947 publication of *Ozark Superstitions* finally earned Randolph academic recognition and a measure of financial independence. He moved to Eureka Springs, a declining Victorian spa that drew a clique of writers celebrating a bygone culture that they claimed was not quite gone.

Randolph treated the rural Ozarkers as both neighbors and subjects, a balancing act that kept him from either rehabilitating or romanticizing them. He reacted harshly to business and town leaders who feared that preoccupation with folk culture perpetuated a hillbilly stereotype that impaired economic ambitions and regional self-respect. Randolph noted the town fathers failed to take into account the widespread nostalgia for the archaic. A 1934 Ozark folk festival in Eureka Springs prompted Randolph to emphasize the profit in the premodern: "The professional Ozark boosters would do well to put more of this primitive stuff into their advertising, and not talk so much about our splendid highways and excellent new hotels. . . . [Tourists] come to see rugged mountain scenery and quaint log cabins and picturesque rail fences and romantic-looking mountaineers." The crass peddling of ersatz goods at the Eureka Springs festival disgusted Randolph, who understood the devil's bargain in tying Ozark folk expression to tourism.

Randolph collected songs and tales primarily for the archives. Through his efforts the ancestral expressions survived in books and libraries even as they faded from contemporary memory. Randolph was not blind to the forces churning Ozark communities. Not only the growing stream of out-migrants but New Deal crop-reduction policies sped the shift from semi-subsistence farms to raising cattle and poultry for the national market. Ozarkers were clearly in the world. Eventually, they also found ways to reward the outsiders' search for the quaint and picturesque.

The folk reclamation project launched by the Ozark salon of writers and propagandists in residence at Eureka Springs did not unfold in a vacuum. Their efforts paralleled the New Deal initiatives to encourage self-sufficiency through developing the commercial potential in traditional crafts, particularly those identified with women. Sewing and quilting were collaborative activities easily overseen by federal workers, who promoted the products as distinctive alternatives to uniform factory goods. In addition, federal resources subsidized not only Randolph but others offering to document through various mediums the latent history of land and people. Commissioned by the Works Progress Administration, Louis Freund captured in his paintings the region's vernacular architecture from cabins to mills. Freund and his wife Elsie soon started an artists' cooperative in Eureka Springs. The objective of the cultural New Deal in the Ozarks was to prolong a way of life upended by the economic New Deal.

Through the continued evangelism of those such as Otto Ernest Rayburn, whose magazine, *Rayburn's Ozark Guide*, informed tourists from 1943 until 1960 where to find both premodern abodes and comfortable hotels, the preservationist vision prevailed. Life in the Ozarks, the image promoted through marketing and literature, was bucolic, unpretentious, and straightforward. Newcomers came to the region with their minds made up. In the mid-1950s a recent migrant exulted about what she found: "A race, a people, quite different from most. Unimpressed by riches, unafraid of poverty, serene, not humble and not proud." Brooks Blevins has authoritatively observed that the romantic Ozarks image arose as forces unleashed by depression and war pushed the region closer to the modern American experience.

THOSE CONSTRUCTING THE IDEA of a common hill culture emphasized the homogenous population that was at various times described as the "white tribe" or "Anglo-Saxon." Indeed, the interior and overwhelmingly rural Ozark counties were entirely or almost completely white after 1930, when the preservationists expanded the pursuit of elusive folk expressions. That was not, however, the ways things had always been. The African American population throughout the region at the beginning of the Depression was thirty-one thousand, about half of what it had been before the Civil War. The folk songs, prized by collectors who were always on the lookout for vestiges of Elizabethan elements, swerved from the Appalachia model due to African American musical influences, including the introduction of the six-string guitar. In contrast to the later white outflow, black Ozarkers migrated during the era of lynchings and ravaging mobs in the early twentieth century to locales offering comparative safety, if not always opportunity.

Since statehood, published travelers' accounts, popular literature, and even cartoons and jokes had fostered a preoccupation with the state's reputation by middle- and upper-class town-dwellers. Observers depicted Arkansas broadly, uplands and lowlands alike, as a backwoods environment defying modern development. The Ozarks heritage movement, buttressed by New Deal cultural uplift, refurbished what had been embarrassing hillbilly stereotypes into affirmative qualities of independence and plain living. The focus of pride and attention on Ozark culture linked the state's cultural identity with that of the upland region. Promotional publications and artistic renderings of the black-majority Delta were rarer. Writers within the state later portrayed the authentic "Arkansawyer" in terms that dovetailed with the revisionist tribute to the unvarnished white hill-dweller. Those Arkansans striving for respectability and consumer comforts were judged to be misguided souls detached from their roots.

Popular entertainment in the 1930s also introduced national audiences to Arkansas as a mountain state. In contrast to the earlier rube cliché on exhibit in mass publications, Arkansans this time were the ones shaping the perceptions of the state.

In 1931 two Mena residents, Chester Lauck and Norris Goff, signed a contract with NBC to go national with a comedy program that had earned an enthusiastic Hot Springs radio audience. Lauck and Goff were the creators of Lum Edwards and Abner Peabody, proprietors of the Jot 'Em Down Store in Pine Ridge, based on the Ouachita Mountain community of Waters. *Lum and Abner* continued on the air for twenty-four years, and the homespun storekeepers appeared in seven RKO movies. A 1936 audience poll identified the program as among the nation's most popular comedy shows.

Another Arkansas native who translated a radio career into movie roles was Bob Burns from Van Buren. He first appeared in 1934 on Bing Crosby's *Kraft Music Hall* and later began a run until 1947 with his own show, *The Arkansas Traveler*, on CBS. Burns had evolved from a joke-telling comedian in his early career to spinning tales that introduced listeners to Uncle Fud and Aunt Dooley. The stories depended upon familiar stereotypes to earn a laugh but also to earn the appreciation of rural families by shunning outlandish farces and ridicule. Burns's signature was playing the bazooka, a homemade musical instrument made from leftover plumbing parts. The device, the namesake for the World War II weapon, implied Arkansans were too poor to afford a proper horn but ingenious enough to improvise.

Arkansans embraced Lum and Abner while the reaction to Burns was mixed. A 1936 advertisement in a state newspaper contained a drawing of two businessmen commiserating, "All those stories that Bob Burns tells on Bing Crosby aren't true." On the other hand, Burns was honored that year with a parade in Little Rock that included state notables such as senator Joseph T. Robinson and Harvey Couch, the powerful utility magnate. Burns had just made his movie debut, and the parade exploited his rising celebrity to rouse national interest and tourist visits during the year-long observance of the Arkansas centennial.

Couch chaired the central committee that coordinated the multitude of local pageants, dramas, and fairs that made this first memorialization of the state's history truly statewide. The distribution of two centennial coins by the U.S. Mint as well as the issuing of an Arkansas stamp by the post office raised funds that were supplemented by private donations. The legislature, however, made no appropriations. The *Arkansas Gazette*, rather than a public organization, commissioned John Gould Fletcher to pen a lengthy verse narrative that encompassed the Arkansas epic from the Hernando de Soto expedition to the Civil War.

In 1936 Texas was also celebrating its secession from Mexico. Couch and state leaders seized every opportunity to deflect attention from the western neighbor, a rivalry that produced in December a clear victory when the University of Arkansas football team defeated in Little Rock the Longhorns of the University of Texas. In April the public relations effort claimed another triumph when the town of Waters was officially rechristened Pine Ridge on a national radio broadcast from the state capitol. The name change was to accommodate visitors disappointed at not finding the home for Lum and Abner's general store. The revision of a community's historic identity in favor of tourism demonstrated state boosters' budding sophistication in marketing the past.

The observance of the state's birth culminated with a visit to Hot Springs and Little Rock in June by Eleanor and Franklin Roosevelt. In the capital the president delivered a speech at a newly constructed amphitheater on the old fair grounds; in contrast to the Texas centennial exposition in Dallas, "Roosevelt Stadium" in Little Rock was built to last only for the occasion. While touring Hot Springs earlier, the First Couple viewed a five-minute school pageant depicting the state's history, visited with one hundred flag-waving orphan children at Our Lady of Charity Convent, and lunched at Harvey Couch's estate. Earlier, the president's secretary informed STFU leaders that Roosevelt's tight schedule precluded a meeting with a union delegation.

NEW DEAL AGENCIES not only altered the view of many in the state toward history and tradition but revealed the natural environment could yield benefits beyond harvesting trees and cultivating crops. The emphasis upon the inherent qualities of relaxation and retreat in a preserved outdoors was familiar in modern America but novel to Arkansans who associated vacation destinations with upland spa centers.

Organized in 1933, the Arkansas district office of the Civilian Conservation Corps (CCC) at one point oversaw up to seventy-seven camps in throughout the state, with around two hundred unemployed young men living five to a tent at each temporary site. The proportion of Arkansans in the state's camps was greater than it was elsewhere in the nation. The CCC in Arkansas fostered rational management of the state's most plentiful resource through planting nearly twenty million seedlings, constructing 133 fire watchtowers, and devoting 167,227 enrollee days battling forest fires. In an episode similar to the conflict over FERA funding, the CCC officials refused to set up camps in the woodlands until the legislature provided funds to support the newly created state forestry commission. The General Assembly refused, but Governor Futrell raised the moneys through private donations.

The CCC not only advanced forest conservation but launched the design of natural spaces for visitors' leisure and aesthetic pleasure. Before 1933 Arkansas had three neglected sites designated as state parks—Petit Jean, Mt. Nebo, and Arkansas Post—but no park system. Prodded by federal officials, the state established a parks commission to acquire land and seek technical expertise from the National Park Service. After the CCC workers developed a park and constructed visitor facilities, the agency transferred operations to the state commission. The state generally did not appropriate money for purchasing acreage for future parks; rather it seized tax-forfeited property, as in the case of Devil's Den Park, or depended upon donated parcels, as was done with the Lake Catherine park. The CCC also introduced a broader conception of conservation through the construction of the White River Migratory Waterfowl Refuge on ninety-five thousand acres spanning four Delta counties.

The CCC based its park building designs upon Adirondack resort models that reflected the New Deal esteem of tradition over contemporary. The lodges, cabins, and pavilions blended into the wooded environment to offer visitors the sense of escape from modern troubles while at the same time furnishing conveniences foreign to many Arkansas rural homes. The native stone and timber buildings demanded a matchless level of craftsmanship and skill that the CCC enlistees would generally find unneeded in the post-Depression economy.

Arkansas towns vied with one another for the location of CCC camps in their vicinities. Local contractors would bid for camp construction, merchants looked forward to selling supplies, and cafe and movie theater owners relished the spending allowances of CCC boys on weekend furloughs. Mena officials estimated their nearby camp infused about $5,000 a month into the town economy. Municipal rivalry, however, dissolved over the prospect of hosting African American camps. The New Dealers appeased powerful Southern congressmen by creating a dual CCC camp system, although Arkansas officials still refused to assign more than a handful of young black men to CCC projects. Leaders in Warren deplored a plan to locate an African American company in place of a white one, and Hamburg relinquished the opportunity for a camp designed to house black enrollees. Eventually African American companies were stationed at Crossett, Strong, Charlotte, DeWitt, and Forrest City.

The presence of the state's black higher education institution in Pine Bluff encouraged the location in the city of one of only five National Youth Administration (NYA) camps in the nation for young black women. Named for Mary McLeod Bethune, the director of the NYA Negro Division, the camp not only provided classes in the liberal arts and vocational training but also gave the students a taste of outdoor life and organized lectures emphasizing individual self-worth. Supervised by Hattie Rutherford Watson, whose husband was the president of Agricultural, Mechanical and Normal College, Camp Bethune closed in 1938 after two years in operation.

———————

ANOTHER SOURCE FOR WORK as well as for the promotion of historical identity was the Works Progress Administration (WPA). Enacted in 1935, the wide-ranging federal jobs program enrolled over thirty thousand Arkansans by the end of the first year. The state was the first in the South to place every eligible woman, 75 percent of whom were assigned to the 123 sewing projects. Before its 1943 liquidation, the WPA sponsored over three thousand construction projects in Arkansas, including bridge and road construction, schools and municipal buildings, and parks and public auditoriums. The WPA in tandem with the Public Works Administration, which provided grants to a number of communities for modern water and sewage systems, laid the foundation for the state's modern infrastructure.

The WPA also funded 138 non-construction ventures, notably the Federal Writers' Project (FWP). The state director of the writers' program was Bernie Babcock, whose 1919 novel, *The Soul of Ann Rutledge*, had earned a national audience entranced by the brief life of the reputed first love of Abraham Lincoln. In 1936 the national FWP director approved Babcock's proposal to compile a black Arkansas history volume as long as African American writers were employed on the project. Babcock argued that no Arkansas blacks on relief were qualified for the task and offered to write the book herself. The national office held firm. Under the auspices of the Little Rock Urban League, six African American researchers collected data later compiled by J. Harvey

Kerns and Samuel S. Taylor to complete *The Social and Economic Life of the Negro in Greater Little Rock* (1941).

Babcock did hire Taylor of Little Rock and Parnella Anderson in El Dorado, who was also African American, along with sixteen white women and two white men to collect accounts by elderly survivors of their experiences as slaves. The 800 interviews with black Arkansans composed the largest portion of the total 2,194 transcripts conducted as part of the overall FWP collection of slave narratives. Taylor's notable interviews were distinguished by their vivid rendering of treatment and work conditions and freedom from the mangled dialect infecting the transcripts of white collectors.

While the oral histories of slavery disappeared for decades into archival shadows, the WPA's valuable *Arkansas: A Guide to the State* found a place on the shelves of the state's libraries. The brief treatment of antebellum Arkansas and the Civil War in the *Guide* largely slighted the homages to aristocratic planters and heroic generals found in the approved state histories sponsored by the United Daughters of the Confederacy since the early twentieth century. Nevertheless, if the white FWP authors of the *Guide* dampened the condescension toward Ozarkers, paternalism haunted their treatment of black Arkansans. The "folklore" chapter in the *Guide* argued that African American culture derived from slave owners: "Customs formerly thought to be of African origin often turned out to be Anglo-Saxon."

A fuller African American history bloomed within the walls of the three-story Paul Laurence Dunbar high school. Dedicated in 1930, the school's "beauty, and modernity, and size" fulfilled the hopes of its community. In 1935 the composer Florence Price returned to her native Little Rock to present a benefit concert of her compositions at the Dunbar auditorium. Both Price and William Grant Still, who was also educated in Little Rock public schools, pioneered the integration of African American vernacular music—folk blues, spirituals, jazz—into the symphonic form. Two years earlier, the Chicago Symphony was the first major orchestra to play the work of an African American female composer when it performed Price's Symphony in E Minor. That same year an Carnegie Hall audience heard the New York Philharmonic perform Still's *Afro-American Symphony.* In 1931 this landmark composition became the first by an African American composer to be performed by a major symphony when the Rochester Philharmonic presented it.

Another notable Dunbar visitor was the historian Carter G. Woodson, founder of the Association for the Study of Negro Life and History. In 1936 Gwendolyn McConico Floyd, a Dunbar teacher educated at Fisk University, began offering what was probably the first black-history class in a southern urban high school. Woodson knew that the popular course used his *The Negro in Our History* as the textbook, and his unannounced visit during a 1938 trip to the state attracted a roomful of students to hear his two hour presentation. Floyd recalled that the historical studies clarified for her students that the familiar acts of discrimination they daily experienced were manifestations of a system of exploitation rather than an embedded social tradition. According to Floyd, the students saw that "[African Americans] were being manipulated; that there were certain jobs we could not get; that we lived in an isolated society."

Although the writers' project did expand the range and diversity of historical topics, determined cultural agents also secured federal subsidies to preserve those vestiges of the Arkansas past that assimilated the state into a heroic American saga.

A descendent of the last Arkansas territorial governor, Louise Loughborough had long brooded that the late nineteenth-century Little Rock red-light district had disfigured a hallowed city block. By 1938 the city was preparing to raze the derelict site. Loughborough, a member of the Mt. Vernon Ladies Association, knew that several endangered structures dated from the territorial period and set out to save remnants of Arkansas's brave origins. Relying on incomplete sources, she declared that the founding fathers of Arkansas had not only lived on but forged a government on that very block. She persuaded the legislature to create what became the state's first history museum, entreated prominent families to donate money, and pressed the state WPA administrator to fund the restoration of the ramshackle buildings. Completed in 1941, the Arkansas Territorial Restoration jumbled characteristics of colonial British America as well as of frontier Arkansas. No reminders of the old brothels survived.

V. When Electricity Came to Arkansas

The largest picnic recorded in Arkansas was celebrated not at a camp meeting nor political rally, but at an Arkansas Power and Light Company (AP&L) stockholders gathering. On July 24, 1930, the families of small shareholders had journeyed from throughout the state to the building site of the utility's second of three planned hydroelectric projects. Congregating in the shadow of the unfinished Carpenter Dam near Hot Springs, the three thousand people were entertained by the AP&L orchestra while being served barbecue from long, custom-made tables. The company officers awarded electrical appliances as prizes to families with the oldest, youngest, and most stockowners.

The gathering conveyed that Arkansas could march into a brilliant modern era without dislodging the personal relationships that anchored rural heritage.

The company was inseparable from the personality and outlook of Harvey Couch, its founder and president. Couch was the first "big man" of twentieth-century Arkansas. Speaking to the stockholders that day, Couch noted that sixteen years earlier the state's only transmission line extended twenty-two miles between Arkadelphia and Malvern, whereas three thousand miles of lines currently electrified most of the towns and cities. Couch did not need to remind his audience that he was responsible for the first Arkansas radio broadcast station or that his company was a major retailer of radio sets. Arkansans were accustomed to accepting nature's devastation, but Couch's hydroelectric projects, beginning with the 1924 Remmel Dam completion, seemed to transform natural forces into agents of prosperity. Little wonder that Couch was placed in charge of state emergency operations during the 1927 flood and again during the crisis of the 1930 drought.

His prestige grew not simply from his reputation as the conductor of technological wonders but from his campaigns to expand the state's industrial and manufacturing sector. Couch reasoned his utility would stagnate without new industrial customers and a growing population of workers. Acknowledging the state's reliance on agriculture, he believed that Arkansas modernization required the encouragement of small industries that could process raw materials into finished goods.

Depending on New York financial firms before his 1926 merger with the giant Electric Bond and Share Company, Couch had struggled throughout his career from lack of local investment credit. Rather than seek the relocation of large-scale manufacturing firms to the state, Couch pursued outside capital to underwrite homegrown operations. Arranging motorcycle police escorts, Couch transported financiers across bumpy roads to Couchwood, his sprawling log-house retreat on Lake Catherine. He believed the rustic and verdant setting best advertised the state's capacity for development.

Couch specifically touted the potential for poultry- and egg-processing plants to create a market for farmers willing to wire their homes for hatcheries and chicken houses. The principle obstacle to this type of diversification, however, was the prohibitive cost to extend power lines to scattered houses in rural corners. With a highly dispersed population, Arkansas largely went dark when the sun set. No more than 3 percent of farms had electric lights, and oil lamps shone from the windows of many small town homes. Before late 1934, neither AP&L nor the other four major electric companies doing business in Arkansas developed alternatives to mitigate the $1500 per mile cost of erecting electric poles along country roads.

The establishment in 1933 of the Tennessee Valley Authority (TVA) just across the Mississippi River and the entrance of the federal government into the power market apparently inspired the private utilities' fresh consideration of the problem of rural electrification.

Couch adamantly opposed public or government power generation and distribution but was eager for an infusion of federal dollars. He had served as a director for the Reconstruction Finance Corporation, created by the Hoover administration to fight the Depression through low-cost business loans, and wanted his old agency to underwrite AP&L's rural electrification costs. Couch's proposed financing structure was part of an overall plan that obligated farmers who wanted lights to work on AP&L construction crews, and that encouraged families to purchase appliances from the utility through an installment schedule. On another front, Couch blocked TVA from stringing transmission lines into his dominion when he negotiated with the public utility to purchase power that was, in turn, transmitted to AP&L customers over AP&L lines. He did not, however, win all the battles.

The 1936 legislation that made the Rural Electrification Administration (REA) an independent agency favored federal loans to rural cooperatives over subsidies to private concerns such as AP&L. Couch adjusted his strategy to secure government financing. He proposed that REA loans to the cooperatives in Arkansas be passed through to AP&L. Couch was foiled by a formidable agricultural coalition headed by the Farm Bureau and the university agricultural extension service. Years of utility reluctance to string wire to distant farms had heightened rancor. REA advocate and future congressman Clyde Ellis recalled that John Hobbs of Rudy had unsuccessfully implored the utility to extend a nearby line to his house for the comfort of his desperately ill wife. Hobbs "used to get so angry and frustrated talking about the power company that tears would stream down his face."

By the end of 1937 the Farm Bureau incorporated seven electrical cooperatives, whose customers paid a five-dollar annual membership fee. The fee was a formidable hurdle for indigent farmers in the state, prompting the federal government to permit installment payments for both it and minimum electrical usage. The practice was extended to other southern states and dubbed the "Arkansas Plan." The cooperatives did not have to construct costly generating plants after governor Carl Bailey's appointees in the state utilities department ordered AP&L to sell electricity to the coops at wholesale rates. The electrical cooperatives multiplied while the cold war with AP&L continued through the 1950s.

Rural electrification was in the long run the most consequential legacy of the New Deal in Arkansas. Ellis remembered one woman's exclaiming, "I just turned on the light and kept looking at pa. It was the first time I'd ever really seen him after dark." Unfortunately, the electric millennium flickered beyond the reach of most farmer families for another decade. By the end of the 1930s transmission lines extended to only 8 percent of Arkansas farms.

Radios preceded electricity into rural Arkansas and alleviated the enduring isolation that marked life outside of town. In nearly 40 percent of farm homes, families could listen to *Lum and Abner* and Bob Burns, although apparently on antiquated battery models. Louise Bryant reminisced that her family had to take their Zenith set to town every three weeks to recharge the battery. James Thompson's grandfather conserved the battery on his radio by listening to only one weekly program. His neighbors without sets gathered to hear the Grand Ole Opry on Saturday nights: "My granddad would let the radio play for an hour and then he would say, 'Folks the show's over!' and would turn it off until the next Saturday night."

The 1950 census was the first to disclose that a majority of rural Arkansas homes had electric power. Home Demonstration and Cooperative Extension agents trailed the incursion of electric poles into vanishing backwoods, introducing families to appliances that had been standard in American homes for decades. The Drew County demonstration agent in the mid-1950s observed, "Many housewives do not use labor-saving equipment to the best advantage in saving time and energy."

According to the experts, farm homes required renovation for families to take full advantage of modern wonders. The Howard County agent in 1954 reported that the demonstration program must continue to emphasize "remodeled homes with more storage space for clothing, household articles, etc." The prosperity that followed the electrification of the farm dwelling was measured by closets stacked with consumer goods. The university agents were continuing to adhere to their original mission to keep families on the farm by closing the gap in amenities and convenience between rural and urban life.

FLOOD, DROUGHT, AND DEPRESSION did not drive Arkansans off the land. During the 1930s the rural proportion of the population fell by only two percentage points. Since the beginning of the century Arkansans in increasing numbers had left the state, but the total pulling up stakes in the Depression was only three-quarters of those who had taken their leave in the 1920s. The Depression did not launch a grand exodus of Arkansas travelers bound for the golden West.

The most significant population shift in the 1930s was the almost 25 percent decline statewide in tenant farmer numbers and the accompanying reduction in the number of black farmers living in the Delta counties. Trucks carrying hundreds of laborers to the Delta farms at harvest time became a familiar sight on the Mississippi River Bridge at Memphis. Escalating investment in the Delta by national insurance companies may have accelerated the shift to a hired work force. Firms such as Prudential acquired large parcels of mortgaged property. Yet the nearly 60 percent rise in the state's gross farm income between 1933 and 1940 was due more to federal agricultural policies than to new operating efficiencies.

The transformation of Delta agriculture through technology was yet to arrive. Overall, the value of implements and machinery used by the state's farm owners did not noticeably increase from 1930 to 1940, and Arkansas inched only from forty-sixth to forty-fifth when compared to other states. The small one-crop farms worked by muscle and despair weathered the Depression, and their survival remained the bulwark of rural poverty. The remaining tenants plowed and planted larger tracts, the additional acreage surrounding empty cabins where families had once lived. The wavering hope of rising from tenancy to independence had dissolved.

The first stop for many black tenants who left the farm was the sawmill. The percentage of mill workers within the African American labor force rose during the decade from 3.8 to 5.7 percent. Those who moved into urban areas other than mill towns were excluded from the better-paying manufacturing, transportation, and retail occupations. Most black families rented small two- or three-room houses, only one-third of which had electricity and only one-fourth, running water. A city address did not ensure city services.

Black women had always been more likely than white women to work for wages, although during the Depression the rising proportion of white females on the job contrasted with the declining percentage of employed African American women. In general, occupations were linked to both gender and racial identity. Working white women punched the clock as sales clerks, telephone operators, apparel mill operatives, and government employees, whereas black female workers were more often domestic servants and agricultural workers. Women of both races held the majority of public-school teaching posts.

In *I Know Why the Caged Bird Sings*, Maya Angelou portrayed the authority and influence of two women in Stamps's black community: her grandmother, the owner of a bustling general store with a steady clientele, and Beulah Flowers, the aristocratic and influential literature teacher. Flowers's husband, Alonzo, had managed his savings from his job as a timekeeper at the local sawmill to become an insurance agent and to build an undertaking parlor. While Mrs. Annie Henderson instructed her granddaughter on how to retain purpose and dignity while negotiating the treacherous shores of segregation, Mrs. Flowers demonstrated how language both liberated the spirit and nourished the appetite for distant, better worlds.

The dreams for ambitious African Americans in 1930s Arkansas were best pursued elsewhere. William Harold Flowers, the son of the Stamps couple, left in 1937 to study law in Washington, D.C. Unlike many, he returned, setting up his practice in Pine Bluff, prepared to confront discrimination and racial brutality.

Harold Flowers grew impatient with the inaction of the older black leadership in the state. In March 1940 he established the Committee on Negro Organizations at a meeting of two hundred people at the Buchanan Baptist Church in Stamps. Flowers expressed the vision of a new generation when he declared that the state's first mass civil rights organization would "revolutionize the thinking of the people of Arkansas." This bold confidence, which once would have been reckless and misplaced, was certainly of the moment. The Depression was fading in the gathering wartime boom, and the old order that had gripped the state since Reconstruction was facing unprecedented challenges.

The dry season was ending.

WARTIME ARKANSAS

Eroding Barriers

N 1941, as Vance Randolph was preserving Ozark folks songs on behalf of the Library of Congress, Alan Lomax, a white archivist and collector, and John Work, an African American folklorist, scoured the Mississippi Delta for bluesmen unspoiled by records and radio. While their recordings of Muddy Waters and Son House for the Library gave the impression of echoes of a vanished primitive era, numerous record companies such as Paramount and OKeh had already recorded a bevy of blues musicians through the 1930s. Waters and the others were professionals who knew to keep their juke joint audiences happy by playing a variety of familiar tunes that seeped beyond the preservationists' definitions of the blues.

In Helena, the transformation of rural music toward an urban sound gathered force in the harmonica solos of Sonny Boy Williamson (Rice Miller) and the guitar work of Robert Lockwood Jr., the stepson of the legendary Robert Johnson. Evictions and want had driven black workers to the Mississippi port city for jobs on the docks or in cotton processing plants. The wages in the pockets of new arrivals charged Saturday night with an electricity that never crackled in the countryside's empty spaces. Unlike white taverns centered opposite the levee along Cherry Street, black juke joints flourished in enclaves scattered throughout Helena. The blues performances were background music to the real business of gambling.

Williamson and Lockwood had larger ambitions. When they heard in November 1941 that Sam Anderson was opening Helena's first radio station, they persuaded food distributor Max Moore to sponsor them in exchange for promoting his King Biscuit Flour. Both white businessmen were familiar with the music and knew it had an audience. The King Biscuit Time's fifteen-minute live broadcast each day at noon on KFFA quickly made the two performers celebrities. "Sonny Boy Corn Meal" was soon advertised alongside the flour.

The acoustic blues music prized by Lomax and other collectors was dwindling to historical artifact. Many aspiring musicians throughout the Delta heard their first electric guitar played by Lockwood on KFFA.

By 1947 Lockwood was in West Memphis, where musicians jostled to be heard on station KWEM in hopes the air time would win them gigs in the raucous clubs up and down Seventh and Eighth Streets. In 1950 Lockwood joined the great migration to Chicago, taking his place among an expatriate class of blues aristocrats recording for Chess Records. At Chess the Delta sound flowed into rhythm and blues before Bo Diddley and Chuck Berry navigated it across racial boundaries into rock and roll. Surviving founding fathers like Lockwood hibernated and then resumed their careers in the 1970s when a blues revival commanded a new, largely white audience.

While the small outmigration of Arkansans in the 1930s was disproportionately white, the massive exodus during the 1940s bore away nearly one-third of the state's African American population as well as 20 percent of the whites. The figures revealed little, however, about the experience of those like Robert Lockwood, who moved from rural places to Arkansas towns before leaving for the anticipated promised land. If fewer African Americans lived in Arkansas after the 1940s, the number who came to live in the state's urban areas—defined by the U.S. Census Bureau as places with 2,500 or more residents—grew by one-third.

Both federal policies and federal revenue during World War II catalyzed social tensions and stimulated economic trends. The widespread protests against the construction of Japanese American internment camps in east Arkansas contrasted with the welcoming of prisoners-of-war as a remedy for the shortage of agricultural labor. Arkansas women, as did American women in general, found work in defense plants. Alarms were raised that changes in family life and the crowding of new migrants into Arkansas towns were shredding the moral fabric. In fact, early marriages and frequent divorces were long-term patterns rather than wartime aberrations.

Urbanization enlarged the congregations of the state's major religious denominations while encouraging clergy and lay leaders to define their responsibilities more broadly. No one felt greater anxiety over the shape of postwar Arkansas than Hamilton Moses of Arkansas Power & Light. AP&L organized a statewide industrial recruitment campaign to compensate for the expected loss of jobs from the government's reconversion of its military production sites. By 1950 manufacturing gained a foothold in Arkansas just as the anti-union movement solidified its aims into law. The shift to a more diversified economy unfolded with minor social disruption and did not stem the population outflow. The racial order, on the other hand, buckled. A new generation of civil rights leaders pivoted history in the wake of seismic federal court rulings.

I. Questions of Loyalty

The eruption of World War II in Asia and Europe prompted the same clash of opinion in Arkansas as throughout America. While isolationist voices warned that the conflict was not this nation's fight, influential Arkansans rallied around President Roosevelt, who was steering the nation into open coopera- tion with the besieged Allies. By June 1940 and well before Pearl Harbor, the influential statewide *Arkansas Gazette* was advocating American entry into the war to avert a possible stateside invasion.

In May 1940 governor Carl Bailey rattled the nerves of Arkansans when he ordered the state police to investigate foreign subversion. Patriotic fervor follow- ing the 1941 U.S. war declaration incited harassment of groups already regarded with suspicion. In January 1942 El Dorado Veterans of Foreign Wars members forced from the town a group proselytizing for the Jehovah's Witnesses, a sect whose pacifism and unwillingness to salute the national flag had also prompted assaults during World War I. In September pipeline-construction workers shot and severely beat Witnesses who had journeyed to Little Rock for an annual meeting. Police arrested and charged the victims of the attack with disturbing the peace.

Apprehensions leading to provocations flared in many American places. On the other hand, the construction of camps in the state for conscientious objec- tors, Japanese American internees, and prisoners of war exacerbated tensions over labor and race never far from the surface in Arkansas.

In response to the 1940 Selective Service or draft law, most registered paci- fists agreed to fill non-combat roles in the armed services. Others who held that even indirect support for military operations compromised their prin- ciples were assigned to camps administered by the historic peace churches. The preponderance of the camps were in Southern states, although most of the objectors were transported from outside the region. Beginning in June 1941 the Church of the Brethren supervised up to one hundred men from nine states (only two from Arkansas) at Civilian Public Service (CPS) Camp No. 7, located on a former CCC site near the Third District A&M College in Magnolia. For many conscientious objectors, the journey south was their first encounter with segregation. Harold Zimmerman recalled that he and fellow black and white objectors refused to comply when the conductor ordered them to split up as the train entered Arkansas. As had the CCC teams, the objectors labored on soil conservation projects, but their dam repair, soil recovery, and tree planting benefited private landowners, owing to the absence of national forests or state parks in the vicinity of the camp.

The camp residents also took on charitable tasks such as making toys at Christmas for area children to ease tensions with those in Magnolia who viewed them as unpatriotic slackers. Local animosity persisted. Most in the camp had refused military service on religious grounds but were rebuffed when they attempted to worship at local churches. Both Magnolia residents and objectors recalled that townspeople believed divine justice was at work when an April 1944 tornado destroyed nearly all the camp structures without causing extensive damage elsewhere. Following the storm, the objectors were relocated to other CPS centers.

Few Arkansans knew of the presence of conscientious objectors, but the forced evacuation in 1943 of West Coast Japanese Americans to internment camps at Jerome in Drew County and Rohwer in Desha County ignited official and citizen protest. In the previous year the federal War Relocation Authority (WRA) had designated the two undeveloped Farm Security Administration (FSA) parcels in the Arkansas Delta as among the ten sites to house the U.S. citizens of Japanese ancestry (Nisei) and the Japanese immigrants legally barred from applying for citizenship (Issei). These natives and long-standing resident aliens were singled out for detention because of their small and concentrated numbers, their absence from vital war industries, and their identification in the popular view with a belligerent nation. The rounding up of these families was also a continuation of a long-standing history of racial animosity.

Arkansas governor Homer Adkins demanded the federal government erect sentry towers around the relocation camps' barbed-wire perimeters and post only white guards. Southeastern Arkansas farmers speculated that the California fruit and vegetable growers association had maneuvered the expulsion of formidable competitors, who would now upend Delta landowner and labor arrangements. In 1943 the Arkansas legislature approved almost unanimously a measure prohibiting property ownership by any person of Japanese descent; the state attorney general's opinion that the law was in conflict with the Arkansas constitution left it unenforceable.

Other anti-internee bills introduced during the session originated more specifically in racial frenzy. The Camden author of a measure to deny Asian student enrollment in white public schools explained, "I know none of you gentleman think Negroes are as good as your children, and I don't think any member of the yellow race is as good as my children or yours either." The bill failed, as opponents cited the virtues of Chinese store owners in such towns as Marianna and the fact that China was an American ally invaded by Japanese troops.

Even if state officials drew back from imposing additional exclusionary restrictions upon the newcomers, WRA administrators recognized that internees venturing outside the camps faced more intense discrimination and ill treatment if viewed as a distinctive race. The director at Rohwer was reluctant to approve the departure of women from the camp to take professional positions with African American institutions: "Japanese-American[s] in the Mid-South have been accepted as 'white people.' . . . If we approve Japanese-Americans to teach in colored schools, we may endanger the social standing of any evacuee relocating in the South."

For their part, the internees, as had the conscientious objectors, first witnessed on public transportation instances of the everyday humiliations faced by black Arkansans. A new resident of the Jerome center had been given a pass to travel by bus to McGehee and surrendered his seat near the front when an African American woman boarded the vehicle. The Japanese American recalled being "stunned and bewildered" when the driver forcefully pushed the woman from the seat toward the congested rear. The internee remained in the whites-only section.

The two internment camps in effect became the last federally organized and constructed agricultural communities in Arkansas. Rohwer and Jerome each encompassed over ten thousand acres and together held around sixteen thousand internees at one point. The mandatory labor requirement for all adult Japanese Americans was fulfilled primarily by completing the construction left unfinished by government contractors: repairing residential barracks, clearing acreage, and digging sewage trenches. The families also chopped firewood from the surrounding swamps to heat the tarpapered barracks, while their cultivation of over six hundred acres of vegetable fields in each camp decreased the WRA food expenses. The internees' industriousness did not silence the criticism from surrounding communities that the authorities were "pampering" the camp residents. The 400-square-foot apartments sectioned off in the barracks and filled with furniture constructed by the families did indeed have electricity but, as was so with most rural Arkansas homes, not running water and plumbing.

In all the camps, the internees organized cooperatives to purchase items and offer services not included in government rations. Leasing the WRA buildings, the cooperatives pooled the internees' meager wages to organize barber and beauty shops, shoe- and watch-repair businesses, and clothing and dry-goods outlets. The WRA schools for the two thousand students in each camp were conducted in unfinished barrack spaces that bore little resemblance to classrooms. Although it paid salaries double the average of those in local public schools, the WRA struggled with a shrinking pool of teachers as women shifted to the more lucrative wartime industries. By encouraging well-educated internees to fill critical positions outside Arkansas, the federal agency made it even harder to staff camp schools.

ALL BUT A FEW Japanese American families left Arkansas after the relocation program ended with the November 1945 closure of Rohwer, the last functioning American internment camp. Already in June 1944, the internees had been transferred from Jerome, which was refurbished as the state's third German prisoner-of-war camp. German POWs began entering the state in 1943 after the victorious Allied campaign in North Africa. Eventually four thousand German prisoners were incarcerated at Camp Chaffee outside Fort Smith, while ten thousand were installed at Camp Joseph T. Robinson near North Little Rock. Seven thousand officers and dedicated Nazi enlistees were dispatched to Camp Dermott, the former Jerome center. By the end of 1944, an Italian prisoner contingent of nearly two thousand, composed primarily of officers, was placed at Camp Monticello. Apparently, most Arkansans took little notice of the POWs, many of whom were held within existing military installations. East Arkansas planters, however, spied a new labor pool.

As the war progressed, employers loudly warned about a shortage of workers. Yet Governor Adkins sternly denied requests forwarded to him through the War Relocation Authority to permit Japanese Americans to take jobs outside the camps. On the other hand, Adkins diligently lobbied the federal War Manpower Commission (WMC) and the War Food Administration (WFA) to authorize the use of POWs in the Delta's cotton and grain fields as well as in the timber industry. Under the international Geneva Convention agreement, enlisted POWs, but not officers, could be assigned non-hazardous jobs unrelated to war production.

Uneasy about the effect of the wartime employment boom on their labor force, Delta planters had been rethinking their growing reliance on wage labor and were using a variety of methods to lock tenants into long-term contracts. They were outraged in 1942 when the WMC identified the Delta region as a labor surplus area, a designation that permitted workers to be transported to other agricultural regions when not engaged in planting and harvesting. Furious lobbying by the Farm Bureau and muscle-flexing by Southern congressmen reversed the policy, and friendlier federal administrators imaginatively pin-pointed Lower Mississippi Valley cotton as critical to the war effort. County extension agents effectively barred tenant families from taking advantage of government programs to migrate to higher-wage regions. Local draft boards threatened those who attempted to bolt with immediate call-up for military service.

The planter-friendly labor regulations curbed but did not halt the exodus of labor. In 1944 Arkansas landowners cited the availability of only two-thirds of the workers needed to harvest a crop already damaged by bad weather as justification for employing prisoners of war. The WMC approved the distribution of German prisoners to thirty branch camps in the state, nearly all of which were located in the Delta. Farmers compensated the federal government at the prevailing wage rate, but this provision acted as a ceiling for pay levels that would have otherwise soared.

Unfamiliar with the demands of cotton farming, some Germans resisted the distasteful chores of chopping and picking through slowdowns and sabotage. Edwin Pelz, who had served in the Luftwaffe, was chagrined on his first day in a field outside of Memphis on seeing his fellow prisoners easily meet their 120-pound quota. He soon discovered their advantage: "They put dirt, stones, and anything else they could find into their sacks." Planters agreed that they endured such insubordination because the cotton would have rotted in the fields otherwise. The prisoners observed and were surprised by the exploitation of African Americans, who were expected to pick two to three times the weight required of the Germans.

Following the Allied victory in Europe in May 1945, agricultural employers throughout the South implored the administration of president Harry Truman to delay the return of the prisoners. It would be another year before the last German contingent was delivered from the cotton rows of Arkansas. After the Germans returned home, laborers from northern Mexico under the contract through the federal *bracero* program shouldered their sacks for the 1948 harvest. Around 300,000 workers poured into Delta fields throughout the life of the program, which lasted until 1964. The migrants sustained the cotton economy while posing a fresh set of challenges to a racial system constructed around boundaries between blacks and whites.

Many braceros recoiled when they were assigned squalid sharecropper cabins and decried financial manipulations embedded in the region's traditional labor relations. Many of the new arrivals felt as helpless as previous generations of laborers. Hector Zavaleta recalled that "there was just not the supervision and adequate checking on these farms of how many people they need, how people were being treated . . . which allowed for a lot of abuse of the program." Others, however, notified the Mexican consulate in Memphis and often won concessions that eluded the STFU and African American tenants when they had petitioned the U.S. government for redress. The consul, to the consternation of Arkansas political officials, had the ability to deny landowners access to braceros if complaints about mistreatment proved valid. The threat of blacklisting also pushed major landowners in northeast Arkansas during the 1950s to compel town businesses to exempt the contract laborers from Jim Crow strictures. In Marked Tree, the "No Mexicans" signs were taken from store windows after the town council, succumbing to pressure, levied fines against proprietors who refused to serve Latinos.

As had been the case for advocates of Japanese American internee rights, the defenders of the braceros understood that identifying Mexicans as white offered some relief from discrimination. For African Americans, the contrast sharpened the lesson that whites could adjust the color line without easing the oppression aimed at their community. Claude Kennedy, who grew up on his father's farm near Marianna, discerned the circumstances of bracero laborers: "It was common knowledge that you could use them, but you've got to give them the respect of being equal to a white man. They could go anywhere they wanted to go."

II. Mobilization: Changes at Home and Work

Nearly 200,000 Arkansans, or about 10 percent of the population, served in the armed forces during World War II. That the state's service percentage slightly trailed the national rate owed much to the fact that a greater proportion of Arkansans were rejected for induction than those from any other state except South Carolina. The inability of young Arkansans to meet the Selective Service education requirements and to pass the medical exams was an outgrowth of poorly funded school districts and the scarcity of doctors and nurses to tend the rural population.

Enlisting the civilian population in the war effort, the federal government encouraged the formation of new organizations that closely resembled traditional community institutions. Downtown shop owners in Arkansas entered the American Legion Auxiliary's National Defense Window Contest to encourage customers to purchase war bonds. Searcy's retail district stood out among towns of a similar size. The Jonesboro American Legion granted membership in the "Slap-A-Jap" club to those who pledged a weekly defense stamp purchase. The combination of patriotism and organized competition also bolstered the collection of scrap and discarded waste for recycling as war material. Martha Newsome of Newport was recognized by the Victory Service League for setting a national record when she accumulated 2,600 pairs of women's hose.

In communities located near military installations, chapters of the United Service Organization (USO) and existing women's service clubs organized entertainments, dinners in homes, and concerts to give the personnel the sense that hometown amenities were around the corner. The Searcy Girls' Service League arranged dances at the local American Legion hut for trainees stationed at the Newport Airfield. As in many similar instances, the local youth also benefited from the endeavor because the base supplied the orchestra for the dances.

In Little Rock, the City Recreation Council set up an elaborate downtown center with game areas, classrooms, and reading rooms for white soldiers from Camp Robinson and for workers at the Jacksonville and Maumelle ordinance plants. Another USO club was located in the former Taborian Temple on Ninth Street, the commercial heart of black Little Rock. The Little Rock Council of Jewish Women provided food for Sabbath services at Camp Robinson, and Reform and Orthodox members invited servicemen to their homes for religious holidays. In 1944 USO centers at the internment camps at Jerome and Rohwer were managed by Mary Nakahara and Mary Tsukamoto to welcome Japanese American soldiers who had recently been permitted to enlist, albeit in separate Army units.

BURGEONING MILITARY INSTALLATIONS jolted the economies and tested the infrastructure of nearby towns. The vast Southwestern Proving Grounds, a munitions testing site, boosted Hope's population from 7,475 in 1940 to 15,475 in 1942. Farmers unhappy that their property was swallowed up by the government's six-fold expansion of Camp Robinson into a troop training center did not gain a sympathetic hearing from North Little Rock business and political figures. Eventually housing around 50,000 personnel, Camp Robinson was eclipsed in population within the state only by Little Rock, which itself had added 25,000 people in the last few months of 1940. The development of the 71,115-acre Camp Chaffee, southeast of Fort Smith, also prompted complaints from landowners who were displaced in favor of three armored divisions. Inductees learned to maneuver twenty-eight-ton tanks across former agricultural tracts. The four training fields for Army Air Corps pilots (Blytheville, Walnut Ridge, Newport, Stuttgart) and the one for glider instruction (Lonoke) were situated near small towns in eastern Arkansas, where the weather and open terrain were opportune.

While training camps boosted customers and revenues for existing local businesses, the massive defense build-up that took off in 1940 reoriented the state's industrial recruitment strategy. Governor Carl Bailey in collaboration with the state Chamber of Commerce organized one of the earliest state organizations to compile and forward to Washington lists of available resources for military production. His successor, governor Homer Adkins, sought to overcome engrained localism through the Arkansas Defense Council. This organization urged counties to do their part to bring jobs to the state by determining what type of defense production might be drawn to their communities. Coordinating local efforts to improve statewide prosperity became the foundation of the postwar economic development campaigns, and the war era endeavors launched the emergence of a modern state out of a collection of rural centers.

The $250 million invested by the U.S. government to construct war production facilities in Arkansas was in line with amounts flowing to other states based upon population. During the New Deal, by comparison, the state had absorbed more than its fair share of federal moneys. Nevertheless, the swift expansion of manufacturing resounded in a state that relied upon crops and turning trees into lumber. The defense plants were not widely distributed, and their location near existing urban centers speeded up rural outmigration. In central Arkansas, the Arkansas Ordinance Plant in Jacksonville employed 13,000, while 800 rotated shifts each week at the Maumelle Ordinance Works in Marche to produce explosives. At the southern end of the state, the Ozark Ordnance Works in El Dorado and the Shumaker Naval Ammunition Depot in Camden required tens of thousands of construction workers but only a few hundred permanent employees in the El Dorado plant and around 5,000 in the Camden facility. Ten thousand civilian and 350 military personnel worked at the $60 million Pine Bluff arsenal that stockpiled reinforced units chemical weapons produced on site and at facilities elsewhere in the nation.

The need for another vital defense material allowed Arkansas to fulfill its long-standing ambition to process native raw materials rather than send them elsewhere. The state possessed nearly all the bauxite reserves in a nation that needed aluminum for airplane production on the West Coast. Despite the natural advantage, state political leaders worried that the vast project would not see the light of day because of what the *St. Louis Post-Dispatch* called "probably the country's outstanding fight between private electric utility corporations and public power agencies."

The national Defense Plants Corporation contracted with Aluminum Company of America to build and operate what became the Hurricane Creek mill in Bauxite to refine alumina from bauxite ore and the Jones Mill reduction plant near Malvern to produce the aluminum ingots. Despite the proximity of Lake Catherine, the Arkansas Power and Light hydroelectric dam could not generate sufficient power to run the Jones Mill plant, which required as much wattage as consumed by all the state's residential customers. The federal administrator of the Rural Electrification Association assured the War Production Board (WPB) that it could supply the needed 100,000 kilowatts through its Arkansas and Louisiana electrical cooperatives from a hydroelectric dam in Oklahoma.

To counter this incursion from public power sources, AP&L executives scrambled in 1941 to expand generating capacity by roping other private utilities from the region into the Southwest Power Pool. The elation of the private corporate heads at signing a contract in December to sell power to the planned aluminum mill was short-lived when they learned that the Defense Plants Corporation had earlier come to a similar agreement with the regional cooperatives. The federal agency was unsure that either of the major suppliers could guarantee reliable power on its own.

The state department that oversaw utility regulation attempted late in the process to remove the rural cooperatives from the power-sharing arrangement by refusing to authorize building the transmission line from the Oklahoma dam site. The federal WPB ordered the state agency to stand down. When Jones Mill went online in 1942, the public cooperatives' kilowatt rate was around three-quarters of that charged by the private power pool.

AP&L continued to insist that the federal hydroelectric dams were massive boondoggles competing unfairly with private companies. The company promoted steam-generating plants fueled from the south Arkansas gas fields as economical alternatives. The federal production czars did grant AP&L permission to construct near Stamps such a unit, which eventually transmitted electricity to factories in other states. Yet federal dam construction continued apace. In 1943 Congress authorized the Southwestern Power Administration (SPA) to manage the electricity produced by U.S. Army Corps of Engineer dams in the region, including the Norfork Dam in the White River Basin.

———————

THE SUDDEN POPULATION INFLUX into Arkansas towns and cities set off a housing crisis that persisted throughout the war and forced hopeful job seekers to bed down in warehouses, tents, and wooden sheds. By 1945 the state's federal housing administrator reported that Little Rock was more densely populated than any other Southern city. Before the war, Little Rock had created a housing authority to clear dilapidated buildings. The wartime boom, however, altered the aims of the program, and only military personnel, government workers, and veterans were accepted for residency in the three 1940s public housing projects. Sunset Terrace and Highland Park, the first two completed complexes with a total of 150 apartments, housed white tenants, while the 100 apartments in the Tuxedo Courts were reserved for African American families.

Real estate investors and developers had long exercised great sway in the Little Rock business community, but the combination of a housing shortage and federal dollars enhanced their influence. Wiley Dan Cammack had not persuaded Little Rock to annex tracts he owned before offering them to the U.S. government. The Federal Housing Authority constructed on the parcel three hundred homes with four basic floor plans that were rented only to white families of military officers. Incorporated in 1943, Cammack Village was perched just across the city's northwestern boundary, an outpost signaling the direction of future urban growth. No African American residents appeared on the federal census for the town before 1970, and the village was once again all-white by the end of the century.

The greater share of rural Arkansans in town censuses did not pose a cultural roadblock to the loosening of restrictions on urban pleasures and leisure. Quite the opposite. The workweek for both Camp Robinson soldiers and the ordnance plant workers extended Monday through Saturday, and turned the once-placid Sunday streets into bustling avenues. The ample shopping crowds persuaded Little Rock police officers that enforcing the Sunday closing or blue laws would be futile and troublesome. Yet the consumer demand for convenience was not the only chink in the moral order. Higher wages and newcomers' escape from family strictures widened the cultural distance between town and village.

John Fergus Ryan recalled that on Saturday nights, farmers, plant operators, railroad men and their families promenaded along North Little Rock's Washington Avenue, which was off-limits to those stationed at Camp Robinson. Located along the street were small cafes, each separating black and white patrons with a board partition; groceries selling the pigs' ears and feet that served as a seasoning substitutes for the rationed salt pork; the three movie theaters ranging from the respectable Rialto, "cooled by 'Washed Air' in the summertime," to the shadowy Liberty that ran louche features such as *Nadine, Queen of the Sun Bathers*. The enviable prosperity of those who worked in the Missouri Pacific Railroad Shops was incarnate in their regal bearing and wardrobe: new dark-brown wing tips polished to a brilliant orange hue and exotic hand-painted neckties set off with steel-sprung collar points.

The Delta evacuation swept into east Arkansas towns favored with military installations. Having reveled in the Saturday excursions to Blytheville from his family's tenant farm, a young B. C. Hall welcomed the decision to move to the town's rapidly expanding section of small houses inhabited by other white migrants. This West End district proved an economic transition between two worlds. Hall's father continued to cultivate land he rented near town, but during the off-season the older children hired on at the shirt factory or in a downtown five-and-dime. Living in Blytheville not only meant the luxury of an extra movie on Saturday, but it also presented Hall with new boundaries to be crossed. He formed a close friendship with Sam Lum, whose Chinese parents owned a store on Ash Street, Blytheville's black mercantile and entertainment center. Too young to sidle into the popular Club Frolic, the two boys perched on a side-alley fire escape to hear the blues players and jazzmen who followed the circuit from Kansas City to New Orleans.

THE RAPIDITY OF SOCIAL CHANGES during the war led Arkansans, as it did other Americans, to exaggerate the extent of the changes. Nationwide, both the marriage and childbirth rates escalated by 20 to 25 percent in the first years of the decade; yet both trends resumed pre-Depression patterns. The doubling of the national divorce rate between 1940 and 1946 was consistent with a long-term development but also accelerated by long separations and the inherent awkwardness of homecomings.

While a number of Arkansans saw ill-advised nuptials and rising divorces as evidence of moral decay let loose by the war, these phenomena were abetted by existing state laws. Brides as young as fourteen and grooms of sixteen could get a marriage license without a waiting period or health certificate. The improving economy leading up to World War II enhanced the attractiveness of Arkansas border towns and resort areas for estranged couples. In 1940 Hot Springs recorded 112 divorces by out-of-staters, an unprecedented tally surpassed by the 1941 total of 532. These statistics raised controversy among politicians, clergy, and social workers because they were linked to the other publicly cited ills of youth crime, child abandonment, and a venereal disease epidemic.

For moralists and reformers, teenage pathology was categorized into male juvenile delinquents who committed various property crimes and female "victory girls," or prostitutes, profiting from the boredom and loneliness of soldiers. Youth disorder increased, but it was not a tidal wave of degeneracy. The numbers of juvenile cases filed in Little Rock courts between 1939 and 1942 grew no faster than the city's population.

The efforts by civic reformers, religious leaders, and police authorities to extend community regulation of personal behavior ran aground against old-fashioned Arkansas political localism. The Little Rock city council rebuffed demands to impose a curfew on adolescents as a usurpation of parental control. County clerks and treasurers, delighted with the rising revenue from marriage license fees, vigorously opposed bills introduced in the 1941 legislative session to stem hasty unions. Companion measures to mandate a venereal disease examination before granting couples licenses fell victim to racist demagoguery. The Blytheville state senator asserted that "only Negroes have syphilis," while the Prescott lawmaker declared that requiring a blood test amounted to "an insult of the white women of the state."

As was true in cities and military bases throughout the era, wartime Little Rock offered space and opportunity for same-sex meetings and liaisons. The assembling of young men from throughout the nation into military units encouraged self-recognition by gay soldiers as well as the realization that they were far from alone. Those on leave from Camp Robinson bypassed the lobby in the downtown Grady Manning to head directly to the understood destination in the hotel's basement bar. Military installations and urbanization also altered the purpose of the familiar small-town drag productions that were often staged by churches and schools to raise donations. The shows in which men appeared as women became urban entertainments, playing to wider audiences. In 1942 Harvey Goodwin, an Arkansan who began his career as a female impersonator in New York, performed before a large crowd of plant workers at the Arkansas Ordnance Plant.

Hardening of attitudes and growing intolerance following World War II compelled gay and lesbian Arkansans to retreat to secluded rural roadhouses. Paradoxically, they found greater freedom and privacy outside the growing cities, which were often assumed to be oases amidst provincial traditions. Urbanization, as it turned out, fired up rather than dampened religious observance.

AMIDST THE CLAMOR that values and piety were ebbing, the pews of Arkansas churches filled after the lean 1930s. Of the largest white religious bodies in the state—Methodist Episcopal Church South (MECS), Southern Baptist Convention, Missionary Baptist Association, and Roman Catholic Church—only the Catholic parishes had grown, albeit slowly, during the Depression era. In the following decade, Roman Catholic membership continued to expand at the same rate to include 2 to 3 percent of the state's population; the Missionary Baptist growth stagnated; the 1939 union of the MECS, the Methodist

Episcopal Church, and the Methodist Protestant Church did not prevent the flourishing Southern Baptists from displacing the Methodists as the state's largest denomination.

Going to church meant a trip across open fields for fewer Arkansans. The new town dwellers found church attendance easier and more appealing because of the urban benefits of full-time clergy and ancillary outreach programs. In 1922, 10 percent of Baptist churches were located in towns of over one thousand residents, while 63.5 percent were classified as open country; by 1946 nearly 19 percent were in urban areas, and 44.4 percent were found in the countryside. In 1951 nearly half of all Baptists were members of urban congregations although only a third of the state's residents lived in towns and cities.

Both increasing prosperity and the new urban surroundings introduced greater uniformity into the order of worship of even the rigorously congregational Baptists. The Southern Baptist Convention's 1940 publication of the *Broadman Hymnal* not only standardized church services but encouraged a fuller integration of congregational singing, calls to worship, and responsive readings. The state Baptist convention created a new department of music to improve church choirs and song leaders. Members' demands during the 1940s for printed orders of service and the delivery of the benediction by noon each Sunday reflected new values of efficiency, individualism, and predictability.

The move to the city had not altered the traditional Baptist skepticism toward the secular reform efforts associated with the social gospel movement. While Baptists shared the era's general anxiety over the wayward adolescents, they shunned agitating for new laws in favor of organizing sports leagues and youth camps. Public lynchings of African Americans provoked statements of regret and pleas for reconciliation, though no support of anti-lynching legislation. In 1948 the Arkansas Southern Baptists continued to insist that an apolitical approach was the best answer to the growing demand for equal citizenship rights: "In the midst of agitated political issues dealing with the Negro problem in our Southland . . . we recommend to the churches in our convention that we hold to the one guiding New Testament principle of Love as the surest way of two racial groups solving the problems incurred in a Christian democracy."

The 1935 repeal of prohibition that had opened liquor outlets in every county was a public issue that incensed the Baptists, but one that remained dormant until the convention set its financial house in order. In 1942 the denomination's Committee on Prohibition and Social Service led the successful campaign to pass an initiated act lowering the percentage of voters who could petition for an election to vote a precinct "wet or dry." The Baptists built upon their success by organizing campaigns that produced victories in thirty-two of the forty local option elections held the next year. Many Arkansans in later years mistakenly assumed that female majorities were able to wring counties dry because the men were away in military service, when in actuality the lower threshold to hold a local option vote was the primary cause.

The white churches' relations with the African American religious community were governed by particular institutional structures. The all-white Southern Baptist Convention contributed monetary support to the National Baptist Convention, although the hard-pressed Southern Baptists halted subsidies to the black religious body during the Depression.

African American clergy in the Methodist Episcopal church had opposed the 1939 unification of the denomination, since their congregations were officially segregated into a separate administrative unit, a condition required by white Southern Methodist leaders to reunite with the Northern Methodist body. The Southwest Conference oversaw black Methodist congregations in Arkansas as well as Oklahoma, although the conference's greatest financial responsibility was the support of Philander Smith College in Little Rock. The African Methodist Episcopal Church (AME) and the Colored Methodist Episcopal Church (CME), which had been organized as independent bodies during the nineteenth century, were the home to the majority of black Methodists.

Arkansas Methodist congregations were not reintegrated until 1972; yet in 1943 the black and white Methodist women on the Little Rock City Mission Board began organizing interracial recreational activities to benefit children. Three years later the church leadership acted upon the suggestion of Harry Bass, the executive secretary of the Little Rock Urban League, to include adults and a wider range of programs at newly established Camp Aldersgate. The Camp was one of the few sites during this era in the South that provided meeting space and overnight accommodations for integrated groups. This refuge in segregated Arkansas was sequestered five miles outside of Little Rock on a former turkey farm.

In contrast to the two largest white Protestant denominations, neither a separate African American Catholic church nor recognized black-led jurisdiction within the diocese existed. Instead, the small number of black Roman Catholics belonged to nine racially identifiable parishes served by religious orders such as the Franciscans and Holy Ghost Fathers. Primarily, Catholic ties to black Arkansans were established within the context of the church's mission and social service objectives.

Founded in 1897 by Charles Harrison Mason in Little Rock, the Church of God in Christ (COGIC), a Pentecostal domination that welcomed African American urban residents who treasured rural traditions of worship, continued its steady growth. By the post-WWII era, Arkansas had the seventh highest number of COGIC congregations in the nation. In the late 1940s, the Reverend M. D. Willett of the St. Paul Church of God in Christ, located in the center of black Little Rock on West Ninth Street, was allotted airtime on a local radio station between 11 p.m. and midnight on Sundays to broadcast a sermon.

World War II profoundly altered the outlook of the Arkansas followers of one religious faith on a significant modern political issue. Before the war, the Arkansas Jewish community reacted tepidly to the call for the establishment of a homeland in Palestine, but reports of Nazi atrocities inspired a strengthened commitment to Zionism. Fearing internal conflict, the Arkansas Jewish Assembly in 1935 had refused to affiliate with the American Jewish Congress because of the national group's Zionist advocacy. By 1944 Dorothy Goldberg and Sarah Scrinopski had organized a Little Rock chapter of Hadassah, the national women's league founded to promote the well-being of the Jewish population in Palestine and advance the cause of statehood.

While each of the major white denominations and faiths depended upon active women's groups to fulfill the churches' proselytizing, social, and charitable obligations in the 1940s, only the Methodists had a female members of the clergy. Esther Mooty was apparently the first woman ordained into the ministry in Arkansas, beginning her pastoral career in 1935 with the Methodist Episcopal Church (ME). The other two major Methodist bodies had not permitted female clergy. While the newly united Methodist church permitted women ordained by the ME before the 1939 merger to serve congregations, no additional female pastors were admitted until 1956.

As early as 1927, the Arkansas Southern Baptist convention had created a Committee on Woman's Work, which delivered a final report that justified an enhanced station for women in church and family. In the following years Baptist women gained additional appointments to permanent boards and committees though no greater authority over church governance. They were disproportionately concentrated on the Orphan's Home and Sunday School committees as well as on the board of an all-female Baptist college in Conway.

THROUGHOUT AMERICA the necessity and willingness to question female roles originated in the changing character of women at work. Simply put, more women earned wages, more women earned those wages in industrial jobs, and those wage-earning women were married and older. Yet discrimination endured. Women were still largely excluded from the better-paying skilled factory tasks and the lack of child care skewed the labor force toward mothers with children old enough to attend school.

About one-fifth of the Arkansas labor force during the war was female, compared to around one-third for the nation as a whole. Defense manufacturing openings expanded the definitions of suitable female labor. Plant supervisors justified the hiring of women in three-quarters of the jobs at the Arkansas Ordnance Works in Jacksonville by claiming that their superior dexterity was an asset in assembling detonators and loading primer mixture.

Women were also called on to operate small businesses and farms as male family members left for military service. This temporary changing of the guard was evident at a number of the state's radio broadcast stations. When her husband joined the Army Air Corps, Veda Beard became the new manager of KBTM-Paragould and was the second woman in the nation to be granted FCC authorization to act in the absence of a station's assigned licensee. Dorothy Weise was program director for Little Rock's KGHI until she took to heart her own public service announcements and joined the Women's Army Corps. The shift of some women from farm to town did not escape the notice of local boosters. After 1942 the Searcy Chamber of Commerce began touting the rising female population as an available source of inexpensive labor for potential industries.

At war's end, Arkansas women, as did American women overall, left the labor market or reverted to old jobs. In 1945 Veda Beard surrendered her managerial position to once again take up the station's bookkeeping tasks. Most women exchanged paid work for homemaking. Yet for those women who had held challenging and higher-paid jobs, the experience revised their ambitions and self-perceptions and encouraged them to respond differently in the future to changing personal and family circumstances. Born in 1922 in the Ozark village of Aurora, Irene Jackson Hunter quit school at fifteen when she began processing tomatoes in a canning factory. Moving to California during the war, she was an electrician and riveter at Douglas Aircraft. In 1945 Irene returned to her native Madison County to marry Olaf Hunter, who was disabled from his wartime service. Although a military pension supplemented their cattle-raising operation, Irene signed on with the U.S. Forest Service in 1954 and eventually became the first female forestry technician assigned to the Ozark National Forest.

Women throughout the nation did edge back into the workplace by the end of the 1940s, and Arkansas women were in step with that trend albeit at a slower pace. The continued march of new factories into the state opened doors for working women who took those jobs more readily than did men. The proportion of employed women in manufacturing rose from about half of men likewise engaged to two-thirds over the course of the decade. Fewer women were limited to the meager wages and long hours of agricultural and household labor, although these workers remained disproportionately African American. Other inequities persisted. Less than 1 percent of women at work filled well-compensated skilled or supervisory positions in factories, and women in manufacturing found themselves concentrated in the lower-paying operations that processed food and made clothing.

These nondurable goods factories became the manufacturing norm in Arkansas. Nevertheless, the profitable, high-wage metal and chemical plants introduced during the war did not close down with the coming of peace. After 1945 the same federal agencies that oversaw war mobilization also took charge in determining who would end up with the industries and installations constructed with federal revenues. During the war, conservatives in Congress killed off New Deal agencies such as the Farm Security Administration and the Works Progress Administration, while liberals failed to slow the rapid postwar conversion away from the wartime system of government investment and mass public employment toward private-sector dominance.

Larger corporations that had secured the bulk of government military contracts during the war were able to acquire government properties at a fraction of their real value. The Reynolds Metals Company first leased and then purchased the two aluminum plants in Arkansas as well as plants in Illinois and Oregon for about 38 percent of the government investment in the facilities. The Lion Oil Chemical Company in El Dorado shifted from production of explosives to processing ammonia into fertilizer after it acquired the Ozark Ordnance Works. The scheduled scuttling of the Shumaker Depot in Camden was halted at the insistence of the state's congressional delegation, and the U.S. Navy continued to procure contracts for rocket production.

Arkansas business and political leaders were relieved that the peacetime conversion of major defense plants allowed the state to retain the complex and sophisticated operations that offered grander hopes than a manufacturing sector based on lumber mills. Their anticipation did not erase their fears that labor organizations would revive with the expansion of heavy industry. As a practical middle road to prosperity, they judged the food and apparel factories less vulnerable to collective bargaining campaigns and less likely to draw workers from existing operations. The rising Arkansas economic model rested upon industries that did not unsettle the traditional agricultural economy or upend labor relations. Owners of these new operations did not demand costly improvements in training or require the proliferation of union apprenticeship programs. The state ably boasted of what it had in great supply—low-cost, reliable workers.

The infusion of federal dollars since 1933 may not have transformed Arkansas but did swing the state off its beaten track. While the New Deal largely maintained the economic status quo, furnishing Arkansans relief from severe want and keeping the financial system from collapse, World War II boosted real incomes and spurred urbanization and factory openings. Yet one cannot comprehend the scope of change in Arkansas without taking into account that wartime policies stimulated hiring in factories throughout America. Arkansans saw these opportunities and streamed for the exits, heading for Midwestern and West Coast cities. Their leaving had as much effect on the state's development as the new manufacturing plants, if not more so. Charles Bolton aptly and inarguably summed it up in his analysis of the economic impact of the war on the state: "For World War II primed the pump of Arkansas's economy, but it also led many Arkansans to go to other wells."

III. Industrialization Without Revolution

In 1943 Hamilton Moses of Arkansas Power and Light did not anticipate the direction of federal reconversion and worried that a rapid shutdown of war industries would trim electricity demand. The author of the state's first utility regulatory act, Moses in 1919 had caught the attention of Harvey Couch, who made the young attorney his company's counsel: "I need a front man; a man who can stand before a crowd and interpret the things which are in my mind, as I envision the possibilities of the future." While Couch was the gregarious industrialist who fashioned a corporation from scratch, a man whose favorite food was hot dogs, Moses was the smooth political gamesman, addressing audiences as if he were harvesting votes and cultivating government officials through friendship and favors. By early summer 1941 Couch was dying of heart disease at Couchwood. Reporters kept vigil outside the home, agreeing out of deference to family wishes not to reveal the severity of the illness. If the scene resembled a royal deathwatch, there was little doubt as to the identity of the successor.

Moses's uneasiness over a postwar energy glut was not based on his company's having excess generating capacity, but on the competition from the now seventeen rural electrical cooperatives. Still under the auspices of the Rural Electrification Administration, the cooperatives became less dependent upon purchasing power from AP&L when the Norfork Dam came online. The legislation establishing the Southwestern Power Authority required it to market hydroelectric power from Norfork and future Corps of Engineers' dams to a preferred client base of farmers' cooperatives, municipal utilities, and military installations in Arkansas, Missouri, Oklahoma, and Texas.

Technically, the cooperatives and AP&L were supposed to coexist rather than battle for customers; under state law the cooperatives served designated rural districts, while AP&L had free rein to wire larger population centers. The legislation, however, was ambiguous, and the uncertainty allowed both sides to attempt territorial raids. In 1946 Newport, served by AP&L, annexed a swath of Jackson County within the boundaries of a cooperative district. AP&L laid claim to the new customers; the cooperative resisted; and the struggle extended for years. At one point the rural residents were asked to choose between the utilities, and Moses himself conducted a local radio "talkathon" to proclaim that the farm families were facing the most critical decision since the Civil War. Eventually, the state Supreme Court settled the matter in favor of AP&L.

In 1957 lawmakers crafted a measure that sealed the boundaries of area served by the utilities to avert future incursions and dampen acrimony. By that time the cooperatives, with new sources for power and redoubled efforts, had brought lights to over two-thirds of Arkansas farms. In 1949 several of the cooperatives formed the Arkansas Electric Cooperative Corporation as a prelude to applying for REA loans to build their own generating plant. Moses, not yet reconciled to the federal dams and fearing that a power surplus would undermine electric rates, fiercely opposed the plant construction and delayed its completion until 1961. Eventually, AP&L would also begin buying power from the Corps hydroelectric projects, and the company continued to prosper even as it shared Arkansas with publicly assisted utilities. Barred from poaching customers, AP&L and the cooperatives withdrew to their protectorates, and the electric wars in Arkansas came to an end.

Throughout the conflicts, Moses not only defended his company's territory but sought to expand the customers in towns already within the AP&L network. Doing this, of course, required those communities to add residents at a time when Arkansas was hemorrhaging population. In March 1943 the utility president convened a summit of state business leaders that evolved into the Arkansas Economic Council (AEC). The AEC revived Harvey Couch's promotion campaign but altered the late utility magnate's development goals. Whereas Couch had sought to lure external capital to underwrite native enterprises, the new plan emphasized persuading national firms to relocate factories in the state. The AEC did not target sprawling industrial complexes resembling the aluminum facilities but preferred a diffusion of plants in smaller towns. This strategy would expand electrical users throughout AP&L's service region without straining the company's generation capacity. The utility continued to influence state economic development and industrial recruitment efforts for the remainder of the century and beyond.

The AEC placed the responsibility on local leaders to wrench their towns from a debilitating reliance on crops and make themselves suitable for manufacturing. Moses led speaking tours, proclaiming that "communities must develop their own assets rather than look to others to do the job." Combining the fervor of a camp revival meeting with new management techniques, the AEC outlined how towns should evaluate themselves through "community clinics." Groups of residents were urged to categorize their town's attributes as either constructive or unhelpful, vote on improvement projects, and then sign cards promising to devote themselves to civic betterment. By 1950 AP&L and allied groups began to sponsor annual "Community Accomplishment" contests akin to the competitions that once marked war bond drives.

AP&L's far-flung local offices expedited the development campaigns, but the utility also fashioned a coalition at the state level. In 1945 the AEC merged with the state Chamber of Commerce, which served as junior partner and the administrative arm for industrial recruitment. That year Moses called for the creation of a state economic agency in an address to the General Assembly. The utility executive knew that it was not his eloquence that insured a favorable outcome. AP&L rewarded legislators through a variety of methods, including paying retainers to members who were attorneys. With the blessings of the governor, the assembly merged a host of nominal economic agencies into the Arkansas Resources and Development Commission. Commission members regularly traveled to northern cities to deliver the message that Arkansas was open for business.

In 1945 the legislature, at the behest of the AEC, also expanded the University of Arkansas's mission by creating the Bureau of Business and Economic Research, a counterpart to the federally supported university Agricultural Experiment Station. In 1955 the university established the Industrial Research and Extension Center that operated as the Little Rock branch of the university's business development program. The blending of public and private interests as well as the links between local and state institutions, framed an industrial development structure resembling the formidable agricultural coalition of university county agents, the Farm Bureau, and powerful local landowners.

THE ARKANSAS MANUFACTURING BOOM did take off following the creation of the Arkansas Economic Council and accelerated during the 1950s. Between 1946 and 1959 the state's manufacturing employment rose by 44 percent in comparison to the 11 percent rise throughout the nation. As the proportion of sawmill workers numbers tumbled, Arkansans took jobs in factories once found exclusively in the northeastern United States. Both business leaders and university economists boasted that the organized industrial development campaigns were responsible for diversifying the state's economy.

Yet the shoe and apparel industries appeared in small communities even before the AEC was fully up and running. The state's first shoe factory started up in Pocahontas in 1945, and Searcy negotiators were in St. Louis on the day Japan surrendered to complete an agreement with the International Shoe Company. By 1950 fourteen shoe plants operated in communities along the rim of the northern uplands and upper Delta, including Piggot, Beebe, Bald Knob, and Russellville. Although textile manufacturing in Arkansas had never matched its importance elsewhere in the South, apparel production gained a foothold and proliferated quickly during the 1940s. In 1949 thirty plants, also concentrated in the northern half of the state, shipped hosiery, shirts, work clothes, and children's garments. Arkansas was attracting industries falling by the wayside in their former home states: leather and apparel manufacturing employment in the state rose 740 percent and 246 percent, respectively, between 1946 and 1959, while declining or stagnating in older industrial regions.

Despite this growth, the combined numbers of shoe and apparel workers by the late 1950s fell short of those employed in another rising industry, one that initially followed the old pattern of processing a raw product. In 1950 about five hundred food manufacturing plants were producing margarine, meat and cheese items, and preserved fruits and vegetables, largely in the same locations as the shoe and clothing factories. The firms' names were familiar labels in postwar kitchens: Kraft, Pet Milk, Swift, Swanson, and Welch's Grape Juice. The eventual success of Arkansas-based companies competing against these established national concerns was a striking reversal of the long-standing colonial relationship between the state and northern corporations.

As they had with the Delta cotton economy, federal agricultural and developmental programs nurtured northwest Arkansas broiler production during the 1930s. National Recovery Administration codes forced the state to develop a poultry inspection program, the agricultural extension agents pressured hill farmers to diversify operations by building brooder houses, and the Works Progress Administration constructed the Highway 71 route to Kansas City to give the northwestern region access to national markets. The necessity for live hauls and the small shipments by scattered growers made truck transportation more feasible than rail. Growers sold their birds to independent truckers such as John Tyson, who would in turn unload the cargo through urban commission houses. Tyson first hauled chickens to Kansas City and St. Louis, but his 1936 nonstop trek to Chicago established a direct link to a lucrative hub.

During World War II, the federal government exempted chicken from rationing limits and included the product in the Lend-Lease food export program. The federal policies rendered poultry the second largest source of agricultural income in the state, and national annual consumption of chicken doubled between 1938 and 1943.

Even with an expanding market, the ten thousand commercial poultry farmers in Arkansas were attached to an industry with critical inherent weaknesses. Getting a bird to a customer involved independent feed operators, hatcheries, breeders, truckers, and processors. This acute segmentation caused the divvying up of unpredictable returns whipsawed by retail price swings. Unprotected by federal allotment policies that limited the production of other commodities, broiler producers also suffered from the continuing reluctance of Arkansas bankers to take a risk on agricultural loans.

Consumer habits after the war also compelled growers to standardize the breeding process through careful management and additional investment. Shoppers at the suburban supermarkets preferred oven-ready birds that were uniform in appearance and size. The surge in demand enticed national processors to construct plants in northwest Arkansas, and the A&P grocery chain sponsored the "Chicken-of-Tomorrow" contest to encourage improved breeds.

The national corporations, however, were not the originators of a vertically integrated system in which one company kept ownership of the product from egg to dressed bird. In the early 1950s the first steps in this direction were taken by Harold Snyder of the Arkansas Valley Feed Mill in Russellville, Collier Wenderoth of OK Mills in Fort Smith, and John Tyson of Tyson Feed and Hatchery in Springdale, as each negotiated feed and broiler purchase agreements with area farmers.

Arkansas producers also pursued advantages by developing one of the first statewide lobbying organizations on behalf of an entire industry. In 1952 they directed surplus funds from the Chicken-of-Tomorrow contests to underwrite the formation of the Arkansas Poultry Federation. Two years later the group threw its support and hefty campaign donations to gubernatorial contender Orval Faubus, who pledged to exempt feed from the state sales tax.

As northwest Arkansas entered the first stages of a new commercial economy, the Delta cotton culture continued the long transition from labor-intensive plantation to mechanized agribusiness. Since the 1920s, John and Mack Rust had experimented with an automatic cotton spindle picker, and in 1933 a prototype harvested five bales at a demonstration in Mississippi. The brothers announced that by 1936 their new company would begin producing mechanical harvesters for sale. While some landowners welcomed the invention, others in the Delta foresaw an apocalypse. The authors of the 1935 *The Collapse of Cotton Tenancy* delivered a grim prediction: "There is impending a violent revolution in cotton production as a result of the development of the mechanical cotton picker. . . . When it comes, it will automatically release hundreds of thousands of cotton workers particularly in the Southeast, creating a new range of social problems."

The Rust invention did not lead the region into a new era. The company dissolved into bankruptcy when the brothers failed to secure credit. During the 1940s the larger, better-capitalized International Harvester Corporation continued to perfect through practice runs on plantations in Arkansas and Mississippi a model that picked two rows at a time. The corporation failed, however, to coax the War Production Board to release scarce supplies of steel, and the machines did not begin coming off the line at an IH factory in Memphis before 1949.

Even with commercial marketing of the harvesters, Delta cotton mechanization proceeded erratically and was not fully in place until the early 1960s. Hiring laborers had remained a cheaper alternative to the machines, and even planters with the mechanical harvesters swore that experienced workers insured a better-quality yield. In the previous decades, the Delta landowners had skillfully adapted to changing conditions and federal intervention to retain control of their labor force. When confronted with new forces rendering field work obsolete, planters hesitated to step over the brink into unfamiliar territory.

In contrast, small farmers and tenants, primarily African American, buried a decaying order by leaving for urban jobs in Arkansas and beyond. The nearly simultaneous phenomena of depopulation and mechanization during the 1940s and 1950s has inspired the "push-pull" explanation: automatic cotton harvesters induced a labor surplus that was drained off by the opportunities in postwar cities. Donald Holley in his closely researched studies demonstrated that planters only fully committed to mechanization after the great migration left them with fewer available hands. Inarguably, Southerners in general packed their bags for good. Nevertheless, Arkansas stood out by losing a greater share of its population. As was true in the adjoining states, African Americans departed Arkansas in greater proportion than white migrants. And yet, none of these other states came close to matching Arkansas in the extent of its white exodus.

East Arkansas planters had been growing accustomed to greater mechanization during World War II when government offered incentives to plant soybeans. Arkansas led the way among Southern states in devoting acreage to a crop easily and profitably harvested by combines. Gradually, landowners began to see that machines were not the mainspring of social revolution. Indeed, the rise of the civil rights movement persuaded planters that automation of cotton production could instead untangle them from workers demanding equality and power. After 1960, federal census workers no longer bothered to record the number of sharecroppers.

WITH THE EXCEPTION OF lumber mill companies, Arkansas manufacturers during the 1940s were largely satisfied with the general tranquility on the labor front and were reluctant to endanger the status quo. In contrast, east Arkansas farmers confronted the continuing activism of the Southern Tenant Farmers Union and the aggressive organizing campaign of agricultural workers by the CIO affiliated Cannery, Agricultural, Packing, and Allied Workers (UCAPAWA). The state's pioneering role in Southern anti-labor legislation predated the expansions of industries in the state. Anti-unionism in Arkansas germinated within the stratified and paternalistic agricultural economy rather than in the expanding urban sector.

After the Christian American Association (CAA) of Houston successfully pressured the Texas legislature to limit labor strikes, the group mobilized to promote the law as a model for other Southern states. Only Arkansas enacted the Texas "anti-violence" bill and did so with solid majorities in both legislative chambers. Introduced during the 1943 session by state senator W. H. Abington of Beebe, the bill made it a felony offense punishable by up two years in prison to threaten or engage in actions that led to violence during a strike at a work site. Employees were subject to the law, but not employers, who might hire toughs to confront strikers.

Opposing legislators fruitlessly underscored the general labor peace outside the Delta and commended the moderation of the American Federation of Labor (AFL). An AFL leader from industrial Union County charged that the bill gained House passage only when "representatives of the Farm Bureau appeared at the legislature with little black grips." A Fort Smith editorial writer echoed the accusation: "Prominent men from eastern Arkansas, whose voices speak with considerable authority in the legislature, came to Little Rock and put on the pressure."

Emboldened by the enactment of the anti-violence law, the CAA mounted a successful petition drive to weaken union recruitment by placing a proposed "right-to-work" amendment to the state constitution on the 1944 ballot. Even business-friendly newspapers in Little Rock and Pine Bluff warned that the amendment was unnecessary and provocative. With the voters' approval of Amendment 34, Arkansas joined Florida as the first two Southern states to prohibit labor contracts that required workers to join a union if they wished to remain employed.

These victories did not quench the anti-labor fervor of eastern Arkansas farm and town leaders. In 1956 the Delta communities of Trumann, Marked Tree, Star City, Lepanto, DeWitt, and Harrisburg enacted ordinances imposing annual permit fees as high as $1,000 on unions. By the mid-1950s urban economic boosters incorporated the anti-labor message into their recruitment arsenal. The state industrial development agency also reproduced the language of the right-to-work amendment in promotional materials.

While other Southern states followed the Arkansas anti-union model, the state retained a higher than average percentage of organized workers within the region. Between 1939 and 1964, union membership rose 348 percent. The aluminum, paper, oil and chemical, and rubber products sector registered the highest percentage of union membership. In contrast, unionization was far from uniform throughout the emerging nondurable goods industries.

Throughout the state, twice as many women as men worked in clothing and food production, although in 1960 their median wages were a little over three-quarters of those paid to men in the plants. Nearly 58 percent of the female employees in these industries lived in rural areas. The background of the new factory workers in addition to formal anti-union drives tested the hardiness of the labor movement.

In 1962 the University of Arkansas Bureau of Industrial Research published a reassuring analysis for its business clientele: "A concentration of high-wage, highly organized industries in a labor surplus area does not raise the levels of wages and union organization for other manufacturing industries of the area." The report examined several industrial centers: the aluminum counties of Clark, Garland, Hot Spring, and Saline; the paper counties of Jefferson and Ouachita; and the petrochemical counties of Columbia and Union. Because the better-paying industries employed less than a third of the overall local manufacturing work force, the wages in those communities' nonunion businesses were no higher than those found in places without heavy industry and organized labor.

The New South dream of late nineteenth-century Arkansas movers and shakers was fulfilled by post–World War II industrialization. The Delta planters overcame their hesitation about mechanization to prosper from the transition to heavily capitalized operations, underwritten by federal crop subsidies and generous grants for irrigation districts. Farming technology and the migration of working adults stranded an impoverished population of seasonal laborers, small children, and elderly non-property owners (although the median age of African Americans in the state plummeted from 24.1 in 1950 to 20.5 in 1960, the proportion of black Arkansans over the age of sixty increased from 10.8

percent to 13.6 percent). Even the growth of 1960's federal transfer payments did not stave off malnutrition and chronic medical infirmities.

The 1950s seemingly confirmed the reassurances of industrial promoters that economic changes brought prosperity without turmoil. Between 1947 and 1957 the number of strikes in Arkansas fell below the Southern average, while 30 percent fewer workers in the state were idled by work stoppages than in the nation as a whole. Employees struck lumber mills more than other industries that were largely untroubled by picket lines. Rising industrial employment, accompanied by declining farm laborers, increased total personal state income by 81 percent between 1946 and 1959, but this improvement straggled behind the 116 percent national rise. The income white rural women earned in the plants often enabled families to remain on farms that were not self-supporting. Arkansas's industrialization did not speed the state toward urbanization.

If persistent ruralism weakened workers' organizations, migration patterns increased the proportion of African Americans living in towns rather than plantations. A new generation of urban black leaders had wider latitude to challenge entrenched discrimination. Just as they favored a manufacturing economy without disruption, white business and political leaders contrived to preserve the racial status quo even as the assaults upon it swelled from within and outside of Arkansas.

IV. Sounding the Trumpet: Early Civil Rights Struggles

Shortly after founding the Committee on Negro Organizations (CNO), in 1940 Harold Flowers mobilized African American civic and professional organizations in a drive to purchase and distribute the $1 poll-tax receipts required for individuals to cast ballots. The campaign increased the number of registered black voters who in turn gave new civil rights organizations political leverage. Flowers toured the state to rally African Americans "to devise a program of action" that ensured their hard-won votes would foster reform. Yet white political monopoly had more than one line of defense. Even those black voters listed on the poll-tax rolls remained barred from the Democratic Party primary elections, the contests that decided who held office in Arkansas.

This barrier collapsed in April 1944 when the U.S. Supreme Court in *Smith v. Allwright* voided the whites-only primary in Texas as an unconstitutional abridgment of the Fifteenth Amendment. The decision sent tremors throughout the South. Homer Adkins, the state's most overtly racist governor in the modern era, first thundered outright defiance of the court ruling but then settled for circumventing it. He approved revisions to party rules that permitted black

Democrats to cast ballots for federal but not state candidates and prohibited African Americans from competing for office in the primary.

Dr. John M. Robinson, the leader of the Arkansas Negro Democratic Association, denounced the party's obstructionist tactics while attempting to mollify Adkins by endorsing him in his primary election bid for the U.S. Senate that same year against the incumbent, Hattie Caraway; his bitter factional adversary, U.S. representative J. William Fulbright; and T. H. Barton, a south Arkansas oil tycoon and philanthropist. Adkins snubbed Robinson: "If I cannot be nominated by the white voters of Arkansas, I do not want the office." The insult was aimed at Fulbright, whom Adkins denounced as sympathetic to black interests. The Fayetteville congressman briskly professed loyalty to racial disfranchisement and coasted to a run-off victory over Adkins that launched his long senatorial career. The campaign demonstrated that court decisions had kindled the revival of race as a political weapon even when no candidate questioned the sanctity of segregation or white political dominance.

During its 1945 session, the General Assembly reinforced the new Democratic Party provisions by enacting a complicated double primary system that restricted African Americans to a diminished slate of candidates at separate polling places. The apparatus fell apart when party officials were unable to manage multiple and closely scheduled elections. In 1950 the delegates to the state Democratic convention reluctantly repealed the party rules that permitted only "white electors." The incendiary threats and scorn in the wake of *Smith* cooled as politics in the state followed the usual course.

White leaders in counties with concentrated black populations had not depended on a racially exclusive primary system to retain authority. A planter explained to V. O. Key why he was untroubled by court decisions: "We're going to follow the law, but I don't care if they vote or not. If they do, they'll vote the way I want 'em to." Most observers agreed that the persistent domination by rural local elites throughout the Delta suppressed African American political independence more effectively than did election regulations. East Arkansas planters clung to the poll tax primarily as a device to assure balloting produced agreeable results. Other, harsher, more violent and extralegal means were available to reinforce racial domination. Rising black political participation corresponded with moves to urban neighborhoods. The 17 percent of registered African American voters in 1947, slightly higher than the Southern average, were primarily residents of Little Rock and Pine Bluff.

ADVOCATES FOR SECURING constitutional rights pointed to favorable federal court rulings as evidence that Jim Crow barriers were impregnable. The NAACP in the 1940s pressed its legal strategy to force Southern locales to meet the "separate but equal" obligations they had flagrantly evaded since the 1896 *Plessy v. Ferguson* decision. Civil rights attorneys discerned opportunities in two sets of cases: equalization of teachers' salaries and admission of African American students to graduate and professional schools. The NAACP knew that Southern states unable to afford separate law and medical institutions for African Americans would have little choice but to integrate those schools. If closing the salary gap between teachers in black and white public schools did not directly challenge segregation, the litigation enlisted the influential African American professional class in the type of public campaigns for equality from which it had often kept its distance.

In 1940 the Supreme Court ruled in *Alston v. School Board of the City of Norfolk* that racially identifiable salary differences for public school teachers failed the constitutional test. This case galvanized educators much as the *Smith* decision later roused the hopes of Arkansas voting rights organizations. As they had done in response to *Smith*, public officials ignored the law until confronted by local residents, resisted its implementation, and finally concocted elaborate evasions. In 1941 the Little Rock Classroom Teachers Association (CTA), a black professional group, compiled evidence of salary disparities. Throughout the state, the average black teacher's salary of $367 foundered below the $625 white average, and the gap in the Little Rock district was only slightly narrower. The difference could not be justified by disparate levels of training. The state black teachers' median education level of 2.5 years of college virtually matched the whites educators' 2.6 years. The CTA filed suit in 1942 after the Little Rock school board responded to a petition for redress by widening the salary gap.

The NAACP had largely stayed away from Arkansas discrimination cases, but the organization's Thurgood Marshall in this instance assisted Scipio A. Jones, a legendary Arkansas black attorney, in preparations for the October 1943 hearing. The lawyers settled on Sue Cowan Morris, head of the Dunbar High School English department, as the lead plaintiff. Morris's well-documented abilities in the classroom and her excellent grades in University of Chicago graduate courses surpassed the credentials of the majority of the district's white teachers. While the lawyers for the defendants carefully attributed different wage scales to "special training, ability, character," they could not always rely upon their witnesses to reiterate a racially neutral justification for discrimination. A white primary school supervisor declared that "regardless of college degrees and teaching experience no white teacher in Little Rock is inferior to the best Negro teacher." For their part, school administrators supplemented their legal defense with selective reprisals. Morris's contract was not renewed following the 1942–43 school year; the Dunbar principal who testified on her notable record was made to resign; and the head of the CTA was relieved of his teaching post.

In January 1944 federal district judge Thomas C. Trimble ruled that the school district's dual-salary system was fair, but his decision was overturned the following year by the Eighth Circuit Court of Appeals in St. Louis. Even before this final ruling, the Little Rock school board determined that halfway measures were more viable than defiance. The district fashioned an evaluation plan that provided immediate raises for some black faculty while maintaining the overall gap between white and African American salary levels. Future lawsuits kept the issue before the courts.

The enrollment of Silas Hunt in February 1948 as the first black student at the University of Arkansas's law school repeated a similar pattern of compliance with federal court decisions while retaining components of segregation. Attempting to stay in line with *Plessy*, Southern states provided African American students tuition at out-of-state institutions rather than permitting enrollment in the public all-white graduate and professional schools. In 1938 the Supreme Court ordered Missouri to halt the practice but the decision triggered defiant circumventions. States such as Texas and Oklahoma succeeded in discouraging black applicants to schools by isolating the few who were admitted to secluded areas away from the main classrooms.

In 1946 Clifford Davis submitted a formal application to the University of Arkansas School of Law. Robert Leflar, dean of the school, quickly began to lobby university and state leaders. He stressed that denying admittance to Davis would lead to a futile court fight that damaged the institution's reputation. Leflar's argument was strengthened by absence of Arkansas statutes barring integration of higher education as well as a resolution by the university's first board of trustees that declared "the institution open to all without regard to race, sex, or sect."

Leflar understood the outcome would be determined by the governor, who could both halt the admission of Davis and stir up popular resentment. Ben Laney, elected governor in 1944, had devoted considerable thought to the best methods to salvage segregation. Aware that the courts would soon shut down the tuition shell game, Laney mulled over the prospect of all-black Southern regional professional schools. The idea soon fizzled in the face of opposition by Arkansas black leaders and the apathy of other state governors. Meeting Leflar in his office, Laney listened wordlessly, frequently gazing out the window, as the law dean explained that any alternative to accepting African American applicants was expensive and divisive. At the end, the governor accepted the logic of Leflar's analysis and agreed not to interfere.

At its January 1948 meeting, the university board formally desegregated the university graduate and professional schools but stipulated that black students would receive instruction separately rather than in lecture halls with whites. From the beginning Leflar had conceded segregation within the law school. Clifford Davis wrote Leflar, even before the board announced its new policy, that he would not attend the university under conditions that failed "to fulfill the requirement of equal opportunity." On February 2, 1948, Harold Flowers accompanied Silas Hunt and Wiley Branton, who wished to enroll in the undergraduate business school, to the Fayetteville campus. Geleve Grice, a photographer from Arkansas A&M in Pine Bluff, the alma mater of the two applicants, was present to document the event for the *Arkansas State Press*, an African American newspaper in Little Rock. Branton knew beforehand that the university had not desegregated its undergraduate programs, while Hunt enrolled in the law school without incident. He was the first African American to begin attending professional school at any previously all-white university in the former Confederacy.

A wounded World War II veteran, Hunt took his classes in a special basement classroom, where he was usually joined by three to five white students who were either sympathetic or eager for the more intensive instruction. Raymond Higgins, a white senior, circulated a poll among members of the law student association that revealed two-thirds of them opposed Hunt's exclusion from general classes. But by the summer Hunt became so ill that he withdrew from the university, and he died from tuberculosis the following April.

Jackie L. Shropshire of Little Rock enrolled that fall and in 1951 became the first black law graduate. On his first class day Shropshire was not consigned to the basement but was seated behind a wooden rail in a corner of the lecture hall. Five law faculty complained to Leflar, who that night surreptitiously tore down the railing. Shropshire, however, remained in the segregated space for the remainder of the year. In 1950 the Supreme Court in a case involving the University of Oklahoma prohibited universities from isolating African American students on their campuses. That year Shropshire and fellow students Chris Mercer, Wiley Branton, and George Haley were free to choose any seat in the room. These early African American graduates from the university law school followed in the footsteps of Harold Flowers to contest segregation both in and outside courtrooms.

The university board of trustees January 1948 policy was not limited to the school of law. That fall, Edith Irby entered the University of Arkansas Medical School, where she sat in classes with other students but was consigned to a separate dining area and bathroom. Her closest friendships were with the other two women in the class, who faced similar pressures to "do twice as much, be even more diligent than the male counterpart." After earning her medical degree in 1952, she set up a practice in Hot Springs before moving in 1959 with her husband, Dr. James Jones, to Houston. There she became the first African American woman resident at Baylor College of Medicine.

THE DESEGREGATION of professional schools in the state became widely-acknowledged landmarks in early civil rights advancement. Less apparent at the time was the long-range significance of the climbing African American urban population that outstripped white growth in such cities as Little Rock. During World War II the Fair Employment Practices Committee had steadily if unevenly removed barriers that impeded black employees from punching defense-plant time clocks at a uniform pay rate. African American neighborhoods expanded in eastern and central Little Rock, orbiting around the bustling six-block West Ninth Street business and entertainment district. There, small retail shops filled multistory buildings, and physicians and attorneys welcomed clients to their offices in fraternal halls. Dr. Oba White recalled that during the 1940s, "You could get the things you wished right in that little area. . . . Someone on the street all the time, during the day, during the night. It was a busy street."

John Kirk's perceptive studies have described how a postwar generation of black leadership mobilized recent migrants and new voters to wrest concessions within the constraints of a Jim Crow society. In a companion development to the widely publicized white "GI Revolt" political reform movement, I. S. McClinton, Charles Bussey, and Jeffrey Hawkins were African American veterans who led groups that called upon Little Rock city officials to provide comparable municipal services to black residential sections. At the forefront of the list of demands was a long-promised city park to be set aside for black families who were barred from the other public parks. In 1949 the intensifying federal judicial scrutiny of segregation arrangements as well as black political pressure led to approval of a bond issue to build Gillam Park on the southeastern edge of Little Rock. Not all African Americans saw victory in the construction of another segregated facility.

L. C. Bates, the editor of the *Arkansas State Press*, was the state's most penetrating and forceful advocate for racial integration. He was impatient with both traditional and new African American leaders who cultivated white patrons to back projects in the black community that did not dismantle segregation.

A Mississippi native, Bates worked as a newspaperman before the Depression took its toll on African American papers and forced him to turn to selling insurance. During his rounds in Arkansas, he met Daisy Gatson, a native of Huttig. In 1941 the couple began publishing the *State Press* shortly after moving to Little Rock and were married the following year. In contrast to the more stolid *Southern Mediator Journal*, the *State Press* publicized discrimination in defense plant hiring during the war and the failure of trade unions to represent black employees. Subscriptions accumulated, and white business advertisers treated the *State Press* as the most efficient conduit to black consumers.

The newspaper's coverage of the murder of Sergeant Thomas B. Foster demonstrated that African Americans who called into question the racial order would lose white backing. In March 1942 Foster, a member of a black engineers battalion, intervened when Little Rock police officers began beating an African American soldier in custody of military policemen. The military police rebuffed Sgt. Foster's attempt to investigate and moved to arrest him. As a crowd gathered at the scene on West Ninth Street, the city officers clubbed Foster to the ground. City police officer Abner Hay then shot the nearly unconscious Foster four times and stood smoking his pipe over the body until the ambulance arrived.

Three days later, the city coroner officially closed the case as a justifiable homicide. Bates's pointed ridicule of the coroner's ruling provoked additional investigations. These came to little. A federal grand jury three months after Foster's death refused to indict Hay. White merchants pulled their advertisements from the *State Press*, but the editorials were unrelenting and the circulation doubled. City officials, buffeted by community anger and warnings from military authorities, appointed eight black police officers to the all-white force. The new hires were kept from patrolling outside the West Ninth Street district and compelled to waive their rights to participate in the department's pension fund.

For Daisy and L. C. Bates, their hard-won independence deepened their disdain for those willing to accommodate segregation and confirmed their belief that softening racial exclusion practices only deferred justice.

An Ozark client of the federal Rural Rehabilitation program, August 1935. The New Deal promoted the practice of traditional crafts such as spinning to encourage small farmers to remain self-sufficient. *Library of Congress, Prints & Photographs Division, FSA/OWI Collection.*

A resident at the Lakeview Resettlement Project grinds sausage for her family, November 1938. The well-constructed houses wired for electricity contrasted with the conditions in tenant dwellings. The federal program did not cross segregation boundaries. Lakeview was one of three projects in Arkansas reserved for African American farmers. *Library of Congress, Prints & Photographs Division, FSA/OWI Collection.*

(*Above*) Workers at the Arkansas
Ordnance Plant, Jacksonville circa 1943.
In August 1943, 75 percent of those on
the assembly line were women, and by
the end of the following year 24 percent
were African American. The plant was
shuttered in 1946, but the Little Rock
Air Force Base was built on a portion
of the site in the 1950s. *Butler Center
for Arkansas Studies, Central Arkansas
Library System.*

(*Right*)Senator Joe T. Robinson examines the business end of a "bazooka"
horn held by radio comedian Bob Burns,
about 1935. The two men were among
the best-known Arkansans of the era.
Robinson exercised legendary influence
as a congressional leader, while Burns
entertained audiences with humorous
sketches based upon his youth in Van
Buren. *Special Collections Division,
University of Arkansas Libraries,
Fayetteville.*

Arkansas Power and Light founder, Harvey P. Couch, seated (left center) on the steps of Couchwood with visiting businessmen about 1930. Couch launched the modern phase of Arkansas industrial recruitment by hosting business prospects as well as Herbert Hoover and Franklin Roosevelt at his log retreat. Couchwood overlooked Lake Catherine, created in 1924 when AP&L constructed Remmel Dam to generate electricity. *Entergy Arkansas.*

Sonny Boy Williamson and Robert Lockwood Jr., along with announcer Sam Anderson, promote "King Biscuit Time" on KFFA in Helena during the 1940s. Williamson became recognized as one of the finest blues harmonica players after he began recording for Chess Records in Chicago. Lockwood was an important figure who bridged the acoustic guitar tradition of Robert Johnson and the electric blues of Muddy Waters and B. B. King. *Ivey Gladin Photographs, Archives and Special Collections, J.D. Williams Library, the University of Mississippi.*

(*Facing page, bottom*) Sidney McMath leads a parade in Little Rock. McMath launched his career as a reformer and fresh face, but old-fashion campaign skills made him governor. The crumpled hat became a familiar prop. *Special Collections Division, University of Arkansas Libraries, Fayetteville.*

Ben Laney, Guy E. Williams, J. William Fulbright, and Carl Bailey at Lake Chicot
in August 1944. Laney won the Democratic nomination for governor that month
after his opponent withdrew from the primary run-off election. Bailey had helped
Fulbright gain the nomination for U.S. senator over the former governor's old rival
Homer Adkins. Attorney General Williams aided Fulbright during a subsequent
Senate investigation into whether voting fraud determined election results. *Bailey
Collection, University of Arkansas at Little Rock Archives.*

A biology class at Dunbar High School in Little Rock in 1947. For over two decades, the city's only African American high school was noted for its strong educational program as well as hosting significant speakers and performers. Nevertheless, crowded classrooms and lack of equipment revealed the effects of segregation. *National Dunbar Alumni Association Collection, University of Arkansas at Little Rock Archives.*

A successful duck hunt at the Bayou Meto Wildlife Management Area near Stuttgart in the early 1950s. In 1948 the Arkansas Game and Fish Commission began acquiring Bayou Meto tracts for a combined public hunting area and refuge. The agency's game management practices established hunting and fishing as the state's most popular recreations. *Arkansas Game and Fish Commission.*

Capitol Avenue, Little Rock, 1958. The capital city's bustling downtown center was replicated in smaller towns throughout the state. Traffic and inconvenient street parking, however, led customers to visit western suburban shopping centers such as Park Plaza, built the following year. *Thomas J. O'Halloran, photographer, Library of Congress, Prints & Photographs Division.*

3 ARKANSAS AT MIDCENTURY

Manufacturing Opportunity

OT SPRINGS WAS A machine town like no other in Arkansas. The ostensible prince of the city-state was a flamboyant boss whose grandiose behavior represented the political organization's magnanimity and its assuredness. Mayor Leo P. McLaughlin's occasional habit of gliding along Central Avenue in a buggy pulled by the smart-stepping Scotch and Soda deepened the popular impression of the Ouachita Mountain spa as a refuge from ordinary rules.

McLaughlin seized office in 1926 when he entrained from outside communities two thousand individuals whose fraudulent poll-tax receipts permitted them to cast ballots in the city's Second Ward. The election outcomes for twenty years afterwards held few surprises. If McLaughlin's vote-getting methods were not unusual, the massive payoffs from the gambling operations brought profits beyond the aims or calculations of other Arkansas bosses. Gambling had flourished throughout the nineteenth century along with the bathing industry. McLaughlin revived gaming in Hot Springs and appointed a crony to oversee the casino operations just as he appointed a director of roads to improve city streets. The gambling houses were expected to play by the machine's rules, and gamblers were to avoid provocations that could incite inconvenient violence.

The machine distributed the take from gambling proprietors to spread goodwill through charitable donations, soft jobs, and supplements to the municipal budget. The casinos, horse book joints, and brothels plied their trade openly, while betting at Oaklawn Park track attracted thousands before becoming legal under the 1935 pari-mutuel law. The new principal industry of Hot Springs even buoyed the traditional one. The numbers of visitors luxuriating in the steamy baths soared to a million by the mid-1940s.

An article on the city in a 1931 issue of *Collier's* magazine portrayed an illicit Shangri-La where judgments were set aside and vice was unmarred by sordid behavior. "The enjoyable truth is that Hot Springs, where you can do practically anything you can pay for, which lacks practically all civic prohibitions, which recognizes none of the conventional prohibitions, and asks only that the visitor observe the right of his neighbor to enjoy himself in his own peculiar way, has no crime wave, and very few crimes."

Like most rulers too long in power, McLaughlin began to confuse the realm with his palace and neglected to blend his self-aggrandizement with disinterested patronage. By the 1940s the criticisms from those who once tolerated the machine began to mount. Many were embarrassed when the city attempted to protect the gangster Lucky Luciano from extradition to New York; residents resented the mayor's decision to name the new airport after himself instead of as a memorial to World War II veterans; and a general outrage erupted when a several downtown stores burned while fire trucks were parked at a political rally for a McLaughlin ally. While gambling in the long run survived the Sid McMath–led 1946 "GI Revolt," McLaughlin's machine was broken. He himself barely escaped a prison sentence on bribery and malfeasance charges. When he died in 1958, looters ransacked his house for hidden spoils and even probed his grave site.

McLaughlin's town also soon disappeared. Trainloads of visitors no longer came to seek cures at the spa for arthritis, rheumatism, and syphilis, and Bathhouse Row acquired a disheveled and forlorn countenance. The bathers were replaced by the tourists who flocked to Oaklawn Park, indulged themselves at the shows and the slot machines in the Belvedere or the Vapors, or simply reclined on the airy verandah of the Arlington Hotel. The old elegance gave way to merchandising Hot Springs as a resort for the vacationing middle class and as a temperate haven for Midwestern retirees tired of long winters.

The Americanization of Arkansas also picked up speed. Voters approved measures to insulate state commissions from direct political influence in favor of professional effectiveness. Governor Ben Laney's desire for efficiency produced a rational budget process and improved legislative operations. His successor Sidney McMath pursued a new progressive agenda of economic development, enhanced schools, and racial moderation. Orval Faubus in his first term as governor endeavored to carry forward a portion of the McMath reform program while sidestepping demands that he shore up segregation. Shunning traditional political institutions, a number of Arkansans joined new organizations, including the White Citizens' Council, that promised no quarter against federal authority.

The legislature continued to endorse industrial recruitment with a series of laws permitting local governments to entice new plants with tax-free financing and low-cost site development. The appetite for capital to start businesses and expand public infrastructure led to the era's most notable success story. Witt Stephens employed his profits from his bond business to purchase Arkansas Louisiana Gas Company while parlaying his influence to dethrone Arkansas Power and Light from uncontested political dominance. If Arkansas incomes did not rise enough to keep residents from leaving the state, those who remained had the means and time to prefer wider choices for recreation and leisure. Traditional hunting and fishing were revamped by game management and the feverish construction of lakes. Notable victories over established football powers elevated the University of Arkansas Razorbacks to a statewide phenomenon.

The state's business elite took credit for moving Arkansas into a new economic era and displayed confidence that wider prosperity blunted discord. The generally peaceful desegregation of schools in Charleston and Fayetteville, along with the defeat of white militants in Hoxie did not contradict their optimism or require them to decide if preserving segregation was worth the danger to their industrial recruitment program.

I. The Managerial Reform of Government

The economic development campaign led by Arkansas Power and Light was accompanied by the gradual professionalization of state government. While a more efficiently managed government historically appealed to urban business interests, voters through statewide referendums clipped the appointive and oversight powers that elected officials had exercised to serve personal agendas.

Shortly after taking office in 1941, governor Homer Adkins appointed all new members to the University of Arkansas board of trustees, which then fired president J. William Fulbright. The deposed academic was the son of Roberta Fulbright, publisher of the Fayetteville *Northwest Arkansas Times* and an influential supporter of Adkins's bitter antagonist, former governor Carl Bailey. Adkins's imperious treatment of the university post as a weapon for political reprisal disturbed alumni and those anxious about the state's reputation. In the 1942 election, voters stood with the reformers by narrowly approving Amendment 33, which set the terms of office for appointees to boards and commissions overseeing state institutions, prevented the governor from either decreasing or increasing the number of board members, and protected members from removal without demonstration of cause. Arkansans in that same year returned Adkins to the governor's office and elected Fulbright to the U.S. House of Representatives.

Both the gubernatorial and legislative prerogatives were trimmed in 1944 when the Arkansas Game and Fish Commission (G&FC) became the first of two constitutionally independent agencies. In 1915 the General Assembly established the G&FC to fend off the endless demands for specific hunting and fishing statutes. However, the G&FC's mandate to develop and enforce game regulations was undermined by low funding and the legislature's continued enactment of local regulations. The 1923 session, for example, put thirty-two laws on the books that governed such matters as the use of nets to catch fish in Chicot County or the setting of quail season in Columbia County.

The drive for professional, non-political oversight of game populations originated with an urban interest group. In 1943 the Pulaski County chapter of the Arkansas Wildlife Federation wrote and led the petition drive for an amendment that vested in the G&FC exclusive authority over game and wildlife management and permitted it to use the income from hunting and fishing license fees to carry out its duties and to acquire land for refuges. Under the proposal, the extended terms of the commissioners allowed them to select an executive director and set policies without deferring to intrusive elected officials.

Overshadowed in 1944 by the controversial right-to-work amendment on the ballot, the proposed G&FC amendment aroused little public opposition and garnered over 60 percent of the votes. In an early test of its independence, the G&FC in 1951 voided an act by holding that the General Assembly had overstepped its authority when it exempted those over age sixty-five from the costs of hunting or fishing licenses. The relative autonomy of the commission and its director irked some powerful legislators, who throughout the 1950s delayed authorization of appropriations for staff salaries and agency operations.

Crippled by the bond default of the 1930s and the low priority for highway construction during World War II, the woeful road system was increasingly burdened by the developing industrial pattern of widely dispersed factories that corresponded to the state's scattered communities. Seven county seats still had no paved outlet. Governor Sidney S. McMath in this first term successfully lobbied the 1949 legislature to submit a $28 million general obligation bond issue to the voters for highway construction and maintenance. Opponents who somberly recalled public insolvency during the Depression were drowned out by the chambers of commerce, civic clubs, and the Farm Bureau. The voters sanctioned the bond issue by a four-to-one margin. Almost 2,300 highway miles were added during the McMath years, but the rapid and massive program exposed the governor to charges of graft and favoritism.

A highway audit commission conducted public hearings in early 1952 to examine accusations that the administration had solicited campaign contributions from contractors and vendors. An implement dealer testified that he had sold the state a road grader following a $500 contribution to the McMath campaign, while other testimony revealed that two contractors who made substantial donations to the campaign received 80 percent of the orders to stockpile crushed rock. The audit commission acknowledged that a long-standing culture of corruption in state government nurtured extensive waste and extravagance in the Highway Department but concluded McMath should have broken with the past: "And while we call attention to the abuses which administration after administration has perpetrated under that system, we realize that in the final analysis it is the present administration which is solely responsible for conditions as they exist at present."

McMath disputed the charges by noting correctly that several audit commission members were political adversaries. The administration staunchly maintained that it followed a policy of favoring friends only when price and quality were equal to those of other bidders. While the commission called on the Pulaski County prosecutor to look into specific instances where bribery may have occurred, no administration officials were indicted. Nevertheless, the practice of old-school politics by a reform administration influenced the voters in 1952 to approve another transfer of prerogatives from the governor to long-term appointees with a degree of independence.

Known as the "Mack-Blackwell Amendment" after its legislative sponsors, Amendment 42 revamped the state Highway Commission. As with the G&FC, the Commission, rather than the governor, hired a director to oversee the department. The commissioners, protected by their staggered ten-year terms, were able to stave off patronage demands and through their lengthy tenures become invested in the professional operations of the agency. Yet the traditional sway of local interests persisted. The appointment of commissioners from each congressional district curbed efforts to create a statewide road system based upon traffic use. One legislator famously explained, "I'd rather have a highway commissioner than a governor from Craighead County."

Touted as fostering honest government, these good-government amendments weakened the ability of the chief executive to manage a growing state bureaucracy. The restrictions on Arkansas governors were among the most binding in the nation. Postwar governors, however, regained influence and clout by taking an interest in fixing local schools.

Arkansas school districts had recovered slightly from the Depression years, when they were wards of the federal government. But the upsurge of state funds from rising wartime incomes did not fully compensate for declining local millage collections in depopulated districts. Teachers took better-paying jobs and left behind overcrowded classrooms. By 1945 over half of those teaching before the war were no longer working in Arkansas schools and were replaced by instructors possessing fewer college credit hours. The length of the average school year fell short of both the Southern and national norms.

The indisputable crisis provoked the first substantial education reform proposals since the 1920s. In 1948 the Arkansas Education Association (AEA), the professional organization of school administrators and teachers, gained critical victories when voters approved a constitutional amendment removing the eighteen-mill limit on local school district taxes and an initiated act abolishing school districts enrolling fewer than 350 students.

While the number of school districts had declined from over 5,000 during the 1920s to 1,598 by 1948, nearly a third, serving 65,000 children, still failed to offer high school classes. Black students suffered particularly from the survival of small rural districts. During the 1941–42 school year, 7 percent of all African American students were enrolled in high school grades compared to 19 percent of whites; by 1950, the 5.6 median number of school years completed by African American adults remained significantly lower than the 8.7 years achieved by whites. Yet throughout the 1940s the gap in comparative outlays for black and white pupils narrowed. In 1950–51 the average per student expenditure for African Americans was 61 percent of that for whites, a notable gain from the consistent 40 percent proportion of the 1930s. These statistical improvements derived from the declining numbers of black students, migration of families to better financed urban schools, and judicial impatience over the blatant inequalities embedded in Southern segregation.

Following the lifting of the millage ceiling, Governor McMath barnstormed the state with dozens of buses and trucks filled with modern classroom equipment to demonstrate that higher property-tax rates were needed if Arkansas children were to keep up with the rest of the nation. His efforts demonstrated that as state government took on greater responsibility for education a governor could command center stage and set the agenda for school reform. Even though over two hundred school districts raised their millage rates, the state contribution to local schools for the first time in history outweighed local funding, rising to 57.8 percent of district revenues by 1951.

In terms of actual dollars, state funding remained insufficient to offset rising salaries, transportation costs among consolidated schools, and razing dilapidated buildings. In addition, the consolidation amendment did not require districts that fell below 350 students in the future to merge with larger neighbors.

By 1966, 116 of the state's 409 districts claimed fewer than 350 students, and none of the 71 high schools that taught fewer than 100 pupils had earned regional accreditation.

The perseverance of small school districts also impaired the state's attempt to have education dollars follow the students. The creation of the 1951 Arkansas minimum foundation program was consistent with the reform effort in other Southern states to provide a funding base to insure students in every district received an adequate education. Ideally, growing schools would obtain more state moneys to hire additional teachers and build new classrooms. Once again the chronic preeminence in Arkansas of local prerogatives dictated that rural districts did not lose revenue even as their enrollments fell. Expanding schools struggled with comparatively less funding on a per student basis. The structural inequities in financing education persisted until state courts in the 1980s ruled that Arkansas failed to meet its constitutional responsibility to maintain a "general, suitable, and efficient" system of schools.

BENJAMIN T. LANEY and Sidney McMath, the postwar governors, both embraced the popular drive to improve efficiency and attract new industries by modernizing government services but disagreed profoundly over what elements from the past should endure in modern Arkansas. Laney was an unflagging fiscal conservative, suspicious of welfare expenditures and resolute in preserving segregation. McMath was sympathetic to organized labor, believed government could help the impoverished, and committed to diminishing the severity of racial discrimination.

Worried that an unprecedented budget surplus would be squandered, Laney introduced the Revenue Stabilization Act as his major legislative proposal for the 1945 session. Although Arkansas was constitutionally obligated to operate within a balanced budget, the allocation of specific taxes to separate state agencies left them hostage to the fluctuations of tax collection. An agency in any given year could find itself flourishing through an unexpected windfall while another was left indigent because temporary conditions interrupted the revenue stream from its particular tax source. This unpredictability reduced the budget process to sorcery and clairvoyance. Approved almost without dissent, the Revenue Stabilization law placed most tax revenue in a general fund and established a mechanism for the legislature to set spending priorities for unanticipated surpluses.

Wishing to apply business techniques to the lawmaking process, Laney in 1947 introduced a measure that nudged the General Assembly closer to the modern era. In effect, legislative sessions had long been biennial conventions in which delegates tended to business primarily at Little Rock's downtown Marion Hotel. Legislative committees met infrequently, kept no minutes, and gave do passes to unread bills. The casual procedures resulted in part from an overcrowded capitol building that housed virtually all state agencies and furnished few rooms for committee sessions.

In any case, the Marion was a more congenial setting. Lobbyists rented and stocked suites to entertain and cajole legislators in myriad ways. To protect hotel manager Ben Shelley from overextended solons, the state paid legislators a daily allowance rather than disbursing the per diem as a lump sum. At the close of each session the secretary of state covered the desks in the chambers with dust cloths and the general assembly ceased to exist.

Pulitzer Prize–winning novelist Richard Ford, Shelley's step-grandson, lived part of his boyhood in the Marion, which represented an oasis of elegance and understood power:

> There was a curving marble fish pond in the lobby; a tranquil, banistered mezzanine with *escritoires* and soft lights; a jet marble front desk; green leather couches, green carpets, bellboys with green twill uniforms and short memories. . . . Ladies from the Delta stayed in on shopping trips. The Optimists and the Rotarians met. Assignations between state officials went on upstairs.

Using a Kansas law as the model, Laney in 1947 persuaded the legislature to organize the Bureau of Legislative Research and to approve the creation of the Legislative Council that reviewed agency budget requests before each session. In 1951 Marcus Halbrook, the bureau director, and his small staff took on bill-writing duties. Previously, either the attorney general or lawyers for private interests groups drafted nearly all the measures. Determined from the beginning that the bureau served only legislators, Halbrook shocked lobbyists by refusing to divulge the contents of bills before they were introduced in the assembly. The impact of the structural reforms was augmented by a host of younger faces; the 1947 legislature included thirteen new senators and sixty-nine freshman representatives.

By the end of his term, Laney turned his attention from good government issues to reinforcing segregation. In February 1948 president Harry S. Truman, who had assumed office upon the death of Roosevelt, placed before Congress a civil rights program that included elimination of the poll tax, enactment of an anti-lynching statute, creation of a federal fair employment committee, and the halting of segregation in interstate transportation. These relatively modest proposals advanced by the leader of their party stunned white Southern Democrats.

In early February, hundreds of Arkansas Democrats who gathered at the Marion Hotel for the annual Jefferson-Jackson dinner to rally support for their party walked out when Truman began an address via a radio broadcast. A few days later Governor Laney plotted strategy with a small group of prominent Southern leaders in the Capitol Hill office of U.S. senator John McClellan of Arkansas to deny Truman the Democratic nomination in the upcoming presidential election.

Throughout the spring, Laney mounted a public campaign against the Truman civil rights program and was at the forefront in organizing the States' Rights Democratic Party to serve as an anti-Truman bloc at the national party convention. At that July 1948 gathering in Philadelphia, Laney was fleetingly promoted as the preferred candidate for president by the States' Rights or Dixiecrat faction, but the movement failed to sidetrack Truman or dislodge a civil rights plank from the Democratic platform.

The Dixiecrats ostensibly launched a third-party campaign, and delegates to a Houston convention chose Governor Strom Thurmond of South Carolina as their presidential candidate. Nevertheless, Dixiecrat leaders intrigued to control rather than compete against Democratic organizations and strived to replace Truman with Thurmond as the party nominee on state ballots. Laney, for his part, confronted unexpectedly strong resistance from Democratic loyalists to a Dixiecrat takeover of the Arkansas party.

Laney's acquiescence to the desegregation of the university law school suggested his basic unwillingness to defy federal-court authority openly. He also advised his Dixiecrat brethren that white supremacy oratory was tactically less effective than denunciations of federal usurpation of state powers. State business groups in 1948 followed Laney's example, emphasizing that national Democratic leaders threatened the Arkansas way of life through championing organized labor. The Arkansas Economic Council, the prodigy of AP&L, accused Truman of abetting Communism.

Nevertheless, racism was close to the surface of the movement. When Laney attempted in 1950 to regain the governor's office, his Dixiecrat credentials attracted the support of white racial radicals who commended him as stalwart against miscegenation. Laney's fall into the company of the strident hard-liners illustrated the dilemma for conservatives who wanted to salvage a racial system losing its constitutional underpinnings. As the legal defenses for segregation crumbled, white Southern officials either searched for evasions to remain within the law without losing political viability or opted for confrontation and defiance. Those who conscientiously met their legal obligations were rare.

In November 1948 Strom Thurmond carried only the four Southern states in which his name appeared on the ballot as a Democrat rather than as a third-party candidate. Arkansas was not one of those states. In September, Sidney McMath, fresh from victory in the gubernatorial run-off primary, had mustered his supporters to block the Dixiecrats' attempted coup at the state party convention.

A MARINE VETERAN of Guadalcanal and the Battle of the Solomons, McMath in 1945 established a law practice in his boyhood home of Hot Springs. The following year he organized other veterans to form the Government Improvement League to run a slate of candidates against the McLaughlin organization. The GI Revolt, which broke out in other Arkansas machine counties and surrounding states, targeted local corruption but shied away from a full-scale reform movement. In 1946 the Hot Springs GIs secured a federal court ruling purging the voting lists of 1,600 suspect poll-tax registrations and then ran successfully as independents in the general election. As the new prosecuting attorney, McMath devoted himself to putting Leo McLaughlin in jail and preparing for a run for governor. Despite securing a change of venue to the rural county seat of Mount Ida, McMath failed to nail down a conviction in McLaughlin's trial.

Unburdened by previous political connections, McMath was a natural candidate whose striking looks and impressive war record fitted him for a statewide campaign. He also proved to be adept at navigating the murky depths of Arkansas factionalism. Aware of Homer Adkins's contempt for McLaughlin and of Carl Bailey's concern that the Hot Springs hero might threaten Senator Fulbright's reelection, McMath was able to draw the two indomitable enemies into his camp. He also enlisted Harry Ashmore, Edwin Dunaway, and Henry Woods, young white liberals who did not shy from plotting strategy with the reactionary Adkins. Their participation signaled that McMath wished to move beyond the narrow political reform goals of the GI Revolt to boost workers' incomes and remove barriers hindering African American opportunity.

Business interests did welcome the new governor's 1949 highway bond program, and McMath hailed the new ribbons of pavement in his own industrial recruitment pitches. When the Eastman Corporation considered a site near Texarkana, McMath promised to construct a four-lane highway between the prospective factory and the city. Yet McMath also publicly questioned the wisdom of maintaining a low-paid labor force to placate the state's employers. His attempts to raise minimum wages and toughen factory-safety regulations reinforced labor-union support for the governor.

In 1949 McMath prodded the General Assembly to approve construction of a teaching hospital to protect the accreditation of the university medical school. The legislature balked at appropriating the full authorized funding, and the medical center was not completed until 1957. Although industrial developers generally favored school improvement measures, legislators considered McMath's 1951 proposal to raise revenue through a higher income tax rather than the more regressive sales tax too steep a price.

The governor's steps to win fairer taxation, improve labor conditions, and lure higher-wage plants countered the economic development approach of the Arkansas Power and Light leaders and their allied business groups. Hamilton Moses had kept the faith of Harvey Couch that the viability of the power company rested on the modernization of the Arkansas economy. Yet Moses, as had his predecessor, reacted virulently to initiatives to rejuvenate the state's economy in ways adverse to AP&L's interests. The continued presence of the Rural Electrification Administration (REA) in Arkansas topped the list of threats.

In 1951 McMath was drawn into the electric wars when over AP&L objections he approved the plan by Arkansas Electric Cooperative Corporation's (AECC) to build a steam-generating plant. Viewing competitive power rates as important incentives to new industry, McMath backed the Public Service Commission (PSC) when it approved the AECC generating station at Ozark, and he lobbied the Truman administration to expedite REA loans for the project. Moses's suspicions of McMath had arisen earlier when the governor neglected to vet his PSC appointees through the utility president. The Ozark plant clash hardened this enmity. McMath perceived the hidden hand of the utility president in the appointment of AP&L friends to the ad hoc highway audit commission that issued the politically damaging report just prior to the upcoming election.

In contrast to these public battles, McMath pursued racial moderation indirectly in an era when rising challenges to segregation stirred the wrath of its adamant defenders. Harry Ashmore, the managing editor of the *Arkansas Gazette* and an advisor to McMath, argued in print and speeches that Southern political leaders should themselves stop depriving African American citizens of the public services and benefits extended to whites. Otherwise, the U.S. Congress and the federal courts would assume the task. Correspondingly, the McMath administration allotted resources more equitably to those institutions serving exclusively African Americans. The governor advocated "achievement of equality of opportunity" but did not endorse desegregation as the means to reach that goal.

McMath had prevailed upon party regulars to repulse the Dixiecrat coup attempt during the 1948 state convention out of loyalty to the national ticket rather than acceptance of Truman's civil rights program. He introduced a measure to use state resources and authority to punish those responsible for the crime of lynching, but his arguments that an Arkansas law was preferable to federal action could not save the bill from a filibuster. He was the first governor to appoint African Americans to the state boards overseeing black institutions, and his 1949 doubling of the appropriation for Agricultural Mechanical and Normal in Pine Bluff gave the black college the means to achieve North Central Association accreditation. Neither these appointments nor his pressure on school administrators to stop diverting funds from black schools within their districts incited marked opposition. McMath's campaign to spur funding for African American public education accelerated a strategy originating with his conservative predecessor.

In 1949 the legislature rebuffed McMath's proposal to repeal the poll tax. While the one-dollar poll tax was losing its potency as a means to discourage citizens from voting, it remained a powerful weapon for east Arkansas county elites to control balloting. Delta landowners solidly opposed McMath because of his racial moderation and alliance with unions. Machine counties elsewhere in the state that were kinder to McMath generally used methods other than the poll tax manipulation to manufacture results.

After he left office in 1953, McMath, serving as the attorney for the state labor organization, campaigned to abolish the poll tax through a state constitutional amendment. In the 1950s large numbers of African Americans paid their poll taxes through drives led by unions. In 1956 these new voters contributed to the defeat of a proposed anti–poll tax amendment. Black leaders feared that the poll tax could be replaced by a more onerous, harsher contrivance to quash African American participation.

McMath was a critical figure in the emergence of a liberal coalition in Arkansas of African American civil rights advocates and union forces; while this alliance based upon common ideological goals and made possible by growing urbanization was a new feature in the state's politics, the engrained tradition of political fragmentation and factionalism undercut liberal solidarity.

McMath elevated a formidable alternative to the business model for Arkansas advancement through his clear advocacy for organized labor, higher-wage jobs, and fair and equal treatment for black citizens. Although the economic

development campaigns that touted a weak regulatory state and official deference to private interests seemed more in line with the state's historic patterns
than the McMath formula, influential corporate heads also had a hand in steering Arkansas politics onto new routes.

To protect their interests, AP&L and the proliferating industry associations during the 1950s weakened the traditional dominance of local elites. A
utility, in particular, did not want to be nibbled by local regulations or foot
the bill of paying off a pack of county machines. If Progressives early in the
century had tied reform to a more robust state government, the rising companies after World War II required responsive state officials—both elected and
bureaucratic—to carry out predictable and advantageous policies. Business
interest groups mobilized clients and employees throughout the state to sway
legislators who customarily had only to oblige hometown big men. Modern
state government in Arkansas originated in the modern private sector.

Other forces tested the once unassailable rural establishments. The isolated
pockets of unionized factories left most members of the General Assembly with
no labor constituency. Candidates for statewide office, however, took notice of
the unions' ability to deliver votes in the party primaries. The growing federal
contribution to the state budget and subsidies for private entities drew congressional officeholders into a complex web of rivalries that went beyond placating
individual county chieftains. Federal dams, for example, created lakes that over-
lapped more than a few local boundaries.

———————

ALTHOUGH DEPOPULATION reduced the size of the state's delegation in
the U.S. House of Representatives from seven in 1940 to four after 1960,
Arkansas held its ground in Congress with long-serving members ascending
to the summit of powerful committees. During their terms in the U.S. Senate,
J. William Fulbright (1945–75) and John L. McClellan (1943–77) successfully
navigated the state's altered political landscape, though their distinct policy
interests and personal styles frustrated those who assumed Southern politicians
were all of a piece.

The erudite Fulbright debunked stereotypes still associated with his native
Ozarks, although his well-known habit of replacing tailored suits with a flan-
nel shirt during election season in Arkansas long amused outsiders. His internationalist perspective began when he was a Rhodes Scholar at Oxford and
deepened with the emergence of the new American globalism in the early
Cold War years. Fulbright's conviction that nations developed in accord with
their particular cultural institutions and were harmed by meddlesome foreign

powers provoked his growing criticism of American containment policy. He objected eloquently during the 1960s to Lyndon Johnson's expansion of American intervention into the middle of what Fulbright considered a civil war in Vietnam. Serving as chair of the Senate Foreign Relations Committee, Fulbright garnered headlines with pointed dissents that infuriated Johnson. Fulbright's resistance to landmark civil rights measures also put him at odds with the president.

As a member of the House of Representatives and continuing after entering the Senate in 1945, Fulbright was as eager as any Southern member of Congress to procure federal funds to reshape the Arkansas economy. His state's reliance upon those dollars did not inhibit his denouncement of the Truman civil rights program as an unconstitutional regulation of his state's racial order. Keeping the Dixiecrats at arm's length and working up a tepid alternative to Truman's proposals, Fulbright in 1948 believed himself a moderate in the mold of McMath. Fulbright would only go as far as to entertain anti-lynching legislation and paring the poll tax. He declared segregation off limits, assuming it was embedded in the cultural fabric of the South rather than an instrument to preserve white supremacy. Throughout the 1950s many white racial moderates shifted to support outright integration while Fulbright stood firm with Southern colleagues in opposing civil rights acts until 1970.

Many Americans outside of Arkansas were puzzled that the author of the momentous Fulbright Exchange Program, created to nurture understanding and tolerance among different peoples throughout the globe, defended a system predicated upon division by color. Fulbright believed himself consistent in his outlook. Shortly after voting against the 1964 civil rights measure, he complained to a state department official that invitations for blacks to attend social functions at the U.S. embassy in Pretoria offended the apartheid government of South Africa: "It does seem to me that we should be guided in the main by the practices of foreign countries in which we have embassies and that we should not try to impose upon them our particular ideas of morality."

Fulbright's preoccupation with international relations did not distract him from tending to Arkansas economic interests, although he generally deferred to the state's senior senator on corralling big ticket federal projects. A rousing speaker, John L. McClellan was not closely identified with the existing party factions in 1938 when he took on Senator Hattie Caraway and the Homer Adkins federal group. Following his defeat, he established a lucrative law practice in Camden before running for an open U.S. Senate seat in 1942. Locked in a bitter primary run-off, McClellan's lack of a political base left him short of funds and on the verge of withdrawing from the race. The encouragement and influence of Ouachita County sheriff Edgar Pryor revived the confidence and finances of the melancholic McClellan. He won the election with a remarkable 61.6 percent margin.

McClellan was more pragmatic than ideological, responsive to state interest groups but far from deferential. He was readily identified as friendly toward AP&L, but his support was not unconditional. McClellan ended Clyde Ellis's dream of an integrated Arkansas River Valley public power system, yet delighted Ellis by pushing through the appropriation process the construction of individual federal hydroelectric power projects. AP&L swallowed hard at this connivance by a legislative ally with their federal adversaries and then became a major customer for the electricity generated by the dams. On a smaller scale, McClellan parceled out drainage projects throughout eastern Arkansas to aid landowners accustomed to losing productive acres to chronic spring flooding.

The calamitous 1937 flood had moved President Roosevelt, who did not share his predecessor's hesitancy about large-scale federal spending, to challenge the U.S. Army Corps of Engineers finally to end the cycle of destruction. The resulting chains of dams, levees, and channels dwarfed the rudimentary system the Corps had erected prior to 1940 in the Lower Mississippi Valley. McClellan led the crusade to construct reservoirs to relieve the effects of dry spells and contain overflow in rainy seasons. Arkansas came to have more than enough water on the surface to meet its needs. Yet, because it was cheaper to pump than to pipe, farmers in east Arkansas drilled into the underground alluvial aquifer with wells fueled first by diesel, then electricity. Federal price supports for rice in World War II spurred farmers to increase irrigated acreage by almost 75 percent during that decade, and cultivation of the grain leapt again during the 1970s. As a result, even the years of plentiful rainfall failed to replenish groundwater reserves in the aquifer.

McClellan relished the investigatory powers of the Senate and authored major revisions of the federal criminal code. As the long-time chair of the Senate Permanent Investigations Committee, he conducted over three hundred investigations and widened the powers of federal prosecutors through his drafting of the 1970 Organized Crime Act. Washington columnist Mary McCrory famously observed that McClellan's questioning of witnesses sounded like "the voice of doom."

In 1957 McClellan combined his zeal for exhaustive inquiries and antipathy toward organized labor when he chaired the Senate select committee hearings into the operations of the Brotherhood of Teamsters. Testimony linking the Teamsters to criminal enterprises angered the public and pressured AFL-CIO leaders to expel its largest and most successful affiliated member. By checking the rise in union membership and influence originating in the New Deal, the McClellan hearings set in motion labor's equally astonishing decline through the end of the century.

Not surprisingly, McClellan clashed with the most prominent Arkansas political figure supported by unions, Sid McMath. McClellan had backed AP&L's campaign to override Governor McMath's approval for financing the Ozark plant that was to generate power for the electrical cooperatives. McClellan's consistent opposition to civil rights measures marked another notable contrast with McMath's positions. In 1952 McClellan joined with Ben Laney to back Francis Cherry in the successful campaign to deny McMath a third term as governor. McMath had been wounded by the highway audit findings and hamstrung by his identification with increasingly unpopular President Truman.

Two years later, McMath failed to even the score in a barebones campaign against McClellan's reelection. Union assistance for McMath was surpassed by the money and votes that flowed to an incumbent steadfastly bringing home the bacon. McClellan, rather than McMath, earned the support of Harold Flowers, the civil rights pioneer who by 1954 had wrenched the state NAACP organization from its conservative, accommodationist leadership toward a more activist stance favoring integration.

In the 1954 senatorial contest, McMath fruitlessly attempted to couple McClellan to AP&L, which in May had received a steep and unpopular rate increase. Orval Faubus exploited the issue more effectively against Gov. Francis Cherry. Only the second twentieth century incumbent denied more than one term, Cherry was among the least politically adroit governors. His foe was one of the best.

––––––––––

A JONESBORO CHANCERY JUDGE when he entered the 1952 governor's race, Cherry overcame his low name recognition and nonexistent political connections by fielding questions from listeners during twenty radio talkathons. Having won office by appealing directly to voters through the media, Cherry summarily rebuffed political bosses who paid courtesy calls on him. He assumed that establishing sound government procedures counted for more than a hard-nosed political organization. Cherry organized a department of finance and administration to supervise the state budget, advocated a property-tax equalization amendment, and stiffened welfare requirements. This last policy change immediately expelled from the rolls about 2,300 people. Cherry's deepening unpopularity revealed that years of federal support for expanded public services made fiscal belt-tightening politically risky.

The property tax proposal would have ended wildly divergent assessments, but greatly increased the levy on agricultural and timber holdings. Most of the 1950s welfare recipients were elderly and white, and many voters considered them the deserving poor rather than "deadheads," as characterized by Cherry. The northwest Arkansas poultry companies forecast ruin arising from his veto of a feed and seed sales tax exemption. Conventional wisdom argued against a cakewalk for his reelection.

In 1954 Orval Faubus broke early from the pack of Cherry's challengers. A Madison County newspaper publisher and highway director in the McMath administration, Faubus had an instinct for speaking the mind of his listeners. Cherry was a diffident campaigner, more comfortable making a pitch from a broadcast booth. At a boisterous Perryville rally, Faubus worked the crowds while Cherry waited in his car, listening to a baseball game before materializing to deliver his scheduled speech. Pushed into an August run-off, the staid Cherry had failed to tarnish his opponent with the highway scandals that had sunk McMath.

Cherry was already on record as promising adherence to court desegregation rulings and said little in the wake of the U.S. Supreme Court's *Brown v. Board of Education of Topeka* decision in May that held school segregation to be unconstitutional. For his part Faubus did not condemn Cherry's subdued reaction although the hill-country politico had opened his campaign by denouncing race mixing in the classroom. Rather than exploit racism, Cherry attempted to whip up fears over Communism. On August 2, he went on statewide television and radio to detail Faubus's enrollment and leadership of the student body at radical Commonwealth College.

Cherry had once again shown a poor sense of timing. By 1954 the excesses of Joseph McCarthy were dampening the postwar Red Scare. John McClellan, the ranking minority member on the McCarthy committee, had a year earlier led a Democratic walkout and returned only when he was allowed to replace the baleful committee counsel, Roy Cohn, with Robert F. Kennedy. Faubus supporters decried Cherry's maneuver as slander against a decorated veteran who fought bravely during the Battle of the Bulge. Faubus intoned his defense in every address: he had remained at Commonwealth a few days as an unenrolled student, never attended classes, and left after the radicalism and atheism of the staff became evident. These were lies, but Cherry reeled from the public backlash.

The Faubus victory also rested on tried and true methods. On election night the Garland County votes remained unreported well into the early morning hours. There the Hot Springs machine, under new management, was fiddling with the vote totals to help out Cherry against the former McMath associate. Finally, Homer Adkins placed a call from Faubus headquarters, explaining that he had a sufficient number of north Arkansas boxes in reserve to counter anything coming out of Hot Springs. The Garland County crowd blinked, and it was over.

Later described by McMath as "the most liberal member of my administration," Orval Faubus reinforced his progressive reputation by withstanding the McCarthyite assault. Yet neither his father's socialism nor the brief stint at Commonwealth College had deflected his preference for mainstream politics. Roy Reed has explained that while an inclination for compromise grew in reaction to Sam Faubus's dogmatism, young Orval also learned from listening to his father and friends that politics greatly mattered to a people living in a poor state. Politics also conveyed status and respect, qualities craved by the young man from Greasy Creek.

The first Faubus legislative session followed the postwar model of modestly expanding and professionalizing government services while banking on the arrival of new industries to lift the state from its chronically low economic rankings. Faubus established a publicity and parks department to promote tourism, although the upgrading and expansion of the state parks was deferred for another era. His backing of a bill to delay the implementation of utility rate increases reflected his sympathy for families whose Ozark homes had only recently replaced lanterns with light bulbs.

Faubus, however, also eagerly collaborated with AP&L and the state Chamber of Commerce to reorganize the state resources commission as the Arkansas Industrial Development Commission (AIDC). Faubus's coaxing of Winthrop Rockefeller from his Petit Jean hilltop retreat to lead the AIDC cheered business leaders. In 1953 Rockefeller had moved to Arkansas from New York to start afresh following a well-publicized divorce and to establish a legacy apart from his illustrious brothers. Business development proponents anticipated that even the prodigal scion of America's first family of capitalism could offer uncommon access to corporate offices. The new AIDC chairman reached into his own deep pockets to lure talented staff for the new agency by augmenting meager state salaries.

The governor also gave his blessings to a measure that state senator Max Howell steered to passage. Arkansas would no longer be among the few remaining states to house developmentally disabled children with the general population of the state mental hospital. The new separate residential center, or Children's Colony, was an innovative village-like arrangement of cottages, classrooms, and dining hall across four hundred acres outside Conway. Mental health officials singled out the colony shortly after its completion in 1959 as a model for the nation. Five similar facilities, termed human development centers, opened in other communities by the late 1970s, but the favorable estimation by professional organizations evaporated in the twenty-first century. The Arkansas policy of placing a high percentage of developmentally disabled adults and youth in centralized institutions had been abandoned throughout the nation, and the federal government sued the state after finding instances in the Conway Center of deficient conditions, questionable treatment of patients, and supervision of staff. In 2011 U.S. District Judge Leon Holmes ruled in favor of Arkansas, finding that the federal allegations were not "supported by the weight of the evidence." In that same year another human development center was closed following an investigation that documented inadequate care of residents.

In 1958, after visiting another state institution for children, Faubus noted squalid and deteriorating conditions but did not reverse the decades-long neglect of Negro Boys Industrial School. Despite the name, this reform school—in contrast to the one for white boys—operated much like the adult prison farms. When twenty-one boys burned to death in a 1959 dormitory fire at the black institution, the governor placed blame primarily on the African American superintendent. Grif Stockely, in his examination, noted that the tragedy was another example of the menace and violence intertwined with racial segregation.

A veteran from Little Rock who first entered the legislature as part of the GI Revolt, Max Howell also sidetracked a 1955 bill to mandate school segregation: "Just because Alabama or some other dyed-in-the-wool Southern state jumped in haste to preserve something doesn't mean Arkansas should." Faubus did not enter the fray over the bill. After the *Brown* decision, Faubus detected little political gain from brazen defiance and decided that occasional segregationist rhetoric would placate white voters. The governor had also taken note of growing urban black political clout and appointed the first African Americans to the state Democratic Party committee.

In May 1955 the Supreme Court in its *Brown II* decision delegated to federal district courts the responsibility to implement school integration with "all deliberate speed." Uncertain that President Dwight Eisenhower would enforce a far-reaching attack on Jim Crow, the Court did not set deadlines for phasing out segregation or stipulate when schools were sufficiently integrated under the law. Faubus calculated that most white Arkansans preferred sidestepping rather than flouting federal authority. He remained confident that this new Court decision allowed him to continue to downplay an issue that he viewed as a distraction from his agenda. Conversely, other white figures grew embold-ened by what they viewed as the Court's retreat from the principles in the orig-inal *Brown* decision. Faubus was unprepared when racial radicals exploited this seeming judicial about-face on integration to move white popular opinion toward outright resistance.

JAMES JOHNSON was a Marine veteran from Crossett whose ambitions had propelled him to the state Senate by the time he was twenty-six. A losing bid for state attorney general in 1954 did not deter him. In contrast to Faubus, Johnson believed he could ride the tiger of race to statewide office. In 1955 he founded the White Citizens' Council of Arkansas, which took its place alongside two other small groups in the state that were agitating to halt school desegregation. Johnson soon overshadowed the other white militant leaders, who were undis-tinguished and lacked his incendiary flair on the speaker's platform.

Johnson possessed the gifts to succeed in a state where personality still counted more than service to party. Yet he was hobbled by the minuscule for-mal membership in the racially extremist organizations and his lack of ties to county elites. In addition the arch-segregationist crudity and appeal to disor-der troubled conservative whites, many of whom remained confident in their power to protect white supremacy. The sheriff of southeastern Lincoln County explained in October 1955 why he canceled a Citizens' Council rally: "We're getting along fine without anybody stirring up trouble."

The Citizens' Council organizations heaped blame on Faubus for not stop-ping several school districts from starting to integrate soon after the *Brown* decision. In the pages of the segregationist paper *Arkansas Faith*, the inac-tion of "Awful Faubus" was explained by his confusion over whether he had been trained at "communist Commonwealth College or a mule barn." In 1956 Johnson, still a relative newcomer to the political arena, ran for governor as segregation's uncompromising defender. Realizing the racism that stirred Citizens' Council members was less effective in the statewide race against Faubus, Johnson sought respectability through appearing publicly with former governor Ben Laney and by arguing that the state could veto the *Brown* deci-sion through the device of "interposition."

In a series of columns the previous year, a Virginia newspaper editor asserted that a state government could interpose its power against Supreme Court deci-sions that overstepped constitutional boundaries. Segregationists wielded the argument to appeal to whites discomforted by a stark racist strategy. In 1956 Johnson put forward an interposition amendment to the Arkansas constitution to require "nullification" of "dangerous invasions" of state authority and popular rule. The so-called Johnson Amendment was inseparable from the Johnson campaign for governor.

In the 1956 campaign, Faubus assured voters he could preserve segregation without radical measures or the hooliganism still associated with Johnson. Faubus trumpeted as feasible alternatives to the Johnson Amendment a less stringent interposition proposal and an act to permit districts under court order to maintain single-race schools through "voluntary" student assignment expedients. Not only was Faubus confident that this circumvention would win over ordinary voters, but he presumed that the east Arkansas landowning elites saw Johnson's fire-eaters as a greater threat to the status quo than the distant federal government. Indeed, Faubus's 58.1 percent statewide victory was reinforced by a 67.7 percent margin in the machine-controlled Crittenden County, a delta province of the sort that had represented Johnson's best hope.

The sting of defeat for Johnson was softened by the approval of his interposition amendment. Militant defiance had a constituency. Faubus nevertheless remained confident that his mastery of the Arkansas political system of machines, corruption, and personal relationships would marginalize the white extremists. Faubus was a moderate by default.

II. Land of Opportunity

Called variously the Bear State, the Wonder State, the Toothpick State (in homage to the bowie knife), Arkansas was officially christened "The Land of Opportunity" by the 1953 General Assembly. If the resolution suggested urban economic development had supplanted the celebration of rural traditions, it also showed that industry leaders worried the 1940s economic boom was subsiding.

Before 1955 the Arkansas Economic Council marketed the benefits of a surplus labor force and compliant local governments to prospective industries. Yet federal minimum wage laws prevented Arkansas from underbidding other Southern states, which in turn were aggressively extending subsidies to new manufacturers. And the continued out-migration sparked business worries that a shortage of available workers could stoke higher wages. The conservatism of Arkansas bankers and the state's shaky reputation in capital markets forced the political and industrial leaders to turn to public financing of private development.

Act 404 of 1955, which created the Arkansas Industrial Development Commission, also authorized local industrial development corporations. These quasi-private organizations raised funds through stock sales to purchase industrial sites and issued tax-free bonds to underwrite low-interest loans for arriving employers. A number of communities immediately jumped on the bandwagon: Searcy developed a parcel and extended a railroad siding for a Frostyaire Frozen Foods warehouse and later raised $500,000 to acquire a ten-acre tract for a California business machine manufacturer; the Morrilton Industrial Corporation leased a building to the Oberman Company, which employed two hundred to produce men's slacks; the El Dorado Corporation arranged for $200,000 in financing to entice Jess Merkle to locate J-M Poultry in Arkansas rather than in Ruston, Louisiana.

With the passage of Amendment 49 in 1957, municipal and county governments were able to issue, following a popular vote, their own tax-exempt bonds to develop industrial parks and erect buildings that met the demands of relocating companies. Three years later the General Assembly smoothed the way under Act 9 for local governments to issue bonds without calling an election. The governments used the modest rents and fees from companies rather than taxes to meet bond payments. Old-fashion localism, in which state government ceded its monopoly on amassing debt or sifting public funds to private companies, was resuscitated with more intricate financial instruments.

By 1966, 151 Arkansas communities boasted at least one economic development organization. In this era Arkansas, along with five other Southern states, issued 87 percent of the industrial bonds in the nation as a whole. Congressional representatives from states that did not resort to municipal financing incentives charged that the federal treasury was being looted to entice industries to relocate from one region to another. Bills to curtail the bond issues disappeared into oblivion in the U.S. House Ways and Means Committee chaired by Wilbur Mills of Arkansas.

Southern communities clearly held a particular attraction for wage-sensitive, highly competitive industries such as food processing and clothing production. Nevertheless, rising industrialization in Dixie depended on a growing consumer market throughout the region and an improving transportation system, major trends beyond the control of local development enterprises.

In general, new Arkansas manufacturing plants were located in areas of white surplus labor rather than in regions with a significant or predominant African American population. This selective pattern owed to the reluctance of eastern planters to see their remaining farm workers siphoned off into other occupations and to the strategies of industrial promoters who believed jobs for whites garnered better publicity and political goodwill. The construction of the J-M Poultry plant demonstrated how even entry-level manufacturing jobs altered the labor markets. African American women won positions on the processing line in sufficient numbers to make Jess Merkle a much-reviled figure in upper-class El Dorado households accustomed to inexpensive domestic workers. The unionization of the plant's workers was neither the exception in a petro-chemical town nor in its industry. In contrast to the apparel factories, many poultry operations in the state's early manufacturing phase were organized.

While black income grew during the 1950s, the practices and policies confining African American workers to arduous and poorly paid work solidified economic inequities. Throughout the decade, black per capita income stagnated at 42–43 percent that of whites. By 1960 over 25 percent of Arkansas black workers were classified as agricultural labors, while 20 percent earned wages in private households. Well over half of the 15 percent of African Americans employed in manufacturing worked in lumber and wood products occupations rather than the newer nondurable good operations.

EVEN THOSE WHO BOASTED that the state could live off its own resources if walled off from the rest of the world had to acknowledge that the fundamental Arkansas scarcity was capital. That one of the dominant figures during the latter half of the century amassed a fortune trading bonds rather than selling timber or cultivating delta soil defied historical precedent. Wilton (Witt) R. Stephens borrowed $15,000 in 1933 to organize his own investment company and to purchase depressed municipal, school, and levee bonds for as low as ten cents on the dollar. With his profits from reselling the debt instruments at nearly face value, Stephens eventually bought an interest in thirty-seven banks. In 1946 he made his younger brother, Jackson, a partner in what became Stephens Incorporated, and the firm began to underwrite bond issues rather than simply buy and sell them. The firm proved invaluable in launching and sustaining firms led by Don Tyson and Sam Walton.

Doing business in Arkansas required close and active attention to politics, particularly for one worried about the credit worthiness of local governments and schools. Witt Stephens worked hard and spent money to have the voters see things his way in 1948 when they approved the lifting of the school mill-age ceiling. Eventually, the Stephens firm and another allied bond house managed the sale of 70 percent of the school bonds in the state. Unerringly flexible, Stephens insinuated himself with governors Adkins, McMath, and Cherry. It required only one day after the 1954 election for Stephens to shake off the dust of Cherry's defeat and be accorded a courteous reception into the Faubus camp. That transfer of loyalties foreshadowed a continental shift in the Arkansas political landscape.

Shortly before the election, the Stephens' interests purchased the ailing Arkansas Louisiana Gas Company (Arkla) and won rate increases the following year from the new Faubus appointees on the Public Service Commission. The favorable decisions hoisted the Arkla stock value well above the Stephens's purchase price while hitting hard the natural gas company's largest consumer, Arkansas Power and Light. The AP&L men and their industrial customers pressed the new governor for relief, but Faubus had not forged close ties with the electric utility and refused to injure his new patron. AP&L then turned to the courts to reverse the commission's adoption of a pricing structure that Stephens had put forward to ensure himself high returns. In February 1957 the state supreme court sided with AP&L. The following day lawmakers introduced bills to enact the Stephens rate system known as the Fair Field Price Law. The overwhelming votes in favor of the measure revealed that Stephens had supplanted AP&L to become the new sovereign of the General Assembly.

It required little imagination to show gratitude to citizen legislators who were attorneys, business proprietors, or landowners. Members who were insurance agents soon provided coverage for Arkla's operations, a service station owner fueled Arkla vehicles, and others went into the banking business with Stephens or found him a reliable lender for farm purchases. The natural-gas mogul also gave legislators a folksy justification for favoring his utility. Upbraiding AP&L for shifting the cost of lower industrial electric rates to residential customers, Stephens declared that Arkla stood with the "biscuit cookers."

Cultivating the image of the country boy who made good through hustle and concealed acumen, Stephens became widely known as "Mr. Witt." On the other hand, Stephens, unlike Couch or Moses, never underwrote industrial development campaigns or took up issues that did not directly touch upon his interests. Throughout his life he was a wealthy and powerful man who continued an indefatigable pursuit of wealth and power: "It's a game with me. That's how they score the game."

State promoters claimed that the financial and corporate achievements of the plainspoken Stephens symbolized a more worldly Arkansas that continued to value personal ties and disdain pretension. The image was not altogether at variance with reality. Most Arkansans remained rural, but the larger urban areas—particularly the cities of Little Rock, North Little Rock, and Fort Smith—grew faster between 1950 and 1960 than the national rate, while the smaller towns and rural areas continued to lose residents. Beyond census designations, the boundary between town and country was etched by the ownership of consumer appliances.

In contrast to the state's farm households, most urban residents by 1960 were warmed by natural gas rather than wood fuel, piled their laundry into automatic washers, placed telephone calls from their homes, and enjoyed the convenience of indoor bathtubs and flush toilets. Yet life in the country was becoming less isolated. Television sets flickered in about 75 percent of Arkansas homes. If the proportion of rural families owning sets was only slightly lower than that of their urban counterparts, viewers distant from broadcast towers were frustrated when trying to tune in Milton Berle, *Playhouse 90*, or *Ozark Jubilee* with Red Foley.

Expanding consumer demand in Arkansas, stimulated by commercials for national products, actually preserved an old economic pattern by drawing the state into the national market. Even though the value added by manufacturing to Arkansas products had increased by fifteen times since 1935, the value of the goods and services the state imported through the 1950s still outstripped its exports. If the industrialization of the state had wrested it from the quagmire of basic processing of natural resources, the higher-priced items purchased by Arkansans were still generally made elsewhere. The one area of a positive balance of payments was in federal spending. In 1958 the state received about $113 million more from the U.S. government than it sent to Washington in taxes and fees. Although the net receipts declined to about $79 million by 1963, federal funds remained an important source of outside capital for state development.

The state's most dramatic net loss continued to be its people. An exodus of 371,000 between 1950 and 1958 forced the 6.5 percent drop in the state's population during the 1950s. Although a reduction in the surplus labor force had the potential to lift wage and income levels, the exit of young adults possessing the information, wherewithal, and ambition to embark on a long-distance move deprived Arkansas of highly productive employees. As in the 1940s, African Americans were more likely to relocate than whites, although the rate of black migration slowed. The youth of the migrants altered the state's demographics, increasing the number of Arkansans who were not earning regular wages. After 1960 the 10.6 percent of Arkansans over sixty-five years of age and 32 percent younger than fourteen were greater than the national proportions of these age groups.

The state attracted few immigrants as permanent residents but more visitors arrived as vacationers. Out-of-state tourist spending doubled between 1948 and 1959, with most of the dollars circulating through Hot Springs and the Ozark region. Organized in 1919 to promote the uplands of southwestern Missouri and northwestern Arkansas, the Ozark Playgrounds Association incorporated the U.S. Corps of Engineers' construction of Norfork (1944), Bull Shoals (1951), Greers Ferry (1962), and Beaver (1963) Lakes into its marketing strategy.

Rather than simply lauding scenery and historic sites, the association highlighted water sports and country music entertainment at resort centers. In 1945 thirteen camps and hotels offered overnight lodging in the vicinity of Baxter County; by 1971, following the creation of Norfork and Bull Shoals Lakes, about 300 businesses had space to serve over 8,000 visitors. The Corps built the lakes for flood control and electrical power generation; recreation was not included in the authorized purpose or mission for the projects but that omission mattered little to Arkansans who carved out unforeseen economic niches.

Soon the advertisements of weekly cabin rentals was supplanted by publicity for retirement communities. In 1955 John C. Cooper, an east Arkansas attorney and farmer, summoned first-term governor Faubus to the dedication of Cherokee Village, his four hundred acres of subdivided housing tracts in Sharp County. Originally intending to promote Cherokee Village to those wanting second or vacation homes, Cooper by 1960 offered expense paid tours for Midwesterners in the market for a permanent retirement residence. Cooper later purchased the older Benton County resort of Bella Vista and also constructed Hot Springs Village near the shores of Lake Ouachita, a Corps project created by the 1955 erection of the Blakely Mountain Dam.

The formation of lakes throughout the state was the most apparent reconstruction of the Arkansas landscape in the latter half of the twentieth century. The restoration of the white-tail deer herd was another environmental modification that redefined leisure. Critical to Arkansas's first economy, hunting gave rise to the narratives and images defining the state's early identity. Beginning in the 1950s, the efficacy of the Game and Fish Commission's wildlife management policies enabled hundreds of thousands of Arkansas hunters to revive a fabled tradition as modern sport.

During the 1927 flood, deer fled for safety to the top of levees where they were easily slaughtered. Although it was thought that the flood had destroyed the deer population in the state, the commission recorded about five hundred by 1930. While game laws limited the number of bucks killed and prohibited outright the taking of does, habitat destruction and the stubborn use of dogs by mountain hunters to run down game depressed the numbers. Realizing that regulations did not solve the problem of habitat recovery, the G&FC developed twelve wildlife refuges throughout the state by 1934 and in 1939 restructured one in Howard County as a "deer farm."

By the time the modern, autonomous G&FC came into existence through Amendment 35, the benefits of the refuge policy could be measured by the increase in the legal deer harvest from 203 in 1938 to 1,606 in 1944. The commission cooperated with federal forest agency officials to trap deer from overstocked herds in the Ozark National Forest and distribute them to the state refuges. The transplanting of the animals led to the establishment of herds in sixty-six counties, and in 1950 the G&FC permitted hunting in several counties for the first time since the war.

In 1943 Alvin Bates saw his first deer when it crossed a Drew County road: "I didn't know what it was, thought it was a curious animal." In 1947 even longtime residents of Augusta believed that the first deer to inhabit the area were those released that year near the wildlife management refuge bordering White and Woodruff Counties. When hunting was authorized locally in 1952, prominent townsmen set up a camp on a bend of the White River. Having no experience in bagging deer, the camp members during the first hunt lined themselves besides trees a few hundred yards apart and waited as another person drove the game toward them. Soon they adopted the common approach of constructing stands up in large trees.

Herbert Lunday of the Buckeye Camp recalled that G&FC-scheduled deer seasons became integrated into the rhythm of community life. "Many citizens of Augusta have enjoyed the excitement of the deer hunts with us. They've wished us safety and good fortune and watched eagerly for us to return to town with our bounty. I especially remember the excellent pies, cakes, and other food sent to us by the women of the community." Within a few years this contemporary recreation, a product of scientific management techniques, became a tradition complete with ritual, folklore, and special knowledge to be passed from father to son. Small school districts excused student absences during the late fall deer hunting season.

A 1998 survey indicated that only about 6 percent of those holding hunting licenses were women, who were more likely than men to hunt with family members. The commission's absolute prohibition against the killing of does became so rooted in the evolving hunting culture that it became difficult to persuade future generations to reverse course when the imbalance of females to males threatened herd size and health.

The white-tail deer slowly began to displace squirrel as the game of choice for hunters. The annual deer harvest did not exceed 10,000 until 1959, although the numbers killed accelerated afterwards and eclipsed 100,000 by 1987. The sale of Arkansas hunting licenses rose steadily after World War II, increasing about

65 percent between 1946 and 1956. With few women taking up the sport, the 209,400 resident licenses in 1960 represented 42.3 percent of the male population in the state between the ages of fourteen and sixty-four.

This hunting boom, however, was dwarfed by the 216.5 percent jump in the issuance of fishing licenses from 1946 to 1956. Wherever the Corps of Engineers went, the fishermen were not far behind. One wildlife historian explained why new equipment rendered fishing in the state's rivers obsolete. "Any up-to-date fisherman in the 1930s and 1940s wanted a rod and reel instead of a pole; plugs and flies instead of minnows and worms; as well as a good-sized boat, preferably one with an outboard motor. Few persons were content anymore to sit on a stump and dangle a line in the water waiting for a fish to bite." In addition to the federal dam-building boom in the 1950s, the G&FC began its own lake development program in 1951 with the construction of the 6,700-acre Lake Conway.

———————

TUNING RADIOS TO BROADCASTS of the University of Arkansas football games was another new fall pastime of the 1950s that ripened into tradition. The only non-Texas member of the Southwest Conference, Arkansas for decades fielded teams that rarely achieved winning seasons. The program, which had adopted the Razorback mascot by 1916, drew primarily upon northwest Arkansas fans before World War II. Until the McMath highway program, the Fayetteville campus was an eight-hour journey from Little Rock. Yet some boosters elsewhere in the state did follow the teams' up-and-down fortunes. Scrambling for programming, T. H. Barton, an oil company owner, set up in 1935 a rudimentary sports network that broadcasted games on his stations in Little Rock, El Dorado, and Jonesboro. Dale Alford, a young ophthalmology student and later a key figure in the segregationist movement, was the game announcer as well as moderator for the "Pigskin Parade."

In 1945 the university board of trustees hired the well-regarded coach John Barnhill from Tennessee to salvage the floundering program. Although professors questioned the expense and merit of big-time football, prominent urban business donors and influential alumni thronged to elevate the Razorback program with a determination equal to their fervor for new industry. During the 1947 legislative session tight-fisted governor Ben Laney loosened the purse strings to push a measure over passionate opposition that authorized revenue bonds to construct a stadium in Little Rock. In September 1948 at the inaugural clash in War Memorial Stadium, Arkansas thumped Abilene Christian, 40–6, before 27,000 fans, the largest crowd ever to view a football game in the state (Razorback Stadium in Fayetteville seated no more than 16,000).

The Barnhill era also marked the emergence of the radio Razorback Network. Bob Cheyne, filling the newly created sports publicity director post, allied with the Southwestern Bell Company to tie together thirty-four stations that would broadcast the play-by-play descriptions delivered over the telephone lines. On fall Saturday afternoons throughout the 1950s, Arkansans from the Delta to the Ozarks heard Wallie Ingalls sign off his coverage of games with his signature admonition: "Win, lose, or draw, let's be sports about it." Whatever the outcome, comprehensive accounts engorged the Sunday *Arkansas Gazette*, which upgraded its coverage through the persistent coaxing of its gifted sports editor Orville Henry. Henry, who remained at the Gazette for forty-seven years, brought on Jim Bailey in 1956 to cover baseball and boxing as well as football. Colleagues in and out of state acknowledged both writers could have easily move on to larger metropolitan newspapers, with one explaining that "they were in a class by themselves."

If promotion and corporate patronage forged the football program into a business-like enterprise, hard-fought battles by underdog squads turned the Razorbacks into a symbol of the state's perseverance against the odds. Although Barnhill's first team won the 1946 conference championship, the 1954 "25 Little Pigs" became the watershed that both institutionalized and mythologized the Razorbacks.

Inexperienced and boasting little depth, Bowden Wyatt's squad easily outdistanced predictions with a 7–0 start that propelled it to a number four national ranking. The play that came to represent the miracle season was a sixty-six-yard, fourth quarter touchdown pass from Buddy Bob Benson to Preston Carpenter that booted offensive juggernaut Ole Miss from the unbeaten ranks. Four years later Frank Broyles began his nineteen-year stint with a below .500 season, but then guided the team to successive conference titles between 1959 and 1961. The habitual top-ten rankings and postseason bowl invitations culminated with the recognition by the Football Writers Association of the team as 1964 national champions (other teams also laid claim to the honor in this era before news organizations settled upon a consensus champion).

The compatibility of politics and sport was on display at the university's most celebrated game, the 1969 shoot-out between number-two Arkansas and the top-ranked University of Texas. With President Richard Nixon in attendance at Fayetteville, the Razorbacks' early two-touchdown lead did not stand, and they fell in a 15–14 heartbreaker.

Even though the Razorback Marching Band included African American members and no longer played "Dixie," the team on the field that day was all-white. In 1965 Darrell Brown had walked on as a freshman, enduring physical and verbal abuse during practices, but was not asked to return the following year. In 1970 Jon Richardson, the first African American football-scholarship player, began a career at the university that would end with his becoming the eighth leading rusher in the program's history. Almer Lee, the first black player to letter in basketball, led the team in scoring during the 1969–70 season, while the first African American female athletes arrived on campus in the mid-1970s.

By the twenty-first century, soaring television contracts upended the economics of college sports. Top-tier universities squeezed their fan base to finance elaborate facilities and bulk up contracts for transient coaches. In 1977 Frank Broyles shifted to the post of athletic director and in 1990 shifted the entire athletic program into the formidable Southeastern Conference (SEC). This relocation was the first shudder in the tectonic realignments throughout the football landscape that eventually produced five elite conferences sufficient in power and wealth to dictate terms to the full National Collegiate Athletic Association. For most seasons throughout their first twenty-five years in the SEC, the Razorback football teams were overmatched and relied upon weaker non-conference foes to hammer out winning records.

The University of Arkansas basketball team fared better during the 1990s under Nolan Richardson, the first African American basketball coach at a major Southern university. After being hired in 1985, he introduced a fast-paced offense and smothering defense that left opponents winded and shell-shocked. He guided the team to a national championship in 1994 and again reached the NCAA championship game the following year. After a series of disappointing seasons and growing tension between the two men, Broyles fired Richardson in 2002. The former coach filed a suit against the university in federal court on the grounds of racial discrimination.

U.S. District Judge Bill Wilson dismissed the suit but was skeptical of the arguments offered by the university's attorneys that Richardson brought the action to secure a multimillion-dollar judgment. Wilson wrote, "It is primarily about wounded pride—wounded pride in a man who started way behind but climbed to the top by hard work, savvy, and most of all, perseverance. Many of us greatly admire, or claim to admire, these traits." The basketball program slumped decidedly following Richardson's dismissal.

Broyles not only established the well-capitalized and aggressive Razorback Inc. but encouraged Arkansans to understand that the operation, like the other rising corporations of Walmart and Tyson Foods, commanded respect for a state more accustomed to condescension. Noted columnist John Brummett reminisced on his boyhood as a Hog fan during the Broyles era: "I also was aware of my state's bad reputation, owing to a backroads economy and backwoods image that got exacerbated by the ugly racist spectacle from Little Rock Central High in 1957. . . . When you're young, you want to believe—or choose to believe, or perhaps truly believe—that a bad image of the sort I describe is wrong and unjust. You look for champions to demonstrate what you think you know—that your state is better than others think, and is as good as any state, better 'n most."

The pride in the University of Arkansas athletic program within the state was matched by uncommon acknowledgement of its significance outside the borders. In 2017 the obituary for the former athletic director in the *New York Times* carried this headline: "Frank Broyles, Football Coach Who Put Arkansas on Map, Dies at 92."

THE ASSEMBLING OF the Razorback Network by the 1950s went against the grain of the revolution that swept away local radio, current-affairs programs and live musical broadcasts in favor of a standard top-forty music playlist. In 1955 KVLC Little Rock became the state's first station to install the new popular music format that also introduced rock and roll music to the airwaves. Working as a salesman for a competing radio station that banked on big band swing outlasting the rock fad, Ray Poindexter assured business owners that the new music appealed only to kids with little spending money. When a middle-aged beauty shop customer interrupted his pitch to the proprietor one day with the declaration, "I like 'Rock Around the Clock'!" Poindexter bowed to the inevitable.

Arkansans tuning in to hear John R. on Nashville's clear channel WLAC or Rufus Thomas on WDIA in Memphis found another sweet spot on the dial when KKOY in Little Rock went on the air in 1956 with a full playlist of gospel and raucous rhythm and blues. More than a few of the R&B records were cut in Sam Phillips's Memphis Recording Service studio. Many of these recordings by African American artists appeared under labels out of Chicago such as Chess or Modern, while others came to bear Phillips's own Sun Records imprint.

In contrast to the traditional Ozark folk artists who largely stayed put, the rural blues musicians had shaken free of the grasp of the preservationists to make sure their audience grew beyond those researching recordings in the vaults of the Library of Congress. Newer R&B performers such as Howling Wolf, James Cotton, and Little Junior Parker, all of whom had perfected their talents in West Memphis clubs and KWEM broadcasts, followed the bluesmen out of the Delta to Chicago. A chagrined Sam Phillips had little choice by the mid-1950s but to unearth less apparent talent, searching for young blue-collar whites who lived across the tracks from genteel neighborhoods and within earshot of black clubs.

Elvis Presley, mulling over a singing career, paid to cut a couple of demo records at Sun Records. Phillips, detecting a sound he believed many would pay to hear, scheduled a recording session that produced a souped-up rendition of "That's All Right," which was not a hit for Arthur Crudup but soared up the charts for Elvis. After Phillips sold Presley's contract for $40,000 to RCA, the record producer had the wherewithal to expand his stable of wild men whose relentless style pushed the needles on the recording equipment into the red. Johnny Cash, Conway Twitty, and Charlie Rich absorbed the crosscurrent of music styles that cut across Arkansas like clashing weather fronts. Gospel shouts, blues echoes, and electric R&B boiled over in rockabilly, an unstable, kinetic mixture performed often by whites who came of age in the northeast section of the state that was neither Ozark nor Delta.

Although the rockabilly bands seemed to defy rules and structure, the musical style proved a dead end. The white patrons of the clubs hunched along a strip of US Highway 67 expected for their dollars from hard jobs not innovation but raw songs that uncorked masculine dreams of cars, women, and good whiskey. Cash, Twitty, and Rich gravitated toward country music and fame, while Sonny Burgess and Billy Lee Riley remained pure and obscure. Marvin Schwartz notes that Burgess in 1959 recorded at Sun Records the last classic rockabilly release.

The evolution of rock and roll out of R&B blurred racial boundaries as white performers who moved closer to the African American wellsprings of the music were both rewarded by young listeners and denounced by those who feared the erosion of segregation. Black artists, while not sharing equally in the growing popularity of the music, found their incomes rising as white kids bought their records and attended their shows. In 1957 a Little Rock television station followed the lead of other urban stations—including WFIL in Philadelphia, the home of the national *American Bandstand* show—to broadcast a music and dance program six afternoons a week.

Legions of white teenagers from throughout Arkansas jammed the KHTV studios to dance to records played by Steve Stephens, a former radio announcer. The live performers on *Steve's Show* were also white, more often playing rockabilly. Robinson Memorial Auditorium, Little Rock's largest concert venue, became the primary site where whites too young or timid to go to clubs could hear black musicians. Seating was segregated, and in 1961 a white music promoter was arrested for sitting with black audience members during a Ray Charles concert.

One veteran dancer from *Steve's Show* recalled African American rock and roll artists played late performances in the Robinson basement following their onstage shows. Both black and white teenagers joined these unauthorized dance parties. In one sense, conservative white apprehensions about the popularity of African American musical forms were on the money. Yet the young white males who angrily, violently defied school desegregation efforts in the 1950s often adopted the style and look of the rock and roll outlaws. Defiance animated the new music, but many of the rebels took up the cause of resisting change.

III. The Springtime of Moderation: Early School Desegregation

In the same month as the May 1954 *Brown* decision, with the beginning of the fall term, two northwest Arkansas school systems became among the first desegregated districts in the former Confederate states. Charleston, a small Franklin County community near Fort Smith, and Fayetteville had each consolidated all black students through the junior-high grades into a single, separate school. Both systems had previously transported their African American high school students to other districts. The school board in Sheridan in south central Arkansas also voted to integrate classrooms shortly after the *Brown* decision, but by that fall no black children were present to enter classes.

Dale Bumpers, the attorney for the Charleston school board, argued the district should take the opportunity offered by the *Brown* decision to forgo the expense of repairing the deteriorating schoolhouse for African American students in the elementary grades. The board voted in July to bring all of the eleven black students into the nearly five hundred white student body. The superintendent won over town business leaders, detailed transition plans with black parents, and persuaded the Fort Smith newspapers to withhold lengthy coverage. The opening day of the semester unfolded without incident or outside notice. During the year, black students suffered verbal harassment from other students and dismissive treatment from some teachers but also formed friendships with whites and participated in extracurricular organizations.

By 1954 the $5,000 annual cost of providing board and tuition at Fort Smith and Hot Springs for its black high school students gnawed through the Fayetteville district's financial balance. One school board member acknowledged that the *Brown* decision "pulled us out of the hole." Given the distances they were forced to travel, the eight to twelve students were separated from their families throughout the school year, some budgeting the limited bus fare money provided by the Fayetteville district to return home only on holidays.

The presence of the university in Fayetteville created a core white constituency for integration that complemented a secure financial and merchant elite whose interests had not rested upon an unskilled black labor force. About 2 percent of the town's 18,000 residents were African American. The Fayetteville school board decided both to enroll African American students into the white high school for the fall 1954 term and to desegregate the junior-high grades gradually. The local newspaper publisher served on the school board, and the implementation was rarely covered leading up to the start of school. If the board decision had the markings of a cautious business decision, private efforts transformed bureaucratic procedure into biracial cooperation.

The United Church Women, an integrated organization already in place before 1954, encouraged support for the school board, while other religious organizations arranged meetings within churches between white and African American teenagers. Critical to the quiet transition was the active collaboration of Minnie B. Dawkins, the principal of the black Lincoln school, and Louise Bell, the principal of the white senior high school. Both women advised students and faculty, arranged tours of the white school for black students, and addressed the misgivings of patrons and parents.

In the wake of the 1957 Little Rock school desegregation crisis, the Fayetteville school board suspended its desegregation schedule and the elementary schools remained racially separate until the advent of a new community movement. Witnessing the 1960s civil rights victories, African Americans formed the Community Concerns on Equality, which in conjunction with interracial groups pressured school leaders to resume desegregation. In 1965 the Lincoln school was shuttered and eventually razed.

Since the Supreme Court in its 1954 decision had deferred ruling on the scope and speed of integration, districts such as Charleston and Fayetteville were acting under financial exigencies rather than legal compulsion. Still, most Southern school districts grappled with similar artificial expenses and chose to continue to pay the bills rather than dismantle a costly dual system.

The Sheridan school board voted to save $4,000 by adding twenty-one black youths to a student population of six hundred whites in the upper grades. A mass protest meeting of incensed whites provoked the resignation of four board members even after they voted to rescind the integration policy. To preclude interracial classrooms irrespective of Supreme Court rulings, the leading employer of African Americans evicted families from company housing at his sawmill and compelled them to move to homes he threw up in an adjacent county. One of the earliest communities to comply with the *Brown* decision thus joined the roll of other nearly all-white or "sundown towns" in the state.

The *Brown* decision had forced a reckoning for white Southerners who had considered themselves moderates on the issue of race. Previously, moderation had meant tolerance, an openness to mitigate the harsher forms of discrimination, a willingness to deliver improved public services to black citizens in lieu of integration. When the Court held that equality was incompatible with exclusion, influential white moderates asserted segregation needed only to be reformed rather than dissolved. Their moderation thinned to a reluctance to incite disorder.

Formed in 1944 by white professionals to bolster education and economic opportunities for black Southerners, the Southern Regional Council lost half its membership after it shifted to public and active support for integration. The reform organization, however, persisted and secured Northern philanthropic funding to nurture grassroots organizations that would help school districts in complying with *Brown*. The Arkansas Council on Human Relations (ACHR) was one of these progenies. From the outset the group was biracial and a training ground for new-style liberals who broke with the older reform tradition in the state that focused upon business development and acceptance of segregation.

Fred Darragh, a white businessman, and Charles C. Walker, an African American clergyman, headed the ACHR's first board of directors. They hired Nat Griswold, a white Methodist minister who had had served as the activities director for families interned at the Rohwer center during World War II, to serve as the first executive director. In line with its philosophy to further integration through expertise and behind-the-scenes negotiations, the ACHR quietly arranged for counsel to help the school board in Hoxie counter the first eruption in Arkansas of organized massive resistance to school integration.

As was so with Charleston and Fayetteville, the Hoxie school board by June 1955 begrudged the financial burden of segregation and believed the relative dearth of black students would stem a white backlash. Nevertheless, the northeast Arkansas community was not far from Mississippi and that state's proliferating brigades of Citizens' Council members. The Hoxie leaders also were unable to dodge media coverage. *Life* magazine documented the tranquil first day of the 1955 school term with photos of African American and white children playing and studying together. What the magazine touted as a tribute to orderly democratic change actually goaded into action Jim Johnson and

Amis Guthridge, the latter a Little Rock attorney who had been prominent in anti-union crusades. They hurried up the road to prop up the hastily assembled Hoxie Citizens' Council chapter.

In contrast to events in Sheridan, the Hoxie school board members refused to heed the petitions demanding their resignations. The attorneys, who intervened on behalf of the board at the behest of the ACHR, secured an injunction to halt the intimidation and harassment that impeded the district from carrying out its lawful obligations.

Defeat at Hoxie invigorated rather than demoralized the radical segregationists. Johnson staged his electoral challenge the following year against Faubus, who had consistently emphasized that the Hoxie standoff did not touch upon his duties as governor. Also in the fall of 1956, various segregationist outfits consolidated into the Association of Citizens' Councils of Arkansas, although the merged group was organizationally disheveled and its small membership transitory. The Arkansas Council operations not only fell well short of the throngs taking up the cause in Mississippi and Alabama but also failed to attract the type of prominent figures who directed the other Deep South Councils.

The absence of elite involvement opened the door for lower-status whites to exert rare authority in their communities through Council agitation and infused their racist program with a class-based defiance of privileged whites. However, these militants were not affiliated with labor organizations, and the Councils continued to revolve around charismatic leaders rather than to mature into an authentic participatory movement. Jim Johnson in particular understood that boisterous rallies and relentless badgering of elected officials amplified the influence of the militant segregationists well beyond their actual numbers.

The Citizens' Council protestors failed to sidetrack integration in Hoxie because school board members and administrators were dedicated to stability, community reputation, and the rule of law. These commitments offered a forceful model for those facing massive resistance in the future.

By 1957 about 940 African American students out of a total black student population of 102,000 were attending integrated public schools. Governor Faubus extended his hands-off approach by not intervening in the desegregation of state-funded higher education, even though his justifications of the inviolability of local authority were less relevant in these cases. All seven of the predominately white colleges accepted black students: Arkansas State in Jonesboro, Arkansas Polytechnic in Russellville, Henderson State Teachers in Arkadelphia, Southern State in Magnolia, Arkansas A&M in Monticello, Arkansas State Teachers in Conway, and the University of Arkansas in

Fayetteville. On some campuses, African American students attended classes only on weekends and evenings. The McMath era building program at Arkansas Agricultural, Mechanical and Normal in Pine Bluff, the land grant college for African American students, had ended and the college would not see significant capital improvements until the civil rights era. None of the private white colleges admitted African American students until the 1960s.

Hot Springs, the soft center in a moral landscape, also stood apart from other Arkansas locales in racial matters. The color line was in place but more porous than elsewhere. Desegregation at the high school by 1957 did not ignite turmoil but went no farther than one auto-mechanics class enrolling ten students.

African American residents claimed better wages and conditions in jobs at the bathhouses, hotels, and medical centers that proliferated in the resort, but the range of occupations was limited. In the craftsmen bungalows along Whittington Avenue, white and black working-class families were neighbors. When it came to pleasure and games in the Spa City, white attitudes were pliant though far from tolerant.

In 1953 the Hot Springs Bathers, a Class C team in the Cotton States baseball league, announced that it had signed Jim and Leander Tugerson, stars from the Negro American League. For the Bathers' owners, just as it had been for strapped school superintendents, money was the basic issue. With four of its eight teams in Mississippi, the Cotton States League was one of only two of the twenty-five professional leagues to prohibit black athletes.

Although Jackie Robinson had entered major league baseball six years earlier, league officials had issued no standing policy on integration. In response to an appeal from the Bathers' management, the national director of the minor leagues announced a precedent: "The employment of Negro players has never been, nor is now, prohibited by any provision in the major-minor league agreement."

On May 20, 1953, the cracker-box ballpark in Hot Springs was filled with 1,800 fans, including the three hundred black spectators consigned to bleachers along the first-base line. They had come to see Jim Tugerson pitch against the Senators from Jackson, Mississippi. The eruption of cheers when Tugerson took the mound soon turned to boos and catcalls as umpires declared the game forfeited. The Cotton States League had not relented and had instructed the umpires beforehand to designate Tugerson as an ineligible player.

The following season the league opened the door for black players but folded in 1955 as television upended another small-town Southern tradition. Jim Tugerson continued to play baseball, although he never donned a major league uniform before his retirement. In Hot Springs, Leo McLaughlin was dead but the gambling casinos flourished with a new, less exclusive clientele who camped at the rows of slot machines rather than match skill and nerve with practiced gamblers at the blackjack table or the roulette wheel.

Shortly after taking office, Orval Faubus announced that law enforcement, like integration of classrooms, was best left to the discretion of local officials. When the governor was asked at press conference whether he knew that illegal gambling occurred in Hot Springs, he replied, remarkably: "I haven't been to Hot Springs." Throughout his administration, the governor had no call to travel to Hot Springs, as casino owners ferried cash packets to Little Rock. On the other hand, Faubus revised his policy of non-intervention when it came to school desegregation.

4 | ARKANSAS DIVIDED

O

N OCTOBER 3, 1963, president John F. Kennedy, in his dedication of the Greers Ferry Dam in Cleburne County, observed how the project tied Arkansas to the national economy. The president predicted the massive federal project would fatten local bank accounts and incline Arkansans to purchase more consumer goods. Arkansas industrial and political leaders had been advancing the same argument since World War II to justify requests for federal revenues. Yet the unraveling of the consensus that had sought growth without social change was evident on that bright autumn day.

In the planning stages for Greers Ferry, the U.S. Army Corps of Engineers was surprised when environmental objections to the hydroelectric initiative surfaced in dam-friendly Arkansas. A state game and fish commissioner, a newspaper writer, and a representative of a wildlife association demanded that the dam be redesigned to release water from the top of the lake as well as from the bottom. The project's detractors knew that the flow of cold bottom-water into the Little Red River below the dam would extinguish the smallmouth bass population. Claiming that this modification would cost $6 million, the Corps almost pulled the plug on the venture. The controversy was settled when the Corps provided land for the U.S. Fish and Wildlife Service to operate a trout hatchery on the river. The outdoors interests were mollified, and by the late 1960s, the Little Red, sans bass, was renowned among area trout fisherman.

The dam testified not only to the Corps's engineering prowess and bureaucratic savvy, but also to the state's congressional clout. With the flower of the Arkansas political aristocracy arrayed behind him, Kennedy observed in his dedication that "pound for pound, the Arkansas delegation in the Congress of the United States wields more influence than any other delegation of any of the other forty-nine states." The House Ways and Means Committee chair Wilbur Mills had just shepherded the president's major tax legislation into law.

Nevertheless, Governor Orval Faubus tailored his remarks for home-front consumption. His use of the National Guard to prevent the 1957 desegregation of Little Rock Central High School had given him national notoriety and an unprecedented stint in office. Faubus's disparagement of the president's pending civil rights legislation was so apparent that it provoked it a congratulatory call from his old nemesis, Jim Johnson.

The president understood fully that U.S. senator J. William Fulbright also opposed integration, although without the public rancor displayed by Faubus. Liberal criticism of the senator's record had persuaded Kennedy following his election not to risk nominating Fulbright for secretary of state. Nevertheless, the two leaders shared an internationalist perspective on the importance of global developments for the American future. In addition, both were repeatedly denounced by strident ultra-right organizations that feared their concern for the perspectives of other nations distracted from the Cold War mission to vanquish Soviet Communism. As they traveled by car from Little Rock to Greers Ferry, Fulbright urged Kennedy to cancel an upcoming trip to a hotbed of extremism: "Dallas is a very dangerous place. I wouldn't go there and don't you go."

In the early afternoon of November 22, 1963, the teacher of the advanced calculus class at Hot Springs High School told his students that Kennedy had been shot while in Dallas. Phil Jamison recalled the reaction of his friend Bill Clinton after the instructor's announcement: "He was motionless. Not even a twitch on his face. Yet you could feel the anger building up inside him."

By 1957 the burgeoning resistance campaigns to court-ordered integration that thundered throughout the Deep South resonated in Arkansas. Governor Faubus's post-*Brown* tactic to appear as a responsible defender of segregation crumbled as more radical figures commanded public support. The unwillingness of the Little Rock business leadership to publicly support gradual desegregation persuaded Faubus that his political survival rested with defiance. The courage of the nine black students who entered Central High School and the resolution of Daisy and L. C. Bates prevented integration from being suspended in the face of violent intimidation by organized segregationists. The radical step of closing the city's high schools eventually prodded influential figures to steer a moderate course that strictly limited the breadth of integration.

White Little Rock's wish to avoid a public debacle similar to the televised riot at Central High School enabled civil rights strategists in the 1960s to push forward the desegregation of downtown stores and public buildings. Yet the flow of retail centers and white residences westward diluted the victories. Real estate developers delayed integration more effectively and without the turmoil associated with the Citizens Council radicals. In the wake of civil rights conflicts, new biracial coalitions became the foundation for urban liberalism. In contrast to the old-fashioned business progressives, the new liberals advocated expansion of rights, aid to the poor, and accountable elected representation.

At the state level, the 1966 election of Winthrop Rockefeller to the governor's office inaugurated a reform program free of the segregationist rationalizations that had accompanied the extension of government services during the Faubus era. While Rockefeller's own Republican party grew ill-disposed toward larger government, a new generation of Democratic aspirants reinvigorated a party that expanded public services and became identified with civil rights. Environmentalism was one emerging issue that cut across the usual boundaries of traditional and modern, conservative and liberal, preservation and economic growth. Campaigns to save rivers, forests, and wetlands did not require redistributing income, surrendering accustomed authority and power, or unsettling what was familiar and cherished.

I. Lines of Resistance: The Little Rock Crisis

When Charlotte, North Carolina, *News* editor Harry S. Ashmore, in the spring of 1947 told his Boston-born wife about an offer to work for the *Arkansas Gazette*, she replied: "Little Rock? Little Rock? Why, it's not even on the way to anywhere." Soon the Ashmores themselves were on their way to Little Rock.

John Netherland Heiskell, *Gazette* owner, had edited his newspaper for forty years and wished to transfer some of the daily editorial responsibilities to Ashmore. In 1927 Heiskell had denounced the lynching and immolation of John Carter in downtown Little Rock in a front-page editorial, and he thought Ashmore's progressive credentials in order. Published since 1819, the *Gazette* enjoyed an ample lead in statewide circulation over the *Arkansas Democrat*, the afternoon rival directed since 1926 by K. A. Engel. While the *Democrat* championed scientific farming and condemned federal authority, Ashmore found the *Gazette* a congenial venue to launch broadsides against Governor Ben Laney and the Dixiecrats. Not content with hoping politicians read his editorials, Ashmore directly advised Sidney McMath and then Orval Faubus at the dawn of his political career. In 1951 when McMath invited him to address the Southern Governors' Conference in Hot Springs, Ashmore discomforted the chief executives by declaring segregation an obstacle to better schools.

Ashmore viewed Southern apartheid as doomed, but his conviction that whites would not give up without a fight made him a gradualist on the pace of its demise. In the months leading up to the 1954 *Brown* decision, Ashmore fretted that a decision to abolish segregated schools on a strict timetable would be unenforceable in the face of a violent backlash. He was relieved that *Brown II* in 1955 permitted school districts to fashion desegregation plans on their own terms as long as progress was discernible. Yet the editor, in his 1957 volume *An Epitaph for Dixie*, regretted that white Southerners had rebuffed this judicial deference: "The South has always contended that given time it could work out its own problems; offered time by the Supreme Court the Southern leaders for the most part have so far refused to use it to make even a tentative start toward the accommodation all of them recognize must ultimately come."

Ashmore had counted on men of influence and power to defuse white resistance through public assurances that the protracted departure of Jim Crow would change little in white lives. Shortly before the *Brown* ruling, Ashmore chatted with Hamilton Moses, one of the architects of Arkansas industrialization. Moses dreaded the demise of segregation but exploded when Ashmore suggested the possibility of white race riots. "One lynching and we've wasted $200,000 in magazine advertising. . . . Hell, what we've been selling is peace and order . . . telling 'em that what we've got down here is stability—friendly politicians who are not going to gut a business with taxes, and workers who are grateful for a job and are not going to be stirring up trouble." Moses assured Ashmore that while he would not publicly urge compliance, he and his fellow business leaders would foil mob rampages.

A NARROW PROFESSIONAL and managerial elite governed the political and economic life of Little Rock. Elizabeth Jacoway has identified roughly thirty-two men who maintained interlocking leadership positions in municipal reform, industrial recruitment, and civic associations. Reflecting an urban progressive outlook unaltered for fifty years, the Little Rock ruling class beat the drum for an efficient, non-partisan local government and modern social amenities to win the hearts of corporate prospects.

The federal government remained an engine for job production as Arkansas officials, along with their Southern counterparts, elbowed aside Northern competitors for Cold War defense dollars. In 1953 ground was broken for the construction of the Little Rock Air Force Base, a Strategic Air Command installation, on the site of the old Arkansas Ordnance Plant. Two years earlier, Everett Tucker had initiated a Chamber of Commerce campaign that eventually amassed sufficient funds to purchase and donate over 6,000 acres for the base. The president of Philander Smith College, the AME-affiliated institution in Little Rock, scoured the African American business community for contributions toward the goal.

The welcoming of a racially integrated military and workforce contingent was proffered as evidence that Little Rock would not endanger jobs by permitting the sort of police brutality suffered by black soldiers stationed at Camp Robinson during World War II. At the same time, the coterie of leaders continued to reinforce the scaffolding of a racially divided city.

The press of rural job-seekers into wartime Little Rock had swelled but not notably altered the contiguous pattern of black and white residential sections. Only single avenues separated white families from the largely African American neighborhoods surrounding Paul Laurence Dunbar High School and near the West Ninth Street black business center.

In 1950 city officials persuaded voters to approve leveraging the bond revenue slated for the construction of Gillam Park to match a grant from the newly established federal urban renewal program. A number of African American leaders who had lobbied for the development of the city's first black park also endorsed the initiative to tear down dilapidated structures owned by white landlords in black neighborhoods.

The first urban renewal project razed blocks of working- and middle-class residences in the Dunbar district. One resident angrily observed that contrary to the advertised goal of slum eradication, "the choicest area of the Negro residential section has been selected for clearance." Many of the families relocated to the black-only Booker Homes housing project, recently built near the isolated and segregated Gillam Park. City officials were beginning to employ federal housing dollars to arrange Little Rock into a constricted black eastern section and mushrooming white settlement in the western wards.

L. C. Bates, the influential editor of the *Arkansas State Press*, was no less sparing of African American proponents who urged approval of the urban renewal initiative than he had been when they supported the Gillam Park bond issue. In a 1953 editorial he remonstrated, "We told you the move was to centralize all Negroes in one area and forget about them while the city progresses in another direction." Daisy Bates shared her husband's uncompromising advocacy for thoroughgoing integration and disdain for the segregationist gratuities that substituted for fair access, power, and opportunity.

Her election in 1952 as president of the Arkansas chapter of the NAACP continued the shift from the older, conservative male leadership. These men had dismissed her as militant, with one asserting, "Mrs. Bates tends to go off the deep end at times on various issues." The media and popular historical accounts of the events composing what became known as the Little Rock crisis would center on Daisy Bates, leaving her husband in the shadows. Yet, a number of inside figures within Little Rock, reflecting inveterate sexism, dismissed her as contributing little beyond attracting media limelight. They insisted that her husband was the consequential strategist and thinker. Such distinctions, of course, ignored the respective strengths of the two and the formidable advantages of their partnership.

The *Brown* decision largely resolved the question within the African American community over whether to settle for amenities within a segregated society or press for integration. Parents were heartened by the prospect of their children's gaining real opportunity by attending schools with adequate resources, modern equipment, and richer curricula. Black students sitting in the same classrooms with whites would not have to settle for second-hand textbooks and obsolete microscopes. The suspicions of African American rivals toward L. C. and Daisy Bates smoldered during the school crisis but did not sidetrack an activist strategy to desegregate Central High school. However, white hostility toward the couple intensified.

By 1955 Daisy and L. C. Bates were the leading and persistent critics of the gradual desegregation plan designed by Virgil Blossom, the Little Rock school superintendent. More than simply a matter of student assignments, Blossom's plan was a school placement strategy that mirrored the developing blueprint for residential segregation. In 1956 the school district transferred African American students to Horace Mann High School, a touted state-of-the art facility located well to the east of the Dunbar school, which in turn became a junior high school. Before the beginning of the 1957 fall term, the district announced the opening of Hall High School to serve middle- and upper-class white families in the western suburbs.

The Blossom Plan stipulated that integration would begin with a handful of African American students admitted solely to Central High School. Completed in 1927, Central High was an imposing structure encompassing two city blocks between white working class and black neighborhoods. Blossom told white patrons such as Sara Murphy that he wished to delay integration of the elementary grades until new facilities could be selectively constructed to insure the effective survival of single-race schools. The superintendent assumed that removing barriers for black students endangered the caliber of education for whites: "Uncontrolled integration would lower the quality of schools." Yet, in walling off the prosperous white neighborhoods from even token desegregation, the Blossom Plan allowed radical segregationists to jeer that the education of lower-income whites was to be forfeited.

In February 1956 Wiley Branton, a protégé of Harold Flowers and one of the pioneer African Americans to graduate from the University of Arkansas School of Law, filed *Cooper v. Aaron* on behalf of thirty-three black students who had been denied admission to four Little Rock white schools the previous month. In selecting Branton to represent the students, the Little Rock NAACP executive committee had resolved earlier divisions within its membership over whether to accept the hesitant steps of the local school board as at least an acknowledgement that desegregation could not be blocked. Yet, as Blossom revised his plan to keep nearly all black students from attending white schools adjacent to their neighborhoods, the committee determined that the superintendent's actions were "more like circumvention than like compliance." Federal judge John E. Miller ruled, however, that the Blossom Plan was a legally acceptable strategy "that will lead to effective and gradual adjustment of the problem." In April a federal appeals panel upheld Miller's finding while also confirming his requirement that desegregation must begin with the 1957 fall term.

Blossom and the school board assumed the judicial blessing of gradualism crippled the efforts by white extremists to rally support against federal intrusion. This optimism was bolstered by the uneventful desegregation in spring 1956 of public transportation in Little Rock, Hot Springs, Pine Bluff, and Fort Smith. In Little Rock, a local union gained the municipal bus franchise and quietly took down the Jim Crow signs, while the other town governments responded to an April Supreme Court decision that appeared to overrule segregation regulations. The anti-segregation bus boycotts in Baton Rouge, Tallahassee, and most famously, Montgomery were not replicated in Arkansas.

The victory in the March 1957 Little Rock school board elections by two supporters of the Blossom Plan over open segregationists also buoyed confidence that whites would accept changes in the racial order as long as those changes were nominal. The superintendent himself was certain that his scores of speeches to civic and education groups would secure a smooth transition. In early 1957 Chamber of Commerce director Everett Tucker gave Blossom partial credit for landing an industrial prospect by alleviating the new corporation's apprehensions over desegregation.

Blossom steadily assured the civic leaders that the center would hold, and they need not risk stirring radical opposition by publicly extolling moderation. Blossom emphasized his plan effectively marginalized both the NAACP and the white Citizens' Councils. The big men of Little Rock need only let matters run their course.

The Fayetteville model to encompass the full community in preparations for desegregation in 1954 was disregarded in Little Rock. Blossom rebuffed the involvement of the local Parent-Teacher Association and dismissed the proposal to form a biracial advisory committee. School officials did not include the black students slated to enroll at Central High in the customary school tours for new students.

In 1956 the state's voters had approved a pupil placement law backed by Faubus that allowed district officials to decide the number of African American students who would desegregate selected schools. Other Southern states had already adopted similar measures. This strategy was an early tactic to evade *Brown* rather than risk outright noncompliance. In the case of Little Rock, Blossom dictated the selection process. After persisting through personal interviews with the superintendent and a series of humiliating questions, seventeen students were chosen to join the nearly two thousand white students at Central High. Seven decided not to attend before the opening day of school.

As Blossom connected the pieces of his plan, the governor of Arkansas remained confident that rhetorical and symbolic allegiance to segregation undercut popular support for extremism. In 1956 Faubus had lobbied Arkansas congressmen Brooks Hays and James W. Trimble to join their colleagues throughout the region to sign a document emerging from the Dixie congressional caucus that came to be known as the "Southern Manifesto." Both representatives were skeptical of the document's assertion that the Supreme Court's *Brown* decision was an "illegal and unconstitutional seizure of power by nine men" as well as its praise for those states pledging to "resist this invasion of their sovereignty by the Court by every lawful means." Hays recalled Faubus insisting that the Manifesto was a palliative to stop "the Ku Klux Klan and the extreme Citizens' Council groups from taking over the political life of the state." The two reluctantly added their names alongside that of every other member of the Arkansas delegation. White moderates, increasingly fearful of the reach of radical segregationists, resigned themselves to appeasement rather than a public defense of judicial authority.

Safely past his election triumph over Citizens' Council leader Jim Johnson, Orval Faubus pushed through the 1957 legislature the first general tax increase since the 1930s Marion Futrell administration. The $22 million package included a one-cent rise in the sales tax, a boost of the severance tax on minerals, and a jump in income tax revenues by replacing the high personal exemption with a tax credit. The new revenue fueled a 40 percent increase in overall education funding during the 1957–58 school year, and underwrote an unprecedented $800 increase in the average public-school teacher salary.

To secure his progressive acts, Faubus decided he had little choice but to sign four segregation measures hatched by a Delta legislative bloc chronically opposed to raising taxes. Among other things, the laws required the NAACP to identify its members to state officials and authorized the establishment of a state sovereignty commission to investigate groups accommodating federal integration efforts. Still certain that he could outflank segregationists, Faubus initially ducked enforcement of these laws.

The governor, however, soon found his space for such maneuverings diminished. Heading into the summer, militant segregationists spoke the loudest and without rebuttal from mainstream white leaders. The Capital Citizens' Council, the Little Rock chapter of the state organization, claimed around five hundred members. Encouraged by Amis Guthridge and the Reverend Wesley Pruden, Council members inundated Faubus with threats of mass rioting if black students entered Central High School. The governor also fielded angry phone messages from outside the city, fruits of Jim Johnson's provocation campaign.

Conceding that whites now believed the state segregation measures armed him to defy court orders, the governor in July convinced Guthridge and Pruden that he would not permit integrated schools in Little Rock. While Faubus shed moderation and hoisted anti-integration colors, he also plotted to avoid a futile showdown with federal officials.

Faubus thought Virgil Blossom would become a collaborator. Besieged as well with vitriolic phone calls and letters, Blossom had sent his daughter to live with out-of-town relatives. "You had better make your piece [sic] with our Good Lord—for your days are very few. . . . We are leaving Florida tomorrow— for Little Rok [sic]. And may God have mercy on your Rotten Soul," read one of the notes in Blossom's mailbox. Faubus thought that the clearly shaken superintendent and school board would welcome a tactic to postpone desegregation and relieve the pressure.

In August the governor choreographed through the segregationist Mothers League of Central High a suit requesting a chancery court judge to enjoin the admission of black students on the grounds the action violated the 1957 segregation statutes and risked civil disorder. Faubus knew those state laws would be overturned by the federal courts but held out hope that a delay would get him off the hook, preferably through the 1958 primary election. The Little Rock school leaders, however, wanted to go forward with desegregation. Blossom angered Faubus when he testified that he did not foresee violence disrupting the opening of school. The school board and the NAACP quickly appealed the state judge's injunction halting the scheduled integration of the high school. When federal judge Ronald N. Davies set aside the injunction and ordered the Blossom Plan carried out, Faubus was left with hard choices.

In a late August visit to Little Rock, Marvin Griffin, the firebrand governor of Georgia, boasted that he would never knuckle under to federal judges and that Faubus should do the same if he wished to stand tall for segregation. Members of the Arkansas congressional delegation remained silent and shielded in Washington. Many clergy implored their congregations to observe the law without defending the principles behind the court decisions. One official of the Arkansas State Baptist Convention assured Blossom in a private note, "A great host of friends believe in you and will be praying for you." The recent decision by voters to replace the mayor-council with a city manager form of government deprived the lame-duck municipal officials of effective authority.

Winthrop Rockefeller, the AIDC chair, explained in a private meeting with Faubus on September 1 that official defiance of federal authority would rupture efforts to lure business operations to the state. Faubus countered that arch segregationists would sweep into power if he stood by while African American students studied in Central High classrooms. The private business interests that effectively governed the city did not echo Rockefeller's assessment of the risk to reputation and economic growth. An admirer of Sid McMath's racial moderation, Witt Stephens, the financier and utility magnate, later explained his inaction by noting that he was on a foreign trip: "If I had been here, I couldn't have done anything about it. Faubus knew how I felt about it." Whether from a mix of fear, resignation, or a commitment to segregated institutions, the abdication of responsibility by powerful and influential whites was astounding in its completeness.

FAUBUS ANNOUNCED in a television broadcast on September 2 that, in response to reports of black youths acquiring weapons and "caravans" of whites heading to Little Rock, he was positioning National Guard troops around Central High. Neither the White Citizens' Council nor the NAACP was sure whether the troops would enforce or prevent integration. The guardsmen encircling the campus were uncertain as well. Faubus knew that a confrontation with federal authority would end with his backing down. He also anticipated that even doomed but showy obstruction sliced away Jim Johnson's constituency in his favor. Whether or not Faubus believed the stories manufactured by Johnson of armed hordes descending upon Central was beside the point.

Faubus was convinced that permitting the African American students to exercise their constitutional rights imperiled his political career, which he was not ready to abandon. He was prepared to obstruct a court order before defying segregationist zealots. Tony Freyer has noted that while Faubus discerned that ambiguous judicial definitions of what constituted integration provided him room to maneuver, the governor also believed himself a victim of the reluctance by officials at other levels of government to enforce the law. In the early hours of September 4, the governor of Arkansas gave the commander of the National Guard clear orders to bar the black students from joining white students entering Central High that morning.

Worried about the safety of the African American students, Daisy Bates arranged to have white and black ministers accompany them to Central. This clerical escort flanked seven of the ten students who approached the National Guard lines. These students—Ernest Green, Carlotta Walls, Gloria Ray, Jefferson Thomas, Minnijean Brown, Thelma Mothershed, and Jane Hill— were halted by Lt. Col. Marion Johnson, who declared, "The school is off-limits to these people."

Melba Pattillo and Terrance Roberts were also rebuffed as they individually approached Central. Roberts soon found Elizabeth Eckford nearby, sitting alone at a bus stop bench, surrounded by livid whites, jeering her with racist taunts and threats. Eckford, also on her own, had been surprised when guardsmen blocked her way and she found no way to escape the frenzied crowd. Wearing a freshly starched school dress, the young black student's dignity and composure in the midst of convulsive bigotry was emblematic of similar scenes in the years to come. Eventually a city bus arrived and Eckford boarded in the company of Grace Lorch, a white woman who rebuked the young men who attempted to block their way.

Urged by her parents to look to her safety, Jane Hill decided to return to Horace Mann. The remaining students wishing to enter Central High school became known as the Little Rock Nine. For nearly three weeks white students came and went at the school, while the African Americans denied entry were tutored in their own homes. During that time, President Dwight Eisenhower met with Faubus at Newport, Rhode Island, but the president did not persuade the governor to comply with the desegregation order.

Shawn Fisher has explained that lawyers in the U.S. Justice Department began to develop arguments for the president to deploy military forces to enforce the court orders in Arkansas. By mid-September Army commanders were also debating whether federalizing or taking control of the Arkansas National Guard away from the governor would spark widespread insubordination by guardsmen sympathetic to the segregationists. These doubts led Pentagon leaders to draft contingency plans to dispatch the 101st Airborne Division from Fort Campbell, Kentucky, if the president issued the order to intervene in Little Rock.

On September 21, Federal Judge Davies granted the NAACP's request for an injunction that required the governor to cease his obstruction of the integration of Central High; such an action was necessary "in order to protect and preserve the judicial process . . . and to protect the constitutional rights of . . . the plaintiffs and other eligible Negro students." A few hours later, Faubus withdrew the Guard and departed for a conference in Georgia. While seemingly a defeat for the governor, the court order allowed him to sidestep the confrontation, his aim from the beginning, and reap the political benefits of his new reputation as a stout defender of segregation.

When the nine African American students entered Central High on September 23, many of the one thousand whites surrounding the school broke through the undermanned police lines surrounding the building. The rioters, a majority of whom were local residents, differed from the all-male toughs seen by later audiences of television broadcasts from the front lines of civil rights battles. With members of the Mothers League encouraging the assault and berating officers, viewers had the impression of an entire community in revolt. The fire chief ignored Mayor Woodrow Mann's instructions to turn fire hoses on the crowd, and police officials panicked at the thought of a full-scale race war if the students were harmed or killed. Even after the students were removed covertly, the terror continued. That evening about one hundred cars rolled into the Bates's neighborhood, and police discovered explosives and arms when they stopped the vehicles short of their goal.

Eisenhower, who regretted the *Brown* decision and had done little to promote compliance by Southern communities, could tolerate neither the public subversion of authority by mob rampage nor the injury to the nation's international reputation as a democratic beacon during the Cold War. With the legal basis established and operational plans in place, the president took command of the state Guard and ordered the 101st Airborne to restore order in Little Rock. On September 24, the nine students were waiting at the Bates home when an army officer came to the door: "Mrs. Bates we are ready for the children. We will return them to your home at three thirty o'clock."

The Army division remained stationed at Central High until November while the National Guard continued to patrol the halls throughout the year. The African American members of the 101st Airborne, however, were encamped at a distance from Central High and not permitted to enter the school where the nine students faced daily hostility and violence. This deference to segregationist feeling was still recalled with bitterness years later by the black veterans.

The military presence outside the classrooms abated but did not suppress the organized harassment campaign. Graeme Cope's incisive studies have revealed that while those whites who bullied the African American students inside Central High already had spotty disciplinary records, adult segregationists on the outside were coordinating many of the attacks. Walls's legs were regularly bruised by blows from steel tipped boots; Thomas was knocked unconscious from a punch that produced an egg-sized lump behind his ear; Ray was followed by a boy swinging a rope fashioned into a hangman's noose; Pattillo was tripped at the head of a flight of stairs; and Brown was doused with hot food and repeatedly kicked.

School officials instructed the African American students not to assist each other if in trouble because doing so might spark a dangerous melee. White assailants were punished if their attacks were observed by an adult; firsthand reports from the black students were not credited as sufficient evidence for fear that white students would begin to fabricate charges. Brown was expelled in February after she retaliated, but was soon placed at a first-rate high school in New York City. The segregationist students claimed a victory and declared they would drive out the remainder of the Nine.

The Citizens' Council members fomented turmoil and disturbance in the school to prove their claims that desegregated education was inherently disruptive and harmful. The national office of the NAACP recognized that the withdrawal of the black students would bolster massive resistance against *Brown*. The civil rights organization supplied funds and counsel to the local chapter to hold the line.

Navigating uncharted territory, Daisy Bates made the students aware that public attention was both an intrusion and an opportunity to educate the audience beyond Little Rock. She coached the students before they spoke to reporters. She also treated these young people as embattled veterans suffering from wounds that few could comprehend. As the mentor for the students, Daisy Bates also became in the public eye the primary leader of the civil rights movement in Little Rock. This status owed in part to her position as head of the state NAACP but also derived from her precise and eloquent expressions of the integrationist viewpoint to the media. Despite the pressure of constant terroristic threats, she successfully adhered to the overall strategy while remaining fiercely protective of the students' well-being. Her ability to balance the cause against the personal cost of daily battles places her at the front rank of the era's combatants for social justice.

The civic leadership, preferring segregation to endure, allowed the white racial radicals to seize control of public life. The Blossom Plan had promised schools that were marginally desegregated. With that plan in ruins, the traditional elite waited to see if the Citizens' Council forces could preserve single-race schools.

The economic and legal sanctions against Faubus's opponents were made more onerous by the complicity of the business movers and shakers.

Spurred by state attorney general Bruce Bennett, North Little Rock and Little Rock city councils approved ordinances requiring membership lists from "certain organizations." The Reverend J. C. Crenshaw, the president of the Little Rock NAACP chapter, and Daisy Bates were arrested and forced to post bond when they refused to reveal members' names. Bennett, the most ardent segregationist among elected state officers, depleted NAACP resources and energy over the next seven months in pursuit of the group's records. Parents of the nine black students lost jobs. Major corporations such as Southwestern Bell Telephone, the Stephens-owned Arkansas Louisiana Gas Company, and Hamilton Moses's Arkansas Power and Light Company removed their advertising from the *State Press,* and by the end of 1959 the Bateses were forced to close the newspaper that was both their livelihood and a forum for new voices.

Ashmore's editorial condemnation of the governor's resistance subjected the *Arkansas Gazette* to reprisals that slashed circulation in 1957 by over 15 percent and lowered revenue by about 7 percent. The popularity of Orville Henry's coverage of the Arkansas Razorbacks and refusal of major department stores to join the advertising boycott helped the newspaper to continue to show a slight profit.

Thriving from its rival's plight, the *Arkansas Democrat* became a ready conduit for Mothers League accusations through its news columns and cheered Faubus with its sympathetic coverage of his justifications. The *Democrat*'s editorials were ambiguous on Faubus's use of the Guard to bar the students but clearer in their skepticism of the judicial rulings on integration. Typical was commentary on September 27, 1957, by the paper's lead opinion writer, Karr Shannon: "Whether [Faubus] was justified in calling upon military forces of the state to 'preserve peace and tranquility' is largely a matter of opinion. But it is significant that the newspapers and magazines blasting away from week to week never once criticized . . . the fact that the 14th Amendment, upon which the 'integration' decree of the U.S. Supreme Court is alleged to have been based, was forced upon the South literally at the point of the bayonet." However, winning two Pulitzer Prizes for commentary and public service was heady consolation for *Gazette* owners and staff.

With Martin Luther King, the head of the newly formed Southern Christian Leadership Conference, attending as the guest of his family, Ernest Green walked with the other graduates during the May 1958 Central High commencement ceremonies. The end of school did not mean victory for equal access. In early 1958 the school board in essence abandoned the Blossom Plan when it petitioned the courts for an extended delay in continuing desegregation. The board's action and the subsequent ruling by the federal district judge granting relief undercut the white moderate argument that overt resistance to integration was futile and less effective than curbing its scope.

Orval Faubus, however, understood that while school integration was stymied throughout the South, the *Brown* decision was not going to be reversed. After a late July 1958 primary victory sealed his third term, the governor called the general assembly into special session to gain the tools to preserve segregation without reviving a vain conflict with the courts. The most formidable weapon among the array of laws rapidly approved by the legislature was Act 4. Under the measure, the governor could shut down schools facing desegregation orders and then have the local voters decide in a referendum whether to integrate the district or keep the schools closed. Faubus did not wish to find himself once again in the spotlight as the only defiant warrior; he now entangled various levels of government in the struggle for segregation.

The U.S. Supreme Court bore much responsibility for the glacial pace of integration, as it left it to Southern federal judges to determine if and when schools would open their doors to African American students. The Court's unusual special hearing in August 1958 on whether or not the Little Rock schools could postpone even minimal desegregation was an exception. Thurgood Marshall, the lead attorney for the Legal Defense Fund of the NAACP, argued that the failure of local government to curtail violence against those exercising constitutional rights should not justify setting aside those rights. On September 12 the Court unanimously agreed that the disorder "which ha[s] followed upon the actions of the Governor and the Legislature" was not a basis to set aside court approved integration plans and confirmed that the *Brown* decision overrode contrary state laws. The justices ordered the district to proceed with the desegregation of the city's high schools. Within hours of the decision, Faubus announced the closing of these schools.

After the governor set the date for the school closure referendum, several of his moneyed supporters set up a corporation to operate a private high school opened only to whites. The Capital Citizens' Council aggressively solicited donations for the proposed T. J. Raney High School from fellow councilors scattered throughout the South.

On September 27 Little Rock citizens voted 3–1 to keep their high schools closed. The decisive margin was likely shaped by the wording on the ballot that only gave voters a choice between integration and segregation rather than closed and opened schools, as well as confident official statements that the public high schools would soon reopen under the auspices of the private school corporation (a federal judge thwarted this stratagem and Raney High School limped along on dwindling contributions). Nevertheless, the outcome reflected strong white hostility, particularly within working-class neighborhoods, to any degree of integration. More prosperous whites, though far from a majority, joined African American voters to support opening the schools. This emerging coalition, fortified by white union leadership, would eventually turn back the radical segregationists.

In the fall of 1958, however, those whites who vowed no surrender to federal rulings were ascendant in Little Rock and the business and political insiders waited on the sidelines. In November Dale Alford, propelled by a segregationist write-in campaign, turned out congressman Brooks Hays, recently reelected as president of the Southern Baptist Convention. Meanwhile, high school teachers fulfilled their contracts and sat at their desks in front of empty classrooms. The football teams, by the stipulation of the governor, continued to hold practices and play games, but no other scholastic activity occurred.

SONDRA GORDY HAS CONFIRMED that displaced Little Rock students pursued alternatives, including living with relatives in other towns, enrolling in parochial schools, or starting college early. Nearly all white families took advantage of such opportunities, while about half of African American students faced exclusion or found the options unrealistic. One student who would have attended Horace Mann recalled, "We had just lost our mother to a serious illness in May of 1958 and there was no way my grandmother could afford to send me anywhere else to school." On the other hand, another dislocated Horace Mann student observed that she and her sister were "fortunate" to locate the father of a friend who traveled to work in Pine Bluff daily: "And so my mother asked if we could ride along with them. So that's what we did."

Before the events of 1957 unfolded, white moderates had been optimistic that business leaders would constrain massive resistance to integration to reassure outside investors. Yet, at the high tide of radical segregation, the economic and civic elite did not waver exalting the city's business climate. A brochure published in April 1959 by the chamber of commerce for visiting conventioneers described the still racially identifiable schools: "The Little Rock Public Schools include sixteen white elementary schools and eight Negro elementary schools, five white junior high schools and one Negro junior high school; three white senior high schools and one Negro senior high school." The publication did not disclose that the high schools were not operating.

The movement to awaken the capital city's elite to the costs of segregation in reputation, job prospects, and educational integrity emerged from the circles that had launched the earlier Progressive reform crusades: white women of privilege and status. No Arkansan boasted a more stately family genealogy than Adolphine Terry, who was the sister of the poet John Gould Fletcher and whose reform activism began with the women's suffrage and anti-lynching campaigns. Vivion Brewer's parents also were part of the Little Rock patrician set, but they atypically encouraged their daughter to enter law school following the customary sojourn at Smith College. Both women married within their class, which buffered them from economic and social coercion. In September 1958 the two convened a meeting of seventeen women at Terry's antebellum family home. There they formed the Women's Emergency Committee to Open Our Schools (WEC) under the portrait of Terry's father in his Confederate uniform.

Terry understood that her own racial liberalism was an anathema even to many of the 1,400 women who eventually joined the WEC, not to mention the business elite who were the objects of WEC pressure. The organization refused to admit African American members in order to reassure moderates that its aim was to return students to public classrooms rather than pushing for social change. Faubus's famous gibe that the WEC represent the "charge of the Cadillac Brigade" was not far off the mark. The incomes of members was about twice that of the Arkansas average; nearly all of them had attended college; and most were Methodist and Presbyterian rather than Baptist.

The members of the WEC, like those of the segregationist Mothers League, used their identity as women to popularize their cause while at the same time challenging traditional gender roles. Both groups highlighted their special responsibility for the welfare of children, marketed their message through mass advertising, demanded accountability from highly placed men, and gained support through telephone chains and canvassing door-to-door. Nevertheless, the groups' differences in background and goals produced distinctive tactics. Like Daisy Bates and the nine students, WEC leaders were plagued with precisely scheduled telephone hate messages. Irene Samuel, for example, parried menacing calls every fifteen minutes on Wednesday and Saturday nights.

Steadily, the WEC promoted their cause as restoring the city back to normal even if not every classroom would be filled with students of the same race. The message finally began to win over the business community. A February survey of Little Rock Chamber of Commerce members revealed an overwhelming majority endorsed a "controlled, minimal plan of integration plan acceptable to the Federal Courts" in order to return the students to the classrooms. In May the tipping point arrived for the well-placed men. After a walkout by moderate members to prevent a quorum, the rump segregationist faction on the Little Rock School Board voted to dismiss forty-four white teachers and administrators who were viewed as sympathetic to integration.

Stop This Outrageous Purge (STOP) became the organizational vehicle for attorneys and businessmen to confront the arch-segregationists. STOP quickly circulated petitions to recall the hard-line school board members. The Mothers League's counter-campaign to remove the moderate directors led to the formation of the Committee to Retain Our Segregated Schools (CROSS). While the men of STOP stated their central aim was to protect teachers, the claims of CROSS that evicting the segregation board members would lead to reopened and desegregated high schools was the more accurate prediction.

Even though the WEC had studiously avoided any identification with integration, STOP leaders believed the women's group too controversial to be more than a silent partner. Yet the WEC's experience in the Brooks Hays congressional campaign and other electioneering efforts made it the moderates' best hope in the weeks leading up to the recall election. Irene Samuels recalled visiting the STOP headquarters early on: "I sat there and those men were running around like chickens with their heads cut off. . . . [This minister] was standing there smoking his pipe, thanking everybody."

The WEC brought to bear modern techniques of data gathering, precinct organization, and direct contact to prod sympathetic voters to cast ballots. Michael Pierce has persuasively called attention to the role of labor union leaders in the recall elections and in the introduction of grassroots, voter turnout electioneering into an Arkansas political culture dominated by machine and boss. Odell Smith, the chair of the state AFL-CIO, had appealed to his members to vote to keep the schools open in the fall 1958 referendum and in May 1959 enlisted other trade unionists to canvass and prod voters.

WEC leaders were aided critically by Henry Woods, now a labor attorney, who drew upon his experience stretching back to the McMath campaigns to figure out likely supporters in a state that did not have a system of voter registration. In the future, coalitions of urban elite white women, labor forces, and black activists formed a liberal vanguard challenging a politics that conflated business interests with the common good.

The May 26, 1959, referendum results that ousted the segregationist school board members and retained the moderates broke solidly along racial lines and less clearly by class. The upper-income white wards voted once more and by similar margins for moderation over outright segregation. Likely due in part to mobilization by union activists, the working-class neighborhoods gave fewer votes to the segregationists, a critical development in this close election. Most importantly, the turnout in African American wards was both larger and united in support of the school opening forces. And, indeed, who went to the polls mattered most of all. Henry Woods explained it starkly: "We got our vote out. And the other side was not that successful. If everybody had voted, we would have lost."

Orval Faubus recognized that the recall election marked the apex of strong segregationist influence, and he adjusted his politics accordingly. The decline of the militant separatists did not hamper Faubus's maneuverability. In 1960 Attorney General Bruce Bennett mounted a primary election challenge by charging that Faubus had turned soft on integration. The governor's reelection demonstrated that his 1957 defiance continued to inspire loyalty among conservative whites.

FAUBUS'S UNPRECEDENTED twelve years in office generated an unprecedented gubernatorial political machine. Despite the authoritarian intent, neither the state sovereignty commission nor the 1958 law requiring that state employees reveal their organizational memberships provoked a statewide purge. On the other hand, the Criminal Investigation Division (CID) of the state police served as the governor's surveillance squad. The CID spied upon and harassed white reformers and civil rights leaders less for ideological reasons than for their identification as political enemies of Faubus. In 1960 he was put forward as a presidential candidate by the National States Rights party, an invention of the Citizens' Council movement. Although Faubus belatedly turned down the nomination, he had clearly become a creature of forces that he set loose in 1957.

In August 1959 a crowd of whites gathered on the capitol steps to hear a brief statement of encouragement from Governor Faubus before they marched toward Central High, where Jefferson Thomas and Carlotta Walls were preparing to resume their education (Elizabeth Eckford was also slated to return to Central but graduated before school opened). Thelma Mothershed and Melba Pattillo had been assigned to Horace Mann, which remained an all-black school, while the rest of the Nine had either graduated or moved from Little Rock. The crowd approaching the school was smaller than the one that had amassed in the fall of 1957, and police chief Eugene Smith directed that fire hoses be opened to scatter the protestors. Three other black students entered Hall High School without incident. Most whites in Little Rock considered the school crisis over.

The reopened schools, however, remained almost completely segregated. With the expulsion of the segregationists, Everett Tucker, one of the members of the school board supported by the STOP campaign, became the new chairman. Tucker intended for the district to comply with the June 1959 federal court ruling that voided the 1958 school closure laws but to hew to a program of minimal desegregation. In August 1959 Tucker revealed his preferences to the *New York Times*: "I think both the whites and the Negroes would be better off in their own schools." The school board made full use of the pupil placement approach pioneered by Blossom and embedded in state statute. Tucker and his fellow members chose the six African American students admitted in 1959 to enter Central and Hall high schools from fifty-nine who applied.

Harry Ashmore's *Arkansas Gazette*, the relentless critic of Orval Faubus, praised the token desegregation solution: "The courts have never required integration. . . . No district is required to merge its white and colored schools." But African American activists and the white liberal core of WEC and union members believed more needed to be done.

James H. Cone attended African American colleges in Little Rock during the lead-up to the use of state troops to halt black enrollment in Central High. He graduated from Philander Smith in 1958, the same year Ernest Green received his high school diploma. Cone witnessed in Little Rock the same white unanimity in defense of segregation that had marked the unquestioned devotion in his hometown of Bearden to a framework of injustice that denied African Americans human dignity. The African Methodist Episcopal Church of his childhood was the refuge where his family and neighbors exercised authority and defined their lives independently of racist customs and deference. Yet Cone, through his years in seminary and religious studies, concluded that the totality of subjugation he had experienced in Arkansas confirmed that Christian institutions must embrace as an overriding vocation a program that went beyond solace to battle poverty and racial oppression. In this seminal 1969 book, *Black Theology and Black Power*, Cone developed the intellectual basis for black liberation theology: "I wanted to speak on behalf of the voiceless black masses in the name of Jesus, whose gospel I believed had been greatly distorted by the preaching theology of white churches."

Throughout the events of the school crisis, the African American community showed fortitude and courage under fire while a small contingent of sympathetic whites more often pursued separate strategies to combat segregationists. Even the most hardened racist had to recognize that stark intimidation was now a blunted weapon. But the strengthened resolve on behalf of racial justice was not a consequence of the governor's clash with the courts. Black solidarity and organizational effectiveness had developed from the emergence of a more forceful leadership after World War II. This legacy would continue with a new set of leaders and the advent of direct action civil rights campaigns in the 1960s. L. C. and Daisy Bates, estranged and then divorced, would not be at the center of the later movements. The *State Press* remained silenced.

The Little Rock crisis was a tragedy. While a number of individuals displayed integrity and social responsibility, the material and psychological toll exacted costs for many years. The failure to desegregate Central High School peacefully was the bitter fruit of a political system dominated by personal opportunism, narrow economic self-interest, and antagonism to the expansion of African American rights.

II. Civil Rights in Little Rock, Civil Rights beyond Little Rock

The struggle for civil rights in Arkansas widened following the Little Rock school crisis. Within the capital, influential whites bruised by the turmoil were prone to seek peaceful resolutions when it appeared recalcitrance could rekindle national media coverage. New civil rights leaders emerged from the city's African American professional class but the intervention of national civil rights organizations was critical to the desegregation of public services and accommodations. Activists faced formidable opposition in the thorny fields of Delta communities even though the confrontations were obscured by the smoke from the fires in Mississippi and Alabama.

In March 1960 about fifty students from Philander Smith College, the historically black Methodist institution, took seats at the Woolworth's lunch counter in downtown Little Rock. They remained seated when refused service, and five were arrested for not leaving after the lunch counter abruptly closed. A month earlier, students from North Carolina Agricultural and Technical College in Greensboro used the sit-in tactic to pressure that city's department stores to serve its black patrons at the counters alongside whites. Within a week, this method of demonstration spread to other Southern cities, and by September about 70,000 blacks and whites had quietly and politely endured taunts and assaults after requesting the right to order a sandwich and soft drink. By that time, twenty-eight cities had opened the lunch counters, but Little Rock was not one of them.

The municipal authorities arrested the Philander Smith students, who were hit with fines and jail sentences for breaching the peace and trespassing. Daisy and L. C. Bates and other NAACP leaders were caught off guard by this new form of protest but soon rallied to raise funds for the legal defense of the students as well as to organize picketing of leading Main Street department stores. Traditional black leaders and the Bateses' adversaries in charge of newer African American organizations viewed the sit-ins with skepticism. Division among community leaders, punitive steps by authorities, and the summer college break curtailed the sit-in movement.

In the absence of federal court orders and embarrassing publicity, holding firm against the lunch-counter movement posed scant cost to Little Rock's reputation. The July 1961 arrival of a delegation of Freedom Riders raised a different challenge. Sponsored by the Congress of Racial Equality, organized interracial groups of travelers journeyed throughout the South, entering bus-station waiting rooms and restaurants to test the enforcement of a 1960 Supreme Court ruling that desegregated interstate travel facilities. Not unexpectedly, the Freedom Riders in May 1961 provoked well-documented violence in Alabama, particularly in Montgomery, where one thousand whites bludgeoned the young group members. Little Rock leaders did not want television cameras lining the city's streets. Shielded by city police from hundreds of white hecklers, the black and white riders were arrested for breaching the peace after they entered the whites-only waiting room.

Pronounced guilty in state court, the five men and women spurned the judge's offer to waive the jail sentence in return for agreeing not to continue their campaign into Louisiana. With the riders threatening a hunger strike in jail, the Little Rock business chieftains persuaded the judge to alter his decision, and the activists departed the next morning. Another group of riders met no hindrances when they disembarked at the Little Rock station the following week. The capital's prominent figures treated demands for civil rights as a problem to be grudgingly managed.

The assuredness of the power brokers in deflecting integration proved the need for an umbrella organization to articulate African American interests more comprehensively and authentically than had individual figures relying on patronage ties to white officials. In the wake of the Freedom Rides in the summer of 1961, several young black medical doctors formed the Council on Community Affairs (COCA). African American leaders holding a variety of views served on COCA committees. The broad representation eased the factionalism that had festered over the actions and prominence of Daisy and L. C. Bates. L. C. Bates signed on with COCA, and the new organization supplanted the old-line NAACP. That state chapter was no longer led by Daisy Bates, who had moved to New York City.

COCA did employ the NAACP approach of negotiation followed by the hammer of litigation when the Little Rock aldermen rebuffed proposals to desegregate municipal parks and public buildings. While a number of prominent African American leaders remained wary of sit-ins, other civil rights activists understood direct actions often stirred a white backlash and exposed segregation's violent underpinnings.

In the fall of 1962 the interracial Arkansas Council on Human Relations (ACHR) asked the Student Nonviolent Coordinating Committee (SNCC), a product of the Southern sit-in movement, to dispatch an activist experienced in mobilizing protest campaigns. After 1960 the ACHR had moved beyond school desegregation to advocate a comprehensive integration program based upon African American goals rather than the hesitant relinquishment by whites. In October 1962 William Hansen, a white veteran of the Freedom Rides and Southern jails, arrived from SNCC's Atlanta headquarters and consulted with Philander Smith student Worth Long, who had attended SNCC conferences. Hansen detected that Little Rock whites on the whole did not recoil from casual racial interaction in public places such as he had witnessed in Deep South locales. Knowing that the business community had been traumatized by the ignominy arising from the 1957 crisis, Hansen decided that talks combined with selective protest actions could pressure downtown stores to serve all customers.

An ad hoc Downtown Negotiating Committee, chaired by banker James Penick, opened talks with a team of two student sit-in activists as well as Philander Smith chaplain Negail Riley and ACHR leader and COCA director Ozell Sutton. When the initial talks broke down, Hansen launched a sit-in campaign at a number of stores. The resulting mass arrests of the protesters stirred over one hundred Philander Smith students to march on Main Street. In contrast to the earlier phase of the campaign when the students were aided sparingly, COCA rallied its members to raise money for bail and legal expenses. Penick began to lean heavily on downtown store managers, using initial capitulations to pressure holdouts to agree to serve all customers without restriction.

The January 1963 desegregation of lunch counters proved to be the first domino, as hotels, restaurants, and movie theaters fell into line. Relieved that discrimination against retail customers had faded without incident, municipal authorities abolished racial restrictions at Robinson Auditorium, the zoo and arts center, and all public parks and golf courses. By the end of 1963 as Southern congressmen continued to bottle up President John F. Kennedy's civil rights legislation, integrated public services were the rule in Little Rock.

The tactics of evasion practiced by white leaders in Little Rock hardened into violence and harsh reprisals when SNCC ventured into Delta communities. William Hansen was attacked and beaten on a public street and pulled off a lunch-counter stool in February 1963 after he arrived in Pine Bluff to support the student-led sit-in movement. President Lawrence A. Davis, fearing white legislators would punish his college with funding cuts, suspended fifteen students from Arkansas Agriculture Mechanical, and Normal for participating in the protests. Robert Whitfield, one of those suspended, formed out of the remnants of the student campaign the Pine Bluff Movement, which targeted cafes, hotels, as well as drugstore counters. Support for the movement grew within the African American community as police arrested activists for even minor infractions. Nevertheless, the official crackdown continued even after the passage of the 1964 Civil Rights Act.

This landmark measure that banned discrimination in public accommodations, employment, and in programs receiving federal funds redoubled the efforts of SNCC to test the extent of integration throughout east Arkansas. The organization's Arkansas Project branched out from field offices in Forrest City, Helena, Gould, and Pine Bluff. Although white and black SNCC teams were often served in restaurants, in some instances only the African American members were handed menus while white civil rights activists were ignored in a silent rebuke. Millard Lowe, a black SNCC worker, recalled visiting a Delta diner: "They were going to serve us to keep from getting in trouble, so what they did was they gave us dirty water, and they gave us food loaded with salt."

Though dogged by beatings and arrests, SNCC workers signed up African American voters throughout 1964, and a slate of black candidates ran for offices in several communities, including eight who filed for state legislative slots. While the election of Arthur Miller to the Pine Bluff school board was the only victory for African American office-seekers, a SNCC field report on one election noted that regardless of the outcome "it finally gave the Negro community a candidate that would serve their interests and therefore have a reason for exercising their franchise." On a personal level, ninety-four-year-old Anna Clay explained simply why she decided to cast a ballot for the first time: "I went down to register to vote to see what that equality was all about."

The SNCC voting drives, building upon the earlier campaigns by civil rights and labor organizations, pushed African American voter registration in the state above the regional norm. The passage of the Voting Rights Act in 1965 did not in the short term directly alter the state's electoral practices. Arkansas had not relied on now-prohibited regulations such as literacy tests, and localities were not under federal supervision since the majority of eligible black voters in the state were registered.

In 1966, however, SNCC prodded the U.S. Civil Rights Commission to conduct hearings in Forrest City on voting irregularities that led the agency to send field workers to monitor polling in the region. Benjamin Grinage, who was then the state SNCC director, outlined in his complaint to the Commission the myriad informal devices used to disfranchise African American voters: "These practices include the destruction of Negro ballots, the mistabulation of votes for Negro candidates, illegal voting of the ballots of illiterates by election officials, probable multiple white voting, segregation of the polling places, and denial of access to Negro poll watchers." Grinage also noted that the ingrained corruption of Arkansas elections rendered meaningless the assurance of a secret ballot.

By 1967 the Arkansas Project had crumbled. The national SNCC office had generally regarded the state as peripheral and diminishing donations to the organization left the field workers in the Delta high and dry. Grinage, who was African American, had strongly objected to SNCC's late 1966 decision to expel whites from the organization and was forced to resign his position. The rising emphasis on black self-determination and pan-African identity evident throughout the nation was represented in Little Rock by the emergence of Black United Youth. Led by the younger brother of Minnijean Brown, one of the Little Rock Nine, the organization believed SNCC too timid in its demands and goals.

Even during the era of direct action by activists, the federal courts remained decisive battlegrounds over the struggle for civil rights. A case involving a privately owned lake outside Little Rock led to a landmark U.S. Supreme Court decision that clarified the scope of the Civil Rights Act. In 1966 John Walker, a young civil rights attorney who had begun practicing in Little Rock the year before, filed suit on behalf of two African American women who had been barred from Lake Nixon after attempting to pay a fee to swim. Whites paying the entrance charge were admitted.

The defendants argued that the Civil Rights Act's coverage of businesses engaged in interstate commerce did not extend to them because all of the Lake Nixon patrons were local. In 1969 the Court ruled in favor of the plaintiffs on the grounds that Lake Nixon was not walled off from interstate commerce regardless of its location or reach of advertising. In a bitter dissent, Justice Hugo Black confirmed that essentially no business could resist or ignore the federal anti-discrimination statute: "This would be stretching the Commerce Clause so as to give the Federal government control over little remote country places of recreation in every nook and cranny of every precinct and county in every one of the 50 states." Proponents of segregation searched in vain for a legal refuge.

IF THE INTEGRATION of retail stores and restaurants after the civil rights laws carried the day in Little Rock, segregation was preserved thoroughly and steadfastly in the school district. In east Arkansas, the most violent resistance assailing SNCC arose from drives to integrate schools as prescribed by law. An estimated 2 percent of black students attended schools with whites in Forrest City. In September 1965 the refusal of that city's school board to upgrade rat-infested buildings in schools attended only by black children generated a nearly universal boycott. Police arrested hundreds of the students and Millard Lowe, the SNCC operative, was severely beaten while held on a prison farm.

Little Rock leaders relied upon lawyers rather than police to retain single-race schools throughout the district. Title VI of the 1964 Civil Rights Act permitted Washington to withhold federal funds from districts that clung to segregation. Federal officials who oversaw education spending rarely shut off funding to localities but did goad districts to come up with more effective integration blueprints than the discredited pupil-assignment approach. After serving as Governor Faubus's trusted legal advisor, William Smith founded the influential practice of Mahaffey, Smith & Williams, later renamed Friday, Eldredge & Clark. The firm devised pioneering "freedom of choice" plans for Little Rock and prospered by drawing up similar templates for districts throughout the state that wished to shirk comprehensive integration.

The freedom of choice plans passed muster with both federal bureaucrats and courts. The stratagems in practice permitted white students to stay where they were and enabled officials to erect barriers against African American students who wished to attend better equipped schools. At the start of the 1966 school year, the Little Rock plan resulted in Horace Mann remaining an all-black high school, Hall High School enrolling seven African Americans among its 429 students, and Central High having a student body that was 85 percent white.

Among the most formidable obstacles in Little Rock was the combination of residential segregation and the district's lack of bus transportation. Through the destruction of black neighborhoods under urban renewal initiatives, federal home lending regulations, and discriminatory real estate practices, Little Rock had become two cities. During the 1960s thousands of whites migrated to the burgeoning neighborhoods west of University Avenue, while African Americans were hemmed into blocks near the central core. The flight of white families away from older neighborhoods predated school integration.

In some smaller towns, where the boundaries between black and white sections were less hardened than in Little Rock, freedom of choice plans did lead to integration, although with costs regretted by the African American community. In 1965 nearly all of the students at the all-black L. W. Sullivan High School in Morrilton chose to enroll in the other high school that had been newly constructed for the town's white students. The school board approved the transfers and fired all of the African American teachers employed at the abandoned Sullivan school. The dismissed instructors and the Arkansas Teachers Association, the professional organization for black teachers, filed a suit requiring reinstatement and the full integration of the elementary schools. The Eighth Circuit Court of Appeals ruled in favor of the teachers in a decision that was cited as precedent in similar cases in other Arkansas communities.

While court decisions also governed the course of desegregation in Little Rock, the housing patterns born of public policy and private interest in turn adulterated the force of judicial rulings.

William F. Rector, a pugnacious insurance and real estate mogul, was a commanding figure even in a city long dominated by real estate developers and investors. Although a segregationist, Rector had opposed the barring of students from Central in 1957 because the unrest unnerved out-of-state investors in his new shopping center at the crossing of University and Markham Avenues. As the crisis cooled, Rector renewed his labors to keep integration at bay. He was little concerned about the fate of Main Street lunch counters. The school district was another matter.

In 1967 Rector deemed a new liberal majority on the school board a threat to the success of his western residential tracts, which were promoted to homebuyers as safe, stable, and racially homogenous. The new board members were affiliated with various reform organizations that had emerged from the school crisis and subsequent civil rights campaigns. These groups included the Panel of American Women, a successor to the Women's Emergency Committee, as well as COCA and the ACHR. Continuing to perfect the get-out-the-vote techniques used during the 1959 school board recall elections, the new class of urban liberals were skeptical of the traditional domination of the city by private interests and encouraged the participation by a range of organized constituencies.

In contrast to alignments in other Southern states, the Arkansas labor movement continued to provide funds and mobilization efforts toward civil rights goals. This trade union and social reform alliance was strengthened in 1964 when J. Bill Becker became president of the state AFL-CIO, a position he retained until 1996. Becker embraced a broader reform agenda than the ones taken up by union leaders elsewhere. Over the course of his stint as the face of Arkansas labor, Becker tenaciously lobbied the legislature to raise unemployment benefits to among the highest in the nation as a percentage of state income, to strengthen the workers' compensation law, to replace the poll tax with a registration system, and to establish the state's first minimum-wage law.

Nevertheless, the urban liberals in Little Rock failed during the 1960s to persuade white voters that maintaining segregation through the freedom of choice plans was a doomed endeavor. Instead, William Rector rallied suburban residents first to defeat school board proposals to extend integration westward and then to vote out the members behind the proposals in subsequent elections. In a series of decisions, the U.S. Supreme Court by 1971 ordered the nation's districts to fully and quickly dismantle dual-school systems and approved as a remedy transporting or busing students across school attendance zones.

In light of these rulings, a federal district judge discarded the Little Rock freedom of choice strategy and prohibited identifiably white and black schools. Given the city's stark racial enclaves, the judge saw no alternative than to require that the district develop by 1972 a plan to have students board buses bound for schools in other neighborhoods. Those riding the new buses the following school year were disproportionately African American. A report by the federal civil rights commission issued after the start of busing in Little Rock noted: "In comparison with other communities, there was little or no appreciable conflict." No longer did angry crowds fill the streets around schools. Softer and more effective methods of resistance unfolded.

Soon after the district court's ruling, William Rector announced to a large assembly of white families that he was bankrolling a private school to be constructed at one of his real estate developments. He exulted to the crowd, "I even hope we'll be allowed to play 'Dixie' if we want to without starting a riot." By the early twenty-first century, nearly half of white students in Little Rock attended private academies rather than public schools. After 1976 African Americans supplanted whites as the majority of students in the district's schools and represented nearly 70 percent of those in public classrooms at the turn of the century, far beyond the proportion of black residents in the city's population.

BY THE TIME OF Rector's death in 1975, his legacy was visible in the shift of population and retail centers westward, a shift that emptied downtown of customers and Main Street stores. The decline of the central shopping district began after World War II, when population growth and surging automobile ownership worsened congestion. Unlike other Southern riverine cities, Little Rock continued to expand westward along the channel of the Arkansas River rather than balloon away from the river. This east-west urban axis fueled demands by real estate interests for a "Crosstown Freeway." Such a route by necessity would bulldoze through existing neighborhoods in contrast to the more familiar metropolitan highway loops that often avoided concentrations of housing.

In 1970 congressman Wilbur Mills browbeat the federal transportation agency to add the freeway to the interstate highway system even as the officials objected that Arkansas would be getting more than its share of federal mileage funds. The congressman's influence spared the city and state significant outlays. Grateful state officials named the new I-630 route after Mills.

The widespread support for the completion of the freeway included business leaders and urban planners who insisted that the faster access for suburban commuters and customers would revive downtown. The most ardent opposition arose from the newly organized Arkansas Community Organization for Reform Now (ACORN). The group, which took on housing discrimination and utility rates in poor neighborhoods, filed objections that prompted a federal judge in 1975 to suspend construction of the Mills Freeway until the state highway department conducted new public hearings.

During these hearings, the maturing urban preservation movement also weighed in on the threats to neighborhood integrity, although not in collaboration with the anti-poverty forces. The state historic preservation office, less than a decade old, had secured recognition from the National Register for Historic Places for an area with a concentration of nineteenth-century homes adjacent to the proposed Mills route. As anticipated by the preservationists, the designation of this historic district gave them leverage in their negotiations with the highway department.

The Quapaw Quarter Association, a well-connected advocacy group founded in 1961, in tandem with the state preservationist officials, won concessions to make certain the district that was once the home of the city's original elite retained the spirit evoked in the nomination submitted to the National Register: "The aesthetic ideals and social patterns of 19th century Little Rock came vividly to life in the McArthur Park Historic District where modern intrusions, incompatible in scale and design with older buildings have not yet marred the visual continuity of the built and natural landscape." The noise of commuters on the Mills thoroughfare would barely reach the shady streets lined by antebellum and Victorian homes.

ACORN opposed the freeway to the end. Nevertheless, the campaign was marred by the group's failure to broaden their coalition and by the formidable odds to stop a project already under way.

Neighborhoods not afforded historical significance remained vulnerable into the 1970s. The I-630 route sliced through the core of black Little Rock, isolating the West Ninth Street commercial district from African American neighborhoods, and accelerated the decline that began with the integration of retail business. Arthur Davis recalled the lively 1940s era: "We would hang out on Ninth Street until 12 o'clock and if you lived out west you better catch that last street car." Davis also reminisced after the demise of the "line" that "for a long time they talked about [urban renewal] and they finally came along. It just broke up our hang-out. . . . That was the demise of the close-knit feeling I think that we had."

According to one estimate, over 5,500 families were relocated in Little Rock during active years of urban renewal. Poor white and black residents in University Park were succeeded by middle-class African American families; West Rock vanished into a retail strip; and the century-old black farming community of Longley was obliterated to pave the way for the Little Rock Industrial Park.

Across the Arkansas River in North Little Rock, Mayor Casey Laman and the city council provided fodder for critics who likened urban renewal to a scorched-earth campaign. In 1960 a city planner announced that a 140-acre tract in the Military Heights section "would be cleared of most of its existing structures." When the city housing authority refused to administer the federal grant program, Mayor Laman secured a tailor-made bill from the state legislature that permitted him to form a separate urban renewal agency.

The uprooting of black families led African American leaders to observe that other areas of North Little Rock suffered from more evident blight than the targeted section that was home to nine churches. Opposition culminated in 1961 when thirty African Americans filed suit in chancery court to prevent the disinterment of over seven hundred graves from the Odd Fellows Cemetery that had been established in 1891 at Military Heights. An unfavorable judicial decision paved the way for the destruction of the cemetery and the building of a hotel.

In 1999 Curtis Sykes, a local historian, organized the dedication of a marker at the original burial site. During the event, the city of North Little Rock issued an apology for the condemnation of the cemetery. Continuing his research, Sykes was unable to determine whether the deceased from the Odd Fellows cemetery were actually relocated to a new resting place, as promised by developers.

By 1963 North Little Rock identified two other sections as future urban renewal projects. Responding to objections from an African American minister, the urban renewal director noted that the transplanted families from

Military Heights were satisfied with their new residences, nearly all of which were outside the city. Between 1960 and 1970, the North Little Rock black population plummeted by over 25 percent.

A 1965 editorial in the *North Little Rock Times* revealed that the displacement was evident well before this census survey of the decade: "The Urban Renewal projects have caused hundreds of people to leave the city—especially Negroes. In one area alone near McAlmont [an unincorporated community populated by African Americans following the Civil War], men on foot checking house numbers . . . counted 431 homes that were occupied in almost every instance by Negro families who used to live in North Little Rock."

As population, wealth, and power discharged from the countryside following World War II, Arkansas public life revolved around Little Rock to an extent found in few other states. The city was the financial capital as well as the home of government. The traditional elite and rising business class treated the renovation of historic neighborhoods as among the cultural advantages that were embellishing and elevating a regional market center. The range of ideological opinions emerging from the contests over civil rights and fair opportunity stimulated a broader participation in policy debates than was evident in other Arkansas communities. The westward expansion of the city sustained these disputes and provoked new political alignments reflecting the racial and class partitioning of the urban landscape. Throughout the 1970s, Arkansas's one big town was evolving into an American city.

III. Politics after Segregation

Winthrop Rockefeller enjoyed widespread admiration for leading the Arkansas Industrial Development Corporation (AIDC) during an era of rising available jobs. The Arkansas Power & Light management and local leaders whose efforts predated the creation of the AIDC credited friendly governments, anti-union regulations, and a lower wage scale. Rockefeller for his part believed Arkansas required a modern setting and services to sustain a modern economy.

To demonstrate that real growth must leap beyond sawmills and cotton gins, Rockefeller emphasized that remaking the Little Rock skyline was more than empty symbolism. He set up a firm to finance and build what became the city's tallest skyscraper, its clean, functional design contrasting with the decorative embellishments on the surrounding structures. Completed in 1960, the eighteen-story Tower Building was a sheer glass and steel representation of a future pointing away from the intimate rural world that prized personal relationships and perpetuated traditional hierarchies.

Rockefeller, a refugee from the skyscraper canyons of New York, also came to believe that the transformation of the state's economy was stillborn without the transformation of the state's politics. This conviction set Rockefeller on a collision course with the governor, who had appointed him to the AIDC and who was unsurpassed in winning Arkansas votes with handshakes and promises.

During his six terms in office, Orval Faubus expanded educational, public welfare, and economic development services while continuing to benefit from his obstructionist stance during the 1957 Little Rock school crisis. Government grew and did more for citizens under his administration. Faubus's denouncements of civil rights during the era of direct action protests, marches, and boycotts outflanked radical segregationists but also made it impossible for moderate candidates to gain traction. In the end, the very public scandals during the last Faubus term opened the door for reformers to gain office by attacking corrupt practices that were falling out of favor.

Federal action paved the way for cleaner Arkansas elections even before the end of the Faubus regime. In 1964 the ratification of the anti–poll tax amendment to the U.S. Constitution outlawed the levy in elections for federal offices. That same year the Supreme Court issued a "one person, one vote" decision in *Reynolds v. Sims*, requiring state legislative districts to contain roughly equivalent numbers of residents.

Arkansas was one of five Southern states still requiring voters to present poll-tax receipts, but was the only one of those to abolish the practice for state elections (the remaining four did not budge until a 1966 Supreme Court decision ruled the requirement unconstitutional). In November 1964, 56 percent of those voting approved a new voter-registration amendment that lifted the poll tax in all Arkansas elections. Reform groups, newspaper editors, and party leaders—including both Faubus and Winthrop Rockefeller, his Republican challenger that election year—backed the measure.

Opposition by the Farm Bureau and a number of county judges doomed the amendment in the Delta counties, but the strong margins of support in urban centers documented the decline in rural political muscle. The new voting system ditched the bewildering complexities of the poll-tax requirements and bolstered the SNCC campaigns to register African American voters. Overall, voter rolls increased by almost 25 percent within five years of the state amendment's passage.

Rural political influence continued its slide in 1965 when state officials reluctantly abided by the Court ruling on equal representation to redraw legislative districts. Previously, each of the seventy-five counties regardless of size had been allotted at least one member in the state House of Representatives. The new House districts crossed county boundaries and added representation to larger towns at the expense of the depopulated row crop regions. Although a few perennial solons exited the scene in 1966, a more thorough revamping of the General Assembly followed the 1970 election. Eleven new senators out of thirty-five and thirty-one freshman out of one hundred representatives took their seats in the 1971 session and backed a package of reform measures that had floundered under the old-guard lawmakers.

The debate over legislative reapportionment did provoke the most notorious political oration in the modern era. First elected to the state House of Representatives during the 1930s, Paul Van Dalsem of Perry County had distinguished himself for rank self-interest and bullying in a setting where opportunism and intimidation flourished. Van Dalsem's success in killing voting registration reform during the 1963 session exposed him to galling criticism from leaders of the American Association of University Women. In a speech that August to a Little Rock civic club, he assured his audience that when any Perry County woman began "poking around in something she doesn't know anything about . . . we get her pregnant and keep her barefoot." Van Dalsem's remarks sparked a public protest by seventy-five local women at the Perryville courthouse but proved no political danger to him until the redrawing of district lines removed his safe seat.

Van Dalsem's defeat in 1966 was viewed at the time as a triumph for good government rather than as a blow for women's rights. Nevertheless, when subsequent redistricting restored a rural stronghold to Van Dalsem, he determined that he could best make amends by sponsoring the resolution for the ratification of the Equal Rights Amendment (ERA). In 1972 the U.S. Congress proposed and sent to the states for ratification the amendment to render unconstitutional actions that denied "equality of rights under the law" on the basis of gender.

In the 1973 General Assembly session Van Dalsem diligently accumulated the votes necessary to gain victory in the House but then fell victim to the sort of personal, factional politics at which he had excelled for decades. Legislators, sympathetic to the ERA but contemptuous of Van Dalsem, delayed consideration of the resolution. The postponement enabled ERA opponents to mount phone campaigns and to bus conservative women to Little Rock to argue that the amendment was not simply an uncontroversial gesture. The ERA and Van Dalsem's rehabilitation sank together. Although introduced in the next three regular sessions of the General Assembly, the ERA resolution never gained a roll-call vote.

The anchors of rural localism, county judges, also forfeited power during the 1970s. Following the revamping of the election system, reformers believed that writing a new state constitution would do more to improve government than piecemeal initiatives. Yet voters in 1970 rejected by a wide margin a new charter drafted in the previous year by a citizens' convention. Various interests objected to specific provisions but no group was more formidable than the country executives who feared that restructuring the quorum courts, the local legislative bodies, would encumber their authority.

The state's constitution mandated a justice of the peace for every two hundred voters in a county. The requirement distended the quorum courts into bloated delegations that only met annually to ratify without debate the judges' recommended budgets. The Pulaski County 467-member quorum court was reportedly the largest legislative assembly in modern politics. The judges padded the county payrolls, rewarded and punished by deciding which roads were graded and what bridges were built, and executed purchasing contracts with negligible oversight. Diane Blair observed that this official "became the closest thing to an uncrowned king that the American political system had to offer."

On the other hand, the county judges fumed that the state constitution imposed on them a $5,000 salary ceiling. With the blessings of the judges' association, the legislature submitted to the voters in 1974 an amendment that stipulated the duties of the judges and invested genuine legislative powers in the quorum court, including setting a judge's salary. The enactment of Amendment 55 did not make the local executives irrelevant but encouraged managerial skills alien to the traditional potentates. Old practices were also discredited during the late 1970s by a four-year FBI probe that produced multiple indictments and convictions of longtime judges. The investigation revealed that kickbacks from vendors as well as the funneling of county-owned materials and labor for personal use were considered the privileges of office. An assistant U.S. attorney observed in 1982 that in the counties subject to the probe "every transaction was illegal and over long periods of time. This was simply a way of life for these men."

THE END OF the poll tax in Arkansas did not end election fraud. Outside the Delta, machine counties had relied upon on absentee ballots that could be easily assigned to voters with or without their consent and used on election day as needed. Marlin Hawkins had parlayed the goodwill he had earned as a federal jobs administrator during the Great Depression to his election in 1950 as sheriff and tax collector of Conway County. He went on to build a rock-solid machine that earned him the deference of statewide officials. Hawkins applied intimidation and harassment to wear down critics of his dominance of local politics but was bested in the mid-1970s by an unlikely group of reformers who referred to themselves as the "Snoop Sisters."

Mindful of the achievements and techniques of the Women's Emergency Committee in Little Rock, Alidene Malone, Dixie Drilling, and Katie Read scrutinized the Conway County election rolls to determine whether names on the registration lists matched real voters. Their support for a reform state Senate candidate in a 1975 special election was aided by Tom Glaze, who directed the Election Laws Institute. The institute recruited law students to serve as poll watchers throughout Conway County to discourage vote tampering in this contest. A deputy from the sheriff's office greeted one of the students at precinct site with a grim warning: "If you want to see your wife tonight you better get out of here. . . . I'll put you under the jail." The poll watchers, however, held their ground and Hawkins's machine failed to prevent senator Stanley Russ from joining the growing company of younger legislators who were more issue-oriented and receptive to consistent government operations.

Hawkins stepped down from office in 1978 following another set of closely monitored elections that confirmed his machine's infirm condition. The retiring sheriff's nephew kept the office in the family but spurned Hawkins's offer to employ the old methods on his behalf. An embittered Hawkins recalled in his memoir: "[The new sheriff] also thought as did most politicians back then, that the old style of campaigning and political leadership was over. . . . There was an almost complete turnover at the courthouse. . . . I then felt like an outsider—even unwelcomed at the courthouse—a place that had been my second home for forty years."

The erosion of traditional, local power bases, the move toward elections that actually represented voter preferences, and the arrival of public-minded legislators characterized the most notable phase of governmental reform since the Progressive era of the early twentieth century. The unseemly twilight of the Faubus administration accelerated the transition to a new political order.

The Faubus formula of expanding public services while denouncing federal intervention had eased public suspicion of a larger state government. State expenditures, which had risen about 60 percent between 1947 and 1955, soared nearly 200 percent during the Faubus years. Although the governor had designated public education as the chief beneficiary of his 1957 tax program, the growth in the school fund slightly trailed the overall budgetary surge.

Official petulance toward Washington edicts masked the deepening state reliance on national revenue. The disbursement of federal funds by state government soared from $9 million in 1957–58 to $46 million in 1966–67. If the twelve-year Faubus administration meant that patronage, rather than professional expertise, dominated the state bureaucracy, broader services and bigger budgets placed Arkansas within the ranks of New South governments. In the ten years following the Faubus era, state spending accelerated even more rapidly although the public school fund's rise once again did not match the arc of total expenditures.

His status as an entrenched incumbent did not prevent Faubus in 1964 from launching a class-based populist campaign against the Republican opponent, Winthrop Rockefeller. Recalling his tenure as first chairman of the AIDC, Rockefeller emphasized government's contribution to economic growth and did not crusade for lower taxes and meager services. In contrast to the Democratic good government advocates, he declared that only a viable two-party competition could permanently end cronyism and graft. Yet civil rights remained the overriding, defining issue for white candidates, and the 1964 campaign demonstrated its potential to outweigh party loyalty.

Although Rockefeller publicly objected to the 1964 Civil Rights Act, Faubus played up his opponent's liberal reputation with the same relish that he pronounced him a playboy interloper. In the short term, Rockefeller's racial moderation brought him few African American votes while alienating the state Republican leadership, who embraced the new conservatism of national standard-bearer Barry Goldwater. Goldwater had vanquished Rockefeller's brother Nelson for the Republican nomination, and the national party platform bristled with anti-government proposals and Cold War rhetoric. At the same time, Faubus was disgruntled by his own party's hoisting the banner of civil rights, and he belatedly and tepidly endorsed the Lyndon Johnson ticket. In 1964 Johnson and Faubus registered almost identical winning margins in Arkansas.

Rockefeller's strategy ran against the current of his party's growing appeal to Southern whites. As Rockefeller harvested votes from urban centers and the traditionally Republican northwest Arkansas, Goldwater scooped up majorities in Democratic south Arkansas. The urban-rural split also characterized black balloting in the gubernatorial contest. Rockefeller won over African American voters in eastern Little Rock precincts while losing badly in rural, black-majority Delta districts.

In 1966 Faubus announced he was retiring to his spacious new house in his native Madison County, leaving not a few to wonder how he managed to afford the residence on his modest governor's salary. In the election that fall, the great majority of the state's African American voters joined the Rockefeller coalition to repulse Jim Johnson's bid to ride rural white resentment into office.

As the first Democrat to surrender the governorship to a Republican since Reconstruction, Johnson compounded his political irrelevancy in 1968 when his challenge to senator J. William Fulbright fell short. The downfall of the state's leading segregationist and the moderation of the Rockefeller administration resurrected progressive candidates who had been unwilling to make the Faubusian bargain with racist sentiment. At the same time, Rockefeller's effort to base a black-white GOP alliance on the middle-of-the-road issues of jobs, schools, and fairer taxes undercut his party's appeal to conservative white Democrats who were alienated by their national party's Great Society liberalism. Arkansas would be the last of the Old Confederacy to abandon the Old Democracy.

THE FIRST ROCKEFELLER TERM was buoyed by the revenue windfall derived from the beginning of income-tax withholding and by public demands to rectify the scandals of the final Faubus years. Rockefeller was not a hands-on administrator but recruited talented and experienced managers to burrow into the intestines of the Faubus network to alleviate graft and favoritism. Commentators and historians have understandably highlighted how Rockefeller altered the state's political culture, but the tedious labor of reforming the state bureaucracy to deliver services responsibly and systematically was perhaps a more significant legacy.

Newly appointed directors of the Insurance Department and Securities Commission halted the chartering of transient companies that sold worthless policies or trafficked in fraudulent securities. Nearly seven hundred insurance operations flowed into the state during the Faubus era, and lax regulation allowed a number to defraud Arkansas investors of an estimated $100 million. Not all the scams originated from out-of-state interlopers. Attorney General Bruce Bennett and Rep. Paul Van Dalsem cooked up a precarious financial enterprise that left stockholders with worthless paper when it crumbled. Federal prosecutors indicted Bennett, who escaped trial when a friendly judge consistently granted him delays based upon ill health.

In both the 1964 and 1966 campaigns, Rockefeller upbraided Faubus for abetting the survival of Hot Springs gambling. The legislature in 1967 confronted the new governor with a bill to authorize a few casinos in the city but failed to override his veto. That year the state police descended upon the clubs and delivered the confiscated slot machines to local law enforcement. When the gambling devices reappeared in the old haunts, the state troopers returned and burned the machines.

No longer a draw for health-seekers, Bathhouse Row's fall from grace was mirrored across Central Avenue by the ghosts of the former clubs. The Southern Club was for a time a museum of celebrity wax figures. Visitors to the city passed under tattered awnings shading storefront jewelry auctions. Only one bathhouse still welcomed clients while another was a museum managed by the National Park Service. Through the 1980s the spa city was a seedy curiosity.

Revelations of brutalities and shocking conditions in Arkansas prisons forced the legislature in a 1968 special session to approve much of Rockefeller's penal reform package. Since the abolition of the convict lease system in 1913, convicts worked the fields at the Tucker and Cummins prison farms to produce their own food and to return a profit for the state through the sale of the surplus. The system's self-sufficiency was reinforced by the use of armed prisoners rather than employed guards to stand watch over inmates. Officials kept order through prolonged whippings and dialing the "Tucker telephone," a battery-powered device that sent an electrical current through wires attached to an inmate's genitals and toes.

A 1966 state police investigation revealed odious housing conditions at the Tucker unit: "The mattresses were filthy and rotten and appeared to be badly discolored. . . . The commodes were stopped up or would not flush. The showers were pouring water from the leaks. . . . The entire barracks area smelled from filth." Meat was served only once a month, and eggs were a Christmas morning treat. Faubus had ordered the investigation of the prison system, but the drawing to a close of his administration postponed meaningful changes until the arrival of the new governor.

The Rockefeller reforms established the Department of Corrections as well as an independent parole board to halt the rampant bribery accompanying the early release of prisoners. Even before the legislature acted on the administration proposals, Rockefeller in 1967 appointed Thomas Murton, an academic penologist from Illinois, first as superintendent of Tucker and then as overall director of prisons. Murton's knowledge and zeal seemed to fit him for the task, but his disdain for policy procedures and bent for dramatic public accusations tested the governor's patience. Rockefeller fired the mercurial Murton after the prison head announced before television cameras that he had discovered the bodies of murdered prisoners in a forgotten graveyard near Tucker.

Murton insisted during a U.S. Senate hearing and in a 1969 book that the administration covered up the fate of those in the mass grave and permitted the reinstitution of brutal treatment following his dismissal. An official state examination of the corpses and a subsequent analysis disputed that the interred had met a violent end. Murton's successor continued to improve treatment and conditions. Nevertheless, Rockefeller could not land a significant appropriation for the corrections department until a federal district judge in February 1970 declared the prison system unconstitutional. Describing Arkansas prisons as a "dark and evil world," Judge J. Smith Henley ordered that the prisoner trustees be disarmed.

Rockefeller benefited from the emergence of the state into a post-segregation political phase but also stumbled at times when attempting to navigate continuing white resistance to expanding African American demands for opportunities beyond service at restaurants and stores.

Alone among Southern governors, Rockefeller paid homage to Martin Luther King Jr. when he and his wife Jeanette sang "We Shall Overcome" hand-in-hand with African American leaders on the capitol steps three days after the assassination of the civil rights leader. Rockefeller appointed the first black members to selective-service boards; named COCA leader Ozell Sutton to the newly formed human resources council; and made William "Sonny" Walker the only African American state director in the South of a federal Office of Economic Opportunity.

Overall, however, Rockefeller displayed the mixture of forthrightness and hesitation to be expected from a leader attempting to mollify both black and white voters. He preferred non-compulsory eradication of barriers rather than aggressive civil rights enforcement. He was reluctant to prod state department heads to recruit black employees or develop procedures to ensure equal services. In 1969 his restrained response to unrest in Forrest City earned him criticism across the spectrum. After the all-white school board fired a teacher active in civil rights efforts, Forrest City black leaders organized a store boycott. Angering white conservatives throughout the state, Rockefeller visited Forrest City, where he openly acknowledged the African American group's grievances. Yet the governor also wished to persuade committee leaders to call off a planned march from Forrest City to Little Rock.

In the end, a small group of protesters set out for the nearly one-hundred-mile walk to the capital. Ignoring those within his party who demanded that he stop the protest, Rockefeller assigned a state police contingent to protect the marchers. Within a week a crowd of whites attacked seven African Americans near the city hall in Forrest City, and Rockefeller sent fifty national guard troops to pacify the divided city. This crisis festered as black leaders became increasingly troubled by Rockefeller's school integration stance, which veered from compliance with federal rulings to tacit support for the "freedom of choice" evasion. The governor's vacillations weakened his biracial coalition and offered an opportunity for a moderate Democrat to recover black support.

Rockefeller's coalition held firm during his 1968 reelection bid, aided by the voters' inclination to grant a second gubernatorial term. In that year a majority of Arkansans at the polls also supported George Wallace's independent bid for president and Fulbright's return to the U.S. Senate. Wallace, the former segregationist governor of Alabama, had converted his firebrand racial politics into a catalog of populistic grievances against an elitist establishment. Fulbright's challenge to President Lyndon Johnson's expansion of the Vietnam War had aligned him with the liberals who continued to be appalled by the Arkansas senator's civil rights record. These election results reflected a white acceptance of the benefits of government services and programs coupled with a reluctance to widen civil rights protections beyond the key acts that had outlawed segregation and voting discrimination. The outcomes also demonstrated that the politics of personality and weak party organizations survived even as the state began to conform to broader regional trends.

Rather than an aberration, the 30.5 percent proportion garnered by 1968 Democratic presidential nominee Hubert Humphrey was barely exceeded four years later by that of George McGovern, who was swamped nationally by Richard Nixon, the GOP standard-bearer. Arkansas Democrats were following the trail of other Southern voters toward becoming presidential Republicans. Southern whites faulted Democratic liberals for the era's turmoil and social divisions, and the Wallace supporters of 1968 migrated to the Republican column in the subsequent decade.

While taking for granted the benefits of pork-barrel projects, farm subsidies, and income for the elderly, loyal Arkansas Democrats deemed increased funding for social and anti-poverty programs to be wasteful. They also regarded the demands by a wider circle of Americans for rights and privileges to foster what they saw as permissiveness and irresponsibility. In contrast to the Democratic Party, the national Republican Party's ideological swing to lean government, lower taxes, and bare-bones regulations fit comfortably within the state's political tradition. A Republican governor, the face of the state party, promoting the expansion of government as a route to prosperity was another matter altogether.

Having spent his first term grappling with the lingering scandals of the Faubus years, Rockefeller resolved to unglue Arkansas from the bottom of the national rankings. He aimed to accelerate the rise in public spending that had been a hallmark of the Faubus years and increase the proportion devoted to education, prisons, healthcare, and state employment salaries.

In his 1969 address to the overwhelmingly Democratic General Assembly, the Republican governor spoke with pointed intensity: "I am angered when I hear it implied that because I and my family are blessed with material things it is easy for me to make bold proposals. . . . So long as thousands of our people go to bed hungry or in pain or in hopelessness, every night, nobody in Arkansas, myself included, has the right to be callous or indifferent." He proposed to more than double the top income-tax rate and boost the sales tax from 3 to 4 percent. As Ernest Dumas noted, no Arkansas governor had introduced a program so ambitious and none saw so little of it enacted.

The state had not increased taxes since 1957. The steady expansion of state services had depended in no small part on federal contributions, particularly under the Great Society programs of Lyndon Johnson. Even the most skilled political wizard would have been stymied by the popular hostility toward taxes as well as by a legislature dominated by the opposition party. In addition, Rockefeller, who attempted to relieve his shyness and public awkwardness with vodka, never mastered the basics of Arkansas retail politics. At an earlier special session, the frustrated Rockefeller was famously overheard to wish "the bastards" would just adjourn and leave town. In 1969 they did indeed leave with little to show for the time spent. Rockefeller was able to lasso the legislators back into another special session that year, during which a majority backed his recommendation to authorize communities to permit mixed-drink sales in restaurants and clubs.

Rockefeller launched a long-shot bid for a third term partly in reaction to the reemergence of Orval Faubus. In the August 1970 balloting, Faubus led the eight-man Democratic primary field but was forced into a run-off with the dark horse runner-up, Dale Bumpers.

The Charleston attorney had considered running for governor in 1968 but feared that the Democratic Party was not yet prepared to nominate a racial moderate. Bumpers in this campaign expanded the politics of personality to a new medium with a series of television spots that featured the candidate seated on a stool, talking directly to the audience. Faubus's ties to rural conservatives had been frayed by his decision to jettison his wife of thirty-seven years and marry a thirty-year-old, divorced mother of two young children. The former governor's run-off loss sealed the defeat of Rockefeller, who could no longer portray his candidacy as the only shield against resurgent corruption and intolerance.

BUMPERS ACCOMPLISHED what his predecessor had been unable to manage: the enactment of much of the Rockefeller program. Using the previous administration's reorganization proposal as a blueprint, Bumpers collapsed about sixty state agencies into thirteen cabinet departments. He also agreed with Rockefeller's assessment that strengthening incomes and the well-being of Arkansans required a tax increase.

Although boosting the sales tax required only a majority vote in the legislature, Bumpers opposed its regressive blow to lower-income families. The governor backed off his original proposal to push the top income-tax rate to 9 percent from the 5 percent level originally set in 1929, accepting 7 percent as a compromise rate in order to assemble the necessary three-fourths majority.

Soon after the bill's passage, income-tax collections climbed nearly 50 percent and raised a total approaching the equivalent of sales-tax revenue. The retention of the $25,000 threshold for the top rate effectively permitted future tax receipts to rise along with inflation. In 1971 only 4 percent of filers were subject to the maximum rate; by the 1990s, the top rate pertained to around two-thirds of those filing returns. Even with the dilution of progressivity, the wealthiest 2 percent of taxpayers in 1990 accounted for over one-fourth of personal income tax revenues. Future Arkansas governors backed higher taxes, but they fought to increase sales taxes rather than replicate Bumpers's gritty campaign to win a super-majority for income-tax revisions.

The income-tax hike subsidized programs and services for Arkansans that residents in other states had long taken for granted. Bumpers pushed the legislature to adopt most of his educational agenda including increases in teachers' salaries and retirement, state support for kindergartens, and free textbooks for high school students. While impressive, the boost in public school appropriations did not match the accelerated funding for higher education, corrections, and social welfare. The state assumed the operational funding for community colleges, launched a major construction program on college campuses, upgraded the unconstitutional prison facilities, expanded services for the physically and developmentally disabled, and promoted childhood immunization and rural healthcare.

Bumpers had been the first candidate for statewide office to incorporate newly awakened environmental concerns into his campaign. In 1971 he declared the twenty-seven state parks an "embarrassment," and the General Assembly with little dissent awarded the parks system an unprecedented $22.5 million for capital refurbishment and expansion.

Bumpers continued Rockefeller's policy of expanding African American appointments to state commissions and agencies. And as had Rockefeller during the Forrest City confrontation, Bumpers was forced to intervene in another east Arkansas community convulsed by post-segregation issues of power and opportunity.

IN LATE 1971 the Farm Bureau and county judges association demanded that Bumpers withdraw state approval of a federal anti-poverty health center in Lee County. The plagues of poverty—gum disease, anemia, skin infection, arrested physical development, intestinal parasites—were epidemic in the county. As throughout the Delta, the plight of low-income sharecroppers had been supplanted by the misery of unemployment. Nearly three-quarters of the population of Lee County fell below the poverty line, but only 15 percent of its residents received federal welfare payments. The school lunch program for children broke the monotony of daily meals of beans, bread, and potatoes, a common diet for those relying almost exclusively on federal food stamps.

The Lee County establishment believed federal moneys were bankrolling social revolution. Neighborhood councils selected low-income representatives to serve as directors of the Marianna medical center where the two Volunteers in Service to America (VISTA) physicians saw about fifty patients a day. In contrast to Delta attitudes, VISTA projects among the white poor in Arkansas mountain counties had not aroused local government hostility.

After mandating a study of the Lee County Cooperative Clinic operations to placate critics, Bumpers announced in April 1972 the authorization of a $1.2 million federal grant to construct a permanent clinic building. Federally funded healthcare began to correct the imbalance in who lived and died in the county. Between 1970 and 1975 the death rate among black infants dropped 50 percent. Nevertheless, the governor's decision flared into an issue during the May 1972 primary as his opponents rehashed accounts of the year of racial turmoil that had splintered Marianna.

Sparked by the arrest of an African American school employee who refused to accept and pay for a pizza she did not order, the black community in June 1971 began a yearlong boycott of Marianna's white-owned businesses. This community action was broadened in January after high school students staged a sitdown strike to protest the cancellation of an assembly to honor Martin Luther King. Class officer Rodney Slater recalled attending a meeting in the principal's office to mediate the dispute when he saw fire hoses directed at students already braving near-freezing temperatures. "All of a sudden we see kids running by the window with this blast of water, in some instances, knocking kids over, picking them up off the ground. It was just bad." The arrest of two hundred students led Slater and fellow black students to stay out of the school the remainder of the year.

Although the VISTA volunteers were ostensibly neutral, clinic director Olly Neal Jr. covertly rallied local residents to stand fast with the business boycott. Neal symbolized a new African American leadership in his evolution from non-violent civil disobedience to a willingness to counter white terrorists on their own terms. He later explained that the bomb threats against the clinic never materialized because of his frequent public declarations as to the certain fate of the bombers. "I promised that if someone messed around—and was slow about it—I would get him with my shotgun. If he was fast, I would tear him up with the 30-06."

The county judge pleaded no contest to charges that he aimed his vehicle at Neal's brother and another man distributing pro-boycott leaflets. The guilty plea netted the official a fine of only $100. Four Marianna businesses went up in flames, and reports surfaced of retributions against black customers who attempted to defy the boycott. Bumpers deployed the National Guard to enforce a curfew to stem clashes, but local whites could not rely on the one-sided suppression of African Americans that motivated governors in past eras.

The business boycott ended in July 1972 when demands for increased private and public employment of African Americans were largely met. On the other hand, many owners closed their shops. A reporter visiting the community a decade later found "no blacks behind the counters at the businesses that rimmed the courthouse square, none in the fire department or on the board of the chamber of commerce." As had been the case before the boycott, almost all white students attended a private academy rather than the public schools. The county's population outflow gathered speed after 1970.

An African American mayor took office in the mid-1990s, but expanding black political power unfolded as Delta economic conditions continued to disintegrate. The Lee Country Cooperative Clinic provided health services into the twenty-first century. Neal himself later completed law school, challenged the Lee County Democratic establishment by aligning with the Republican Party, and in 1991 became the first African American district prosecuting attorney in the state upon his appointment by governor Jim Guy Tucker. He later became one of the first three black judges on the state Court of Appeals.

In 1974 Bumpers was nearing the end of his second term with solid popular support and a list of accomplishments that persuaded future scholars to judge him the state's finest twentieth-century governor. Bumpers also knew voters were unkind to governors scrambling for third terms, and he had never shaken his long-held Washington ambitions. When in March he announced his candidacy for the U.S. Senate, he acknowledged that his views largely mirrored those of the incumbent, J. William Fulbright. Rather than the persistence of issueless politics, this confluence of political outlooks reflected a new moderate consensus on race and the federal government's role in moving Arkansas up the economic ladder.

Fulbright had moved in recent years to win the allegiance of labor and African Americans through support for a minimum-wage boost and sponsorship of a jobs program. By 1974 he was the most liberal member of the state's congressional delegation. On the other hand, Bumpers's progressive accomplishments appealed to voters loath to overlook the senator's votes against civil rights measures. Both Bumpers and Fulbright in past campaigns had depended on the white urban middle class, and it was this group of voters who agonized over the choice between the urbane and eloquent candidates. "It is a contest that has divided families, marriages, business partners, and old friends," noted one newspaper columnist. African Americans, who would vote against Fulbright, 4–1, were far from ambivalent.

In the May primary, Bumpers carried all but four counties, and his 65–35 percent margin mirrored the early polling that had persuaded him to make the challenge. His victory indicated a pathway for Democrats who reconciled reform, civil rights, and job creation to assemble the biracial coalition that eluded Rockefeller.

IV. Many Rivers to Cross: The New Environmentalism

The shift from rank exploitation to the managed development of natural resources left its mark on the face of twentieth-century Arkansas. The Theodore Roosevelt administration created the Ouachita and Ozark National Forests, the largest federal landholdings in the state, to supply a perpetual source of timber for harvest. Only with the 1930s expansion of state parks through the Civilian Conservation Corps program were natural environments showcased as tourist destinations. As Arkansas Power & Light's objections to federal dam construction faded, elected officials scrambled to welcome U.S. Army Corps of Engineers' flood control, irrigation, and navigation projects.

If the Arkansas congressional delegation warily regarded federal officials charged with enforcing labor and civil rights regulations, they cultivated those bureaucrats who could straighten rivers and manufacture lakes. The first stirrings of resistance within the state to the Corps of Engineers' endeavors predated the late 1960s national environmental movement and revolved around individual crusaders rather than cohesive organizations.

Senator John McClellan had trimmed the ambitious plan of Rep. Clyde Ellis, the champion of the electrical cooperatives, for a vast Arkansas River

Valley Authority to a more modest proposal. Yet, for a decade, even the formidable McClellan was unable to snare funding for a system of dams to ease flooding, support barge traffic, and generate electricity. Then in 1956 he and Robert S. Kerr of Oklahoma, the Senate public works chair, overcame opposition to the project by President Dwight Eisenhower by calling in congressional favors and informing the president that Oklahoma would lose a Republican congressman in the next election if he held up the funding for four dams.

The Corps of Engineers struggled with the project that was unprecedented in its size and complexity, while the state's congressional powerhouses parried skeptical federal budget directors to keep construction on track. In 1963 *Life* magazine published a blistering critique in which an anonymous Corps engineer exclaimed that "the Arkansas is the most godawful, cantankerous river in the county." Governor Faubus retorted that the magazine targeted Arkansas because its citizens were "too decent, honest, God-fearing and patriotic." When the Corps determined that several railroad and automobile bridges across the river would need to be modified to accommodate new barge traffic, McClellan compelled the federal government to absorb nearly all of the $36 million required to replace or alter the bridges serving cars. The final bill for the system was almost $1.4 billion.

On June 5, 1971, President Richard M. Nixon in a ceremony at the Catoosa port in Oklahoma dedicated the McClellan-Kerr Arkansas River Navigation system. Nixon echoed John F. Kennedy's Greers Ferry observations nine years earlier by proclaiming that the project would boost agriculture and discourage rural migration when area industries got off the ground.

During the project's first two decades of operation, materials (sand, gravel, and rock) used in the maintenance of the waterway itself represented the greatest tonnage piled on the river's barges. Into the early twenty-first century, iron and steel as well as chemical fertilizers were the most valuable products, usually shipped up the channel to a port just short of Tulsa. At best the Oklahoma and Arkansas boosters for the system cited modest transportation savings for shippers and a reduced need for highway maintenance as major economic benefits. By the second decade of the new century, Arkansas was third among states with miles of navigable rivers but the ranking was hardly proof of a rebirth of the state's nineteenth-century transportation network. Waterborne tonnage in landlocked Arkansas was a fraction of that shipped in and out of coastal regions, and two-thirds of the state's total flowed through the Mississippi River ports at Memphis and Helena.

The Ouachita River navigation, the other inland waterway system in Arkansas, was among the earliest of the Corps's projects in the Lower Mississippi

Valley. By 1925 the engineers had gouged a shallow navigation channel north from the river's mouth in Louisiana to Camden. Barge traffic dwindled during World War II, but the intervention of U.S. Representative Oren Harris and Senator McClellan forced the Corps to give up plans to abandon the waterway. When Harris in the 1950s gained a commitment from the Corps to dredge a deeper channel to boost shipping into the Camden port, he met unexpected opposition from wildlife advocates.

The Arkansas River project had not kindled objections on environmental grounds, in part because of its historic status as a major transportation artery. In addition, the transformation of that river benefited a wider range of the population than simply shippers and barge operators. Those fishing for sport welcomed stabilization of banks that led to a cleaner river. Recreational boating also boomed on a river less subject to dramatic fluctuations in water levels. In 2013 over three thousand of these vessels passed through the locks. In the case of the Ouachita, hunters, fishing enthusiasts, and recreational users were the ones who feared the consequences of a river made viable for modern navigation.

In 1970 McClellan brokered a compromise by pushing through appropriations for a wildlife refuge along the Ouachita and for the construction of two new locks and dams. The agreement did not hold. The Corps concluded in the early 1980s that accommodating larger barges required slicing through bends to straighten the course of the river. Local conservationists called upon state environmental groups, including the Arkansas Wildlife Federation and the Audubon Society, to mobilize grassroots opposition to the plan. Since the swifter river current would likely erode natural sandbars that were popular sites for picnics and boisterous parties as well as disturb favorite hunting and fishing spots, the defenders of the Ouachita were not dismissed locally as "tree-huggers" or cranks who valued nature over humans.

Of course, the Ouachita had not been a natural river since the early twentieth century. The opponents of the Corps's channelization did indeed wish for the agency to maintain the river for recreational purposes through dredging operations to remove underwater snags and silt build-up. Yet navigation and flood control rather than recreation were the authorized goals that permitted the Corps to keep the current unimpeded by natural obstacles. Elected officials and economic interests tended to favor expanded shipping partly out of fear that the Corps would curtail its operations and allow the river to rise and fall with flood and drought. The defeat in the 1992 Democratic primary of U.S. representative Beryl Anthony, a proponent of river navigation, suggested little political advantage if not political peril in supporting heavier barge traffic.

The Corps did not cut through any bends, and barges on the river were few and far between. After 2000 the Ouachita found another calling that was also outside the its authorized purpose. A critical groundwater shortage that threatened the future of a vital aquifer led manufacturers in industrialized Union County to begin drawing water directly from the river rather than from underground wells. This alternative source of water depended upon the pooling of water behind the uppermost lock and dam on the Ouachita River. Economic developers and conservationists and those who loved the outdoors all agreed in this case that federal money and management was a benefit that should be preserved.

The Arkansas lowlands through which the Ouachita flowed were not regarded by visitors or state tourism boosters as scenic. Hunting and fishing were the primary recreational draws. In contrast, the green and leafy Ozarks were marketed and celebrated as both an aesthetic wonder and the remnant of an authentic Arkansas landscape.

BY THE MID-1950s the Corps of Engineers' White River basin project had underwritten north Arkansas tourism through the creation of Norfork and Bull Shoals lakes. The first public alert that dam building threatened the integrity of the Ozark panorama was issued by state game and fish commission biologist Harold Alexander in a series of 1956 *Arkansas Gazette* articles. Alexander's essays troubled Bentonville physician Neil Compton, who was drawn home after World War II by memories of the region's unspoiled beauty. Compton's apprehensions were deepened by the Corps's intention to dam sections of the Buffalo River and flood the picturesque Lost Valley in Newton County. In 1961 Compton founded the Ozark Society, although he often grew impatient with the fractious group's inability to settle on a common strategy.

Compton's solid Republican and civic leadership credentials gave his crusade a mainstream cast, but his sharp instinct for publicity opportunities proved even more decisive. In 1962 the anti-dam movement achieved a public relations coup when Supreme Court justice William O. Douglas made a canoe trip down the Buffalo River under the watchful eyes of national reporters. The environmental case was continually aired thanks to sympathetic journalists writing articles that reached a statewide audience. The Ozarks Playground Association, fearing the Buffalo River dams would divert the tourists already flocking to the Corps lakes along the White River, proved an unexpected ally.

The Corps refused to strike its colors when faced with citizen mobilization. Eager for federal largesse, U.S. representative James W. Trimble continually steadied the agency's resolve, as did the pro-development Buffalo River Improvement Association (BRIA), led by Marshall newspaper editor John Tudor. BRIA insisted the new dams would insure affordable electricity for rural customers, a reliable source of drinking water, and welcomed dollars from visitors.

In 1965 Governor Faubus, a native Ozarker, weighed in against the damming the Buffalo. He unleashed his objections in a florid letter to the chief of engineers of the Corps: "In so many places, the giant power-driven machines of man are flattening the hedges, fence rows, and nooks, where the song birds nested . . . leveling the forests where once roamed the wild deer; scarring the mountains and pushing down the lofty crags where perched the eagles." The Corps had long followed a policy of never undertaking in a state a project opposed by the governor. The victory of Republican John Paul Hammerschmidt over Trimble in the 1966 general election marked the final demise of the dam projects and the survival of a free-flowing river.

The movement to designate the Buffalo an official national river stimulated the imagination of developers, who hatched such schemes as an "Ozarkland" theme park and the resuscitation of an old zinc mining boom town into a tourist center. While these speculative ventures came to nothing, the 1972 law that turned the Buffalo River over to the National Park Service did refashion the area. A contingent of landowners along the river who had backed the environmentalists in hope that their farms could be saved from inundation bitterly denounced their former compatriots when the national government moved to buy up acres for the new preserve.

Stretching for 135 miles across three counties, the Buffalo River park's limestone bluffs and clear water lured over one million visitors annually by the second decade of the twenty-first century. Many sightseers stuck to the hiking trails, but the large number floating the more placid stretches of the river provided a booming business for outfitters and triggered occasional canoe bottlenecks.

Unlike advocates for mountain folk culture, Compton had not insisted that a natural waterway would be a cash machine for local economies as opposed to the uptick in tourism springing from a new lake. Indeed, into the new century, the three national river counties remained poorer than the rest of the state and lagged well behind the nearly threefold population growth of Cleburne County, the gateway to Greers Ferry Lake. By the fiftieth anniversary of the dedication by President Kennedy, this Corps lake welcomed seven million annually and the adjoining trout hatchery alone, according to the U.S. Fish and Wildlife Service, had a comparable economic impact to overall Buffalo River tourism.

The "battle for the Buffalo" was not only iconic for the Arkansas environ-mental movement but soon came to be understood widely as a good fight won on behalf of all Arkansans. In 2013 the location of C&H Hog Farm, housing 6,500 swine, within the Buffalo River watershed ignited outrage that spanned partisan and ideological camps in a manner rarely seen with other public issues. The state Department of Environmental Quality had granted a permit to the concentrated feeding operation after limited review and public comment. In 2015 governor Asa Hutchinson, a Republican, and the legislature, with a Republican majority, agreed to impose a five-year moratorium on future indus-trial animal feeding operations in the area, a decision praised by environmental-ists and groups dedicated to preserving the Buffalo.

Nevertheless, the consensus on excluding large-scale livestock raising sites within the river's watershed cracked open when the state's traditionally domi-nant economic sector and formidable lobbying organization perceived a general threat to landowners. In 2018 the Arkansas Farm Bureau, with the avid sup-port of its members, objected to a decision by the state's environmental regula-tory agency to deny the existing farm in the Buffalo watershed an additional required permit. C&H could not stay in business without the permit. Farmers throughout the state became apprehensive that state regulators had estab-lished a precedent to suspend other types of ongoing agricultural operations. The Farm Bureau on its website called attention to its campaign "to support the family owned and operated C&H Hog Farm in Mt. Judea and stand up for the property rights of farmers across the state." During that year's session, the General Assembly enacted a measure to restrict the issues that could be raised by the public in a challenge to a holder of an existing liquid animal-waste permit. The sponsors of the bill insisted it would only soothe farmers without changing environmental regulations, although opponents feared that problems arising after feed lot operations gained permits from state regulators could not be addressed or corrected.

The Oklahoma attorney general in 2005 also ignited a united response by Arkansas political leaders, this time on behalf of poultry producers and pro-cessors. This official presented evidence in a federal lawsuit that chicken waste leached across the state boundary to pollute the Illinois River. Years passed without a ruling on the suit in an Oklahoma federal court, and Scott Pruitt, the new Oklahoma attorney general, became an ally for the Arkansas interests in declining to press ahead with new court filings to secure a decision. Pruitt's critics contrasted this inaction with the flurry of suits he filed to scale back reg-ulation of air and water in Oklahoma by the federal Environmental Protection Agency (EPA). Pruitt, who would become the first director of the EPA in the

Donald Trump administration, excoriated his predecessor under President Barack Obama for resorting to "regulation through litigation."

The controversy between the two states prompted the General Assembly to authorize the Arkansas Natural Resources Commission to compel landowners to file plans for disposal of those nutrients that posed a threat to water ways. The phosphorus levels in the Illinois between 2004 and 2016 fell after chicken growers in northwest Arkansas counties spread around 30 percent less chicken litter across pastures draining into the watershed. By 2017, despite the steady declines, the levels of phosphorous still exceeded the Oklahoma water quality standard.

TEN YEARS AFTER Faubus instructed the Corp of Engineers to cease and desist over destruction of the Buffalo, another Arkansas governor informed the engineer of the Little Rock Corps District that he opposed the damming of a free-flowing river in the north central upland region. Governor David Pryor, who succeeded Bumpers, had toured by helicopter a section of what he later called the "noble Strawberry." Unlike the Buffalo, this river had many detractors eager for its disappearance under a twelve-thousand-acre lake but few defenders.

Bereft of dramatic, photo-friendly bluffs, isolated from a large university community, and not serving as a major destination for canoeists, the Strawberry River did not inspire outside environmentalists to rally on its behalf. Yet many who lived along the waterway's seventy-mile stretch treasured it all the same. These residents confronted unsympathetic federal and state lawmakers. Influential legislators pushed through the General Assembly an appropriation to partially meet the costs for recreational amenities on the new lake. When Governor Pryor vetoed the measure he cited the many letters from long-standing property owners who did not want to move. "I have drank it, fished in it, swam and played in it, used water from it to wash my clothes. I love it as it is," wrote one.

In the following decades, the activities of the residents, including cattle grazing and road construction, endangered the Strawberry. The buildup of sediment choked fauna in the stream and threatened an impressive diversity of species. In 2000 the Nature Conservancy, an unusually flush environmental organization able to tap wealthy donors and corporations, began buying parcels from willing landowners to stitch together a 950-acre preserve. The Conservancy mustered local volunteers to plant two thousand trees to check erosion and established a buffer zone off-limits to cattle herds. The organization's leaders were drawing upon experience to revive the Strawberry River. Years before, the Conservancy reaped public attention and praise for its intervention to rescue a river watershed in the Delta.

If the proliferation of lakes was the most dramatic reshaping of the Arkansas landscape in the second half of the twentieth century, the first half was marked by the eradication of the east Arkansas bottomland forests, the fabled Great Swamp. The clearing of the land continued after World War II with rising soybean and then rice markets. Farmers relentlessly petitioned members of Congress for additional flood and drainage control projects to wrest acres from swamp bottoms. By 1970 Senator John McClellan and U.S. Representative Bill Alexander obliged by securing funding for the Corps of Engineers to straighten and deepen the Cache River, a waterway that flowed from near the Missouri Boot Heel until merging into the White River at Clarendon. Upon completion, the waterway would be little more than a ditch and the floodplain given over to sweeping crop fields.

The Delta, endlessly refashioned to suit the demands of agriculture, was the unlikeliest of battlegrounds between the Corps and the environmentalists. Then migratory ducks became the unexpected wild card.

Mallards, in particular, had long alighted along east Arkansas rivers and by the 1920s flocked to the harvested rice fields and irrigation impoundments surrounding Stuttgart. While the 1930 drought sparked fears that ducks would go the way of the passenger pigeon, the population quickly recovered. By 1947 a St. Louis reporter described a season in which the migrating waterfowl turned the sky dark: "I watched mallards sitting in vast and solid rafts on the Arkansas reservoirs quacking raucously and happily, and at dusk, saw them start for the rice fields. They took off in successive roars like fleets of miniature B-29's."

For a variety of reasons—the emphasis on marksmanship, the necessity for trained dogs, the advantage of securing a leased site—duck hunting held special appeal for wealthy individuals. Organized into shooting clubs or paying duck camp fees, hunters had generally observed bag limits and restricted the killing of hens prior to the setting of public game regulations. This informal tradition of game management influenced Rex Hancock, a Stuttgart dentist and duck hunter, to form the Citizens Committee to Save the Cache River Basin.

As with the unfolding of the Buffalo and Ouachita River battles, well-regarded local figures formed alliances with established environmental organizations, lobbied sympathetic state federal agencies, and relied upon friendly media coverage. The Arkansas Game and Fish Commission in 1971 signed on to a suit filed by the Arkansas Wildlife Federation to stop the ditching. During the controversy, the *Arkansas Gazette* ran an editorial entitled "The Rape of the Cache," and *Gazette* cartoonist George Fisher fixed the image of Corps bureaucrats as befuddled men in Bermuda shorts and pith helmets that sported badges reading "Keep Busy."

McClellan's death in 1977 and a subsequent government study documenting the Cache River Basin as vital for waterfowl habitat terminated full-scale channelization. In 1980 the U.S. Fish and Wildlife Service (USFWS) outlined the boundaries of a national wildlife refuge in the middle section of the basin, but the new presidential administration of Ronald Reagan scratched the necessary appropriations to purchase land.

By the mid-1980s, plummeting agricultural prices provided an opening for the Nature Conservancy to buy up depressed farm acreage. In 1986 the USFWS began to purchase what the Conservancy held in reserve. Seven years later U.S. senator Dale Bumpers induced Potlatch Corporation to transfer its substantial holdings of Delta wetlands to the USFWS in exchange for federal forest acreage in Idaho. The expanded White River and the Cache River wildlife refuges made up a large portion of the 550,000 acres that came to be known as the Big Woods of Arkansas.

Nancy DeLamar, director of the Conservancy, coined the term one evening as she and colleagues volleyed names to stir support for the diminished remnant of the once sprawling forest canopy. She recalled the phrase from a William Faulkner story: "It was of the wilderness, the big woods, bigger and older than any recorded document."

Through the twenty-first century both the duck population and the length of the hunting season steadily climbed. Over forty commercial hunting clubs around Stuttgart alone allowed corporations to entertain out-of-state clients with a good shoot and a fine dinner at a well-appointed lodge. As one club proprietor explained, "It's one of the few hunting sports where you can get a group of people in a blind. They have a captive audience with their customers." In 1947 Lion Oil Company of El Dorado built near Casscoe in Arkansas County a 4,800-square-foot lodge along with auxiliary buildings including a caretaker's house, a laundry building, apartment units, and a water tower. Potlatch acquired the property in the early 1970s and continued to host both prominent business and political figures, including president George H. W. Bush. As in past decades, important national business leaders thought of Arkansas first as a hunters' paradise.

Beginning in 2005, a surge of out-of-state visitors to the Big Woods were bird watchers rather than duck hunters. Early in the previous year, Gene Sparling posted on social media that while boating through the Cache River Basin he had spotted what appeared to be an ivory-billed woodpecker. Sixty years earlier scientists concluded that the largest woodpecker in the United States fell into extinction because of the loss of habitat. The bird fed almost exclusively on a beetle found in the disappearing bottom-land hardwoods throughout the South. Other sightings and brief video footage led the Cornell Lab of Ornithology in April 2005 to pronounce the survival of at least one male ivory-billed woodpecker.

Stores in Brinkley began selling woodpecker souvenirs to tourists and duck hunting guides branched out to take birders into the Big Woods (although duck hunters remained, unsurprisingly, the greater source of profit). Yet futility dogged scientists hoping to find additional evidence, and in 2010 the Cornell team called off the search. In 2014 the U.S. Committee of the North American Bird Conservation Initiative judged that the ivory-billed woodpecker was "probably extinct."

Beginning in the 1960s, Arkansas environmentalists skillfully tied their goals to the popular and historical traditions that appealed to prominent elites who influenced public opinion through modern media and organization. In a state still half-covered by forests and largely rural, outdoor pursuits blended into everyday life. Environmentalism, like other reforms, required the growth of the urban professional class, and city dwellers in Arkansas did not have to venture far beyond the suburbs to locate rivers and deep woods. Business and political figures generally viewed the new ecological awareness as compatible with economic development.

Environmental initiatives that did not directly impinge on exploitation of resources or industrial expansion were widely regarded as opportunities to market scenic landscapes and attract a new cohort of tourists. For a time in the late twentieth century, Arkansas was not unique in the softening of partisan or ideological brawls over preservation of remote natural spots. In October 1984 the U.S. Congress approved a series of measures that extended protections to wilderness areas in ten states. Senator Dale Bumpers sponsored the first of these bills, which sailed through the Senate due to the decisive support of his conservative Republican colleague from Texas, Senator John Tower. Ed Bethune, the Republican representative of the urban central Arkansas congressional district, ushered the Arkansas Wilderness Act, which covered 95,000 acres in the Ozark and Ouachita National Forests, through the House.

In the early 1970s the Parks and Tourism department contracted with a marketing firm to develop a slogan that could be used for out-of-state advertising campaigns. The phrase "Arkansas is a Natural" caught on, and in 1995 the legislature replaced the "Land of Opportunity" motto with "The Natural State" as the official state nickname. Promoters appreciated that communities with little manufacturing could still erect an economy built on tourists and retirees. This new industry did not require a skilled workforce, disrupt community patterns, or command significant state government outlays. Tourism became the meeting ground between the new environmentalism and New South boosterism.

Gov. Orval Faubus meets the press at the state capitol, October 2, 1957. The Little Rock crisis offered American viewers the first television images from the front lines of the new struggle for civil rights. National reporters were not above resorting to stereotypes. A *Time* magazine article referred to Faubus as a "slightly sophisticated hillbilly." *Special Collections Division, University of Arkansas Libraries, Fayetteville.*

Little Rock police detectives look on as Daisy and L. C. Bates inspect remnants of a burned cross outside their home in 1957. Years of experience as activists prepared the two civil rights leaders to sustain their commitment to desegregation in the face of unrelenting harassment during the school crisis. *Special Collections Division, University of Arkansas Libraries, Fayetteville.*

A sit-in demonstration at Woolworth's in Little Rock, November, 7 1962. Unlike the sit-in movements elsewhere, the Little Rock effort did not yield immediate results. However, downtown Little Rock stores were desegregated before the passage of the 1964 Civil Rights Act. *J. N. Heiskell Collection, University of Arkansas at Little Rock Archives.*

Orville Henry interviews Frank Broyles as assistant football coach Borys Malczycki observes, circa early 1970s. Both Broyles, the long-time football coach and then athletic director at the University of Arkansas, Fayetteville, and Henry, the long-time sports editor and columnist for the *Arkansas Gazette* and later the *Arkansas Democrat*, were pivotal in establishing the Razorback program as a source of pride and fervor for the state's residents. *Courtesy of the Henry family.*

Gov. Winthrop Rockefeller joins community leaders in "We Shall Overcome" at a memorial service for Martin Luther King Jr. at the state capitol, April 7, 1968. The only southern governor to publicly honor the civil rights leader after his assassination, Rockefeller wished to include African Americans in a Republican coalition to challenge Democratic dominance. *Winthrop Rockefeller Collection, University of Arkansas at Little Rock Archives.*

(*Facing page, bottom*) Supreme Court Justice William O. Douglas fishes in the Buffalo River, May 1962. Advocates for preserving the river had gained the support of key state journalists, but Douglas's three-day canoe trip attracted national attention. Environmental leader Neil Compton observed that with the justice's visit, "We knew that we had a cause not to be denied." *Special Collections Division, University of Arkansas Libraries, Fayetteville.*

Working on the line at the Tyson chicken processing plant in Springdale in 1978. Women were a significant portion of the new Arkansas manufacturing labor force after World War II. *Bob Besom, photographer, Shiloh Museum of Ozark History.*

Fay Jones in front of his design for a home on Eden Isle near Heber Springs, circa early 1970s. Having built tree houses as a child in El Dorado, Jones earned worldwide recognition for his design of Thorncrown Chapel near Eureka Springs and the Cooper Memorial Chapel in Bella Vista. *Al Drap, photographer, Fay Jones Collection, Special Collections Division, University of Arkansas Libraries, Fayetteville.*

Asa Hutchinson, Tim Hutchinson, Frank White, attend the Republican National Convention, New Orleans, 1988. Neither the election of White as governor in 1980 nor Tim Hutchinson as senator in 1996 ignited a Republican surge to challenge Democratic Party rule. The inauguration of Asa Hutchinson as governor in 2015 fortified his party's dominance of state government. *Courtesy of Gay White.*

Mike and Janet Huckabee with their children (l. to r.) David, Sarah, and John Mark, circa early 1990s. Following his tenure as governor, Mike Huckabee made presidential runs in 2008 and in 2016. His daughter was an advisor in both campaigns as well as those of other Arkansas Republicans. She later became the press secretary for President Donald Trump. *Courtesy of Mike Huckabee, Archives and Special Collections, Ouachita Baptist University.*

Dale Bumpers, David Pryor, Bill Clinton, Jim Guy Tucker, and Mike Beebe, Little Rock, March, 2009. By the time of the opening of the Arkansas Studies Institute, the political era represented by these major figures was drawing to a close as the state shifted from Democratic to Republican sway. In 2017 the Central Arkansas Library System's Arkansas Studies Institute building became the Bobby L. Roberts Library of Arkansas History & Art in recognition of the library's influential director. *Michael Keckhaver, photographer, Butler Center for Arkansas Studies, Central Arkansas Library System.*

Gloria Ray Karlmark and Ernest Green stand next to their bronze likeness during the August 2005 dedication of "Testament," a monument on the grounds of the state capitol. John Deering, editorial cartoonist for the *Arkansas Democrat-Gazette,* sculpted statues of each of the Little Rock Nine based upon pictures taken by Will Counts, a photographer with the *Arkansas Democrat.* Commemorations of the students' struggles renewed debates over the progress made in the years that followed the school crisis. *Courtesy of the Arkansas Secretary of State.*

5 | AN AMERICAN STATE

I N SPRING 1981 Berton Rouché, a writer for *The New Yorker*, spent nearly a month in Hope, gathering material for a series of essays on American small towns. When the magazine published his profile of Hope, copies quickly disappeared from local news racks, and reprints of the article circulated widely. The enthusiasm seemed warranted by the Edenic introduction: "The sun shone every day of my stay but one, and the nights were mild, and many of them were moonlit, and almost every night I fell asleep to the long, slow, faraway whistle of a freight train."

Rouché praised the downtown Crescent Drug as a "beguiling relic of the long-gone days when the corner drugstore was a social center." Yet the comments of townspeople revealed that even in Hope the old soda fountain was a quaint reminder of an unrecoverable past. Confirming both the importance of broiler production to the local economy and the ebbing of home-cooked meals, one man observed: "We love chicken here in Hope. We've got Colonel Sanders and Chicken Country both." Residents shopped the national grocery chain store, but its selections were tailored to the hometown palate. The butcher explained, "We don't carry veal or any kind of lamb. Folks here just won't eat it."

As throughout the nation, local preferences smoothly blended into a standardized consumer economy. Yet Arkansas had only recently begun to look like the rest of America, and debates over the gains and losses were far from silenced. The owner of a men's clothing store welcomed absorption into the mainstream: "We're not all barefooted hillbillies settin' on the front porch and spittin' tobacco juice. We're the Sun Belt now. We've got more new people coming into town than you would believe possible." The mayor was doubtful about the consequences of the economic development campaigns: "There's a trend these days toward thinking what's good for business is good for Arkansas. I don't agree. This is still an unspoiled state, and Hope is an unspoiled town. We have a good industrial base. It's clean and pleasant. It accepts the environment."

Roueché had not been in town long before learning he was in "the water-melon capital of the world." Hempstead County's light, sandy soil enticed farmers early in the century to plant fruit as a buffer to the vagaries of the cotton market. Before World War I, a seed salesman began offering prizes for the largest watermelon. The contest evolved by the mid-1920s into a fair or "festival" that coincided with the August harvest. In September 2005 Lloyd Bright hauled to the local feed-store scales a melon that captured the world record at 268.8 pounds.

The Hope Watermelon Festival event was not an isolated phenomenon. Dozens of communities tapped the tourism market through showcasing festivals. Most of these weekend events self-consciously evoked particular local traditions either through an agricultural commodity (Warren Pink Tomato Festival, Emerson Purple Hull Pea Festival, Atkins Picklefest), or an older industry (Malvern Brickfest, Smackover Oil Town Festival, Fordyce on the Cotton Belt), or folk arts and games (Rison Pioneer Craft Festival, Mena Lum and Abner Days, Harrison Bluegrass Festival). A town no longer required a lake or mountain vista to rebrand its cultural identity as a product in the growing leisure industry.

Sixteen years after Roueché's visit, two natives of Hope stood on the steps of Little Rock Central High School to open the large wooden doors for the nine men and women who had crossed that threshold forty years earlier under the protection of the United States Army. During this commemoration of the 1957 integration crisis, both President Bill Clinton and Governor Mike Huckabee praised the courage of the former students and emphasized that in 1997 many doors remained shut. Clinton noted, "Segregation is no longer the law but too often separation is still the rule," while Huckabee answered Arkansans who wondered when the consequences of the crisis would fade: "Until justice is the same for every human being, whether he or she is black or white we will deal with it."

Ernest Green, who had been the lone senior among the students, declared their goals were larger than entering classrooms once reserved only for whites. "What we needed was the same thing to which all people are entitled, a community that wants its children to blossom and not bleed, a society that encourages us to reach for our dreams and recognizes us as whole persons." Listening to the speeches that day was the First Lady of the United States, who would become the first woman nominated for the presidency of the United States by a major party.

During the years between the lyrical profile in *The New Yorker* and the 2016 presidential campaign of Hillary Rodham Clinton, the prosperity of Hope and the surrounding region faltered even as the state's major urban centers closed the gap on national economic benchmarks. Hope's downtown retail center, with the stores that had stirred Roueché's wistful tributes, did not endure.

An ambitious plan to preserve Main Street as a site where shoppers could walk and visit along storefronts contributed to the downfall of the central district. A nationwide urban experiment in the 1970s to lure business from shopping malls by limiting traffic and turning downtown streets into pedestrian spaces was tried with little success in several Arkansas communities. In 1978 urban developers in Little Rock capped years of planning with the opening of the Metrocentre Mall. Cars were banished from six city blocks of Main Street. After about a third of the retail operations fled, the corridor was reopened in 1989 to traffic.

In Hope, downtown stores relocated and chains surfaced along a formerly residential avenue that became a commercial artery emptying traffic into the brimming parking lots of the Walmart discount store near Interstate 30. The usual evolution of Walmart operations was completed in 2001 when a Supercenter that sold groceries opened at a site the company purchased from a local Baptist church.

The sunny expectations of town leaders reported by Roueché dimmed as Hope remained home to fewer people. The decline, however, was intermittent and followed, to a point, the fortunes of the state as a whole. The town suffered the greatest population loss in the harsh 1980s, when Arkansas buckled under a series of economic gales. Hope and Hempstead County made up ground in the next decade but stumbled after 2000. The state's metro areas flourished in the new century while disappointment stalked the rural quarters of southwest and east Arkansas. Thirty-six of the seventy-five counties lost population in a state that grew 9 percent overall during the first decade of the twenty-first century (a rate that still lagged behind national growth).

Hope's population ebb reflected the slowing of an earlier robust migration of newcomers. Roueché likely encountered few if any Latinos, but their proportion of the population soared roughly thirteen fold in the 1990s, a rate that tracked the rise of manufacturing employment from 33.3 to 42 percent of the local workforce. The subsequent collapse in these manufacturing jobs was equally dramatic in scope and speed. By 2014 only around 22 percent of those working in Hope were employed in plants, a drop that even surpassed the relentless decline of manufacturing jobs statewide. Although fewer Latinos arrived in Hope, they comprised in that year more than two in ten residents in the town. Rather than merchandising nostalgic wares, Latino retail entrepreneurs offered a range of products and services for a place less of the Sun Belt and more in the Nuevo South.

Huckabee famously noted, "In my little hometown of Hope, Arkansas, the three sacred heroes were Jesus, Elvis and FDR, not necessarily in that order." In 2016 the presidential nominee of the party of FDR was overwhelmed in Hempstead County by Donald Trump, the Republican candidate. Hillary Clinton netted only one-third of the county's and the state's voters. The county had long followed the Southern political pattern of mustering majorities for GOP presidential contenders but persisted in supporting Democratic hopefuls further down ballot. Democrats angling for statewide office had been competitive in this rural swing county, one of twenty-six crucial to their electoral success. But the Republican realm bulged beyond the Ozarks and suburban enclaves to claim precincts that had been once up for grabs. In 2014 Hempstead County voters aligned with the rest of the state by shifting to Republican candidates across the board, including the county judge and a state representative. The race for governor was much closer in the county than in the state as a whole. Mike Ross, the Democratic aspirant, hailed from neighboring Nevada County and had represented Hempstead County in the U.S. House of Representatives for six terms. Nevertheless, even he failed to carry Bill Clinton's home ground.

Bill Clinton would likely not have been elected president in 1992 if the state he governed had not reformed an intrinsically corrupt political system, diversified an economy overly reliant on resource exploitation, and evolved into a more equitable society. On the other hand, Bill Clinton running for a statewide office in 2016 would likely have lost.

In a twist on the old notion that the state was a colonial pawn of Northern capitalists, Arkansas entrepreneurs such as Walton, Tyson, Murphy, and Dillard became familiar names to shoppers throughout the nation. The thriving metropolitan corridor lining the state's northwest boundary challenged the accustomed preeminence of Little Rock. Tourism campaigns beat the drums for Bill Clinton's presidential library and Alice Walton's Crystal Bridges Museum of Art without neglecting to extol the upgraded state parks. The marketing of cultural institutions to visitors was a new element but did not eclipse the celebration of Arkansas as a place of clear skies and silent spaces. Native writers and artists produced works with a rich blending of tradition and modern awareness that avoided the cloudy uplands of nostalgia.

A larger and more professional state government after World War II followed the evolution of modern business enterprises that required expanded public services and spending to underwrite infrastructure, financing, and labor productivity. The sturdy consensus in the late twentieth century for this economic model dissolved as the Republican Party began to prevail at all levels of government. The generation that succeeded the founders of the legacy companies grew more engaged with causes and movements beyond their immediate business interests. These new movers and shakers became influential advocates for transferring public funds and resources directly into private hands based upon their skeptical assessment of government effectiveness and competence.

The drive to shrink government size and expense reopened debates over civil rights. In the twenty years since the speeches by President Clinton and Governor Huckabee on the steps of Central High, newly elected officeholders insisted that individuals pursuing their goals in an open marketplace would erase barriers to a fair society without the need for extensive government oversight and enforcement. The debate over alternatives to public education illustrated the divide over whether transferring government revenue to private interests served all families. Once again, the schools became the battleground over how Arkansas could become "a community that wants its children to blossom."

I. Uneven Progress:
Corporate Growth on the Edge of the Sun Belt

"We're the Sun Belt now."

In the 1970s scholars and commentators contrasted the growing prosperity of a region sweeping from the Carolinas to Southern California with the woes of the slumping industrial Midwest. The Sunbelt locales attracted not only retirees escaping Northern winters but also migrants streaming into cities swelled by defense industry dollars, surging energy production, and manufacturers turning to technology rather than workers. This recognition of an unmistakable socioeconomic Southern rim stretching to the West underscored that neither the traditional American South endured as an enclosed region nor was prosperity universal throughout the old Confederacy. Overviews of the Sunbelt slotted Arkansas on the margins of the region, both in terms of geography and economic dynamics. The state was better off but still had considerable ground to make up to match national benchmarks.

Arkansas's population growth failed to match the overall Sunbelt climb through the last half of the twentieth century. Arkansans continued to benefit from the favorable balance of payments between outgoing federal taxes and incoming federal spending, but the slice of the state's economy tied to Cold War operations and bases was not on par with agriculture or food and clothing production. If the ascent of the metropolis in the Sunbelt was indisputable to commuters in sprawling Atlanta, Houston, Phoenix, or San Diego, Arkansas remained a majority rural state until the 1970s (the 1970 state census actually recorded a 50/50 split between town and country; nationally, 73.6 percent of the population was listed as urban). The increase in urban Arkansans slowed in the subsequent decades leading up to 2000, and by that year only 13 of the 102 incorporated municipalities with a population of 2,500 (the boundary between rural and urban for the census bureau) reached or exceeded 25,000 residents.

On the other hand, economic reports that measured Arkansas with 1970s powerhouses such as Texas, Florida, and California obscured the extent and rate of change in the state since World War II. While the United States had become urban by 1920 because of the flood of immigrants seeking factory jobs, Arkansas towns and cities grew in population by two-thirds between 1950 and 1970 despite the continued out-migration of its citizens. The countryside, of course, was emptier. During the 1960s, the state exceeded the national growth rates in personal income, increased employment, value added by manufacturing, residential construction, retail sales, and, not surprisingly, agricultural cash receipts. Arkansas farmers prospered even more dramatically during the following decade as they embraced mechanization and relished a shift in federal farm policy that rewarded planting more acres. Between 1970 and 1978 statewide total net farm income increased 279 percent.

The chronic inflation that fueled soaring crop prices in the 1970s combined with festering unemployment to curdle the American economy. While a number of Sunbelt states relied upon new technologically oriented industries to weather the storm, agriculture buoyed Arkansas and advanced the state's century-long quest to "catch up" with the rest of the nation. Arkansas's marked economic progress was often measured by analysts in the state with the imperfect but useful comparison of state and national per capita income.

In 1950, as the take-off of manufacturing began to reshape the state's economy, per capita income was just over half of the national measure and only Mississippi fell lower. By the end of the 1970s, Arkansas boosters had reasons to celebrate reaching 78 percent of the national per capita income and achieving near parity with the states in the southeastern region. Wages grew throughout the state and, in contrast to the Sunbelt pattern, were not notably higher in metropolitan centers than in non-metropolitan counties. The unprecedented economic gains were accompanied by a singular change in population. For the first time since the nineteenth century, more people moved to Arkansas than left.

But not everyone stayed. Black Arkansans continued to seek opportunities elsewhere throughout the remainder of the century, even as African Americans moved from reeling Northern states to Atlanta, Dallas, Charlotte, and Memphis in what demographers called a reverse of the Great Migration. The heft of the Arkansas economic renaissance did not lift all families and regions. Poverty and structures of exploitation embedded in the old order persisted alongside new ways of making a living and building wealth to create a selective prosperity.

The 1970s population growth rested on the band of counties stretching from the urban center of the state up the Arkansas River Valley and encompassing the northwest rim of the Ozark Plateau. An internal boundary, roughly following the long-standing transportation route slicing diagonally from northeast to southwest, began to distinguish a modernizing west from a languishing rural south and east, where wealth and power had historically resided. Arkansas was a state with brightening Sunbelt enclaves overshadowing vacant rural patches.

In the early 1970s Juanita Sandford required students in an advanced sociology course at Henderson State University to not only read studies of poverty but visit low-income households throughout the state. One student reported a mother and five children in southeastern Ashley County were crowded into a three-room house: "They have an outdoor privy and one water hydrant, outside. There are rags stuffed in the holes of the walls to keep out the cold. On the wall in the living room is a picture of Christ, and on the TV is a picture of Dr. Martin Luther King." Another student observed a family of fourteen in eastern St. Francis County also living in a three-room shanty: "There were holes in the walls large enough to put a hand through. There was no gas and no running water."

Electric lights and appliances arrived in rural Arkansas before indoor plumbing. Whereas, two-thirds of rural homes had electricity by 1950, just 58 percent boasted the basic plumbing amenities by 1960. The incorporation of the Arkansas countryside into the American market not unexpectedly continued, and the 1970 census recorded that nearly three-quarters of rural houses had running water and bathroom fixtures. The surviving divide over what most Americans regarded as necessary for a decent lifestyle was not drawn between town and country in Arkansas but between black and white. Only 30 percent of rural African American households in 1970 had full plumbing.

The continued exodus of African Americans from rural areas already short of hope extended the most consequential demographic transformation since the flight of refugees from the state during the Civil War. By 1990 the proportion of the state's black population had declined from 22 percent in 1950 to slightly under 16 percent; in addition, those living outside urban areas plummeted from over two-thirds of the African American population to 6.5 percent. Black Arkansans were more likely to reside in town than whites. Better jobs and salaries in urban areas pushed African American median family income between 1959 and 1989 to grow faster than that of whites. The percentage of black professionals and managers in 1990 was over four times higher than what it had been thirty years earlier. This statistical increase was evident in the expansion of the African American middle class, historically concentrated in Pine Bluff and Little Rock. These two cities became home to half of the black-owned firms in the state.

But these notable gains barely eroded the persistent gap between white and black economic status, whether in town or countryside. Holding jobs in low-wage service and resource-processing enterprises, African American men and women in Arkansas had a greater distance to go to approach white income levels than was the case nationwide. In an astute analysis of 1990 census data, Lawrence Santi concluded that only about half of the racial disparity in Arkansas incomes originated in divergent social backgrounds. Black households were generally younger and less-educated, but those with experienced and trained workers still did not enjoy the same financial rewards as white households with similar backgrounds. The exclusion of African Americans with appropriate credentials from higher-paying occupations reinforced inequality.

CLIMBING THE ECONOMIC LADDER in the state slowed as the boom era of the 1970s crashed against the all too familiar barrier of a weather-induced natural disaster. The heat wave and drought that struck Arkansas in 1980 approached those of the apocalyptic years of 1930 and 1954 and fostered losses within the state of about $1 billion as well as directly causing the deaths of over 130 residents. Not only were the crop fields parched, but millions of chickens died from the heat. The dry spell eased, but a general agricultural crisis resulting from overproduction and diminishing international markets weighed down Arkansas farmers throughout the decade. At the same time, manufacturing employment fell as the state could not sustain its low-wage advantage against developing nations that welcomed apparel and shoe factories. A third fewer clothing workers labored in Arkansas plants by the mid-1980s, when the decline paused before resuming in the following decade. The U.S. economy surged following the end of a deep recession in 1982, but Arkansas fortunes nevertheless lagged.

Undoubtedly, the state's economic woes within the context of a flourishing national economy arose in part from the continued dependence on the traditional sectors of agriculture and processing natural resources. Yet hard times also kindled modernization. State economic leaders confidently pointed to the expansion of plants turning out electric motors, refrigerators, automobile tires, power tools, and fabricated metals. By 1984 employment in the electrical equipment industry surpassed that in lumber and wood products, the century's perennial top job producer among manufacturers of durable goods.

In 1987 Nucor, a pioneer in developing steel mini-mills that processed scrap metal into construction materials, joined a Japanese company to open a plant in Mississippi County. Smaller and less complex than the integrated operations in Northern cities, these new steel factories, reminiscent of the non-durable good operations in the 1950s, were located in lightly populated areas in the South and Midwest. Recruiting a nonunion labor force at lower wages, the mills sped the loss of jobs and production in the Rust Belt. In 1992 Nucor constructed another mini-mill in Mississippi County, and in 2017 a rival firm opened the Big River Steel mill on 1,300 acres outside Osceola.

The southwest section of Arkansas grappled, as had Ohio and Pennsylvania, with the downfall of large metal-production operations. In 1985 Reynolds Metals Company, which had acquired the major aluminum production plants from Alcoa after World War II, closed down the Hurricane Creek and Jones Mills factories because of a softening market and expensive power. In the 1950s Alcoa had opened an alumina refinery near Bauxite that it transferred in 2004 to a former subsidiary. By 2017 this plant employed only 142, a comparable figure to those working at a Reynolds rolling mill near Malvern. These numbers were a fraction of those on the job when the industry was at full throttle.

––––––––––

THE ROUNDS OF BUSINESS FAILURES that preoccupied Arkansans most keenly in the 1980s were the closures of financial institutions. Declining commodity prices were not, perhaps surprisingly, the culprit. The engrained caution of Arkansas bankers had limited their exposure to shaky farm loans. More so than in nearly every other state, Arkansas farmers had been forced to look to the federal Farmers Home Administration, a traditional lender of last resort.

Savings and loan associations (S&Ls), on the other hand, were less risk adverse due to a wave of federal deregulation measures early in the decade that awarded them advantages that banks did not enjoy. The S&Ls had been confined for decades to the safe and staid home mortgage market but were now able with nominal oversight to speculate in a broader array of properties. These Arkansas financial institutions dived into surging land and commercial developments with the same frenzy as their Sunbelt counterparts. The S&Ls offered depositors unsustainable rates on savings accounts that in turn prodded them to extend loans to questionable projects. With insufficient funds to make depositors whole, the Federal Home Loan Bank board allowed many failing S&Ls to continue even thought they were fiscally moribund.

Eventually, Congress had little choice but to approve a massive bailout package for the industry that spiraled to an estimated final reckoning of $341 billion in taxpayer dollars. In Arkansas federal regulators closed and assumed the obligations for S&Ls ranging from large entities such as FirstSouth in Pine Bluff and Savers in Little Rock to the smaller Madison Guaranty, whose owner, James McDougal, was brought to trial but acquitted on four counts of federal bank fraud.

As the S&Ls began to vanish from Arkansas in the following decade, business news headlines tracked the acquisition of long-standing banks by out-of-state firms. By the end of the 1990s, the names Worthen (Little Rock, established in 1877), First Commercial (Little Rock, 1934), and Twin City (North Little Rock, 1904) were replaced on the front of downtown buildings by institutions headquartered in St. Louis, Charlotte, Milwaukee, and Birmingham. For the first time since the territorial era, the state's political capital was not the financial capital. Nevertheless, the nationwide drive toward financial consolidation sputtered in a state with a population and institutions that remained stubbornly dispersed.

A study published in 1999 by John R. Hall Jr. and Ralph B. Shull revealed that small hometown banks, comprising two-thirds of all commercial banks in the state, held 25 percent of the total assets all Arkansas banks. Comparable institutions throughout the nation accounted for only 5 percent of assets. By examining balance sheets, the authors discovered that these community institutions had increased their lending in the 1990s and issued a greater number of agricultural production mortgages than had larger banks. The study concluded the inherent uncertainty of such loans made the trend "especially problematic for the smallest banks." That worry was misplaced.

Arkansas banks not only largely withstood the financial crisis and 2007–2010 Great Recession, but several of the state-based firms moved aggressively to snap up the assets of distressed banks within and outside the state. By 2017 only four banks in Arkansas were on the Federal Deposit Insurance Corporation's list of institutions that had failed since 2000, a stark contrast to hard-hit states such as Florida, Georgia, and Illinois, where toxic real-estate loans drove dozens of institutions into receivership. But the emerging metropolitan center extending from Fayetteville through Springdale to Bentonville took a spill. Construction permits fell by a greater percentage there than both the national average and the rest of the state. Real estate developers, including one firm that owed $120 million to thirteen banks in the area, fled to bankruptcy court for relief. Nevertheless, the portfolios of most Arkansas banks had not been overloaded with home mortgages, and this restraint paid off as the northwest section, though hit the hardest, began to recover ahead of the rest of the state.

In the 1990s Arkansans proudly noted that Little Rock, at least for a short period of time, was the home to the largest investment firm outside of New York. After Witt Stephens took over Arkla Gas he passed on control of Stephens Inc., the investment company he founded in 1933, to Jackson Stephens, his brother. Jack Stephens enlarged the company's portfolio well beyond municipal and school bonds while continuing to assist Arkansas enterprises. The firm oversaw public stock offerings of companies that became familiar to American households: Walmart, Tyson, Alltel, Dillard's, and J.B. Hunt Trucking.

Securing financing for start-ups in the state became increasingly critical as the national economy in the late twentieth century began its transition toward technology-centered enterprises. Charles Morgan, who in 1975 took over the information management services company that became Acxiom, grumbled about the barriers his business faced before going public in 1983: "The large banks wouldn't talk to us. They didn't believe anything sophisticated and good could come out of Arkansas." The expansion of Stephens and emergence of larger banking operations within the state loosened the capital logjam. By 1999 the thirty-six publicly traded Arkansas-based companies tripled the number operating in the mid-1980s.

Bank of the Ozarks, chartered in Little Rock, and Home BancShares, based in Conway, boomed in the wake of their successful bids at FDIC auctions for banks undone by the Great Recession. Stephens Inc. had underwritten the public offerings for both before they muscled to the top of the list of largest state banking companies. If historically Arkansas had been starved for adequate capital, its economy in the twenty-first century was unable to provide an adequate investment market for growing Arkansas banks.

In 2011 Bank of the Ozarks began doing business in New York City, followed in 2014 by Home BancShares, which saw its stock soar after the move to Manhattan. By 2016 most of Bank of the Ozarks's loans were through its New York branches. In that year, George Gleason, the firm's CEO, observed that his bank was "probably one of the dominant, if not the top, construction and development lenders in New York." Although in 2018 the bank constructed a new operations center in the small town of Ozark, it also blurred its identity with that locale by changing its name to Bank OZK. The institution's chief administrative officer explained, "We wanted our new name to free us from geographic limitations, be modern and distinctive. . . . We wanted a name that would embrace our heritage."

The agricultural production loans on the books of community and small banks that worried the authors of the 1999 study actually proved a foundation for a healthy financial sector. This boon was thanks to the longstanding underwriter of the Arkansas modern economy—the national government. Increasingly in the 1990s the Farm Services Agency, a division within the federal agricultural department, insured by up to 90 percent every loan those banks extended to landowners wanting to raise chickens. These farmers needed hefty lines of credit to build grow-out houses that met the specifications of processing companies such as Tyson Foods, ConAgra, and Pilgrim's Pride. This federal safety net permitted rural banks to remain whole even as owners of broiler houses were more likely than other farmers to fall into insolvency.

BY 1952, WHEN DON TYSON dropped out of the University of Arkansas to join his father's business, John W. Tyson had already pushed the industry toward vertical integration by contracting with farmers in the region around the company's headquarters in Springdale. Within seven years, the younger Tyson, an aggressive innovator in the mode of his father, shifted the company from a feed and hatchery operation to a fully integrated poultry firm by opening a processing plant that turned live chickens into table fare. Tyson, and the other companies that survived low commodity prices during the 1950s, directly owned every stage of the process except for the farms that grew chicks into broilers ready for slaughter. The poultry companies had learned through failed experiments that contracting with farmers who took on the debt to construct the growing houses was safer and more profitable than buying tracts of land and building their own structures.

Growing crops in the Ozarks, particularly since the collapse of the fruit-growing enterprises, was traditionally precarious, and agreeing to contracts that preset prices seemed to farmers a better bet than hoping the market broke in their favor. Processors furnished chicks and feed and paid the growers according to the weight of the broilers after the company trucks collected the birds. Growers came out ahead as long as they kept in check expenses tied up in labor, utilities, as well as debt on equipment and chicken houses. But they increasingly faced an uphill battle to control these costs owing to volatile commodity returns and the processors' tenacious drive for efficiency through research and technology. The growers who survived submitted to greater oversight and stipulations to earn contracts that usually covered only the delivery of single flocks. Even as Arkansas in the 1960s displaced the older commercial poultry regions in the mid-Atlantic states, the larger hauls of chickens headed for the plants were grown by fewer Arkansas farmers.

The University of Arkansas became the research and development arm of the industry and never flagged in pursuit of the better bird. In the 1950s a broiler required fifteen pounds of feed and fifteen weeks to grow to three pounds, but by the early twenty-first century nearly ten pounds of feed and five weeks produced a five-and-a-half-pound chicken. In addition to modifying the cocktail of feed ingredients and drugs, the poultry companies compelled growers to install equipment that improved ventilation and grain distribution in the chicken houses. By the end of the twentieth century the emergence of the "tournament system" of compensation reinforced the processor's prodding of growers to take on additional debt to refit chicken houses. Under this system, processors ranked growers against one another to calculate remuneration and bonus payments, putting farmers with older houses at a disadvantage to those who had recently entered the business with new structures.

The poultry companies praised the system for rewarding the superior, more diligent growers. Confronting mounting skepticism of the payment model, the poultry industry's national lobbying association in 2014 issued a pointed defense: "The term 'tournament' is used by critics to imply that there is only one winner in modern chicken production. In reality, it is a performance-based system where everyone benefits, including the farmers, who are compensated according to the quality and care of their chickens." By that year, however, Tyson and the other integrated companies had already fended off a serious drive for expanded federal regulation of production contracts. The support for government oversight had mounted as Tyson introduced its established management techniques to its new holdings in beef and pork production.

Even before Don Tyson took over the company following his father's death in 1967, the hard knocks of the boom-and-bust poultry market had convinced him that even an elaborate vertical integration system was an inadequate buffer. He launched a dual campaign to forge new markets for his company's products and to pare competition.

Tyson Foods spearheaded a branding revolution in the late 1960s when it marketed small chickens boasting more white meat as "Rock Cornish Hens," a convenient frozen item sold at a fixed cost per bird rather than by the pound. Brent Riffel in his comprehensive history of the company emphasized the importance to the company's growth in developing value-added goods. Riffel's study underscored Don Tyson's explanation: "We found out that if we could do something more to chickens we could sell them for more." As married women entered the workforce, the assortment of Tyson's convenience foods—chilled chicken portions, pre-cooked fried chicken, chicken patties, and processed sandwich meat—occupied larger sections of the grocery display cases. By 1990 only 20 percent of retail chicken sales were whole birds.

Chicken meals sold to restaurant customers were even less vulnerable to price swings than specialty offerings in grocery markets. Don Tyson's fervent fourteen-year courtship with McDonald's was rewarded in 1979 when the fast-food franchise contracted with the processor to supply the meat that would go into the newly invented "McNugget." By 1984, when Tyson Foods obtained Valmac Poultry, the main supplier for Kentucky Fried Chicken, the company distributed ready-to-cook products for forty-two of the fifty largest fast-food chains. The acquisition of Valmac illustrated the interconnections of the state's tight-knit business establishment.

Cliff Lane, whose poultry firm in Grannis had risen to among the largest after he bought Arkansas Valley Industries, was engulfed in debt but refused to raise capital by selling his Valmac state-of-the art processing operations to Don Tyson. Lane Poultry secured from Worthen Bank a $10 million loan that Stephens Inc. purchased and then sold to Tyson Foods. With his company's fate in the hands of a rival, Cliff Lane attempted to frustrate Tyson by selling the Valmac property to a Texas investment firm. Don Tyson dispatched Jim Blair, the company's attorney, to extend an exorbitant offer for Valmac that the Texas company readily accepted. When Lane Poultry went into receivership the following year, the bankruptcy panel over the objections of Lane permitted Tyson to snap up the stock and dissolve the company.

In 1989 Stephens Inc. again was the financial advisor for Tyson during the protracted, monumental struggle with ConAgra over the purchase of Holly Farms, the third-ranking poultry firm. With the Holly Farms plants under its wing, Tyson Foods solidified its position as the top poultry producer nationally and expanded its reach globally, particularly in Asia, where consumers preferred the dark-meat portions that were the second choice of Americans. The acquisitions campaign continued after 1991, when Don Tyson stepped down as chief executive officer. The company, however, looked beyond chickens to mitigate market twists and turns. Cobbling together a group of seafood operations was a rare misstep. The contract-grower model could not be transferred into that industry, but Tyson company leaders did view the approach as viable in pork and beef production. Don Tyson, though, was skeptical of the risks accompanying the next takeover initiative.

In 2000 he opposed the campaign by the company's CEO and his son, John H. Tyson, to battle with Smithfield Foods for Iowa Beef Processors (IBP), the nation's dominant beef and pork packer. Tyson Foods won the fight and became the nation's largest meat company. With Tyson taking up a portion of nearly every American dinner plate, the company also became the focus for critics of modern agricultural production and processing. The Arkansas firm confronted resistance when it moved to impose the contract-grower system upon cattle feedlots and hog farms. Dogged objections by Midwestern livestock farmers stirred a response initially in Iowa and then from Washington.

In its home state, Tyson Foods had stymied regulation of the company's standard contract arrangements. Dissatisfaction over contracts in which the parties were far from equal drove the emergence of short-lived Arkansas-based growers' associations in 1962 and 1991. The complaints often revolved around the plight of a grower saddled with expensive chicken-growing houses (generally requiring $300,000 to build) and unable to recover costs if the processor stopped extending contracts. Companies insisted that such decisions were governed by performance, while growers suspected reprisals for supposed malcontents. In 1997 a grower wrote, in a letter to the USDA that supported a federal rule to overhaul the system, "I will sign my name but would appreciate it if you don't use it. Fear is a terrible thing." Another communication to the federal agency read, "I have never written to anyone like you before. I didn't even know there was anyone who could help us." Tyson Foods and other processors countered by citing a large number of growers who, in the words of John Tyson, "get the pleasure of being on the farm and living a lifestyle that's fast disappearing in America today."

In 1999 the USDA after receiving the comments from growers issued a narrow rule to verify the weight of broilers upon delivery by growers to the processors. Earlier attempts to introduce legislation on behalf of growers in the Arkansas General Assembly and the U.S. Congress were stillborn. Nevertheless, in the following year, the attorney general of Iowa paid heed to hog producers who in the wake of mega-mergers feared processors would "chickenize" their operations through one-sided contracts. Tom Miller drafted model legislation endorsed by fifteen other state attorneys general (none in the poultry-centered Southern states) to mandate transparent contracts, outlaw reprisals against growers, and scrap the tournament system. The measure, however, failed in the Iowa legislature, and the other states backed off.

Livestock producers and poultry growers wanting to improve their bargaining position with the dominant meatpacking firms advocated for revisions in the 1921 Packers and Stockyards Act but made no headway during the administrations of Bill Clinton and George W. Bush. In 2010 Barack Obama's Department of Agriculture proposed a regulation that incorporated elements of the Iowa model law as well as allowing individual growers to bring suits against processors. Insisting that setting aside a production system in place for decades would disrupt supplies and confront shoppers with soaring prices, the integrated processors directed their formidable influence and financial firepower at Congress. The administration was thrown back on its heels, and the resulting compromise stripped most of the provisions opposed by the industry. In 2011 Congress voted to pull funding for enforcement of the surviving regulations.

In its final days the Obama administration recast the 2010 proposal as the "Farmer Fair Practices Interim Rule" and set implementation for April 2017. The rule did not abolish the tournament system but required processors to justify decisions when growers complained that lower rates of compensation were arbitrary, retaliatory, or an outgrowth of deceptive practices. The USDA in accompanying documents argued for the necessity of the regulations: "In this country, we expect fair treatment and fair wages for services rendered. But for chicken growers in particular, the deck is stacked against them and they have nowhere to turn if they are unfairly cut out of the business."

As agencies in the opening months of the Donald Trump presidency scrutinized regulatory actions taken by the Obama administration, the USDA postponed implementing the meat production rule before formally quashing it in October 2017. The trade and lobbying groups for the processing companies were unstinting and uniform in praising a decision that confirmed their immense influence. The president of the National Pork Producers Council warned that the new rule would have turned every "contract dispute into a federal case subject to triple damages," thinning the ranks of farmers as processors abandoned contractual arrangements to raise livestock directly.

The divisions among growers who viewed themselves either as an unprotected labor force or as independent farm operators undermined sustained challenges to large-scale companies that could count on backing from all levels of government. For many growers in the twenty-first century, raising chickens was a way to stay on the land and in agriculture rather than a means to a stable livelihood. Just as north Arkansas women in the 1950s worked in shirt or shoe factories to supplement farm income, families who owned broiler operations relied upon other earnings to hold on each year. The modern way of bringing chickens to market proved to be among the forces keeping Arkansas distinctively rural.

———————

DISSATISFACTION AMONG GROWERS had mounted over the decades as processors restructured contracts and hardened their negotiations to hammer out additional efficiencies in production. The drive to lower costs within the processing plants themselves also strained relations with the other set of poultry laborers—those who worked the line.

As Tyson and other processors ventured into selling chilled birds to stores and processed meat to fast-food chains, the processing plants evolved from slaughter houses to manufacturing operations that deboned, cut up, and "fabricated the carcass." These steps to turning chickens into tender chunks or seasoned breast meat began in 1973 for Tyson with a state-of-the art plant in Nashville. The new technology to produce the value-added products did not reduce the overall plant employee force but did accelerate the pace needed to perform the repetitive tasks. Increased complaints in the 1980s led the Occupational Safety and Health Administration to begin to monitor and document rising instances of musculoskeletal disorders and carpel tunnel syndrome among processing workers, although employees also emphasized that cuts and falls associated with line speed were common injuries. A north Arkansas plant worker surveyed in 2015 by the Northwest Arkansas Workers' Justice Center explained, "There might be 20-plus chickens that we cut [in] one minute. The line is going so fast that sometimes we accidentally cut our hands."

In her study of the conditions in the former J-M processing plant in El Dorado, purchased by ConAgra in the 1980s, LaGuana Gray dramatically revealed that not only did the carcasses rapidly stream through the plant but did so without pause. An employee recalled that a female coworker became ill and called out for help before slumping over: "A supervisor had walked up to her, and the lady fell back into her arms, and she died in her arms. . . . They pulled her back from the line sitting on the stool, and another person walked up in her position. They never stopped the line."

The local chapters in the state of the United Food and Commercial Workers Union (UFCW, formed in 1979 from a merger of meatpacking and retail-workers unions) confronted the processors over health and safety conditions arising from plant mechanization but made little headway. The preponderance of organized processing plants wilted by the late 1970s as Tyson Foods launched an effective campaign to decertify union representation. The company defied investigations into its tactics by the National Labor Relations Board, claiming immunity based on its federally recognized status as a "family farm." In 1986 the federal government curtailed the substantial tax break associated with this status, but Tyson Foods continued to fend off union challenges.

The UFCW retained a collective bargaining contract with the ConAgra plant in El Dorado, although many of the rank and file accosted the union leadership for being remote and deferential to management. The union could do little when Pilgrim's Pride purchased the operation in 2008 and shut it down to reduce production in the midst of collapsing prices during the Great Recession. The maneuver did not, however, salvage the overextended corporation. After entering bankruptcy, the firm fell into the grasp of JBS SA, a Brazilian company that became the world's leading beef producer following its purchase of Smithfield Foods's U.S. beef division. The El Dorado plant was not reopened under new management. Hundreds of its former employees struggled to find work in the midst of a manufacturing depression, capsizing one of the state's oldest industrial centers. Nearly a hundred growers who had supplied birds for the plant sued Pilgrim's Pride for market manipulation but failed to win damages after a favorable decision by a federal magistrate was overturned by an appeals court panel.

Most of the line workers in the El Dorado plant had been African American women, but the continued historic concentration of plants in white-majority counties—Benton, Washington, Sebastian, Independence—limited the proportion of black workers in the industry. The 1990s wave of Hispanic migrants, a result in some cases of recruiting efforts by the poultry companies, left the workforce in the processing factories proportionally less Anglo. The percentage of African Americans employed in food processing between 1990 and 2012 remained largely unchanged. Buoyed by a steady arrival of workers, poultry processing operations did not markedly reduce their labor force to the same extent as did factories in other sectors. The number of poultry plant workers in 2014 was 8.5 percent fewer than in 2004 while Arkansas manufacturing jobs fell by 25 percent. Even with the influx of newcomers, unemployment in northwest Arkansas remained below the state average. Wages in the poultry industry did continue to rise in the first decade of the new century but trailed the overall private sector increase. The low compensation for those laboring in the state's largest manufacturing industry hindered the state's drive to advance up the national income scale.

Don Tyson died in 2011 as his company was emerging from the upheavals of recession. In 2014 Tyson Foods bested JBS in a battle of titans for Hillshire Brands, a producer of well-known brands of hot dogs and sausage, to remain the largest American meat processor and among the top three national food-and-beverage operations based on sales. The firm had surmounted periods of soaring grain prices due to federal export policies as well as subsidies to turn corn into ethanol, immigration service raids, federal investigations for employing undocumented workers, and test findings of salmonella contamination of its products. The company prevailed in court against charges of smuggling workers from Mexico and agreed to manageable health inspection regimens that did not slow line speed.

Early in the twenty-first century, Tyson Foods moved to outflank critics of its environmental and health legacy by using its formidable market reach to craft a model of corporate citizenship for the industry. The company hired both a chief sustainability officer and director of animal well-being. It set up a well-publicized collaboration with the World Resources Institute and the Nature Conservancy to control pollution and greenhouse gases.

Whether or not detractors were mollified, the flexibility of the company impressed other executives and corporate directors in the industry. In early 2017, Tyson Foods topped other food companies on *Fortune* magazine's list of "World's Most Admired Companies." Although "social responsibility" was one of the criteria, the company's peers recognized that a strategy of cost control and acquisitions throughout the years had brought Tyson Foods to a commanding position in an economy far different than the one when John Tyson began hauling chickens to Chicago.

ANOTHER, BETTER-KNOWN international corporation headquartered in Arkansas found itself outranked on the 2017 *Fortune* list by formidable competitors. Walmart, like Tyson, had also followed a course of stringently limiting expenses and supplanting rivals, but technological breakthroughs at the start of the new century transformed both retailing and consumer expectations. The company's executives acknowledged Walmart needed to break from its past to sustain the growth and retain the advantage it had enjoyed under its founder, Sam Walton.

In 1950, after his landlord refused to renew the lease on his successful Newport variety store, Sam Walton opened Walton 5 & 10 on the town square in Bentonville. By the early 1960s he owned sixteen variety stores affiliated with the Ben Franklin chain throughout Arkansas, Kansas, and Missouri. Even so, Walton spied the advantages enjoyed by full-scale discount merchandisers such as Gibson Products, a Texas chain, and knew his five-and-dime outlets were outmoded. He did, however, have breathing space. Arkansas had comparatively few discount operations in July 1962, when Walton welcomed the first customers to his Wal-Mart Discount City in Rogers.

Nelson Lichtenstein in his history of Walmart explained that Walton's decision to relocate to northwest Arkansas insulated the company from showdowns sparked by the civil rights movement. Store managers in biracial locales would have had to decide whether to knuckle under to segregation diehards or to employ and serve equally African American residents. By the time Walmart expanded outside its core Ozark region, the fires had dampened, and the company compiled an estimable record in fair hiring.

The other benefit of the uplands location for Walton was the availability of the same set of workers who had been drawn to the apparel and chicken plants. For white rural women, a Walmart paycheck not only underwrote a family's ability to stay on an unprofitable farm but also conferred a degree of status and autonomy absent from the factory floor. Bea Scott of Pea Ridge recalled her first days at a store during the Christmas season: "Every day there was something different in Walmart. You didn't do an assembly-line job at all."

Walmart employees, Bethany Moreton noted, found themselves able to serve their neighbors in the shopping aisles with the same friendship and care that earned respect in churches and other community institutions. Sustaining traditional Arkansas practices not only steadied the blue-vested Walmart workers but also eased their transition to a sphere governed by sales performance standards and technological innovations. Coming from a high school in Huntsville that only had two classroom typewriters, Alice Martin was leery of computers. "I thought, 'There's no way I can learn a computer'—I was scared to death of it. They provided the equipment and the training to learn it, and I will always be thankful for that." Taking a job at Walmart revealed once more that Ozark residents welcomed the accoutrements of modernization if the personal ties, religious faith, and family hierarchy woven into rural life endured.

Far from wishing to chip away at long-standing customs, the Walmart leadership strove to transfer the tight-knit culture of small towns into loyalty to the company, deference to store managers, and mutual effort toward a collective goal. Female employees choosing the Walmart way shunned traditional tasks but labored under traditional inequities. Many fellow workers agreed with Ann Tuttle's sentiments: "I've always appreciated Walmart for the opportunity to grow and have a job that let you go as far in the company as you want to go." Yet while women, who made up two-thirds of the hourly workers, shaped the climate and operations of Walmart stores through daily initiatives and guidance, the title of manager eluded them.

During the company's expansion era, the differential treatment of men and women was not viewed as exceptional in the locales that welcomed the new Walmarts, and few workers protested. In return for an easier route to management, men were expected to listen and embrace "service leadership," a managerial approach that emphasized mutual obligation. The concept blended easily into an evangelical religious culture. Walton preferred to recruit executives from small religious colleges, including the University of the Ozarks in Clarksville and John Brown University in Siloam Springs, out of a conviction that these graduates would devote their hearts and energy to the company more fully than those from elite schools.

Sam Walton originally confined his store placements to small towns to avoid direct competition with the national retailers. He staked his company's growth on the bet that these overlooked consumers would choose the better bargain and greater selection over loyalty to hometown merchants. Downtown retailers offering items available at a Walmart on the edge of the community suffered from the chain's loss-leader inducements and volume pricing. On the other hand, restaurants, specialty shops, and other service establishments rose by catering to the out-of-town Walmart patrons. Walton insisted his stores kept out-of-the way towns viable by stocking an array of products that saved residents a trip to the nearest urban center.

As Walmart molded its workers into a self-contained community devoted to the well-being of the company, the stores themselves remained separate and apart from the actual communities. The standard format and goods offered few concessions to local taste. The long hours demanded of store managers left them little time for civic involvement, and the company limited donations to those local organizations endorsed by store employees. The company reinforced its claim that a store's success rested on the contributions of everyone by calling hourly workers "associates." Employee testimonials in the company newsletter disclosed that many saw themselves as working, not for a corporation, but for "Mr. Sam." Piloting his own plane to stores throughout his growing empire, Walton led the associates in the Walmart cheer that in Arkansas vied in volume and ubiquity with the "Woo Pig Sooie" chant for the university Razorback teams.

Walton in this autobiography insisted that his cardinal rule for running a company was to "break all the rules." Millennial-era digital tycoons would come to define innovation as synonymous with disruption, a repudiation of experience and tradition. In contrast, the folksy, unaffected Walton celebrated rural and village conventions even as he reshaped the retail landscape of the nation's heartland. Walton stood as the prominent model of how one gained purpose through service to Walmart and its employees. His careful attention to the company's bottom line was touted as reflecting the thrift of a billionaire who drove a pick-up truck around Bentonville. Of course, not a small part of the down-home persona was performance; Walton did live in a spacious home designed by the noted architect E. Fay Jones. In addition, Walton's ingrained conservatism led him at times to deviate from his own prescribed path to success: "Swim upstream. Go the other way. Ignore the conventional wisdom."

While its northwest Arkansas location conferred advantages, Walmart struggled in its early years to secure competitive service from national distributors and large trucking lines to its isolated operations. If not a visionary, Walton understood the nuts and bolts of merchandising, and his answer to this bottleneck was the turning point in his company's fortunes. In late 1969 the firm began supplying Walmart stores from its own 60,000-square-foot distribution center adjacent to the company's headquarters. This breakthrough in supply-chain management paved the way for future distribution centers that were hubs to newly constructed stores planted in shopping hinterlands throughout the nation. Hundreds of trucks loaded and unloaded goods each day in the newer 1.2-million-square-foot centers.

Walton, however, balked at moving into the next stage of supply management, due to his suspicion of computers as trendy and unnecessary overhead. The persistence of David Glass, Walton's eventual successor, and Jack Shewmaker, president of the company, bore fruit in the mid-1980s when the company adopted a technological advance already familiar to supermarket shoppers. After linking the Universal Product Code or bar-code readers at store registers to a state-of-the art satellite network, Walmart executives knew precisely which goods flew off the shelves or gathered dust. The company weaponized this data to wrestle rock-bottom prices from vendors, who in turn had to recover costs at the expense of Walmart's competitors. By 1991, a year before Walton's death, Walmart surged past Kmart and Sears to become the nation's largest retailer.

Walmart leaders also took notice that supermarkets were venturing beyond groceries to lure customers who welcomed the convenience of purchasing cosmetics, housewares, and medicines without having to make an additional stop at another store. Perhaps, even a Walmart store. In the late 1980s, the company began opening "Supercenters" that offered under one giant roof the products found in the traditional Walmart outlets as well as fully stocked grocery display cases. Even though home-owned grocery stores were already distant memories in small communities, Supercenters forced the next stage of retail consolidation when regional and national chain food stores were driven from towns. Few of these outlets could compete with the around-the-clock hours, cut-rate prices, and low wages of a nonunion workforce. By 2003 Walmart edged out Kroger as the nation's largest seller of groceries.

Organized labor had a precarious foothold in the Arkansas Ozarks, and the Walton business plan to curtail labor costs made no provision for allowing unions in stores or distribution centers outside the core region. The company single-mindedly used soft power—extolling the Walmart "family," extending stock options to associates—and hard-edged tactics—intimidation, threats to close operations, dismissals—in response to scattered unionization campaigns. The Walmart Supercenters' victories over supermarket chains also took a toll on the United Food and Commercial Workers Union. The UFCW was no more successful in winning certification elections in Walmart stores than it had been in attempting to organize poultry processing plants. Company executives shrugged off fines and adverse rulings by the National Labor Relations Board over its heavy-handed methods.

The UFCW and the service-workers union abandoned the futile organizing campaigns after 2000 and formed activist organizations that portrayed Walmart as razing the American dream through suppressing wages, relying on overseas factories, and limiting consumer choice when competitors folded. Critics of the corporation highlighted evidence that not only did Walmart benefit from favorable tax policies and direct subsidies but that a large proportion of its hourly workers qualified for food stamps, Medicaid, and other public assistance programs. The aim of these broadsides was to spark public pressure upon Walmart to change the way it had done business since its inception. The company's questionable employment practices moved from the court of public opinion to actual courts when a suit filed by six female employees in 2004 became the nation's largest class-action case. The 1.5 million women working at Walmart were added to the list of plaintiffs.

Attorneys representing the original plaintiffs in *Dukes v. Wal-Mart Stores* suggested the failure of women to gain promotions into management reflected a corporate culture that had not evolved from antiquated Southern mores. On the other hand, depositions by longtime employees argued they lost status and dignity when the company shed small-town intimacy in favor of corporate goals. One witness in *Dukes* acknowledged about the early years, "We always knew that the guys made more than we did"; but any resentment was mitigated by "the family atmosphere. . . . We attended weddings and funerals and baby showers." Discrimination began to rankle as the women found themselves taking orders from young men they had tutored. Another witness noted, "The way we felt about things was no longer considered."

By 2011 when the U.S. Supreme court ruled 5–4 that the case could not go forward as a class-action suit, Walmart began to post openings for managerial jobs rather than rely on word of mouth and standardized its qualifications for promotions rather than deferring to the preferences of store managers. The proportion of female managers rose notably after the filing of the *Dukes* suit although still well below the percentage of women working at Walmart (the "manager" title covered a wide range of positions at Walmart, some with limited responsibilities and compensation).

In 2015 Walmart, its policies under scrutiny in academic studies as well as on activists' websites, announced that within two years all of its workers would earn at least nearly three dollars above the hourly minimum wage. Although most employees saw little gain and Walmart did reduce its workforce over the course of the following year, the company's investors were displeased by the estimated billion-dollar cost tag that accompanied the raise. The unhappiness on Wall Street was not a sudden chill. Walmart's stock had barely nudged upwards since the beginning of the century, and analysts wondered if the company had become too large to turn around.

In 2008, as the nation's economy sank into recession, the business press viewed hard times as tonic for a retailer that had thrived when customers were desperate for bargains. Not this time. Walmart piled up successive unprofitable quarters as it lost business to deep-discount dollar-store chains. But even more formidable challenges emerged along the digital frontier. Sam Walton's revolutionary paradigm was upended by merchandisers with no shopping aisles, no parking lots, and no rows of cashiers.

At the 2017 Walmart shareholders' meeting in Bentonville, Doug McMillon, who had been CEO since 2014, described a "new Walmart" that would gain a greater share of its revenue from e-commerce. The announcement arose not from entrepreneurial inspiration but from necessity. Reflecting Sam Walton's confidence that low prices trumped other considerations for consumers, the company had not kept pace with brash online retailers such as Amazon.com that had gone from selling books in the mid-1990s to just about everything by the early 2000s. By 2011 Walmart had belatedly boosted its investment in digital technology and services, yet had risen only to fourth place by 2016 in online sales, a startling contrast to its dominance in brick-and-mortar operations. These old-economy outlets, however, absorbed much of the cost to position and equip the company to take on Amazon. Walmart's new acquisition strategy pinpointed specialty online retailers, while the corporation tested approaches to move products from warehouse to home rather than to a store.

Just as McMillon outlined to shareholders and employees the future of a company that broke from Mr. Sam's expense-slashing strictures, he also invoked a managerial credo that had been fundamental to the extraordinary rise of the company from its Ozark beginnings: "We will compete with technology but win with people.... We will win because we are purpose-driven, with clear and meaningful values and an effective and resilient culture." This was the longstanding reassurance that Walmart did not dislodge traditions and beliefs as it ushered its "family" and its customers into new eras that rocked livelihoods and institutions. The corporation's self-conscious veneration of rural conventions in a reordered society evolved from how Arkansans were making their peace with the modern era.

———————

DECLINES IN MANUFACTURING JOBS and increases in immigration by the early twenty-first century fanned distress in Arkansas and other rural states that "globalization" washed away opportunity. Tyson Foods and Walmart were not only outsized influences in the global system but also the largest private employers in the state. In Arkansas the firms counted on not only the deference of state government officials and the media but their identification as homegrown success stories to mute any popular backlash over the pitfalls of an international economy.

By the start of the new century Arkansas, in comparison to surrounding and Southern states (Texas excepted), boasted a disproportionate share of large corporations. In addition to Walmart and Tyson, these included Alltel, the wireless communications company in Little Rock; Acxiom, the data-mining firm in Conway; Beverly Enterprises, the nation's largest nursing-home chain in Fort Smith; Dillard's, the department store company originally founded in Nashville; J.B. Hunt Transport Services, the trucking firm in Lowell; and Murphy Oil in El Dorado.

A 1998 study in the *Arkansas Business and Economic Review* drew the obvious conclusion that the growth of firms with immense assets and sales did not stem from the state's "resource base and general composition of its economy." Chickens had long been raised in other states, and Sam Walton could have started out in an isolated upland section of his native Oklahoma. That Arkansas was not uniquely suited to breed corporate success was implicitly acknowledged by political and business leaders who continually sought ways through policy and incentives to make the state appealing to investors from elsewhere. Most Arkansans simply savored the fact that corporate empires straddling the globe were rooted in a place still dependent upon agriculture and still not taken seriously.

As with Don Tyson and Sam Walton, the other major Arkansas companies were known by those in charge. The legacy of these figures survived, not simply in the endurance of their enterprises (which in some cases were acquired and renamed) but as the human faces of a new economy. To shake hands with Walton in one of his stores or see Tyson wearing the khaki company uniform was to shrink globalization to the intimate, the local, the recognizable.

Arkansans viewing the corporate founding fathers as neighbors linked their success to the state's self-image of overcoming the odds through native pluck and vernacular versatility. In 2017 a former speaker of the state House of representatives cited famous entrepreneurs as proof that the state's citizens were well-equipped to meet modern challenges: "Arkansans are innovative people. From farmers who engineer their own equipment when there are no other options to entrepreneurs like J. B. Hunt and Sam Walton who used groundbreaking concepts to build Fortune 500 companies, our state is embedded with a history of innovation." Still, such boosterism offered little to those Arkansans who were falling behind by persevering in ebbing industries and communities that remained afloat on government favor and aid.

II. Uneven Progress:
A Rural Economy in a Global System

Tyson and Walmart sparked a boom in the northwest corner that did not carry far into the rest of the state. The urban counties along the western border atop the Springfield Plateau (Benton and Washington) and rural counties to the east (Carroll and Boone) boasted assets that suited the needs of ambitious capitalists. The area was not tied to a narrow range of crops but still offered a surplus of inexpensive labor readily available for new plants and stores. The proximity to major Midwestern markets and shipping terminals trimmed transportation costs and promoted the development of trucking as an auxiliary business to the processing of local resources.

Public funds compounded private investment. Residents and those attending Razorback sports events had long agitated for an alternative to bypass the meandering and treacherous routes serving the chain of cities on the plateau (Fayetteville, Springdale, Rogers, and Bentonville). Completed in 1999 at a cost of nearly $500 million, Interstate 540 (later I-49) took travelers driving between Alma and Bella Vista through the only highway tunnel in the state.

In 1998 President Bill Clinton dedicated the Northwest Arkansas Regional Airport that offered the region's first nonstop flights to major American cities. After the Federal Aviation Administration (FAA) in 1994 had approved the project, critics of Clinton, spurred by an ABC News investigation, detected undue influence behind the FAA's decision to commit sizeable grants that represented the preponderance of the total cost to construct the airport. Financing was delayed until the Government Accounting Office (GAO) completed an investigation demanded by Senator John McCain, the Republican lion from Arizona. The GAO concluded the FAA did not veer from federal regulations but questioned the agency's scoring of the applications that found the airport to be eligible for funding.

Even before the advent of the Clinton presidency, the region's corporate heavyweights had drawn the attention of Washington policymakers toward the area's transportation aspirations. In 1990 Sam Walton transfixed visiting members of the U.S. House Public Works and Transportation Committee at a lavish barbeque at Don Tyson's home on Beaver Lake by noting that he had paid large sums in federal taxes and believed it was time for the national government to do its part to help his home section, which was now bursting at the seams. The U.S. secretary of transportation dropped by northwest Arkansas three weeks later to assess the need for a new airport.

The region's major figures institutionalized their influence and resources by forming the Northwest Arkansas Council that same year and recruiting two community development professionals to set it in motion. Carol and Uvalde Lindsey scoured grant sources and navigated federal bureaucratic byways but the Council's architects did not remain behind the scenes. Alice Walton, the daughter of the Walmart founder, became the first chair of the council, and her advocacy for the project was acknowledged in President Clinton's dedication remarks: "Alice Walton wore me out."

The push for the airport also sparked a debate within the region over whether distinct communities were dissolving into an upland hub of international corporate headquarters and auxiliary enterprises. Nevertheless, the steady rise in incomes and abundant job opportunities rendered quixotic any movement to reset the economy. The Northwest Arkansas Council continued to be a private nonprofit organization that generated initiatives to tackle infrastructure shortcomings. The Council's directors understood the perils of bypassing government entities and openly submitted their plans and funding proposals to region-wide boards of public officials.

Local leaders historically had welcomed federal lake construction as key to capturing tourists and luring retirement communities. The influx of residents to the region obliged developers and officeholders alike to recognize scenic lakes also as reservoirs. The 1950s population wave into Northwest Arkansas strained the supply of drinking and industrial water, provoking major business owners in 1959 to take advantage of recently approved Arkansas Act 114 to set up the first water district in the state. In the previous year the Arkansas congressional delegation had flexed its muscle to permit the Corps of Engineers to include municipal water supply as an authorized purpose when it built dams. After the Beaver Water District reached an agreement in 1960 with the Corps for favorable cost sharing on water storage rights, the federal agency began construction on the Beaver Lake Dam, completing the project in 1966. The District pioneered formation of a regional framework to coordinate and apportion infrastructure costs to insure water flowed to Bentonville, Fayetteville, Rogers and Springdale.

During the years the Northwest Arkansas Council grappled with funding for the regional airport, it won government grants to move forward the construction of a large-scale distribution system that supplied water to outlying rural areas overwhelmed by exploding real estate developments. Established in 1992, the regional water authority, referred to locally as "Two-Ton" after the last syllable in the names of Washington and Benton counties, began delivering water to customers in 1999. Federal assistance on a grand scale gave Northwest Arkansas the means to escape the water shortages that beset other areas of the state.

The cities up and down the northwest metropolitan corridor had distinct economic bases (Fayetteville, the University of Arkansas; Springdale, Tyson Foods; Rogers-Lowell, J. B. Hunt; Bentonville, Walmart). Cooperation made greater sense than competition. A rising tax base, a durable middle-class core, corporate leaders interested in promoting an urban quality of life for their employees, and a well-placed confidence in future growth encouraged regional solutions for common problems. The predominately white demographics allowed community leaders to sidestep taking stands on issues of equity and power-sharing required in other Arkansas cities with larger African American populations.

Other sections in the state lacked this confluence of traits and similar region-wide development associations struggled to match the effectiveness of the Northwest Arkansas Council. By 2015 the Fayetteville-Springdale-Rogers-Bentonville urban chain was the only metropolitan statistical area in the state to have reached and exceeded the national per capita income average.

THE CHRONIC POVERTY dogging interior Ozark counties triggered arguments over whether the retail and poultry-processing revolutions conveyed widespread benefits or rewarded the haves without relieving the have-nots. Newton, Searcy, and Stone Counties headed into the twenty-first century without an urban center and with a significant share of jobs relying on the marketing of mountain culture and the natural environment. The 2000 census found sixteen Arkansas counties still completely rural. The Buffalo National River ran through Newton and Searcy, while Stone County promoted itself as a sanctuary for folk music and crafts. Landowners raised chickens but no poultry-processing operation appeared in any of the three counties. By 2010 manufacturing played a small role in Newton County, and only Searcy County among the three kept a small contingent of apparel workers busy. Wood-products plants, the perennial rural industry, were responsible for the majority of manufacturing payrolls in these counties. Although generally keeping pace between 1980 and 2010 with the rate of income growth statewide, these three Ozark counties fell among the bottom ten in per capita income levels.

Earnings for manufacturing workers in Arkansas and the nation overall exceeded what those employed in the service and other nonprofessional sectors made. Factory pay, however, in Newton, Searcy, and Stone counties between 1990 and 2010 was not significantly higher than the overall local wage level. The counties were not insulated from the inexorable closure of plants after 2000 but those able to find work stocking store shelves or catering to visitors generally did not experience a notable wage decline. Public school jobs, as in most rural places, furnished the best income.

Over the course of the twentieth century, manufacturing had curbed deprivation in Ozark communities. Nevertheless, by 2000 the low wages for both plant jobs and tourism-related occupations weighed down the prospects for locals who chose to stay. The civic leadership in the three counties emphasized unspoiled scenery for tourists rather than resources of interest to business investors. In contrast to chambers of commerce websites for most Arkansas localities, visitors to the sites for these counties in 2017 spied few references to existing industry or appeals for plant relocations. The slogans on the front web pages confirmed that the economic development plan was to keep economic development at bay: Newton County was "Nature's Paradise"; Searcy County was "Your Authentic Ozark Family Playground"; and Mountain View in Stone County was "Your Place in the Mountains."

However deep the commitment to pristine Ozark environs, most of those living in the three counties would have welcomed the natural-gas drilling rigs and wells producing sizable royalty checks for landowners sitting atop the Fayetteville Shale. The primary exploration activity was nearby but a bit to the south, extending from the southeastern edge of Pope County to southwestern Independence County. As is often the case with natural resource booms, this shale play brought sudden wealth to the core region without leaving behind an auxiliary industry to employ drilling-rig workers after the predictable bust.

George P. Mitchell and the engineers with his Texas energy company developed an unconventional horizontal drilling technology that used hydraulic pressure or "fracking" to extract natural gas from a sedimentary formation. The company's success in the Barnett Shale in north Texas spurred explorations in promising formations throughout Texas and the surrounding region.

Southwestern Energy Company began quietly purchasing leases in Arkansas before revealing in 2004 that a discovery well confirmed an ample reserve. Landmen, or leasing agents, crowded into county courthouses to unearth title deed owners while the state Oil and Gas Commission issued hundreds of drilling permits annually.

A 2012 University of Arkansas study calculated that the Fayetteville Shale led to $18.5 billion in economic activity. This estimate included over $1 billion in royalties, roughneck jobs that paid $100,000, and upsurges in local tax revenues reaching $2 billion. One small Van Buren County school district was able to not only catch up on basic maintenance but to purchase computers for students and hire specialists in developmental education. At peak production in 2008, around two thousand wells made Arkansas the eighth highest natural-gas producer in the nation. The windfall persisted long enough to shield the shale counties from the worst effects of the Great Recession before oversupply drove down prices from around $10 per million Btu (British thermal units) to $2 by 2012.

Not unexpectedly, the state's regulatory system was overwhelmed by both the unprecedented activity and the unfamiliar technology. Insufficient numbers of inspectors generated incomplete reports based on infrequent inspections. The agencies overseeing the industry soon rewrote rules that governed a range of drilling actions, including the wells that injected waste water from fracking into impermeable subterranean layers of rock. Geologists pointed to this technique as responsible for a host of small earthquake eruptions centered in Faulkner County. Arkansas stood apart from the other industry-friendly shale-producing states when the Oil and Gas Commission shut down those wells in the county.

With prices plunging, energy companies concentrated on more productive formations outside Arkansas. Few anticipated even a modest revival of exploration in the near future after the last Fayetteville Shale well was drilled in December 2015. One farmer who acknowledged that royalty payments made his family wealthy for a time mused in 2016 on the rise and fall of his fortunes: "I may have wasted my money on frivolous things like vacations, but it's been good for me."

The shale gas boom in the state's north central region likely delayed these counties from suffering the population loss that had been the rule in the rest of rural Arkansas. By 2012 the state's cities regained employment levels that had dipped during the Great Recession, but the rural sections continued to reel from the aftershocks of the downturn.

FOR DECADES, manufacturing operations had employed a large share of the rural labor force. Not only the outflow of plant jobs but the winnowing of agricultural and forestry occupations lashed these workers. Poverty rates in the metro areas were higher than the national average (with the exception of the northwest Arkansas urban show horses), but the even greater destitution throughout rural provinces lodged Arkansas among the five poorest states in the nation.

In 2006 Sanyo Manufacturing, a Japanese consumer electronics firm, announced the end of production at its television production plant in Forrest City that had employed 500 at the beginning of that year. Sanyo bought the factory in 1979 and initially established good relations with the union representing the 2,000 line workers, 60 percent of whom were African American. Tensions mounted by the mid-1980s as television sets flooded the market. In 1985 the company's request for wage reductions provoked a bitter strike that led management at the Osaka headquarters to consider leaving Arkansas. In 1988 Governor Bill Clinton may have saved the operation from fully shutting down when he prevailed upon Walmart to purchase sets from the factory after Sears cut back on orders.

Nevertheless, by that year, employment at the Forrest City plant had fallen to 650, of whom only 190 were hourly wage workers. Sanyo had been steadily transferring production to factories in Tijuana, Mexico. The border factories or "maquiladoras" benefited from favorable tariff treatment when components assembled by local workers, earning a fraction of American pay, were made in the United States. In 2006 the company decided not to reconfigure the Arkansas assembly lines to turn out new flat-screen televisions following an impasse over additional salary cuts.

While touring Arkansas in 2013, Paul Theroux, a noted writer of travel books and novels, spoke to two women in Forrest City who earned a pittance at part-time stints in the discount motel where he stayed. One had worked at the Sanyo factory before the layoffs took hold, and the other lost jobs following the closure of a shirt factory and then a labor force reduction in her furniture plant. She explained that a promised pension from the latter employer was pending: "Under arbitration, they say. So here I am. I work here, if you want to call it work. That's about it." Having witnessed firsthand deep poverty in agrarian regions throughout the world, Theroux was surprised to find comparable conditions in secluded corners of the Ozarks and Delta. His descriptions of the rural poor echoed the disquieting astonishment of travelers reaching the state in the

1930s: "Living in buried hinterland, in fractured communities and dying towns and on the sidelines, they exist in obscurity."

The University of Arkansas Cooperative Extension Service through its ongoing research identified the places where poverty endured season after season. Each of the 1990, 2000, and 2010 census counts revealed that over 20 percent of all residents in the same seventeen counties lived below the poverty line. Throughout that thirty-year period, over 20 percent of children in the same thirty-nine counties dwelled in poor households. Nearly all of these "persistent poverty" counties were largely rural and located in the tarnished jewel of the traditional economy, the Delta.

Appalachia introduced American political leaders and the public at large to rural poverty. In 1964 President Lyndon Johnson, on the porch of a shanty in eastern Kentucky, committed the nation to a war on poverty. The Mississippi Delta, however, was also a familiar landscape of scarcity and want, first captured through the lens of New Deal photographers. In 1990 the Lower Mississippi Delta Development Commission, created through a bill sponsored by Senator Dale Bumpers and chaired by Governor Bill Clinton, reported that federal grants for infrastructure, healthcare, and economic development were potential seed money to revive distressed communities up and down the Big River from southern Illinois to Louisiana. In 2000 as Clinton prepared to leave the White House, Congress acted upon the report and approved legislation drafted by Senator Blanche Lincoln of Arkansas to establish the Delta Regional Authority.

Modeled after the Appalachian Regional Commission, the measure provided only a fraction of the money proposed by Clinton to counter the weight of unemployment and a diminished tax base. Ten years later the congressman representing east Arkansas suggested that the federal government would need to allocate $300–500 million to the authority if Delta residents were "going to see any magic." By that time, the organization, obligated to serve 252 counties, had distributed a total of $75 million over the course of the decade for water, sewer, and road projects. The annual budget of the Appalachian Regional Commission was several times greater than that of its Delta counterpart. No New Deal arrived in the new century for a ruined land swept by economic devastation comparable to the Great Depression.

Through mechanization and use of chemicals, landowners raised row crops on expanding farms with little need for labor. The 33,000 Arkansas farmworkers in 2012 composed 70 percent of the total employed in 1997 and nearly 60 percent labored no more than 150 days annually. Rural manufacturing until the late twentieth century had been for Delta residents a promising successor to the labor-intensive plantation. While the massive exodus of labor after World

War II had prodded landowners to turn to machines, boarded-up factories fed continued depopulation, if at a more measured rate.

The Delta lacked not only jobs but also workers. In 2015 for every 100 Arkansans of working age, 66 of those living in the state were either too young or too old to be counted in the federal census tables as part of the labor force. Nationally, 61 out 100 Americans were younger than eighteen or older than sixty-four and not considered by demographers to be of working age. Retirees had boosted the percentage of those past working age in the north central counties, but their pensions, savings, and Social Security payments actually alleviated the poverty rates in this region. The "dependency ratio" of youth and older adults to the general population was conspicuous in east Arkansas, the location of the four counties with the greatest proportion of impoverished. This ratio in Chicot, Desha, Monroe, and Phillips Counties ranged from 73 to 77 per 100 residents. The income for the young and elderly rarely came from wages they earned.

As direct federal assistance payments to the poor declined throughout the nation, payments in Arkansas fell off at an even faster rate. Aid to Families of Dependent Children (AFDC), a provision in the 1935 Social Security Act, reached fewer Arkansas recipients during the 1980s and remittance amounts trailed inflation rates. Monthly Social Security checks to retirees, indexed to the cost of living, became the dominant income support system in the state.

The 1996 Personal Responsibility and Work Opportunity Reconciliation Act replaced AFDC with a program that gave states the leeway to spend federal grants on programs they identified as anti-poverty and the authority to limit how long households could collect benefits. No state adopted a briefer eligibility period for lifetime cash assistance than Arkansas, and few spent a smaller proportion of the block grant funds to help families with cash for basic needs, job preparation, and childcare. State officials continued the modern tradition in Arkansas of distributing federal moneys to meet priorities they, not Washington, authorized.

In 2015 Arkansas devoted 19 percent of its combined state and federal welfare program funds to core family assistance as defined by federal guidelines; only two states allotted a lower proportion. From the mid-1990s the national government failed to boost welfare block grants to keep pace with inflation or counteract economic downturns. Accordingly, Arkansas officials methodically curtailed direct cash assistance to impoverished families rather than redirect a share of government welfare dollars from non-welfare activities. In 1995 federal welfare payments were awarded to 40 out of every 100 poor Arkansas families, but in 2015 only 5 out of 100 families gained cash support—and what they got was bare-bones. The $204 monthly benefit to a family of three with one parent in the household left Arkansas in the company of the ten states that sent the smallest checks to the very poorest.

The backers of the 1996 act, including President Bill Clinton who proclaimed the measure would "end welfare as we know it," insisted it was a critical reform to move recipients off the dole and into the workforce. Arkansas structured the program to shrink welfare rolls even as poverty rates climbed. No longer eligible for cash assistance, poor households relied upon other forms of government aid, especially the nutritional assistance program that provided families a debit card to purchase food at grocery stores. These cards were commonly presented at checkout counters in east Arkansas counties where over half of the children were eligible for the food benefits.

Nutritional assistance, however, did not banish nutritional deficiencies. In 2014 Arkansas was among five states where the greatest percentage of children experienced "food insecurity," characterized by the federal agricultural department as ranging from a limited and low-quality diet to repeated incidences of "disrupted eating patterns and reduced food intake." Thirty percent or more of children in a third of the state's counties, primarily in the Delta, lived in food-insecure households.

———————————

GOVERNMENT SUBSIDIES kept Delta farms—primarily the largest ones—above water. The post–World War II decline in the number of Arkansas farms continued into the new millennium with 12 percent fewer in 2017 than twenty-five years earlier. During that period, the number of farming operations covering at least 2,000 acres rose by 70 percent while the total of those under 500 acres ebbed.

Beginning in 1994, the Environmental Working Group extracted from federal agricultural records the destination of federal aid dollars. From 1995 to 2016, about 60 percent of the $12.4 billion in total payments (including commodity programs, crop insurance subsidies, disaster programs, and conservation programs) went to 5 percent of the Arkansas operations obtaining subsidies. Three-quarters of the state's farms garnered no assistance. Payments peaked between 1999 and 2003 during that time period, with the bulk of commodity payments headed toward those who raised rice, cotton, and soybeans. The subsidies for rice operations were nearly three times the amount allotted for cotton farmers, who gained almost twice the payments sent to soybean growers. In Arkansas, as throughout rural America, most surviving farms were small and depended upon income earned by family members off the farm rather than checks transferred from a county USDA office.

National news stories reporting on the annual updates to the Environmental Working Group databases noted that Riceland Foods Inc. of Stuttgart was the top recipient in the United States of federal agricultural payments. Riceland, which began in 1921 as a farmers' marketing cooperative, was indeed an immense operation. By the twenty-first century, the company milled and marketed more rice than any other operation in the world. Grocery shoppers as well as food manufacturers ranging from breweries to breakfast-cereal makers purchased Riceland's processed product. The six thousand farmer members, some of whom grew soybeans and wheat, elected the twenty-four board of directors of the cooperative from their own ranks.

In 2007 the Environmental Working Group plowed deeper into USDA data to track federal payouts to the cooperative's individual farmers rather than attribute the lump sum of total benefits to Riceland Inc. Thus, researchers scanning the database noted that whereas Riceland during the peak era of crop subsidies in the early twentieth century was annually credited with over $100 million in payments, the company from 2007 onwards was shown as receiving no funds.

African American farmers throughout the decades had been ensnared between hostile local bankers and dismissive federal lending officials. A farmer in Monroe County explained his predicament to Paul Theroux: "If you're in a bind, in serious default, white farmers want to buy your land. They're just waiting for you to fail. They're on one side, bankers on the other. My bankers are all right, but I have to explain a lot to them to get them to understand my situation. There are no black loan officers. It's not talked about, it's not written about. There's none."

In 1999 the U.S. Department of Agriculture agreed to settle a lawsuit filed by the National Black Farmers Association and to pay millions in claims to thousands of farmers who had been denied loans, disaster compensation, and technical assistance. Yet a 2008 report by the Government Accountability Office revealed the USDA had mishandled the settlement cases. A large number of farmers who were not permitted to participate in the original litigation filed a second suit. In 2011 a federal judge approved a new settlement of $1.25 billion that brought to a belated close the drawn-out case.

For many it was too late. Between 1982 and 1992 the number of African American farm owners in Arkansas fell by nearly 40 percent. A resurgence of black farmers between 1997 and 2007 followed the initial settlement and the reinstatement of a civil rights division at USDA. The 2012 census registered a slight decline, and the uncertain prospects for younger operators kept the mean age of African American farmers above that of their white counterparts. Many African American farmers who stayed the course were saddled with debts and aging equipment. During the years when he could not secure a federal loan, James Stephenson of Chicot County had little choice but to farm "out-of-pocket," renting acreage for his rice crop and combing scrap metal yards to keep his tractors in working order. He estimated for a reporter in 1999 that fifteen years of rejected applications for federal loans cost him $4 million in lost income, repossession of equipment, and debt payments on commercial loans.

Delta counties prevailed among the state's twenty where agricultural enterprises claimed the greatest subsidy totals. Farms in the four counties marked by chronic and pervasive poverty—Chicot, Desha, Monroe, and Phillips—received over $1.6 billion in the twenty-one-year period surveyed by the Environmental Working Group. In 2014 the state's human services agency issued $23 million in food assistance benefits to families in these counties.

Although commodity subsidies in east Arkansas usually outstripped the amounts available to help families in those counties to buy food, the supplemental nutritional assistance outlays dominated successive federal farm acts. Partisan quarreling over the level of funding for nutritional support delayed approval of the 2014 Farm Bill until the Republican congressional majority conceded to smaller decreases than originally proposed for the program. Deviating from earlier farm bills, this measure replaced the long-standing direct payments to row crop farms with programs intended to mitigate income loss resulting from lower yields and sharp market downturns. Under the old system, the government had sometimes sent checks to farms where no crops were grown.

Supporters of the 2014 bill anticipated that subsidy expenses would decline, but falling crop prices following its passage actually fueled higher farm commodity and disaster program remittances. In 2016 the total of agricultural payments was twice as high as the amount reaching Arkansas farmers two years earlier. A drop in the market price for the state's leading commodity accounted for the boost. A university economist observed, "If you grew long-grain rice in Arkansas, you likely got a check."

Although Arkansas had long been among the leading rice-growing states, a little-noticed shift in agricultural policy in the final quarter of the twentieth century elevated the state to the leading national producer of the grain and set in motion the most extensive reshaping of Arkansas's agricultural economy since the mechanization of cotton production.

IN 1973 THE U.S. agricultural secretary anxiously eyed declining rice stocks and lifted allotment restrictions that had only allowed those already raising the crop to cultivate additional acres. Numerous Arkansas farmers planted rice for the first time, doubling within two years the total acreage in the state devoted to the crop. A university extension agent recalled that "people were on a waiting list to get a tractor." Yet by 1976 soaring national rice production reached the level slated to trigger the reimposition of the allotments.

Lawrence County farmers rallied against a retrenchment of rice production and beat a path to Washington. They found a sympathetic listener in Richard Bell, an assistant agricultural secretary and free-market advocate who later became president of Riceland Foods and then the first director of the Arkansas Department of Agriculture. Senator John McClellan, who had previously attempted to pass a bill to lift the restrictions, and senator Dale Bumpers were on board although long-established rice farmers in Arkansas who had benefited from a statutory lid on supply were skeptical. The proposed reform evaded death at many junctures before emerging as the Rice Production Act of 1975. Price protections for existing allotment holders survived until 1981 when Congress eliminated allotments completely.

With some hyperbole that contained more than a grain of truth, U.S. representative Bill Alexander lauded the legislation that expanded rice planting in Arkansas beyond the Grand Prairie region: "[The 1975 bill] created more wealth in Arkansas than any other single event in the history of the state, including the introduction of cottonseed back over a hundred years ago." Planted acreage rose from 442,000 in 1972 to a high point of 1,791,000 in 2010. In line with Alexander's assertion, the value of rice production at $1.3 billion in 2010 was six times higher than in 1972.

In Arkansas most of the acres planted in corn, cotton, and soybeans were irrigated; in the case of rice, all of the acres were under irrigation. The shift of cotton farming in the 1940s to western states demonstrated that agricultural production could flourish in an arid region where cataclysmic weather was rare but irrigation a necessity. Rain in the Delta by contrast was abundant but unpredictable and often excessive. Millennial floods did not inflict the epic pre–World War II era havoc but high-water events in 2008 and 2017 exposed vulnerabilities arising from unregulated levee districts and private levees erected by farmers to channel torrents away from their fields. In 2011 a massive flood tested even the infrastructure designed and constructed by the Corps of Engineers over decades.

While drought in 2011 baked southwest Arkansas, late spring rains and record snowmelt swelled the Mississippi River to levels unseen since 1937. Monitoring the historic flood crests upriver, the Corps shielded New Orleans and Baton Rouge by opening two spillways, one of which forced the evacuation of over 3,000 residents in the Atchafalaya basin. A late April swarm of hundreds of tornadoes caused most of the Arkansas weather-related deaths that spring.

The Corps maintained an around-the-clock watch on sand boils and seepage in east Arkansas levees. In May the local county judge convened a public meeting in Arkansas City to dampen alarm. He recalled the apprehensions of his Desha County constituents: "You can see panic in their eyes. When you hear those rumors—and some of them heard the stories of the '27 flood—they are concerned, should be concerned. But not panicked."

The levees generally held throughout the Delta, and town residents dismantled banks of sandbags by summer. The president authorized disaster aid for twenty-six Arkansas counties that coped with flooded highways, evacuations from outlying communities, and washed-out farm acreage. Despite the record high waters, the Corps concluded that its system could have withstood an even greater assault from Old Man River.

From the late 1990s through the second decade of the new century, drought seared the western United States. Competition for the surface water stored in massive federal reservoirs intensified between urban centers and agricultural regions as well as among states that were parties to historic river compacts. The conflicts revived a vintage aphorism into a contemporary cliché: "Whiskey is for drinking and water is for fighting." Farm owners in the scorched West feverishly drilled wells to tap the groundwater lodged in aquifers. Based on 2010 findings, the U.S. Geological Survey (USGS) reported that California led the nation in groundwater extraction; Arkansas was second, and Texas ranked third. While Arkansas fell short of its 50-to-60-inch average rainfall during occasional dry years, rampant depletion of aquifers rather than drought precipitated water shortages in Arkansas. Receding groundwater levels was a not unforeseen consequence of the federal decision to give landowners the freedom to farm rice.

In 1931 the USGS identified a broad cone of depression or trough in the Grand Prairie section of the Alluvial Aquifer, a formation under south and east Arkansas and parts of neighboring states. It was not long before the falling water tables drove some farmers to stomach expensive drilling costs to tap into the deeper Sparta Sands Aquifer. In contrast to the shallow Alluvial, which could be replenished in wet years, the Sparta was only marginally recharged by annual precipitation and vulnerable to permanent damage if overused.

Nevertheless, the drawdowns accelerated as cultivation exploded throughout the Grand Prairie and northeast Cache River Basin rice belts. In the five years after the passage of the 1975 Rice Production Act, groundwater usage rose 56 percent, with irrigation accounting for nearly 90 percent of the withdrawals.

In 1998 the Arkansas Natural Resources Commission (ANRC) identified the Grand Prairie and in 2009 the Cache Basin as official Critical Groundwater Areas, a designation that did not impose penalties or regulations but gently encouraged the areas to protect "groundwater through conservation and use of excess surface water." The ANRC had previously classified industrial south central Arkansas as a critical area where overuse imperiled the Sparta Aquifer. Union County, home to many of the plants, levied a conservation fee on water users and secured government grants and private support to divert Ouachita River water for use by those industries that had been tapping into the Sparta. By 2005 monitoring wells charted the reversal of groundwater declines and confirmed the county to be the first site in the nation to achieve rising groundwater levels in an endangered aquifer.

As far back as the U.S. 1950 Flood Control Act, agricultural policy makers and conservation officials had been urging a similar diversion from large rivers to the fields in the two Arkansas core rice regions. For their part, farmers and state officials were reluctant to assume the expense of constructing the necessary pump stations, canals, and pipeline grid without drawing on federal coffers. In 1992 the U.S. Army Corps of Engineers revised its criteria to add water conservation to the list of justifications required to fund a project. A Corps official examining the condition of the east Arkansas aquifers noted his agency was breaking new ground: "It's really the first major irrigation project in the eastern side of the country. The needs of the project are so great, and the projected loss of the aquifers is going to be so great that something has to be done."

In 1999 the state authorized the establishment of the Grand Prairie Irrigation District to bring water from the Arkansas River to rice fields. The district was to entice federal support by raising a portion of the project's cost through assessments on landowners. Farmers throughout the area fell into conflict over the proposal. Those opposed to the levies and possible regulations forged an unlikely alliance with environmental organizations. One landowner leading the resistance to the diversion enterprise also excoriated the classification of the Grand Prairie counties as a critical groundwater area: "The designation is the first step by [state officials] to regulate water in this state. That means they can tax you into submission." As dissident farmers insisted that their individual conservation techniques would resolve the water crisis, the environmentalists strained the alliance by suggesting the key was to curtail rice acreage.

"The question I have is whether we have to find an alternative water source for farmers. Whether we should make more water available to farmers," observed a representative of the Wildlife Management Institute.

What became the Grand Prairie Demonstration Project survived but faced another delay in 2006, when a federal judge suspended construction after the reported sighting of an ivory-billed woodpecker called into question the undertaking's impact on the bird's habitat. By the time work resumed on the project two years later the Corps and the state had drawn up plans to add another surface water diversion project to relieve the overstrained aquifers. The Bayou Meto Water Management Project first received funds in 2010 to pump an allocated portion of the Arkansas River to nearly 270,000 acres in sections of the Grand Prairie. With organized opposition subsiding, Arkansas reached an agreement with the Corps to come up with 35 percent of the nearly $1 billion dollar cost of both projects. A portion of the state's share was based upon Grand Prairie landowners purchasing the river water delivered through the system of canals and pipes.

Federal appropriations and grants secured by grower associations trickled toward both projects, but the completion dates remained uncertain as the close of the century's second decade approached. The Grand Prairie and Bayou Meto diversion programs, however, were designed to save only 15 percent of the groundwater expended for irrigation; in fact, Delta rivers and lakes did not contain enough excess or unallocated water to fill the gap between rising crop-production demands and available groundwater. The ANRC often noted in its literature that "Arkansas is a water-rich state." Nevertheless, that agency's flow of reports and studies demonstrated that without vast public, particularly federal, outlays for infrastructure or an extraordinary reversal of decades of agricultural practices Arkansas faced a water-insolvent future.

GROWING AND PROCESSING resources remained central to the Arkansas economy and set it apart from those of other states. The Arkansas Agricultural Experiment Station noted that while production, processing, and selling of agricultural products were a shrinking portion of Arkansas's gross domestic product after 2000, this sector continued to represent a much higher share of the state GDP than was the case regionally or nationally. The state braved the high winds of the Great Recession thanks in part to the sturdy performance of the agricultural economy during those years.

In the first fifteen years of the twenty-fist century, over 40 percent of the manufacturing GDP in the state depended upon processing raw materials, even as employee numbers in those low-wage factories declined. Job loss followed the shifting of plants to other nations, particularly for apparel operations—2015 employment was about 11 percent of 1997 levels–as well as the mechanization of resource production stages. Poultry processing employment remained stable: 95 percent of the workforce that did the job in 1997 were employed in 2015. In contrast, other resource industries endured downturns: wood products (63 percent of 1997 levels), paper manufacturing (71 percent), and furniture manufacturing (32 percent). With the exception of apparel and furniture factories, annual payrolls rose in the other industries despite fewer workers. Nevertheless, the overall personal income in the state grew more slowly after 2000 than during decades of job growth in the last half of the twentieth century.

State leaders at the turn of the twentieth century had abided by the New South gospel that Arkansas could modernize through industrialization without corroding the agricultural foundations of its society and economy. State leaders at the turn of the twenty-first century retained faith in the Sunbelt formula. They fervently sought to attract technologically based enterprises requiring highly educated employees to a state more rural and more tied to planting and harvesting than nearly any other.

And what of Arkansas Power and Light, the parent of modern economic development? Jerry Maulden, who became president in 1979, followed the path of Couch and Moses, delivering around a hundred speeches a year, exhorting civic club gatherings to prepare their communities for an economic revival: "Arkansas has all this unrealized potential, and it's just around the corner." But a 1984 ruling by an administrative judge for the Federal Energy Regulatory Commission (FERC) to force Arkansas customers to pay for a Mississippi nuclear power plant turned the state's largest electrical utility into a pariah.

Middle South Utilities (MSU), AP&L's parent holding company, had constructed the Grand Gulf plant near Vicksburg to generate energy for its other utilities in Mississippi and Louisiana. Cost overruns propelled these Middle South subsidiaries to renege on an earlier agreement and demand that AP&L be assigned part of the construction bill even though it would not use the generated power. In 1985 FERC agreed to assign AP&L a greater share of the expenses than it did the other MSU utilities. Arkansas lawmakers that year introduced bills in the General Assembly enabling the state to take over the company.

These proposals failed to pass, and the company regained enough political influence within a decade to repel an existential threat to its financial structure. By the mid-1990s, major industries within Arkansas grew confident they could lower their power costs by haggling with a variety of providers. Manufacturers banded into associations, such as the Alliance for Lower Electric Rates Today, to guide the deregulation of electrical utilities through the legislature.

Fearful that it could not recover its substantial capital investment in generating plants in a competitive market, Entergy Arkansas (the rechristened AP&L brand) arrayed its forces under Cecil Alexander, a lobbyist of legendary prowess. Alexander, a former speaker of the House known as "Slick," lassoed the industrial bloc to get behind a variant of deregulation during the 1999 legislative session that improved the utility's already favorable odds in getting what it wanted from the Public Service Commission, the agency that approved rate requests. The measure was so one-sided that it reignited a battle with Entergy's old adversary, the state electrical cooperative association. The cooperatives in league with the state attorney general forged a compromise on deregulation that commanded the usual overwhelming legislative majority, and Entergy Arkansas remained whole and formidable. And, as it turned out, the old-line utility would not be called upon to compete in an open market for energy consumers.

In 2003 the General Assembly formally killed the deregulation of the electrical utilities, which had never gone into effect, in the wake of the spectacular failure of deregulation in California and of the equally spectacular collapse of the Enron Corporation, an energy giant that had bet heavily on supplying power to states shutting down their regulatory apparatus. In the same period, FERC began promoting the expansion of regional transmission grids that permitted utility companies to snare better prices by venturing into wholesale power markets.

In 2005 the federal energy agency once again required the Arkansas utility's customers to reimburse another company in the Entergy system grappling with punishing generating costs. The FERC commissioners determined that the terms of a system agreement did not permit Entergy Arkansas to use the savings from its less expensive nuclear and coal-fired plants to benefit only the customers in its immediate service region. By this point, Arkansas ratepayers had already ponied up $3 billion for the Grand Gulf plant that supplied them no electricity. Entergy Arkansas demanded a release from the system agreement but only extricated itself after eight years and an additional $1 billion in payments beyond those still on its tab for Grand Gulf.

In 2010 the state Public Service Commission pushed Entergy Arkansas toward affiliating with one of the emerging regional transmission organizations when the parent system agreement lapsed. In late 2013, its centennial year, Entergy Arkansas transferred its own transmission grid to Midcontinent

Independent System Operator (MISO), an organization that managed similar networks in fifteen states from the Great Lakes to the Gulf of Mexico. The state's electricity customers gained an immediate reduction in their bills with the exit from the Entergy power pooling agreement, even though the Arkansas utility remained a subsidiary of the Entergy holding company. Oversight by MISO of the Entergy transmission network also benefited rate payers. The firm sought the best price from generating companies throughout its region. Power plants owned by Entergy Arkansas were no longer the invariable supplier of electricity coming into the homes and businesses of the utility's customers. In 2013 an Entergy Arkansas executive acknowledged the advantage of a neutral manager of the transmission system: "Many generators participate in the market, and that presents the opportunity to come up with a lower-cost solution to benefit all customers."

III. State Government, National Politics

The reform goals originating in the Winthrop Rockefeller administration persisted after Dale Bumpers left the statehouse for the U.S. Senate and became the guiding principles of a new era in Arkansas politics rather than mere remedies for the maladies of the Orval Faubus regime. White officeholders continued to dominate the elected positions but were no longer able to rebuff out of hand African American insistence upon shared authority and fair distribution of government services. Public officials still deferred to business interests and responded readily to the demands of prospective employers but acknowledged that old-style corruption and inept government agencies were out of step with the direction of the new economy. Candidates did not shirk the exhausting face-to-face, retail electioneering that remained the DNA of Arkansas political culture. Yet in this new era, those in office strenuously maneuvered to build public coalitions for programs that previous generations of politicians would have viewed as unwarranted and disruptive of the accustomed order.

For Faubus there was no life after politics. He had neither wealth nor profession. Being governor had been his only vocation. For the 1974 gubernatorial campaign, Witt Stephens and other power brokers jilted Faubus in his second comeback bid and backed a young upstart from Ouachita County who two years earlier had challenged the old warhorse from Ouachita County, John McClellan. David Pryor, a three-term congressman, had forced Senator McClellan into a Democratic Party primary run-off, usually a death-knell for incumbents. Stephens rejuvenated McClellan's prospects by passing the hat among well-heeled businessmen, and the five-term senator closed the deal with a fiery televised debate performance tarnishing Pryor as the minion of organized labor.

Stephens grasped Pryor's talents and potential. He remained a crusty benefactor of McClellan and senator J. William Fulbright but believed that Faubus's heyday had passed. In early 1974 the wily financier telephoned Pryor, who was mulling a bid for governor: "I'm going to help you. I beat you last time, and I owe you one." Stephens in that year could not salvage Fulbright but retained his standing as a decisive power broker with Pryor's capture of the governor's office.

Pryor continued the reformist programs of Rockefeller and Bumpers on a modest scale. He consolidated government agencies, including the establishment of the natural and cultural heritage department; supported the calling of a constitutional convention; and appointed the first women and black representatives to several judicial and administrative department posts. The movement for a new constitution, another thwarted initiative from the Rockefeller years, stalled in the General Assembly and courts before a convention finally convened after Pryor left office. Reflecting a growing national backlash against federal big-ticket projects, Pryor slowed expenditure growth after two decades of exponential increases. His contests with McClellan and Faubus had led observers to take for granted that Pryor was wedded to a liberal agenda. "Much to the surprise of many, the 'Old Liberal' David Pryor turned out to be a true fiscal conservative," approvingly noted an Arkadelphia editorialist.

After his reelection, Pryor urged the 1977 General Assembly to reverse decades of consolidation of services at the state level. The governor proposed in his "Arkansas Plan" to reduce state income taxes by a quarter while granting the counties the authority to raise revenue through any method of taxation rather than to depend solely on the property levy. In a series of town meetings, Pryor explained to his listeners that they could apply their windfall from the income-tax cut to maintain local services or for "a new shotgun or coon dog." Since what came to be dubbed the "Coon Dog Plan" would also lead to the end of state turn-back funds to local governments, county officials quickly realized they would be saddled with additional obligations while hostage to the willingness of their constituents to vote new taxes. County judges did not wish to regain independence at that price. The rough handling of his plan by the General Assembly relegated Pryor to the customary irrelevancy of second-term governors.

Despite the setback, Pryor in 1978 overcame strong opposition to win the U.S. Senate seat that became vacant following McClellan's death the year before. Personality continued to matter more than a legislative scorecard. Voters deemed the amiable Pryor as exceptionally approachable, even when compared to ambitious contemporaries who relished working crowds large and small. In 1990, before what turned out to be Senator David Pryor's final term, no candidate bothered to file against him.

The misfortunes of Pryor's agenda as governor highlighted the new unwillingness of legislators to cede influence over statewide issues. Election reform and newly redrawn urban districts diminished the sway of local power blocs over the general assembly while strengthening the influence of larger business interest groups. The new generation that had entered the General Assembly in 1971 had a keener sense of institutional responsibility, while the restructured committee system made lawmaking more open and less arbitrary. Legislators expected creditable information along with the usual favors from lobbyists.

The incremental reforms eventually pared away most of the buffoonery and rowdiness. Diane Blair aptly noted that by the 1990s the change in the legislative culture was unmistakable: "Both lobbyists and liquor have been officially banished from the chamber floors, and the occasional hog calling or fiddle playing is a rare tension-reliever rather than a routine occurrence." Yet remnants of the shadowy, less savory practices endured even as the legislature matured.

Bill Lancaster, who became the first chief of staff of the state Senate in 1985, recalled in his memoir how practiced lobbyists secured favorable treatment for their clients with steady payments to key legislators. During one late-night conversation, an insurance company lobbyist poured out his fury over a lawmaker who had betrayed him on a critical committee vote: "I paid the guy's filing fee. I funded his entire reelection campaign. I buy his suits and silk ties at the finest men's store in Little Rock. I pay for his wife's shopping trips to Dallas, fly her down there, and pay for all of her clothes, and then he stabs me in the back."

Nevertheless, the making of law in Arkansas in the last quarter of the twentieth century could not be boiled down to backroom quid pro quo transactions. The functioning of the General Assembly and the pressures swaying legislators grew more complex if not always more principled. The legislature altered its rules in the late 1960s to deprive the speaker of the House and the lieutenant governor, the Senate's presiding officer, of their powers to assign members and bills to committees. In the Senate, Knox Nelson and Max Howell leveraged their chairmanships of crucial committees to manage and oversee that chamber's proceedings. Nelson softened his dominance by remaining mindful of members' self-regard and their obligations to local patrons. On the other hand, Howell's bluster and intimidation were famously summed up by Bill Clinton: "He just wants to be treated like every other Roman emperor." Nick Wilson, a member of the 1971 class, challenged the two tribunes of the Senate in his own quest for influence and self-enrichment. Nevertheless, a new front in the factional wars opened with the entrance of a cohort of good government activists, derisively labeled by Wilson as the "young golfers."

Wilson shared the ideological commitment to expand government services and fend off socially conservative propositions (from banning rock music festivals to restricting abortion) with Mike Beebe, Morril Harriman, and other newcomers in the 1980s but bristled at attempts to disinfect venal legislative practices. In 1988 Wilson quashed a wide-ranging ethics measure backed by governor Bill Clinton that required lobbyists to register with the state and disclose their favors and gifts to officeholders. The governor in tandem with Beebe and his legislative allies enacted the reform through a successful popular referendum campaign.

In 1999 Nick Wilson resigned from the Senate following his conviction on tax evasion counts. He accepted a reduced prison sentence through a plea bargain on related federal charges that he had diverted funds for his personal use from state contracts to administer child-support enforcement and workers' compensation. Investigations ensnared other prominent officeholders in the 1990s. State representative Lloyd George and senator Ben McGee also surrendered their seats upon pleading guilty to federal indictments arising from abuses of public office. In 1990 attorney general Steve Clark resigned after his conviction for using state credit cards to entertain friends, and former secretary of state Bill McCuen in 1996 was sentenced to seventeen years in prison for accepting bribes and kickbacks.

The new state ethics commission inconsistently applied the 1988 voter-approved ethics initiative. Trade associations employed sitting legislators to represent their interests to colleagues until a 1995 statute prohibited members of the General Assembly from becoming paid lobbyists. Observers of the General Assembly ranked former legislators who became "government relations" executives for businesses and interest groups as the most effective lobbyists in an era when no single company dominated proceedings as Arkansas Power & Light or Arkla Gas had once done. In 1973 Witt Stephens relinquished control of Arkla to his protégé Sheffield Nelson only to discover that his heir intended to break off the utility's ties with other portions of the Stephens empire. Mr. Witt discovered his loosening grip on the legislature during the 1977 session. Nelson's supporters blocked a bill that would have boosted natural gas prices by forcing Arkla to renegotiate a supply contract with Stephens Production Company.

While the number of lobbyists descending on the capitol during legislative sessions rose into the hundreds, a few companies and associations predominated and were rarely thwarted unless arrayed on the opposite sides of an issue. Utilities, regulated by the state and dependent upon the Public Service Commission for rate increases, mustered the largest army of lobbyists. Southwestern Bell, the telecommunications heavyweight that became AT&T, stood out within this group. The agricultural and resource economic sectors were represented by the formidable Poultry Federation, the wood products industry, and the Farm Bureau. Financial institutions, trucking firms, and construction contractors did their part to entertain legislators afterhours at receptions and dinners. The Arkansas State Chamber of Commerce/Associated Industries of Arkansas remained, as it had for decades, a formidable influence over policy and law although at times twisted in knots, much like the General Assembly, when powerful corporations fell out over conflicting interests.

With a couple of thousand bills introduced during each regular session, lawmakers were often guided by the assurance of those sponsoring the measures. The ease of passing a bill in the General Assembly encouraged the introduction of local and minor items unseen in other state legislatures. One lawmaker sharply made the point in 1995: "Got a problem up in Imboden? Hey, solve it at the state capitol—get legislators involved who've never heard of Imboden and don't care."

The influence of lobbyists over lawmaking deepened after voters in 1992 approved a stringent term-limits amendment that limited executive officers as well as state senators to two four-year terms and state representatives to three two-year stints. With seniority rendered irrelevant, committee appointments and assignment of bills were centralized once more. The newcomers who entered in unprecedented numbers each session were often more ideologically committed to issues that reflected national movements, generally attentive to state policies over district interests, and quick to forage for other elective offices they might fill after their brief legislative stints. The dwindling of institutional experience and knowledge within the General Assembly not only worked to the advantage of lobbyists but also reinforced the leverage of the governor's office. By dislodging those who seemed to have taken up permanent residence in the General Assembly, term limits opened the way for those hailing from different backgrounds. A door ajar, however, did not assure access.

THE REPUBLICAN PARTY stirred to life in a changed political landscape. Term limits cost Democrats the privilege of incumbency. Booming migration into the party's northwest core heralded additional legislative seats at the expense of the wilting Democratic Delta when decennial apportionment rolled around. Historically, the state GOP was organizationally anemic and unable to recruit candidates for the full range of elective offices. Before the 1990s the party followed a top-down strategy in hopes that support for Republican presidential candidates would lead Arkansans to provide a supporting cast of Republican members in Congress. Party leaders were cheered when Ed Bethune (1978) and Jay Dickey (1992) netted congressional seats outside the upland Third District.

By 1998, when term limits had scoured open half the seats in the state House of Representatives, a popular Republican governor, Mike Huckabee, fortified the party's campaign assets. The GOP executive director chortled, "We are in play, and we're combating images of the good ol' boy system with young, attractive candidates." Following that year's election, Republicans represented 23 percent of all members of the General Assembly, a long way from 1991 when fewer than 10 percent served in the body. Even with the new structural advantages, parity for the GOP remained prospective rather than inevitable.

Of course, new boys were not the only alternative to good old boys. In 1964 when Dorathy Allen of Brinkley was elected as the first female state senator, three women were serving in the House of Representatives. By the end of the 1990s the female percentage in the House approached the national average for state legislatures, but in 1999 the absence of any women left the state Senate as the only all-male legislative chamber in the nation. After 2000 more women ran successful races for Senate posts while the percentage of women in the House remained stable. By 2015 the proportion of women sitting in both chambers continued to trail national averages although it was greater than those serving other states in the Old Confederacy with the exception of Florida, North Carolina, and Texas.

In 1999 Blanche Lincoln, who had been the congressional representative for the Delta district, became the first woman since Hattie Caraway to represent the state in the U.S. Senate. Following her 2010 election defeat, only white men filled out the Arkansas congressional delegation. In 2002 Jimmie Lou Fisher, a Democrat, was the first female nominee by a major party for governor, but her defeat preserved the historically male line of chief executives.

The election in 2014 of Attorney General Leslie Rutledge, a Republican, placed a woman for the first time in the constitutional office second only to that of the governor in the range of its powers and public profile. Nancy Hall had been the first woman elected to a constitutional office when she easily defeated her male opponent in the 1962 Democratic primary to become state treasurer. She served nine terms in the office before her retirement. Following the 2016 election, the majority of state Supreme Court justices were female. Although Arkansas compared favorably with other Southern states in the proportion of women in elected positions, the low percentage of women registered to vote and casting ballots led the Institute for Women's Policy Research in 2016 to rank the state near the bottom in the region for women's political participation. The proportion of African Americans reaching office in the term-limits era did not match that of white women winning elections. In 2015, 3 percent of Arkansas legislators were African American women compared to 17 percent of white female state lawmakers. A greater share of female members of other Southern state legislatures were African American than was true in Arkansas. This discrepancy was due in part to the lower percentage of black Arkansans (nearly 15 percent of the voting-age population) in comparison to African American citizens in most Southern states. Black residents were 26 percent of the voting age population in Alabama, 31.5 percent in Louisiana, 35.5 percent in Mississippi, and 16 percent in Tennessee. The concentration of African Americans in a relative handful of dispersed Arkansas counties hindered the creation of black-majority or near-majority legislative districts as well as the configuration of a congressional district in which a black candidate had a practical and reasonable chance of winning. The 2010 census recorded African Americans in the majority in three of the state's seventy-five counties and at least a quarter of the population in eleven others throughout the eastern and southern lowlands as well as metropolitan Pulaski County. Historically only a small proportion of white voters cast ballots for black candidates. In 1991 African American legislators and the state Republican Party challenged the legislature's apportionment plan that kept overwhelmingly white congressional districts intact, but federal courts did not find in their favor. Arkansas remained before the 2020 elections the only former Confederate state not to have elected an African American to statewide office or to serve in Congress.

As part of evolving black political activism, the century's first African American legislators—one senator and three representatives—were elected in 1972, all from Little Rock and Pine Bluff. By 1976 a larger proportion of eligible black Arkansas voters were registered than in any other Southern state. In 1988 Ben McGee ended the long political drought in eastern Arkansas. He won his House seat after filing a successful federal lawsuit that found Crittenden County officials had designed a multimember district to ensure an all-white delegation.

In December 1989 a federal panel concluded in response to a suit by African American plaintiffs that the state's apportionment of legislative districts left black voters with "less opportunity than other members of the electorate to elect representatives of their choice." A subsequent decision created nine additional legislative districts and also required the state to gain permission from federal authorities if officials altered the rules on the proportion of votes needed to win an election. Thus, Arkansas, which had not been subject originally to the 1965 Voting Rights Act, was narrowly obligated to follow this "preclearance" procedure as outlined under Section 3 of the Act. Most Southern states had been subject to preclearance oversight under the broader Section 5, which was voided in 2013 by the U.S. Supreme Court's ruling in *Shelby County v. Holder.* In 1998 fifteen African Americans were elected to the state General Assembly, the highest number since the 1891 disfranchisement laws. Those numbers remained largely unchanged in the following years.

Moderate Democratic candidates for statewide office garnered white votes without resorting to the racially charged appeals and thinly veiled bigotry that infected the political rhetoric in other Southern states. Most Arkansas whites lived in localities where they were the dominant voting bloc and were largely unaffected by the modest civil rights initiatives backed by Democratic leaders. White Arkansans were less moved than their counterparts in the region to abandon the party of their ancestors even as it welcomed African American supporters. Yet white Democratic officeholders instinctively understood the tripwires of reform. They avoided liberal remedies that redistributed resources and authority, instead widening the scope and generosity of government services for the general population.

AFRICAN AMERICAN VOTERS were critical supporters for Bill Clinton, who as governor was also named a defendant in the 1989 lawsuit to halt the dilution of black voting rights. Clinton's backers were disappointed when the governor decided to defend the state's apportionment plan. Yet he judged his biracial coalition was more likely to fracture if he repudiated that plan as discriminatory. Under Clinton, the state first appealed the ruling requiring preclearance under the Voting Rights Act but then dropped the appeal. The U.S. Justice Department by that time sided with the African American plaintiffs, with a brief submitted by solicitor general Kenneth W. Starr, who would again cross paths with Clinton.

Throughout his time as governor, Clinton's commitment to power-sharing was exercised primarily through the diversity of his appointments. He named the first African Americans to a wide number of boards and commissions as well as directors of the top-echelon departments of finance (Mahlon Martin), human services (Walter C. Patterson), and health (Joycelyn Elders).

At the beginning of his first term in 1979, Clinton proposed an ambitious transportation, education, and environmental agenda, a seeming return to the days of

Rockefeller and Bumpers. The legislature agreed to fund an extensive highway construction program, and Clinton defended the assessment of higher taxes on the largest vehicles with the impeccable logic that they caused the greatest road damage. Yet poorer Arkansans tended to drive older and heavier cars and were hit with the full increase when they renewed their annual vehicle registration.

Misfortune magnified Clinton's political miscalculation. In May 1980 President Jimmy Carter transferred to Fort Chaffee about 18,000 refugees who had fled Cuba after Fidel Castro, the country's Communist ruler, threw open the gates at the port of Mariel. In June several hundred refugees left the base and clashed with state police near the small town of Barling. In that fall's general election campaign, Frank White, a former savings and loan executive and recent GOP convert, aired footage of the melee to dramatize his charge that Clinton sacrificed public safety to placate the Democratic president. Clinton lost two-thirds of the counties that year, abandoned by rural voters in numbers that outstripped his urban majorities. An internal poll had alerted Clinton to the likely outcome, but White appeared surprised by his victory, which he attributed to divine favor.

White had been director of the Arkansas Industrial Development Commission in the Pryor administration, but he was drawn to the Republican Party for reasons other than its pro-business orientation. Deeply religious, White and his wife Gay were among the founders in the late 1970s of the Fellowship Bible Church, a non-sectarian fundamentalist congregation in Little Rock that had grown rapidly in numbers and influence. At Ronald Reagan's inauguration festivities, White was a minor celebrity, a socially conservative, fiscally prudent businessman who had brought down one of the Democratic Party's rising stars.

For the 1981 session, the new governor's program was little more than undoing a number of the Clinton initiatives and trimming agency budgets. He did endorse legislation that permitted voters to levy municipal and county sales taxes through referendums. Through this progeny of Pryor's Arkansas Plan, state lawmakers shifted the responsibility for tax increases to local officials who retained the buffer of state turn-back moneys. With the Ronald Reagan administration's liquidation of federal revenue sharing, local governments used the new authority to replenish their budgets. In future years the combined state and local levies drove sales-tax levels in Arkansas to among the highest in the nation and became the largest sources of revenue for cities and counties.

Rather than for this significant shift in taxation, White was in later years identified more closely with a measure that replicated a model bill circulated by religious activists throughout the nation. The governor did not read what became known as the creation science law before signing it, but firmly defended its purpose and constitutionality in the face of derisive public opposition.

Approved by solid majorities after perfunctory debate, Act 590 effectively mandated science teachers to inform their students that an equally plausible alternative to biological evolution was that existing species were unchanged since the sudden and recent creation of the universe. The American Civil Liberties Union filed a suit on the grounds that the act violated the constitutional protections against government establishment of religion. The ensuing proceedings in *McLean v. Arkansas Board of Education* prompted unflattering comparisons to the 1925 Scopes trial in Tennessee. One of the witnesses offered during his testimony on behalf of the measure that UFOs were a demonic manifestation. After federal district judge William Overton struck down the law, Arkansas attorney general Steve Clark refrained from appealing the decision. In contrast to the reaction to unpopular court findings during the civil rights era, neither White nor legislative leaders set out to arouse popular outrage to pressure Clark to keep up the fight. Nevertheless, George Fisher, the dean of editorial cartoonists in the state, consistently portrayed the governor on the editorial page of the *Arkansas Gazette* with a half-eaten banana in hand.

Like Winthrop Rockefeller, White had not been elected by a stable coalition, nor did his tenure foster Republican Party competitiveness. And while the congenial governor was generally well-liked, his political stumbles were reminiscent of Rockefeller's miscues. The outcome of the rematch in the 1982 gubernatorial contest was a personal triumph for Bill Clinton, while it also reconfirmed Democratic supremacy. Throughout the race, Clinton was a chastened figure who situated himself on the side of the cultural divide that extolled faith, family, and responsibility. He campaigned fervently in African American communities, knowing his political comeback was fruitless if he failed to net those votes by strong margins.

Clinton offered a modest program at the opening of the 1983 legislative session that matched his campaign's aversion to bold initiatives. He followed his predecessors' well-worn path by centering his agenda on improving schools. A May 1983 state Supreme Court decision provided him the fortunate rationale to more thoroughly restructure education.

The *Alma v. Dupree* ruling required that the state revamp its distribution of aid to narrow the gaping disparities in school-district income. Hillary Clinton chaired an education standards committee that in its tour of the state that summer discovered at least half the school districts did not offer physics, advanced math, foreign languages, and music. The First Lady also later recalled parents listing disturbing examples of teachers lacking rudimentary knowledge and skills.

Preparing for a special fall legislative session, the governor crafted his wife's widely praised recommendations into a package of proposed bills that went beyond the court-ordered remedies. Clinton directed the one-cent increase in the state sales tax not only to finance equalization among districts but also to underwrite the mandate that schools offer students a minimum set of courses and services. Clinton sidestepped the persistent controversy over consolidation, a political litmus test in rural communities, by endorsing the survival of small school districts if they met the basic standards.

Both popular and key legislative support for the tax program rested upon the approval of a mandatory competency examination for all employed teachers. Clinton steadfastly defended the tests against sustained and passionate opposition from the Arkansas Education Association (AEA) and in the face of evidence that those most likely to be forced to leave the profession were disproportionately African American. During the same session, Clinton promised to back a tax rebate for low-income families if labor activists set aside their distaste for regressive taxes and endorsed the sales-tax boost. He reneged, however, after state Senate opposition to the rebate threatened to derail approval of the tax. In this school-reform fight Clinton followed the blueprint for moderate Democratic leaders. He linked the expansion of government services and expense to personal responsibility, while publicly stranding liberal interest groups.

If previous governors had made education a centerpiece of their administrations, none had thrown themselves so completely into the enterprise as Clinton or sought to extend its benefits beyond the schoolhouse doors and across generations. He pursued increased funding for adult training and literacy programs while touting early childhood development initiatives as critical to improving student academic performance. The Home Instruction Program for Preschool Youngsters (HIPPY), for example, trained lower-income mothers to teach the skills and concepts that would start their own children on the same footing as all their classmates. Clinton treated education as an instrument for moving individuals up the economic ladder.

Those advocating social-justice principles became disenchanted with his insistence that educational improvements were more realistic avenues for progress than contentious measures directly benefiting the impoverished and shifting political power from traditional gatekeepers. On the other hand, many in the business community and a hardened portion of the white electorate distrusted Clinton's character and motives well beyond the usual skepticism faced by other Arkansas politicians. A banker in the late 1980s grumbled about the governor's record to his coffee group one morning at a southern Arkansas restaurant. When reminded that Clinton had generally heeded the wishes of the financial industry, the critic acknowledged the assistance: "But I don't think he really meant it when he did those things."

The AEA failed to impose a political cost upon the governor or force the repeal of the teacher testing program, unmistakable evidence of its eroding influence. The AEA along with other unions had held their own in the early post-segregation era. Liberal activists not only delivered votes to favored candidates but resuscitated the Democratic state committee, traditionally disregarded by officeholders who banked on private and local interests to service their campaigns. The labor-progressive coalition partners, however, began losing ground even before Clinton's extended tenure loosened their hold upon the levers of the party machinery.

Specifically, union membership shrank. By the 1970s the collective bargaining decertification campaigns in the poultry-processing plants, the zeal of Tyson and Walmart to keep their trucking lines and warehouses off-limits to labor organizers, and competitive pressures brewing at low-wage plants abroad renewed the anti-union movement. The proportion of union workers declined from a peak of 17.5 percent in 1970 to slightly over 6 percent in 1998, placing Arkansas ninth among thirteen Southern states. The slide continued with the acceleration of deindustrialization, leaving less than 4 percent of organized workers in 2016. That year the state agency in charge of business recruitment boasted in its materials that Arkansas was among five states in the nation with the lowest union membership.

As their ranks dwindled, labor groups sought legislative relief to parry the corporate offensives. Elected officials, however, could count. David Pryor kept his distance from the labor movement after John McClellan in 1972 secured reelection by homing in on the challenger's union ties. Citing public safety, Governor Pryor in 1975 deployed the state National Guard after Pine Bluff firefighters walked off the job. The strike, backed by the local civil rights associations, crumbled, and state union officials faulted the governor for resorting to coercion rather than mediation. In the Senate, Pryor and Dale Bumpers did not back union proposals broadly supported by their Democratic Party colleagues, including other moderate Southerners. In 1994 Arkansas union leaders lobbied both senators to support a measure to keep firms from hiring permanent replacements for striking workers. The two lawmakers frankly expressed their doubts that labor forces could deliver sufficient support in their upcoming reelections to counter the toll inflicted by well-financed business groups.

The 1994 proposal did have the nominal support of another Arkansan in the nation's capital. Union leaders concluded, however, that President Bill Clinton was lukewarm on the measure after he failed to corral his home-state senators. Leading up to 1992 presidential race, J. Bill Becker, the state AFL-CIO leader, had graded Governor Clinton poorly in a report on his labor record to the national trade union. Becker still fumed that Clinton had backtracked on the bargain to supply a tax break for low-income Arkansans as part of the 1983 school-reform package.

CLINTON'S RECONSTRUCTION of education in his second gubernatorial term was an impressive political and policy accomplishment, but it appeared for a time to be the zenith rather than a foundation for his legacy. The shaky 1980s economy along with the cuts by Ronald Reagan in federal aid to states lowered new revenues slated for the schools and hobbled the introduction of new reforms. In 1989 Clinton once again attempted to enlist support for another sales-tax boost by erasing the income tax for 260,000 poor residents. The plan came up one vote short in the Senate.

The tax proposal was not the only tinder fueling acrimony in the 1989 session. John Walker, the lead attorney representing African American students known as the Joshua Intervenors, and the lawyers for Little Rock, North Little Rock, and Pulaski County Special school districts reached a settlement to release the state of Arkansas as a party from the ongoing desegregation lawsuit. In return, the state would make annual payments to help the districts comply with court remedies to achieve equal education. A host of lawmakers balked at an ongoing appropriation that lacked a sunset provision, and claimed that rural communities would be plundered to provide magnet schools, compensatory programs, teacher insurance for big-city kids. Settlement supporters, however, played upon the opponents' dread of capricious federal judges to secure approval on the last day of the session.

By 2013 the state had directed over $1 billion to the three districts. Walker, then a member of the state House of Representatives, observed that the funds had not been adequately monitored to ensure they were used for the original purposes, while other legislators, impatient with the expense, backed bills to close out the disbursements. In 2014 a federal district judge approved a settlement, negotiated by the state attorney general, that set a 2018 deadline for the state's final payments.

The successive years of belt-tightening and retrenchment had wearied Clinton, but in 1990 he decided with some reluctance to bid for a fifth term (an amendment extending constitutional officers' terms from two to four years had taken effect in 1987). The Republican primary that year included the type of drama involving outsized personalities, deep-seated grudges, and controversial financial deals usually reserved for Democratic Party free-for-alls.

Tommy Robinson had served as director of public safety during Clinton's first term before launching a successful campaign for sheriff of Pulaski County. He became a conspicuous presence on statewide media for racially charged tirades against judges, televised arrests of county officials who ignored his funding demands, and the dumping of county prisoners outside a state correctional facility. In the 1990 GOP primary, Robinson was opposed by Sheffield Nelson, another former Democrat and Clinton appointee to the Economic Development Commission. Nelson had been an early backer of Robinson, who gained a seat in 1985 in the U.S. House of Representatives, but the ambitions of both men in a state with few outlets for large ambitions provoked a falling out.

Nelson had retired from Arkla Gas, but Witt and Jack Stephens had not forgiven what they regarded as his betrayal of their trust and bankrolled Robinson's primary run. Robinson slashed at Nelson over a controversial transaction involving natural-gas reserves that had produced a windfall for Jerry Jones, another friend and benefactor of Robinson. In the previous year, Jones committed much of his personal wealth to buy the Dallas Cowboys football franchise for $140 million (in 2017 *Forbes* magazine put the franchise value at $4.8 billion). Angered by the charges over his business practices, Jones ended a farming partnership with Robinson and no longer paid his family medical expenses. Nelson won the primary thanks to crossover votes from urban Democrats who feared the prospect of the erratic Robinson as governor. The Stephens brothers had favored Frank White over Clinton in previous races but wanted the incumbent governor to humble the detested Nelson.

In the general election, Clinton won again, this time with 57 percent of the vote. Another wave of reformers picked up legislative seats that year and brightened Clinton's hopes for dusting off his shelved policy goals. The governor's turn of fortunes owed much to his failure to set aside the federal court order that enlarged African American representation through redrawn districts. In addition to a larger black caucus in the General Assembly, the reworking of a Pine Bluff senatorial district enabled Jay Bradford, a white progressive, to overthrow Knox Nelson, the kingpin who had sabotaged Clinton's 1989 tax proposal.

Addressing a more sympathetic General Assembly, Clinton proposed higher taxes for new programs that he asserted were investments to improve workforce preparation, infrastructure, and the overall business climate. This justification for expanding government beyond what conservatives believed wise and short of what liberals dreamed necessary was a tenet of modern Arkansas public policy. It became the foundation of the economic program of the first Arkansas president.

The legislature earmarked a half-percent sales tax increase for education. Moneys not only benefited public school districts but also established a state-supported residential math-and-science high school, offered grants for pre-school enrichment programs for poor children, and extended college tuition scholarships for students from middle- and lower-income families. The heads of large business enterprises defied chamber of commerce orthodoxy to accept a corporate income-tax hike to upgrade the state's poorly equipped vocational schools into technical colleges. The heavyweight leadership of the Arkansas Business Council—Tyson, Walton, and Murphy—shared the growing apprehension that a dearth of trained workers effectively saddled modernizing industries with a labor shortage. Higher gasoline taxes were put into place to jump-start road maintenance and new construction. A measure to exempt a portion of Arkansans below the poverty line from the state income tax finally made it through the legislature although the state remained among the very few imposing the income tax on a portion of low wage earners.

POLITICAL OBSERVERS ranked the 1991 session as the most constructive and activist since the 1971 legislature, which had enacted the Bumpers's reforms. Without the new measures, Bill Clinton would have entered his first presidential campaign with a shorter resume that tilted toward the early repairs to school financing. On October 3, 1991, declaring that he represented a new generation of leadership free from sterile ideological divisions, Clinton announced his candidacy for president in front of the Old State House in Little Rock. Outside the gates stood unnoticed a former governor who had raised taxes for education, formalized the state's industrial recruitment campaigns, and displayed an uncanny gift for connecting with ordinary Arkansans. Still incensed that Clinton had dismissed him in 1983 from a state patronage post, Orval Faubus was not among the cheering supporters.

As the crowds thinned that fine autumn day, Faubus crossed the street to the Stephens Inc. offices, where the patriarch, Witt, held court at daily lunches attended by politicians, reporters, and business leaders. Presiding over the closest approximation to an Arkansas salon, Witt Stephens took puckish delight in inviting guests with contrary opinions and then introducing a controversial topic to judge its effect. On this occasion Faubus found himself sitting at the same table with J. O. Powell, the former *Arkansas Gazette* editorialist who had written few kind words over the years about his dining companion. Whatever their observations on Clinton's prospects—conversations at Stephens's lunches were always off the record—these astute and knowledgeable men had helped shaped the era that had just culminated on the portico of the old capitol. Though suffering from failing health, Orval Faubus would live another three years. Making deals almost to the end, Witt Stephens died in December. The *Arkansas Gazette* did not survive the month.

Reverence for the *Gazette* had deepened in the post-segregation era, when many looked back proudly at its editorial criticisms of Faubus during the Little Rock crisis. Its traditional layout and paucity of feature stories earned the Gazette the affectionate nickname of "the old gray lady." Although the uniformly liberal editorials and columns ran counter to grassroots opinion, few questioned its primacy as the state's newspaper of record. By the mid-1970s the *Gazette* had almost a two-to-one advantage over the rival *Arkansas Democrat* in circulation and advertising revenue.

In 1977 Walter E. Hussman Jr., the owner of the *Democrat*, offered to surrender to its competitor if his paper could remain alive as a subsidiary publication within a joint operation. He resented the rebuff to his proposal by the *Gazette* owners and began pouring money into his publication without any hope of recouping the losses. His new managing editor, John Robert Starr, relished the underdog status and continually reminded readers of his daily column that he was making war on the *Gazette*: "I'm a street fighter and I know how to compete." A larger staff and expanded news coverage raised the *Democrat*'s credibility, and color graphics reinforced the contrast with its competitor. For its part, the *Gazette* strengthened its investigative reporting and devoted space to extended analyses of politics and education. In the end, however, improvement in the papers' overall quality was a sideshow to the war.

In 1986 *Gazette* publisher, Hugh B. Patterson, whose father-in-law's family had owned the newspaper since 1902, withdrew from the fray. Drawing upon revenue from his profitable media operations in southwest Arkansas, Hussman had been able to discount *Democrat* commercial advertising rates as well as win over readers with free classified ads. The Patterson family income came only from the *Gazette*. While Hussman insisted that he merely sought to reach parity with the *Gazette*, Patterson understood that Little Rock would not withstand the pressures toward a monopoly market any more successfully than other American cities.

The sale of the *Gazette* in 1986 to the Gannett Corporation seemed the most unlikely of pairings. The style of the expansionist chain was typified by its national daily, *USA Today*, which offered casual readers vivid illustrations, abbreviated hard-news stories, and an abundance of human-interest features. The Gannett makeover of the *Gazette* represented a consumer trend that did not take hold in Arkansas. Those who had grown up with the *Gazette* resented the changes, and the new owners could not boost readership to compensate for their ample investments in production facilities. The *Democrat* continued to hemorrhage cash but by 1991 had closed the gap in daily circulation and was ahead in Sunday edition numbers. Impatient with losses exceeding $100 million over the course of five years, Gannett surrendered. On October 19, 1991, the day following the announcement that Hussman had paid $68.5 million to Gannett for what had been the oldest surviving newspaper west of the Mississippi River, *Gazette* and *Democrat* subscribers alike unfolded an edition of the *Arkansas Democrat-Gazette*.

Notwithstanding the rechristened banner or the *Democrat-Gazette*'s official history, which traced its origins to William Woodruff's founding in 1819 of the *Gazette*, the war ended with an acquisition and not a merger. The *Democrat* endured and the *Gazette* died. Hussman did not attempt to recover from the years of red ink by slashing operating expenses; in fact, the *Democrat-Gazette* increased its column inches. The publisher recognized his newspaper faced continued competition from television and emerging digital news sources. Expanded coverage of state developments outside Little Rock prepared the *Democrat-Gazette* to begin publishing in 1998 a special regional edition for the thriving northwest corner.

In 2005 Hussman acquired a number of smaller newspapers in that region and sharpened the rivalry with Stephens Media, which published among its several newspapers one that served Springdale and Rogers. Warren Stephens, who had taken the helm at Stephens Inc. after his father, Jack, retired, also owned the media company. In a predictable reprise to the central Arkansas war, both operations lost money until 2009 when the two magnates agreed to a merger that permitted the Northwest edition of the *Democrat-Gazette* to be distributed with the Stephens's newspapers. Eventually all of the daily newspapers controlled by the two companies were consolidated into the *Northwest Arkansas Democrat-Gazette*.

At the time of the merger, a former publisher in the northwest corner underscored the pressures for consolidation in the news business, particularly in a region where towns were melding into a single urban sprawl: "From what were basically four distinct markets just 20 years ago, we really now have one major metropolitan market. The fundamentals of the newspaper business are changing rapidly and there is no space for profit in competing daily newspapers in a single market." By 2016 national media companies, including Gannett, acquired a flock of urban newspapers, a development coming on the heels of out-of-town ownership of local television stations. A single newspaper corporation dominated the Arkansas market but it was Arkansas-based.

Arkansas Gazette loyalists gave Walter Hussman grudging respect for sustaining the quality and breadth of a state newspaper that was superior to Gannett news dailies throughout the nation, even those in larger markets. But they deplored the persistence of the *Arkansas Democrat*'s unblinking, conservative editorial thrust. The *Arkansas Gazette* had dependably favored Democratic candidates, although its editorials during the Bumpers, Pryor, and Clinton eras would not uncommonly range to the left of their policies and voting record. Republican leaders took comfort in a sympathetic *Arkansas Democrat-Gazette* as the party advanced in the state.

John Robert Starr, the managing editor who retired in late 1992, and Paul Greenberg, the head editorial writer, were contemptuous of Bill Clinton. Greenberg had won the Pulitzer Prize for his editorials during the civil rights campaigns in Pine Bluff and in 1980 coined the "Slick Willie" nickname for the young governor. The epithet did not catch on in Arkansas but resurfaced along with harsh and dismissive stereotypes of the state during the Clinton presidency. Former reporters and editors for the *Arkansas Gazette* agreed their newspaper would have concentrated its resources to probe and rectify the flawed accounts appearing in national publications on state government operations and influence during the Clinton era. The *Arkansas Democrat-Gazette* generally ceded coverage of purported official wrongdoing and corruption to national outlets.

NOT UNEXPECTEDLY, President George H. W. Bush during the 1992 campaign questioned if leading "a small state" prepared one for the presidency. Normally, partisan depictions of Arkansas would have subsequently faded as critics retrained their assaults on Clinton's presidential policies; and, indeed, in 1996 Senator Robert Dole said little about the state during his unsuccessful run to unseat the incumbent. In contrast, the national media examinations accompanying the official Whitewater investigations customarily outlined an intricate scandal with its roots in "Arkansas political mores."

In March 1992 a *New York Times* article suggested that in the early 1980s Governor Clinton intervened with state regulators on behalf of an insolvent savings and loan owned by James McDougal, a coinvestor with the governor and his wife in the Whitewater real estate development in Marion County.

Accumulating demands for a full accounting prompted U.S. Attorney General Janet Reno in January to appoint Robert Fiske as special prosecutor to probe all matters relating to the financial ties between Clinton and McDougal. In August 1994 a panel of federal judges replaced Fiske with Kenneth Starr, the former Bush administration solicitor general.

By September 1998, when he delivered his findings to the U.S. House of Representatives, Starr acknowledged that his lengthy investigation into transactions related to the Whitewater investment or Arkansas government operations had not uncovered wrongdoing by Hillary and Bill Clinton. Nevertheless, the special prosecutor advised the House in his report that the president committed acts while contesting a sexual harassment civil suit filed by Paula Jones, an Arkansas state employee, that "may constitute grounds for an impeachment." On February 12, 1999, the U.S. Senate acquitted President Bill Clinton on the two articles of impeachment that the House had approved on party-line votes the previous December. The votes in the Arkansas delegation mirrored the partisan split on the issue. Asa Hutchinson, the Republican representative of the northwest Arkansas congressional district, was a prosecutor during the Senate trial, while former senator Dale Bumpers, who had completed his final term in January, delivered the closing argument in defense of the president.

The prevailing thumbnail sketch of Arkansas lingered during the years of the Clinton presidency: members of an entrenched elite hold and exchange political offices to advance their common financial interests in a system devoid of the normal checks and balances. In late 1998 Republican presidential speechwriter Peggy Noonan characterized the president's efforts to counter the impeachment proceedings: "He acted as if he were still in Little Rock, still up against legislators in plaid suits who own the Chevy dealership. When Bill Clinton was governor and it was Yalie vs. the yokels, the yokels folded when you leaned on them. But Washington is not Little Rock."

Many Southerners had viewed the election of Jimmy Carter to the presidency in 1976 as both redemption and confirmation that the region's hard-won experiences in overcoming a legacy of racial oppression, rooted poverty, and deficient public institutions prepared the South to offer leadership in the aftermath of the Watergate scandals. Similarly, Arkansans hoped for a reappraisal based upon the recognition that no American president could emerge from a state lacking a diverse economy, maturing political structures, and openness to contemporary influences. Instead, the glare of official investigations and journalistic excavations coiled the state into the lurid opening act of a new era of partisan rancor and ideological combats. Arkansas not only remained saddled with embedded stereotypes of insularity, corruption, and clandestine dealing but the campaigns of total warfare that slandered the state metastasized into the virulence and distrust that dominated early twenty-first-century political culture. Arkansas closed its historic gap with America in becoming a harbinger of American fragmentation.

THE WHITEWATER INQUIRIES may not have forced Clinton from the presidency but did lead to the resignation of his successor as governor and altered the course of the state's politics. Jim Guy Tucker had previously lost contentious races to David Pryor and Bill Clinton and decided to settle in 1990 for the winnable lieutenant governor's spot rather than challenge Clinton once more. Tucker gained his ultimate goal when Clinton resigned as governor to move to Washington and easily won two years later a full gubernatorial term.

Tucker had tilted rightward after Pryor battered him during the 1978 race for the U.S. Senate as a liberal foil for the labor movement. In his first session, Tucker increased the education budget by transferring revenue from other state agencies rather than through tax measures. He later summoned a special session that endorsed his proposals to stiffen laws and sentences for juvenile defenders over protests that young African Americans would bear the brunt of the crackdown. In 1993 Tucker supported and signed a civil rights act that had emerged from a task force set up by Clinton. Lacking an enforcement mechanism, the measure was weaker than federal statutes. Subsequent state court rulings left gay and transgendered Arkansans largely unprotected.

In 1994 Sheffield Nelson once again captured the Republican nomination to challenge an incumbent governor but amassed a slightly lower proportion of the vote in the general election than he had secured four years earlier against Clinton. Despite his electoral strength, Tucker was frustrated during his new term by the fate of two major initiatives. Voters overwhelmingly rejected an ambitious highway bond program and a proposed constitutional convention that would have begun its work from a draft already written by the governor and slightly revised by the legislature.

Union leaders had once centered their hopes on Tucker after other major Democratic figures had spurned labor reform but became disillusioned with him as well. In 1993 J. Bill Becker failed to persuade Tucker to veto an overhaul of the workers compensation system that raised obstacles to obtaining payments and limited the range of medical care for injured employees. Led by Tyson Foods, business lobbyists were not open to compromise on the proposal, and Tucker had little chance of sustaining a veto when backers needed only a bare majority in the General Assembly for an override. An embittered Becker declared, "Congratulations to business and industry; let them enjoy their bloody victory."

In 1994 Arkansas delegates touted the new law during a session at the annual meeting of the American Legislative Exchange Council, organized in the 1970s by leaders of the fledging New Right movement to promote model conservative legislation. The Arkansas approach, which did produce one-third fewer claims in the first six years, became a useful model for states set on retrenching workers' compensation costs.

Tucker not only aligned with past governors in his relations with labor but also expanded assistance to those firms promising more jobs. As fewer plants migrated from the evacuated Rust Belt, Arkansas development leaders became more attentive to operations within the state. In 1993 the Economic Development Incentive Act, endorsed by Tucker, authorized the Department of Economic Development to reward companies hiring additional workers with a rebate equivalent to a portion of the expanded payroll. Under a provision in the act, companies that purchased existing plants could become eligible for state payments by counting employees who were already on the job.

Still, about two-thirds of the over $500 million in corporate subsidies during the 1990s flowed from the 1985 Manufacturer's Investment Tax Credit. Governor Bill Clinton coaxed the legislature during that year's session to approve the tax credit after International Paper announced plans to close its plants in Pine Bluff and Camden. The measure allowed firms to waive sales and use taxes for up to 7 percent of the cost of plant expansions. Both paper mills hung on, but in 2001 the company shut its seventy-three-year-old Camden operation.

The sum of government incentives continued to rise during the early twenty-first century, while manufacturing employment continued to decline. The state campaign to subsidize job creation had revolved around industrial expansion since the post-WWII era but extending assistance to a broader range of enterprises did not silence a growing number of critics. In 2005 a conservative economist emphasized that ladling benefits to certain operations was a "function that ought to be left up to the marketplace." The economic development agency asserted that companies securing state incentives would otherwise not have added jobs or expanded production without the tax-payer funded enticements. Surveys of company heads throughout the nation downplayed the importance of subsidies in locating plant sites, but Arkansas leaders claimed that they could not disarm if other states continued to extend corporate favors.

IN 1995 KENNETH STARR secured an indictment of Tucker in the midst of his investigations into James McDougal's Whitewater and other rickety financial intrigues. Tucker during his time away from public office had invested in a number of different enterprises, both in the United States and abroad, and the federal charges hinged on loans he had secured through the Small Business Administration (SBA). The prosecution's principal witness, who had pleaded guilty to bilking millions of dollars through his financial services firm from the SBA, insisted Tucker concocted a scheme in league with McDougal to defraud the SBA of $825,000. The witness, a former Little Rock traffic judge, had leveled similar charges against Bill Clinton.

On May 28, 1996, a jury convicted Tucker, who was tried along with McDougal and his wife Susan, on one count of conspiracy and one of mail fraud. The verdict held the governor responsible for incorrect information the former judge and confessed embezzler had submitted in an application on behalf of Tucker to the SBA for an otherwise legal loan to purchase a utility. The prosecutors did not present evidence that Tucker had been shown the errant application.

The state constitution prohibited those convicted of a felony from holding public office, and the governor announced he would step down July 15. On that date, Tucker stunned those who gathered at the capitol to witness lieutenant governor Mike Huckabee's installation by declaring that he would not formally resign until the presiding judge ruled on whether a juror at his trial had been tainted. Late in the day, the state teetered on the edge of a constitutional crisis as both Huckabee, a Republican, and Tucker asserted their right to be governor. By evening, however, Tucker submitted his resignation after Democratic leaders insisted they would not block his removal from office.

Huckabee's poise during the brief standoff won him admiration from rank-and-file Democrats while boosting the hope of Republicans that their party had turned a corner. Five years earlier, Huckabee had deftly reconciled fundamentalist and moderate factions during his tenure as president of the Arkansas Southern Baptist Convention. The respect and familiarity he enjoyed within the state's largest religious denomination had sustained his win over a Democratic opponent in a 1993 special election for the lieutenant governor's post, vacated when Tucker succeeded Clinton as governor.

The Republican Party itself was moving toward greater ideological cohesion. The social and anti-tax conservatives in northwest Arkansas appeared to eclipse the business establishment and Rockefeller reform wings of the party. In 1996 Tim Hutchinson, the U.S. representative from the mountain Third District, became the first Republican sent to the U.S. Senate since Reconstruction when he defeated the state's attorney general for the seat vacated by Senator David Pryor. U.S. Representative Jay Dickey, a Republican, continued to represent traditionally Democratic south Arkansas, while Asa Hutchinson won the seat his brother had given up in the U.S. House to run for the Senate. Term limits swelled the GOP delegation in the General Assembly.

Nevertheless, Arkansas at the edge of the new century was not, as it turned out, on the verge of crowding under the GOP tent with the rest of the South. In 2000 Mike Ross ousted Dickey to recoup the Fourth District for the Democrats, and David Pryor's son Mark in 2002 prevented Tim Hutchinson from gaining a second Senate term. Huckabee completed the two terms allotted him under term-limits strictures but could not transfer his popular majorities to Asa Hutchinson, the Republican nominee for the 2006 governor's race. Mike Beebe, the Young Turk who became the master of the state Senate when the old horses went to pasture or prison, became the new chief executive. He was also titular head of a party occupying every state constitutional office, boasting solid majorities in the General Assembly, and claiming every seat in Congress, save for the unobtainable upland district. Surveying the melancholy returns, Asa Hutchinson judged the outcome of the races a "huge setback" for the Republicans and concluded, "It's going to take a lot of rebuilding."

Victories for Democratic politicians in Arkansas grew from fusing their overwhelming support among African Americans with a sufficient proportion of white voters to produce electoral majorities. Consistently successful Democrats reaped their critical margin of white support from what Diane Blair and Jay Barth identified as the "rural swing counties." These locales stretched in a broken band from southwest to northeast, angling between the Delta and the Ozarks, more racially balanced and less politically predictable. The white majority in the twenty-six counties commonly favored a state government strong enough to improve schools, upgrade roads and utilities, and subsidize community organizations and local enterprises. These rural citizens also believed government should uphold moral and religious traditions, push the legal limits to prevent abortions, resist same-sex marriages, and not impair what guns could be owned or where they could be carried.

Voters in these counties turned on Bill Clinton in 1980, but he regained their support two years after this defeat by emphasizing his trip to the woodshed brought him closer to his faith and convinced him not to overlook those dislodged by economic upheavals. Mike Huckabee captured and held the swing counties with a greater emphasis upon social conservatism but also drummed up support for economic policies remarkably consistent with the approach of the Democratic governors. Democratic office holders crafted a guarded civil rights template that produced African American appointments to state agencies and commissions as well as initiatives to assist lower-income and working-class households. These political leaders hesitated to embrace programs to dismantle long-standing social and economic obstacles specifically burdening black communities.

Swing-county residents saw clearly the growing gap between their home-towns and the prospering metropolitan centers. White voters living in similar locales in other states became apprehensive over being left behind and turned toward the Republican Party.

Democratic leaders knew if they lost the rural swing counties, they would lose Arkansas.

IV. Life in New Arkansas, Life in Old Arkansas

Since 1947 when AT&T established area codes, every Arkansas phone number began the same way: 501. Early in the twenty-first century the state's area-code map revealed a new set of boundaries overlaying the traditional geographical regions. In 1997 the North American Numbering Plan Administration assigned the 501 area code to metropolitan central Arkansas and five years later designated 479 for the northwest Arkansas metro corridor. Calls to the remainder of the state, fifty-six of the seventy-five counties, began with 870. The need to provide the large urban centers with their own area codes reflected not only population consolidation but also the digital gaps within the state.

The proliferation of cellular phones in central and northwest Arkansas households exhausted all the possible configurations of phone numbers. The state public service commission anticipated that the 870 service area—more rural, tied more closely to the historic economies and institutions—would need to be subdivided by 2013, but the continued loss of population in many of these counties postponed any new demarcation. Cultural identifications tied to living in the hills, or in the lowlands, or along ridges and rivers blurred in a technological era when one's phone number revealed a great deal about life and livelihood.

Urbanization slowed in Arkansas. Forty years after the census revealed the state crossed the threshold from majority rural to urban, the 2010 count reported slightly over 56 percent of residents living in incorporated towns of 2,500 or more compared to 80 percent of Americans overall. Among southern states, only Mississippi had a smaller proportion of town dwellers. Not unexpectedly, the average number of Arkansans per square mile was only 64 percent of that for the nation overall.

In contrast to lightly settled western states where the few towns were separated by empty spaces, Arkansas communities were scattered and numerous. Nearly 23 percent of the population lived in towns with 50,000 or more residents, but those centers totaled only 9 out of the 541 populated places identified by the census bureau. Around a fifth of the state's communities had fewer than two hundred people, and these were home to a mere 0.5 percent of the population. Even as the state's larger towns claimed a greater share of the population, the total number of places where people resided had continued to rise since 1970 when the census located 476 such enclaves.

The appliances and consumer amenities enjoyed by town residents were no longer beyond the reach of rural households in the years leading up to the twenty-first century. Satellite dishes blossomed in front of country houses located beyond cable television lines, and local Internet service providers, the mom-and-pop enterprises of the early digital era, cast a wide net throughout the state. By 2000 users impatient with slow speeds and inconvenience discarded the once ubiquitous dial-up modems that had been attached to existing telephone lines. Those households without access to broadband digital service trudged in virtual space on the wrong side of a new urban-rural divide.

By 2015 the state floundered at the bottom of connectivity rankings. Only a third of rural Arkansans compared to slightly over half of rural Americans were able navigate the web at the Federal Communications Commission's (FCC) minimum broadband standard of 25 megabits per second (mbps) download speed. On accepting an appointment to the FCC's Broadband Deployment Advisory Committee, an executive for an Arkansas technology company insisted more than idle surfing was at stake: "There are many unserved and underserved people in our state, and broadband is a huge economic driver."

In the 1930s farmers were generally early adopters of technology that made economic sense, whether radios that delivered weather forecasts and commodity reports or vehicles that could reach markets over rutted roads. In the 2010s Arkansas farmers dispatched drones over their fields to monitor crops and soil conditions. Yet the expense of the infrastructure, just as it had once kept farm houses in the dark, checked the transmission of broadband.

In 2016 the heads of three electrical cooperatives, citing the years when their companies battled the investor-owned utilities to string power lines into the countryside, set up partnerships to speed Internet to rural areas over fiber optic wires. Their for-profit competitors who wanted the same internet customers disputed the history lesson, although continuing to rely upon solicitous legislators. In 2011 the General Assembly checked competition by restricting municipalities seeking to offer broadband to residential or business customers.

In one sense, the telecommunications companies, which along with cable operations dominated the broadband market, were on target in arguing things had changed. In the earlier era, Harvey Couch, the utility magnate, failed to secure for AP&L the federal support that instead went to the cooperatives. In 2015 the FCC awarded federal grants through its "Connect America" program to communications companies to extend services to "rural areas where the cost of broadband deployment might otherwise be prohibitive." AT&T gained $428 million each year to connect underserved areas in eighteen states, including Arkansas. After initially balking, the telecommunications giant gave in to the FCC demand to deliver 10 mbps download speeds to customers rather than a sluggish 4 mbps. In 2019 Arkansas still had a higher proportion of residents without access to adequate broadband speeds than almost any other state. The legislature that year modified constraints that kept municipalities from providing broadband service. Under a new measure the government entities could apply for grants and loans to build infrastructure to speed internet access to underserved areas. The sponsor of the bill observed that Arkansas stood out in raising roadblocks to widespread broadband delivery.

Private telecommunications companies also emerged victorious in competition for public dollars to bring broadband speeds to all Arkansas school districts, an advantage that only a fraction of the districts enjoyed before 2015. The legislature refused to allow schools to tie into the public high-speed network serving state-supported higher education institutions and eventually twenty private firms contracted to wire the districts. In 2017 Arkansas was among a handful of states in which all districts provided their classes broadband speeds. An out-of-state consultant on technology use in education commended the accomplishment: "Look, Arkansas took a situation where the state was one of the worst in the nation in terms of effectively using the resources that they have, and they've turned it into one of the best." The bulk of those resources deployed by the state for the project came from federal coffers.

INTO THE TWENTY-FIRST CENTURY, Arkansans continued to take jobs in cities without moving to them. They put more miles on their vehicles than other Americans, and the daily commuting time in a state without a large metropolitan center still approached the national average. In central Arkansas, about 85 percent of the over 300,000 residents traveling to work drove alone while less than 1 percent took mass transit. The solo commuters pushed the region to eighth among the 100 largest urbanized areas for freeway use. Little Rock had extended its biking trails, but they were primarily used for recreation.

In fact, in 2015 the area ranked 230th among the nation's 392 metro regions in the number of people cycling to a job.

In 2014 the state highway department proposed adding additional traffic lanes to ease daily snarls on a section of the interstate highway adjacent to Little Rock's business center. Opposition arose and the debates revived familiar charges that municipal and business elites prized development and suburbanization over neighborhood integrity and invigorating low-income precincts. Supporters for widening the highway, labeled the "30 Crossing," charged that concocting alternative routes to the existing corridor ignored traffic patterns and risked pushing the highway department to spend its millions elsewhere. The chair of the metro regional chamber of commerce challenged those who insisted road expansion fed sprawl, noise, and pollution: "I've been in the real estate business for almost 35 years. If you look at downtown Little Rock, there's a freeway there now. I heard someone say it was depressing. There's beautiful, active development going on in downtown Little Rock, and there's a freeway there."

Opponents to widening the freeway cited the destruction of the African American commercial district along Ninth Street as the poisoned legacy of the Wilbur Mills Expressway, the freeway smoothing the commute to the western suburbs. A 2016 essay in *The Atlantic* that scoffed at the ambitious 30 Crossing concluded with a description of a ghost walk along the once vital "Line": "Now, there are few homes, and those that exist seem empty. There are also few local stores. We walked down the street, and as the highway hummed nearby, we found a sidewalk where people used to walk. Today, it disappears into overgrown grass."

While community organizations insisted that the new project was a concrete boundary dividing neighborhoods, an African American city-council member defended enlarging the freeway by emphasizing that her constituents had little choice but to travel that route to work. Early in the 30 Crossing's development, preservation forces moved quietly to create a buffer between the section of a neighborhood near MacArthur Park that was listed on the National Register of Historic Places and the proposed thoroughfare.

Urban liberals in Little Rock, much as their counterparts in other American cities, incorporated into their agenda advocacy for a compact residential downtown sector that was pedestrian-friendly and offered niche retail outlets as well as entertainment venues. These goals, as opposed to those touching upon race and class, dovetailed with the investment strategies of sundry real estate developers, historically the nemeses of the progressives. Taking note of the success of urban revitalization in Memphis during the 1990s, Jimmy Moses and Rett

Tucker (whose father, Everett Tucker, was a moderate segregationist board member during the Little Rock crisis) led the way in launching mixed commercial and condominium developments. They grasped the opportunities for downtown in the wake of the failed Metrocentre Mall experiment that had blockaded Main Street. The area offered other advantages; investors setting their sights on older buildings reaped federal restoration tax credits based on the fieldwork of preservationist experts keen to save historic properties.

Municipal leaders and media commentators credited entrepreneurial drive oiled by public subsidies for giving rise to what was dubbed the River Market District. The William Jefferson Clinton Presidential Center and Library opened in 2004 in a nearby warehouse quarter. The adjacent Clinton School of Public Service, established as part of the University of Arkansas system in 2004, along with the nearby Heifer Project International headquarters, an anti-poverty nonprofit that provided livestock to communities in developing nations, and Winrock International, established by the former governor to boost economic growth in tandem with resource development, made Little Rock the unexpected home of philanthropic enterprises with a global reach. These centers along with the subsequent Main Street residencies of fine arts organizations and arrival in 2017 of the Little Rock Technology Park, bolstered claims by downtown promoters that the capital city was finally in step with the New Urbanism movement. "In cities big and small, trends across the country show the live, work and play mantra is working. Each piece enhances the next to create a part of town where people want to be and to be seen. Downtown has become cool again," observed the director of the tech park, an entity underpinned by local taxes.

Yet population growth in the central Arkansas metro area, spanning six counties, rose faster outside the Little Rock city limits. The urban core's proportion of jobs dropped as well. Jobs in the central business district declined nearly 40 percent between 1980 and 2010 while they increased in the western suburbs and the surrounding cities. In 2017 Metroplan, the region's planning agency, calculated that 44 percent of the population in the metropolitan area lived outside Pulaski County, the location of the principal cities of Little Rock and North Little Rock, compared to 32 percent in 1990. Even with new residents snapping up condominiums in downtown high-rises, the number of people moving to Pulaski County between 2001 and 2015 roughly equaled the number who left. Migration did not contribute to the county's population rise. Little Rock officials could take heart that the shift away from the big city was even more pronounced nationwide; by 2000 American suburbanites outnumbered those residing in central cities.

In late 2017 the small congregation of the Quapaw Quarter United Methodist Church voted to sell the impressive but deteriorating building that had once been home to the largest Methodist membership in the state. The 1920s-era building was on the National Register, but the church pews emptied as members moved from the historic downtown neighborhood to the western developments. One member after the vote summarized the dilemma facing historic structures: "Who wants to be part of a sinking ship? Even if it's a beautiful ship."

Little Rock/North Little Rock continued to record the highest rates of poverty in the central Arkansas metropolitan region, although the rise of low-wage retail and service jobs with few benefits led to a growing share of residents in the commuter towns treading water below the poverty line.

Between 1990 and 2010 the black population rose in three of the five suburban central Arkansas counties. Yet, as had been true throughout the late twentieth century, the African American proportion of the population in Pulaski County exceeded that of the state as a whole while the orbiting counties were whiter than other Arkansas locales, with the exception of the upland regions. In 2010 whites slightly outnumbered blacks within Little Rock, but the exponential growth of Latino residents shifted the capital to a "majority-minority" city. Little Rock was more ethnically diverse than other, larger urban places in Arkansas, which were predominantly white. Pine Bluff was the only metro area within the state in which the majority of the population was African American. Nevertheless, the residential segregation in Little Rock, which evolved from municipal policies and real estate practices after World War II, persisted. African American and Latino neighborhoods rarely extended north of I-630 and west of I-430.

LaVerne Bell-Tolliver recalled suspicion and hostility when her middle-class family in the early 1960s moved into a white residential area west of their former neighborhood. She was the only black student in her junior high school. Eventually the white families took flight, and African Americans purchased the houses in what became once more a single-race area. John Walker, the civil rights attorney, commented in 2016 on the effect of hardening residential divisions upon the education for black students: "It's another form of segregation that precedes *Brown*. It's almost the same as *Brown*, except at the time of *Brown*, black and white people lived in proximity to each other."

THE LITTLE ROCK STORY of race and class was a familiar chapter in urban development. Little Rock was the Arkansas city that most came to resemble urban centers throughout the nation. The Fayetteville-Springdale-Rogers metro area (which also included Bentonville) traced an alternative model during a growth spurt matched by few American cities. Northwest Arkansas did not contain a single high-population core circled by suburbs and commuter towns. Instead, the major cities along the I-49 corridor, edging toward one another's municipal limits, had distinct economies and identities. Each revolved around a dominant industry. Tyson Foods (Springdale) was the second-largest area employer, followed by the University of Arkansas (Fayetteville) and J. B. Hunt (Lowell/Rogers). Bentonville, propelled by the ascent of Walmart and the influx of vendors seeking favor with the retailer, outdistanced the others in both personal wealth and fresh subdivisions.

By the twenty-first century, downtown Bentonville, like many Arkansas small town squares, exhibited the melancholy pall of a once vibrant center that had faded with the closing of each store and professional office. A city planner in 2015 recalled what he saw upon arriving twenty years earlier: "There was a bail bondsman, a couple of smaller retail stores and a bank." Town leaders throughout the state who had learned from the folly of transforming main streets into outdoor malls took interest in big-city attempts to convert their downtown areas into high-density, walk-around retail areas that encouraged personal interactions. While the New Urbanism intended to reconfigure urban grids into intimate small-town spaces, boosters of actual small towns hoped to rejuvenate their economies by emphasizing that New Urbanism amenities were already in place. Nevertheless, friendly greetings and personal attention of shop proprietors were unlikely to lure young professionals to a town square still dominated by hardware stores, discount clothing shops, and beauty salons. Forging future prosperity through a rosy past required a great deal of work and resources.

Municipal leaders made good use of the expertise of the staff of the Arkansas Historic Preservation Program (AHPP) or employed the growing number of preservation consultant firms to reinforce the historical bona fides of their locales and secure tax credits to rehabilitate tottering but significant structures. Dozens of small town commercial districts across the state gained a listing on the National Register of Historic Places. The Main Street program of the AHPP provided assistance in design and business startups and accrued an estimable record of new ventures and store relocations to downtowns. However, town leaders discovered that recovering the bustle and energy on squares at a time before interstates, Internet, and Walmart usually demanded substantial financial investments by those willing to wait on profits and return. Downtown Bentonville was not listed on the National Register, but money was available.

Shortly after Alice Walton, the daughter of Helen and Sam Walton, announced in 2005 she was building the Crystal Bridges Museum of American Art on family land near the Bentonville square, restaurants and specialty shops began taking up leases. In 2007 voters approved a bond issue to support improvements throughout downtown, whose previous major attraction had been the Walmart museum located in the original Walton's Five and Dime. When Crystal Bridges opened in 2011 downtown space was already occupied and valuable. The 2012 total sales-tax receipts for transactions around the square was eleven times the 2008 total. Visitors could not help but be struck by the anomaly of an almost cinematic town square situated in a super-charged metropolitan growth region dominated by several of the nation's largest corporations.

Those visitors came primarily to see the art. Alice Walton and those fanning out to collect works during the museum's construction confronted wariness, indignation, and resentment that major works obtained by industrial buccaneers of the first Gilded Age were to be shifted to Arkansas thanks to the fortune of a discount retailer. That transferal of art to the American interior was, however, the point; with free admission underwritten by the Walmart corporation, school children and others throughout the region viewed pieces formerly ensconced on the coasts. Five years into its operation, the majority of the 2.7 million visitors to Crystal Bridges were Arkansans.

By that point, critics and commentators acknowledged the museum ranked among the finest in the country. The praise mounted in 2014 when the museum organized a massive exhibit based upon the travels of curators to meet and confer with nearly 1,000 artists throughout the nation. The *New York Times* called the unprecedented show "a snapshot of unheralded 21st century art." Formerly unheralded Bentonville thrived. The museum's executive director acknowledged the effect of the Walton endeavor: "While economic impact is not our purpose, it's a welcome residual benefit for the region."

In 2014 the Bentonville mayor explained that he, like many others in his booming city, had resettled from a different part of the country and found that small-town cordiality turned strangers into neighbors: "I will tell you it's been my experience that I've never seen a region that assimilates outsiders any better than Northwest Arkansas." However, one group of arrivals was not universally welcomed.

THROUGHOUT THE 1990S Hispanic migrants journeyed to the overwhelmingly Anglo locales to take up work in the poultry-processing plants. The region's civic and business establishment was confident this formula to ease the chronic labor turnover for Tyson Foods would also stimulate the economy as a whole. The mayor of Rogers did his part by forming a soccer club and encouraging banks to finance home loans.

A backlash followed. The Americans for Immigration Moratorium emerged and gained members who charged that the newcomers, who overwhelmingly had moved from the western United States, were responsible for rising crime and unwarranted burdens on public services. The movement consolidated in 1998 around the candidacy of Steve Womack, who ousted the incumbent Rogers mayor with a promise of "zero toleration for illegal immigration." In 2007 Mayor Womack along with county officials in northwest Arkansas became among the few local government leaders in the United States to sign up law-enforcement personnel for training to enforce federal immigration regulations.

Following his election, Womack set up a community center that scheduled English language classes and supplied guides for local services and assistance. Nevertheless, those in the pioneering Latino wave into Arkansas from the western United States relied upon family and neighbors before developing more formal support associations. In 1996 Margarita Solorzano moved from California to find that her new home offered little else beyond employment: "This part of Arkansas did not have the infrastructure to support the needs of any diversity. When the Latinos started to come, people did not understand their needs or didn't know how to provide services." In 1999 she along with others formed the Hispanic Women's Organization of Arkansas, which first offered mentoring to girls before proceeding to prepare residents for naturalization and voter registration. Despite these efforts, the proportion of naturalized citizens among the state's immigrant population in 2010 was well below the national average

By 2000 the state's central urban core drew a greater share of Arkansas-bound Latinos, many of whom found reasonable housing near the African American working class section of southwest Little Rock. In this neighborhood emerged markets and panaderías that sold corn husks for tamales, mole sauce, and *roscas de Reyes*, while taquerías, first confined to small storefronts then igniting the food-truck wave, offered customers an antidote to commercial Tex-Mex cuisine. One of the early migrants to Little Rock, Maria Rodriquez echoed the sense of displacement and initial isolation expressed by Solorzano: "At first we felt alone. I still miss my family in Mexico, but now there are many Hispanic families." A significant proportion of the Latino population, though never the majority, were foreign born (primarily from Mexico and El Salvador) but these immigrants had also lived elsewhere in the United States before shifting to Arkansas.

Latinos made the move to the state from California and Texas to not only find stable employment and low housing costs but also from a conviction that crime and violence were less rampant in smaller towns and cities. Into the twenty-first century the dispersion of the Hispanic population penetrated the rural sections of the state that were outside the high-growth areas but still in need of workers for animal-processing operations. Latinos made up nearly eleven percent of DeQueen's population in 1990 and a majority of the nearly 7,000 residents twenty years later. The town, however, was the only urban area in the state with those demographics. In 2010, 7 percent of Arkansans were Hispanic.

The ninefold increase in the Latino population between 1990 and 2010 propelled Arkansas to among the top states in the growth of its immigrant and Hispanic population. The Pew Hispanic Center estimated that in 2010 unauthorized residents represented 42 percent of the state's immigrants, a proportion that exceeded the national average but one that held steady during the Great Recession. Although fewer found their way to Arkansas after 2010, Latinos were still more likely to be found living in the Northwest section and working in poultry plants and construction. They remained a rising share of Arkansas workers, particularly compared to whites, whose workforce participation declined after 2000. Arkansas's unemployment rate coming out of the Great Recession fell below the national rate, but the state had a greater proportion of people who had stopped looking for work altogether due to retirement or discouragement.

Not only had the numbers of manufacturing jobs diminished nationally in the century's second decade, but employees were abandoning those positions for less strenuous work with a more promising future. In a comprehensive 2013 analysis of the effect of immigration on Arkansas, the Winthrop Rockefeller Foundation concluded that the availability of immigrants in the tight manufacturing labor market saved employers $52 million in wages: "These labor costs savings kept Arkansas's businesses competitive, while being passed on in the form of lower prices to US consumers." Those in Arkansas who asserted that the newcomers undermined wage levels and disrupted cultural traditions countered that the economic benefits did not extend far beyond corporate suites.

When the debate over curbing immigration flared once more during the 2016 presidential campaign, a state newspaper reporter checked on the mood in DeQueen. The proprietors of Panaderia La Colmena bakery, El Paisano food stand, and La Carniceria Nueva meat market emphasized immigrants buoyed the local economy and were self-sufficient strivers: "They're honorable, decent, dependable family people with kids who go to college," explained Israel Ortiz, a native of Mexico, whose son had earned a degree from the University of Arkansas at Little Rock.

The state's voters strongly supported in that election Donald Trump, who pledged to shutdown crossings at the border with Mexico and apprehend large numbers of unauthorized migrants. Yet independent polling of state residents revealed a range of views on the status of immigrants. In the 2015 Arkansas Poll, 60 percent of respondents favored a pathway to citizenship for undocumented immigrants, while 25 percent supported deportation of all such individuals. Sixty-five percent of respondents to a 2015 nationwide survey by the Gallup Poll also backed a plan to permit immigrants to remain and seek legal status, while 19 percent preferred deportation. In June 2018 Arkansans in Benton and Washington Counties participating in a Talk Business/Hendrix college poll split over whether they backed the Trump administration's policy, announced that April but reversed in June, to separate children from parents accused of entering the United States illegally. In the survey, 47 percent of those questioned opposed the policy, while 40 percent endorsed it. A Quinnipiac University poll conducted at roughly the same time showed two-thirds of Americans overall objecting to the administration's approach.

BEFORE LATINO MIGRANTS spied opportunity in Northwest Arkansas industries, another set of newcomers deemed the rural Ozarks a haven from industrialization and the consumer mainstream. The 1930s back-to-the-landers were refugees from the collapse of the modern economy, but the 1970s wave settled into upland farm tracts as a utopian alternative to a society that had sacrificed authentic and plain living for stultifying prosperity. Natives warily regarded the outsiders' counterculture garb and outlook but were won over in part by their new neighbors' deference to those who knew the lay of the land and how to live off of it. A youthful settler recalled that a nearby family sheltered her and her husband when winter caught them unprepared: "I'm sure they thought that we were crazy but they wanted to teach us their ways [because] we were interested. They embraced us. We embraced them." By some estimates, up to six thousand back-to-the-landers moved to the region but the migration and many of their farms did not endure deep into the 1980s.

Another group in the 1970s, mistaking the Ozarks for a wilderness offering space and isolation for defiant alternatives to modern America, conspicuously kept their distance from the local population. In 1976 James Ellison carved out a compound in Marion County a few miles south of the Missouri line as the new redoubt for a militant racist organization he had founded five years earlier. The Covenant, the Sword, and the Arm of the Lord (CSA), which may at one point have enlisted up to one hundred members, stockpiled weapons and supplies to prepare for an anticipated confrontation with a despotic government hostile to whites and controlled by Jewish financiers. In April 1985 after a four-day standoff, federal, state, and local law enforcement entered the CSA site, confiscated weapons, and arrested key leaders. The nonviolent resolution followed negotiations involving Robert Millar, Ellison's self-described spiritual advisor, and the U.S. Attorney, Asa Hutchinson, who memorably donned a flak jacket before entering the compound. Ellison agreed to supply evidence against other violent white supremacists in exchange for a reduced sentence.

The following year, Hutchinson was the Republican nominee for the U.S. Senate but failed to turn Dale Bumpers out of office. After serving his sentence, Ellison settled in Elohim City, another anti-Semitic, racial-purity movement outpost founded by Millar in the Oklahoma Ozarks west of Fort Smith. The site was a hilly way station for radical right figures in transit and for residents awaiting the fulfillment of the founder's prediction: "We're going to have civil war and race riots. . . . I believe that the inheritors of the promises of the 12 tribes of Israel are primarily the Celtic tribes."

Before the 1970s the prevalence of evangelical Protestant churches and absence of African Americans persuaded a long-standing advocate of religiously oriented movements of intolerance that the Ozarks had the makings of the Promised Land. In 1964 Gerald L. K. Smith, a perpetual candidate for high office and publisher of the anti-Semitic *The Cross and the Flag* magazine, retired to Eureka Springs and decided to make it the site for outsized commemorations to his career. The following year he commissioned the building of a seventy-foot statue of Jesus Christ. A rigid concrete rendering without grace or realism, the *Christ of the Ozarks* was the first stage of Smith's quest for immortality. By 1968 he had built a 6,000-seat amphitheater hollowed out of the side of a mountain to stage a production of the final days before the crucifixion of Christ. The sold-out performances during the warm months left *The Great Passion Play* with few peers among the nation's outdoor spectacles. The drama included a cast of 150 local actors, as well as camels, horses, sheep, and donkeys moving across a 400-foot-long stage representing a section of ancient Jerusalem.

Shortly before his death, Smith planned an amusement park duplicating the Middle Eastern shrines revered by Christians. He intended for his New Holy Land to spare devout tourists from having to visit Israel and finding themselves "paying cash to a Jew." The vision expired with its creator. Smith's crypt at the foot of the gigantic statue of Christ came to be largely ignored by those who traveled to see his handiwork. The audiences to *The Great Passion Play* dwindled after the early 1990s, and the production faced foreclosure in 2012 before last-ditch fundraising efforts allowed the curtain to go up on the 2013 season. Similar calls for donations in 2015 were needed to give the *Christ of the Ozarks* what executives for the Smith estate called "a face-lift" to smooth out "several blemishes that amounted to deteriorated concrete."

Eureka Springs flowered for decades as a center for Christian tourism, but the lovingly preserved Victorian village also drew counterculture migrants attracted by its seemingly eccentric detachment from contemporary tumult. The long-haired free spirits jostled against the devout *Passion Play* ticket-holders along the narrow streets of shops filled with mountain craft kitsch. Otto Earnest Rayburn and other promoters of the Ozark Romance from the 1930s might have been satisfied that hill traditions became less often the source of humor while regretting their preservation as consumer artifacts.

Another set of entrepreneurs, seeing how Smith's Sacred Projects drew profit from those with common beliefs and backgrounds, catered to a community whose shared identity ranged outside the *Passion Play*'s target demographic. Brock Thompson inarguably observed that just as evangelicals throughout the region made the pilgrimage to Smith's unfinished New Jerusalem, so also did gays and lesbians, who patronized "with the power-wielding tourist dollars in their pockets" recently opened bars and bathhouses.

In 1972 Barbara Scott, late of New Orleans, bought the New Orleans Hotel in Eureka Springs as a restful escape from urban stress for other lesbians. She soon leased the hotel bar to gay and lesbian proprietors who also perceived more opportunity in an Ozark niche than in their Crescent City home. Their success set in motion an LGBT chain migration that raised the shutters on boarded-up businesses and created venues that reflected the identity, taste, and culture of the new owners and clientele. Gay and lesbian newcomers encountered some hostility but generally fell into the same informal coexistence that had marked the interactions of hippies and middle-American churchgoers. Barbara Scott recalled the diversity of the hotel bar customers: "The straights came in because it was the happening place to be." Jan Ridenhour, who moved from Boulder, Colorado, in the late 1980s with her partner, noted in 2008: "In Eureka, there are no gay bars, but no straight bars. Everyone's accepted here." Steve Roberson and his partner advertised their Rock Cottage Gardens in both general tourism papers and LGBT publications as a romantic weekend respite, but "no children, please." Both straight and gay couples regularly and repeatedly booked stays.

A tottering spa in the interior Ozarks that gained a reprieve through the investment of proceeds from a career promulgating bigotry seemed an unlikely destination for those all too familiar with bigotry. Michael Walsh wished to trade Chicago for a rural residence but was doubtful when friends explained that Eureka Springs was a rare small town that would welcome a gay man: "I had the northerners' perspective of Arkansas as a backward, hillbilly place." After his relocation, Walsh discovered that Eureka Springs was "a mosaic of people." A town that depended upon its appeal to travelers and outsiders had successively accommodated itself to the summer crowd drawn by embalmed quaintness, those curious about Ozark folkways, the audiences moved by the *Passion Play*, the hippies, and the LGBT entrepreneurs. The isolation of the mountain community gave space for divergence and crisscrossed paths.

Kristin Seaton and Jennifer Rambo of Fort Smith slept in their car overnight in Eureka Springs and were waiting at the Carroll County courthouse on Saturday, May 10, 2014, when the county clerk's office opened. That day they became the first same-sex couple to receive an Arkansas marriage license. Chris Piazza, a Little Rock circuit judge, the day before had struck down a 2004 state constitutional amendment and a statute prohibiting same-sex unions: "A marriage license is a civil document and is not, nor can it be, based upon any particular faith. Same-sex couples are a morally disliked minority and the constitutional amendment to ban same-sex marriages is driven by animus rather than a rational basis. This violates the United States Constitution." The Carroll County clerk's office was the only one in the state that kept Saturday business hours; the clerk issued fourteen additional licenses to gay and lesbian couples after providing one to Seaton and Rambo. Arkansas became the first Southern state in which same-sex couples secured licenses.

Five days after Piazza's decision, the Arkansas Supreme Court ruled that the circuit judge had not addressed the full range of issues and ordered the county clerks to comply with the state law that forbade same-sex unions. By that time several hundred licenses had been issued to same-sex couples, and the Supreme Court ruling left the status of the Arkansas recipients uncertain. The state Court held off delivering a final decision until the U.S. Supreme Court the following year ruled in *Obergefell v. Hodges* that the federal Constitution protected the right of same-sex couples to marry.

Before that ruling was issued, the Eureka Springs city council had approved the state's most far-reaching ordinance prohibiting discrimination on the basis of sexual orientation or gender identity. Municipal officials slated a referendum for May 2015 after local religious leaders, including those affiliated with the Smith enterprises, circulated petitions calling for repeal of the ordinance. The executive director of *The Great Passion Play* was bitter after voters validated the council's decision by a 70 percent margin. "There is an infill of very vile, radical, vicious people in this town. They have gone around intimidating people to the point that they were afraid to get out of their homes today," asserted Randall Christy. Yet he also insisted that the faithful from out-of-town should not alter their plans to see the *Passion Play.* "I think Eureka Springs is beautiful. I think it is a wonderful place for people to come to. I don't think tourists have anything to worry about at all."

The ordinance was nullified two months later when Act 137 (2015) took effect. The Arkansas General Assembly, in anticipation of proposals headed for approval in Eureka Springs and Fayetteville, banned local measures that prevented discriminatory actions against LGBT individuals. In February 2017 the state Supreme Court upheld the act, unanimously setting aside the Fayetteville anti-discrimination ordinance. The ruling stipulated that the state's 1993 civil rights measure did not include sexual orientation or gender identity among protected classes. A Carroll County justice of the peace acknowledged that while Eureka Springs could not enforce its anti-discrimination measure it could advertise to visitors the popular support for the ordinance: "You are safe and welcome here. That's really all we can do."

A Pew Research Center study of 2014 poll results reported that slightly over a third of Arkansans favored same-sex marriage; only two other states posted a lower proportion of support. The Arkansas Poll, conducted by the Blair Center of Southern Politics and Society, found in its survey a slight increase in acceptance of the unions between 2013 and 2016, while the Pew Center surveys revealed that Arkansans who responded that homosexuality should be accepted rose from 27 to 45 percent between 2007 and 2014.

CHURCH ATTENDANCE in Arkansas largely mirrored the rest of the South, although an even greater percentage of white Arkansans were evangelical Protestants and affiliated with congregations in the Southern Baptist Convention. Reflecting the pattern throughout the South, the number of African Americans who were members of the National Baptist Convention was about double that of those who were adherents of the Church of God in Christ (COGIC), a denomination whose origins rested in the state. The 2010 Religious Census revealed that Arkansas was nineteenth in the United States in National Baptist membership; COGIC followers in the state worshipped in almost as many if smaller congregations than the Baptists, and their numbers placed the state fifteenth in comparison to the denomination's members nationwide.

Overall, the state's residents were as likely as those throughout the region to attend religious services at least once a week. Those sitting in the pews of white Protestant churches shared a socially conservative outlook that molded the state's political culture. Nevertheless, the modern evangelical consensus did not infallibly mirror the stands of earlier generations of Protestant activists. Individual behaviors once denounced from pulpits achieved legal standing in Arkansas.

In 2005 Governor Mike Huckabee, who was also a Southern Baptist preacher, allowed to become law without his signature a measure that opened casinos at the Oaklawn Park horse-race track in Hot Springs and the Southland Greyhound racing track in West Memphis. The proliferation of casinos across the Mississippi River from Arkansas as well as the tribal-owned gaming operations just over the Oklahoma line left lawmakers sympathetic to pleas for relief from the owners of the Arkansas pari-mutuel sites. The Arkansas Supreme Court in 2007 cited the "competitive disadvantage" faced by the two tracks in upholding the 2005 act that reserved for Oaklawn and Southland the right to install what the court labeled "electronic games of skill." The constitution, according to a 1956 Court decision, prohibited "games of chance."

Both racing venues expanded their facilities to house massive casino wings. Particularly after the 2011 floods shut down its competitors in Mississippi for an extended time, Southland flourished with increasing numbers of gamblers trying their luck at electronic slot machines and poker devices. Upstairs, only a handful of patrons in the stands watched the greyhounds tear after "Rusty," the mechanical rabbit lure. Even when the high waters subsided, customers continued to flock to Southland's casino. The wagering on the electronic games at Southland rose from $240 million in 2007 to $2.7 billion in 2015, while betting totals on dog racing fell 45 percent during roughly the same period. Despite warnings on the perils to family stability by a religious advocacy organization, voters in November 2018 amended the constitution to permit the full range of games at the Oaklawn and Southland casinos as well as at two new sites. Within a few months both of the historic gambling operations announced a high-rolling expansion that included hotels and more acreage for gamblers.

The revival of casino gaming in Hot Springs contributed to the city's strengthening economy, but those walking up and down Central Avenue in the second decade of the twenty-first century passed numerous vacant and deteriorating buildings, historic structures exempted from municipal code regulations. In 2014 fires destroyed the Majestic Hotel, first opened in 1902, and the Baxter building that had housed an African American hotel during the Jim Crow era. Yet the gamblers and the tourists were not deterred, and the city trailed only Little Rock in visitor numbers and dollars.

Nevertheless, the largest source of modern employment in a city that had been built on its curative waters was the health-services industry. The percentage of Garland County residents age sixty-five or older was greater than state and national levels. Retirees living in new lakefront homes required professional, technological, and pharmaceutical ministrations for their ailments rather than a vigorous massage and soaking bath. Fewer and fewer people from surrounding areas came to fill their containers with the spring waters from public jug fountains along Central Avenue. The National Park Service continued to offer treatments at the Buckstaff Bathhouse but by 2017 had leased several of the other dowagers of Bathhouse Row to private investors. Innovative and careful renovations of several buildings to house local businesses as well as an upscale hotel contributed to the hopes of city leaders that this time, braced by gambling's reprise, Hot Springs would recover its swagger.

While health considerations had been part of the arsenal of anti-alcohol proponents, moralism and religious tenets continued to be at the forefront of local option elections following World War II. Both sides, however, wearied of the expense and rancor of the wars over drink and backed a 1993 act that pushed the required number of signatures to launch a local option contest beyond what was thought politically feasible. The singular Arkansas arrangement of a balance of dry and wet counties, which often included dry townships, seemed destined to hold. Except it did not.

After 2005 a wave of long-dry counties hurdled the high bar for collecting signatures to put the demon rum question before the voters, who in most cases decided they were ready for retail liquor sales. The ranks of dry counties, most already dampened by private clubs, diminished from forty-three to thirty-five between 2000 and 2017. Both urban centers with a growing population tired of inconvenient drives to liquor stores in nearby wet counties and small towns hoping to regain economic viability and tax revenue joined in the movement. This turn away from tradition was often propelled by campaign donations from Walmart, which anticipated adding beer and wine to the grocery side of Supercenters in newly wet locations.

Liquor retailers adjacent to dry localities wrote sizable checks in bids to defeat the initiatives and preserve their customer base. A minister fighting to keep liquor sellers out of Jacksonville acknowledged his discomfort accepting aid from time-honored adversaries: "In fairness, I talked to many churches and individuals that are against it, and they were not willing to put up a dime. I utilized who was willing to help fight it. [The liquor stores] were honest with me, and I was honest with them."

In 2017 the General Assembly agreed with Walmart lobbyists that grocery stores in the state should be able to expand their wine selections beyond the authorized small winery labels. Arkansas vintners had been granted privilege of place on grocery shelves although constitutional interstate-commerce considerations required that protections be technically extended to all operations producing under 250,000 gallons a year regardless of location. The liquor store owners' association fought to no avail against the behemoth from Bentonville but were also hobbled by division among their members. County-line package stores jumped on the Walmart wagon after the retailer assured those proprietors it would not back drives to shift more counties into the wet column for eight years.

Just as grassroots local option elections (albeit with corporate cash) had introduced drink in churchly communities, Arkansas joined Florida as a groundbreaker in the South when its voters approved the legalization of medical marijuana (proposals in both states won in the same November 2016 election; the *Washington Post* insisted Florida was "the first Southern state to enact a robust medical marijuana regime" while the *Arkansas Democrat-Gazette* concluded the vote in favor of the proposed constitutional amendment "made Arkansas the first Bible Belt state" to provide marijuana to those with specified medical conditions). In the 2017 session, legislators introduced over fifty bills related to the production and dispensing of marijuana for medical purposes, several of which were designed to sabotage the purpose of the new amendment.

When the smoke cleared, the author of the amendment gave the General Assembly good grades for approving balanced regulations for the new industry. He and other advocates for prescribing medical marijuana singled out for praise Rep. Douglas House of North Little Rock, an opponent of the amendment who introduced and worked to pass measures to implement it. House explained that his antipathy toward the treatment softened when members of his church quietly admitted they had resorted to marijuana to ease acute pain and escape the ravages of opioid addiction.

The Centers for Disease Control and Prevention (CDC) tracked a quadrupling between 1999 and 2015 of deaths throughout the nation related to opioids that were either prescribed or gained illegally. By 2017 Americans under the age of fifty were more likely to die from drug overdose than other causes, and the toll was pronounced in rural communities. The CDC reported that 392 Arkansans in 2015 succumbed to overdoses and that all but nine Arkansas counties registered opioid prescription rates beyond the national average, rates placing the state behind only Alabama.

———————

ARKANSAS WAS ACCUSTOMED TO unwanted distinction during national public-health crises. The turn of the twentieth century maladies of hookworm, anemia, pellagra, typhoid fever, and tuberculosis had been vanquished by breakthroughs in medical treatments, expanding health services, and subsiding of deep rural poverty. Those twenty-first century Arkansans continuing to live in the most impoverished rural counties suffered tragically from modern ailments that insured the state's consistent ranking as among the unhealthiest in the nation. In 2015 personal behaviors—smoking, obesity, inactivity—associated with and amplified by social and economic conditions—low income, substandard housing, violent crime—placed Arkansas near the bottom nationally in premature deaths. Arkansas was among the five states that had the highest rate of residents dying of cancer, heart disease, stroke, and chronic lower respiratory diseases such as emphysema and bronchitis. The Robert Wood Johnson Foundation drew a striking conclusion from the data: "Each year, over 1,300 deaths in Arkansas could be avoided if all residents in the state had a fair chance to be healthy."

Of all the forms of dying that were more common in Arkansas than in the rest of the United States, infant mortality was among the most preventable. Babies born prematurely often suffered from illness and death before their first birthdays. Teenage mothers more often than older women gave birth before term, and Arkansas was unremittingly one of the leading states in the number of teenage births. The state followed the national trend of a declining birth rate to mothers between the ages of fifteen and nineteen but at a slower pace; between 1991 and 2015 the nation's teenage birth rate fell by 67 percent compared to the state decrease of 56 percent. This decline was greater in Arkansas for African American women than for whites. The percentage of unmarried teenagers becoming mothers was only slightly less in Arkansas than for the nation because teens in the state were more likely to be wed. The overall Arkansas fertility rate (proportion of births for every 1,000 women, ages 15 to 44) historically lagged behind the United States; but this demographic trend was reversed in the mid-1990s, and the state annually surpassed the national birth rate into the twenty-first century.

Despite the state's comparatively high birth rate, the size of Arkansas households fell below the national average. The state's families fractured often. Arkansans not only married earlier but also filed for divorce more frequently. Children in the state were less likely than those in the nation as a whole to be in two-parent families and more often living with neither parent. The smaller households of the state's large number of retirees were balanced by the many elderly Arkansans who took in grandchildren to rear.

More than 40 percent of single-parent families struggled below the poverty line between 2012 and 2015, compared to just over 10 percent of married-couple households. Single women were predominately the earners in these Arkansas families, and the wage gap between them and single fathers was even larger than the overall divide between that of men and women employees. Yet women in the state after 2000 were less and less likely to be employed. By 2014 Arkansas was near the bottom among states in the percentage of women earning money on the job. In addition, that income was less than that earned by women in nearly every other state, although the annual earnings had not declined for the state's women as it had for Arkansas men in the new century. Arkansas women remained concentrated in healthcare support (88 percent of the workers in this profession were female according to the 2011–2015 U.S. Census Bureau survey), teaching and library services (77 percent), and office support positions (75 percent). Women also continued to hold down jobs in the apparel and food-processing sectors.

Arkansas women along with those in other states made up an increasing proportion of those sitting in college classrooms, and after 2010 a larger percentage held bachelor and higher degrees than male Arkansans. Arkansas usually surpassed only one state in percentage of total higher-education degree holders, but women's heavy representation in education fields led to a greater proportion of female employees holding professional or managerial posts compared to men. An analysis of census figures by American Express found that the number of Arkansas firms owned by women between 2007 and 2016 had grown by over 42 percent, not far behind the national 45 percent growth. The report also noted that employment in those businesses had dropped 10 percent and that sales over the period edged up an anemic 2 percent.

NEVERTHELESS, a number of start-ups prospered by offering new products welcomed by unforeseen niche markets. In 1982 Patricia Upton added home-made scent to a collection of pine cones, berries, and acorns to help a storeowner friend in Heber Springs boost her Christmas trade. Upton had pioneered the decorative home fragrance industry and her company, Aromatique, grew to serve an international clientele. Kerry McCoy parlayed $400 to jumpstart Arkansas Flag & Banner in Little Rock. She expanded the company from catalog and mail-order sales to designing and producing a variety of flags for retail outlets, including Walmart, as well as for individuals.

A story appearing in *Arkansas Business* shortly before Olivia Farrell made the weekly publication the flagship of her Arkansas Business Publishing Group documented that only 3 percent of the state's corporate board members were women. Farrell recalled the uniformity of the boards "really flew all over me, because that was ridiculous, just ridiculous," and in 1995 she published the first edition of the "Top 100 Women in Arkansas" to demonstrate the abundance of candidates who had escaped the notice of business heads.

The annual lists provided Pat Lile a reservoir of donors to establish the Women's Foundation of Arkansas. The organization produced reports on the status of women in the state and launched initiatives to promote career development, particularly in the sciences and mathematics. In addition to Lile, who headed the Arkansas Community Foundation, the numerous other founders hailed generally from law (including Audrey R. Evans, chief judge of the U.S. Bankruptcy Court), politics (Charlotte T. Schexnayder, former state representative and president of the National Federation of Press Women), and education (Cora McHenry, former president of the Arkansas Education Association).

The 1994 *Arkansas Business* story also highlighted that the proportion of African Americans on company boards was even lower than those filled by white women. In the 1990s black men tended to work in the older, lower-paid lumber sector of manufacturing, while white men were over-represented in the more lucrative metal and machinery production industries. The difference between black and white income in Arkansas was even more profoundly unequal than the gap existing for the nation as a whole. This disparity endured. The 2011–2015 census survey revealed the income gap persisted as African Americans continued to earn less than whites. Arkansas white households also enjoyed higher levels of Social Security and public cash assistance payments than black residents.

By 2015 African American men and women filled jobs disproportionately in service occupations as well those involving the moving and hauling of goods. Yet the steady growth in numbers of black professionals since 1959 continued into the new century. African American women were more likely to hold management positions than were black men, while a greater percentage of African American employees than whites worked at various levels of government. The long-standing urban addresses of black Arkansans were critical in providing a wider range of professions and occupational opportunities than in the collapsed rural economies. In 2015 62 percent of African Americans were residing in urban centers while 55 percent of white Arkansans called such places home. The heart of contemporary black Arkansas remained the central metro region; nearly 40 percent of African Americans in the state lived in Jefferson and Pulaski Counties alone.

The number of both white and black Arkansans holding bachelor's degrees or higher grew by two-thirds between 1989 and 2015. In that same time span, the proportion of white households bringing in an income of $50,000 and higher grew by 170 percent while the percentage of African American households in that income range increased four times. Beginning in 2003, the Anderson Institute of Race and Ethnicity at the University of Arkansas, Little Rock, conducted annual surveys of African American and white residents in Pulaski County. The participants revealed diverse reactions toward discernible black progress in an economy still marked by racial inequality.

A larger number of white respondents were satisfied with their current circumstances and believed they had obtained the "American Dream," but African Americans were more confident they would reach the American Dream and that their children would fare better than the current generation. All of those surveyed cited hard work as the key to advancement, but African Americans more often than whites noted that connecting with influential people opened doors. Blacks were more likely than whites to underscore the importance of a college degree. The respondents agreed that money, success, and freedom were the hallmarks of the American Dream. In 2014 African Americans calculated the minimum income that gave access to middle-class status was higher than what whites believed necessary. The successive surveys uncovered the more tenuous status of African American households and a keener appreciation for what was required to insure financial security. Black respondents were more apprehensive at the prospect of job loss, rising housing expenses, and falling short of a decent retirement than were whites.

African Americans polled over the course of the survey increasingly related that they made a point to do business with black-owned firms. A smaller proportion of African Americans ran their own businesses than did whites but, as was so with female entrepreneurs, found profit in serving neglected sectors. Myron Jackson established his communications firm in 2007 to help companies reach diverse ethnic markets. Jackson noted that marketing campaigns had not reached all customers even in a city with an abundance of advertising enterprises: "Brands were struggling, and we made the point that when companies were spending 100 percent of their advertising dollars to reach the general market, i.e. white people, in a town like Little Rock, that meant tearing a dollar bill in half and throwing half away." The Arkansas Economic Development Commission counted 460 minority-owned companies, ranging from those providing behavioral and counseling treatments, translations and Spanish-language materials, security consultation for medical marijuana operations to more traditional construction contractors and suppliers of office materials for government agencies.

Arkansas established a goal that 10 percent of state government discretionary procurement budgets be extended to minority-owned firms and in 2017 set a 5 percent goal for firms owned by women. In neither case were the goals mandatory. But state spending with minority companies did increase from 2.5 percent in 2011 to 7.5 percent in 2015.

V. Arkansas Culture:
Fields of Memory, Stones of History

In 1991 Kerry McCoy purchased Taborian Hall in Little Rock to house her Arkansas Flag and Banner. The Knights and Daughters of the Tabor, a black-owned fraternal insurance association, opened for business in 1918, and during World War II the USO hosted dances for African American soldiers at the Dreamland Ballroom on the hall's third floor. McCoy soon fixed the hole in the roof as the first step in restoring what had been one of the anchors of the Ninth Street commercial and cultural district. A fundraising campaign underwrote the beginning in 2010 of the restoration of the Dreamland Ballroom. Soon supporters raised additional funds by renting out for events the space that had once hosted Duke Ellington and Count Basie. By that time, Taborian Hall was the only remaining structure from Ninth Street's halcyon era. After the original 1913 headquarters of the Mosaic Templars Mutual Aid Society burned in 2005, the state and the city provided funds to construct a three-story replica to house the Mosaic Templars Cultural Center.

Opening in 2008, the center was the museum within the Department of Arkansas Heritage (DAH) system established "to collect, preserve, interpret and celebrate Arkansas's African American history, culture, and community from 1870 to the present." The growth of an intellectual infrastructure to support and promote the study of the state's history had encouraged the exploration of topics and developments that had been either ignored or warped by celebratory preconceptions.

The University of Arkansas Press, beginning in 1980, brought out valuable studies that would have been of little interest to publishers outside the state. Launched in 2006 by the Butler Center for Arkansas Studies of the Central Arkansas Library System, the online *Encyclopedia of Arkansas History and Culture* soon snared over a million and half visits annually because of its authoritativeness and its wiki-like expanse of entries (though vetted by editors and specialists). The Arkansas Historical Association prospered with healthy fund balances along with steady membership, and its journal published scholarship that provoked reconsideration of topics first covered by essays in its earliest editions. The Association's annual meetings recognized through a cavalcade of awards the robust health and energy of local historical associations and their journals.

The state's first rediscovery of its history in the 1930s had been subsidized by federal dollars, but state funds underwrote the late twentieth-century renaissance. In 1987 the General Assembly increased the tax on real estate transfers and allotted a portion to the DAH and to the Arkansas Historic Preservation Program. The staff of the preservation program aggressively combed the state to locate properties for possible inclusion on the National Register of Historic Places. Sites on the Register were eligible for rehabilitation grants and tax credits. Moving beyond Victorian homes and dramatic architectural showplaces, the program documented the significance of main-street commercial buildings, highway bridges, crop storage facilities, and New Deal–era water towers in the lives of the wider population. The state agency was buttressed by the Historic Preservation Alliance, a nonprofit advocacy group. Professionals and lay activists in the field understood that lawmakers needed proof of larger economic benefits to justify protecting historically significant properties with public funds.

The state preservation program distilled findings from a study released in 2006 by the Center for Urban Policy Research at Rutgers University into a digestible overview and a brochure entitled "A Profitable Past." The materials announced that historic preservation contributed $970 million and over 23,000 jobs annually to the state's economy. About 90 percent of that $970 million derived from visitors seeking out historic sites, while the economic activity associated with the rehabilitation of properties accounted for much of the balance. The study's author concluded that heritage tourists made up about 16 percent of all those traveling in the state, while acknowledging that "due to limited information on heritage tourism in Arkansas, a number of estimates were necessary in order to quantify the economic impacts."

Well before the advent of the new century, a number of Arkansas communities that despaired of reopening derelict manufacturing plants or jumpstarting a resource-based economy took steps to compete for tourists by marketing elusive pasts.

By the 1980s, Helena, the old capital of the Delta blues empire, resurfaced as a destination for enthusiasts of the music pioneered by Sonny Boy Williamson and Robert Lockwood Jr. Inaugurated in 1986, each October the King Biscuit

Blues Festival attracted leading musicians and sizable crowds to the Cherry Street Historic District. The old city blocks served as period backdrops for the performances onstage, while vendors hawking crafts sidled around the street musicians hoping for attention and a few dollars.

Previously, Helena leaders had highlighted antebellum romance and Civil War campaigns as saleable pasts: "Helena. Long ago is not so far away." Those themes steadily lost favor with new leaders in Helena (which merged with West Helena in 2006), but the blues revival also wheezed as an engine of economic resurgence. The festival lost the rights to the King Biscuit name for several years after 2005, but the event continued to add more stages and attract crowds that had to be housed in a temporary campground. In 1990 DAH opened the Delta Cultural Center to bolster the community's tourism arsenal. In a mock-up studio nestled among the exhibits, John "Sunshine Sonny" Payne hosted until his death in 2018 the weekday King Biscuit Time broadcast over KFFA as he had done since 1951. Payne had begun doing odd jobs even earlier when Sonny Boy Williamson and Robert Lockwood performed at the station on the eve of the Great Migration, which left Helena a shrinking island in the deserted Delta.

The music retained legions of fans, but the blues alone could not revitalize the town in the second decade of the century. A November 2016 *Arkansas Democrat-Gazette* article covering the seventy-fifth anniversary of the radio program observed, "The museum is one of the bright spots on Cherry Street in downtown Helena-West Helena, where old and new businesses are interspersed between abandoned and crumbling historic buildings." A trickling of newcomers with high hopes opened retail shops, and a promoter organized a second music festival to fill a springtime weekend. The city also circled back to Civil War tourism, although instigating a more comprehensive and relevant focus upon emancipation and the African American military experience.

El Dorado, once among the state's leading industrial centers, reeled from the outflow of people as jobs with solid pay and benefits above the south Arkansas norm evaporated with successive factory closings. Community leaders believed the downfall of the area's signature heavy industries created an opportunity to promote a new identification with the performing arts. But the Union County town took a path more closely resembling the one followed in Bentonville that endowed cultural institutions rather than the Helena-West Helena focus upon seasonal festivals.

The Murphy Arts District, underwritten by substantial donations from the family members with a controlling interest in the oil company, inaugurated its year-round schedule of musical and theatrical events during a fall 2017 weekend that drew 21,000 to hear a range of popular music performers. A dedicated local tax and a state grant were included in the mix of funds that built an outdoor amphitheater and transformed a former automobile dealership into a music hall. The new arts district built upon the earlier revival of the courthouse square. The Mason family had purchased and restored a number of buildings that brought shops and customers into what had been a retail desert. Yet few struggling towns in Arkansas had the philanthropic wherewithal available in El Dorado to reanimate ghostly downtowns.

Jodie Mahony, who represented El Dorado in the General Assembly for nearly four decades, sponsored the 1987 bill that furnished the wherewithal to preserve historic sites through the tax on real estate transactions. While his imprint was affixed to most of the era's public education legislation, Mahony with this measure provided an incentive for state institutions and agencies to acquire vintage structures as well as to restore rather than leave to molder older properties in their inventory. The act created the Arkansas Natural and Cultural Resources Council (ANCRC), which annually awarded grants to successful applicants. Between 1989 and 2018 the Council awarded over $360 million in grants, including those that subsidized extensive repairs to the Governor's Mansion following an infestation of rats, the restoration of the campus bell tower at the University of Arkansas, Pine Bluff, and preserving local newspapers by the staff of the Arkansas History Commission (renamed Arkansas State Archives in 2016).

The Heritage Sites Office at Arkansas State University, directed by Ruth Hawkins, skillfully reaped funding from the ANCRC and from other sources to establish an eclectic set of places that represented haunting chapters in the history of the Delta: the uncharacteristically grand Lakeport Plantation near Lake Village, the Southern Tenant Farmers Museum housed in the building in Tyronza where Clay East and H. L. Mitchell operated their businesses; the home of Mary and Paul Pfeiffer in Piggott where their son-in-law, Ernest Hemingway, drafted portions of *A Farewell to Arms*; the Administration Building and childhood home of Johnny Cash, the storied country music performer, at the New Deal–era Dyess Colony; and the silent witness of the camp cemetery and lone smokestack from the hospital that once served the Rohwer Japanese American internment center in Desha County.

The Arkansas State University office earned preservation awards for attracting visitors to museum sites that authentically conveyed the history of pain and endurance in a troubled land. Cultivating heritage tourism was a tall order in the Delta. Upland communities, on the other hand, benefited from decades of promotions that constructed a past softened by the commercialization of anti-commercial habits and expressions.

THE PUBLICLY FUNDED CAMPAIGN to collect Ozark folk music before the form was compromised by commercial media was largely wrapped up by 1963, when the Arkansas Folk Festival was first staged in Mountain View in Stone County. Modern admirers of Ozark lore held that the early to mid-twentieth century versions of music and stories preserved on tape and in print were representative artifacts from an earlier, if ill-defined, era. The contemporary trek of musicians from front porch to the stage inspired a new phase of performance tourism, though one still reliant upon government support.

Jimmy Driftwood, the composer of the popular commercial ballads "Battle of New Orleans" and "Tennessee Stud," wrestled the Folk Festival from the original backers who planned to lure audiences with familiar popular tunes. Driftwood instead insisted on spotlighting performers of traditional music even as their numbers in the Ozarks dwindled. The festival nevertheless took off, and each April tens of thousands of visitors congested the Mountain View arteries to listen to a lineup of musicians who often were from outside the region.

The state director of the federal regional agency that funneled grants for rural development reckoned that the audience for the folk revival might stoke a revival in Mountain View fortunes—at least enough to upgrade the water system—if the festival had an institutional anchor. The agency head believed that establishing an Ozark Folk Center could resurrect fading artisanal traditions, but these plans were complicated by the lack of practitioners. Ozarkers realistically had gravitated toward modern livelihoods rather than trust capricious consumers of handmade crafts. When U.S. Representative Wilbur Mills smoothed the awarding of the federal grant through his customary dexterity and influence, the Center backers acknowledged that passing along folk skills was now a matter of training and pursued an affiliation with a nearby state vocational school.

No students, however, graduated with a certificate in the folk arts. The state tourism department took over the construction of the Ozarks Folk Center after the original contractor filed for bankruptcy. Department officials had little choice but to organize the center as a self-supporting state park and were uninterested in expanding their agency mission to operate a post-secondary training institute. In 1973 visitors to the new park strolled through a spacious outdoor museum with an expanded performance area, craft shops, a restaurant, and a lodge.

The early years were rocky. In 1975 Governor David Pryor cut short Driftwood's tenure as the center's musical director after the temperamental songwriter provoked quarrels among musicians when he banned amplified instruments and favored older performers. Driftwood and remnants of the traditionalist Rackensack Folklore Society retreated and entertained tourists in a venue outside Mountain View. These performances were intended as plaintive echoes of lost sounds. In reality, generations of Ozark residents had revised and shaped their musical expressions out of the tensions arising from the introduction of modern forms into rural isolation. These practical adaptions continued apart from and at odds with the long quest for authenticity.

Some investors in mountain tourism treated the Ozarks as a blank canvas for extravagant ambitions. The state tourism agency was leery when a group of Harrison business owners began to construct a theme park in Newton County modeled after the hill village in Al Capp's *Lil' Abner* newspaper comic strip. Nevertheless, official apprehensions that a showcase of un-distilled cornpone in the heart of the Ozarks would detract from the state's other attractions faded by the May 1968 opening of Dogpatch USA. Although falling short of the investors' soaring projections, solid crowds looked over the shoulders of crafters in quirky shops and applauded songs delivered by young performers costumed as Capp's characters. Former governor Orval Faubus, biding his time until his next and last campaign, accepted the invitation to manage the park, linking the state's most famous upland native to a fabricated hillbilly settlement.

Dogpatch was more profitable than other ersatz tourism venues in the hills but stumbled when a new owner began diverting revenue to construct a nearby ski resort and snow-making apparatus. This venture did not gain traction on the icy but snowless slopes of the Ozark highlands. Visitors to the region also began to bypass Dogpatch to hear once-famous musical performers stage a last hurrah at Branson, Missouri, or take amusement park rides at Silver Dollar City that promised more thrills than paddle boats, antique cars, and a mini-train circling the Newton County valley. Dogpatch gave up the ghost in 1993.

In early 2017 one of the owners of the property explained to a reporter his dream to erect a settlement where tourists could view artisans and organic growers practicing a true mountain ethic of premodern self-sufficiency rather than chuckle at market-tested stereotypes. Later that year, he leased the property to an entertainment company that trumpeted a conservative mission to confront "the desecration of American historical sites and the rise of anti-American sentiment within America's entertainment culture." The owners of Heritage USA Ozarks Resort at Historic Dogpatch, Arkansas, reported in February 2018 to an appreciative group of Jasper residents that the new park would preserve elements of the history of Dogpatch as well as offset the corrosive influence of contemporary media on families. This latest quest to wrench Ozark history in service of a cultural agenda apparently fizzled by August when Heritage USA, behind on lease payments, vacated the site.

————————————

THE MUSICAL INFLUENCES and traditions in the state were too myriad, too disparate to birth a singular Arkansas music. Arkansas musicians who were honed in those cross-currents were hard put to launch recording and touring careers by staying close to home. More than a few of those who broke out made their mark on modern popular music through innovation, experimentation, and defiance. Few Arkansans in any other line of work exerted comparable influence on American life and culture. As the raw conditions that birthed the music from cropland and ridges melted away in the twilight of the twentieth century, the succeeding generation of Arkansas-based musicians struggled to break through in an industry in which genres were endlessly sliced and blended into recombinant forms tailored to micro-audiences.

By the 1990s a coterie of performers blending rural genres that echoed past eras were grouped under the spacious umbrella of "Americana" or "roots music." Among the precursors was The Band, a group of Canadian musicians and one native of Phillips County who began as members of an Arkansas rockabilly outfit led by Ronnie Hawkins. The Band on its initial albums in the late 1960s rowed against the current of what was playing on turntables or over the radio. "It was as though psychedelia, and the so-called British Invasion, had never happened; the group played and sang like five distinct individuals working toward the same goal, not mixing together smoothly. There was a collective sound to 'the band,' but it made up five distinct individual voices and instruments mixing folk, blues, gospel, R&B, classical, and rock & roll," wrote Bruce Eder on the Allmusic.com website.

In his later solo career and after a bout with throat cancer weathered his voice, Levon Helm, the group's drummer hailing from Turkey Scratch, wrote spare, hard-furrowed songs that updated authenticity as a rebuke to hyper-technology. In 2008 the newly formed Americana Music Association named him artist of the year. Two of his albums garnered Grammy awards under the Americana category, which in 2009 had been broken off from the Contemporary Folk classification.

In 2017 the Americana Music Association presented its Trailblazer Award to Iris Dement, whose 1992 *Infamous Angel* evoked static-laced radio broadcasts from the Ryman Auditorium. The record was widely ignored by contemporary country radio stations. Dement often ascended to a keening pitch that divided listeners who associated her uncompromising austerity with the self-reliance of an

Ozark homestead. In truth, she was born near the rockabilly corridor of northeast Arkansas. Her family, like many others, could not make a living where they were and set out for California when she was only three. Charred by the Pentecostal faith, Dement composed songs respectful of her childhood hymns but acknowledging belief's ragged comfort when inexplicable misfortune and desolation blanketed individuals. She was not a traditionalist, even if she sounded like one.

Arkansas musicians in the twentieth century who made their mark nationally were steeped in gospel, blues, and fence-line country music but did narrow their sweep to register hits in specific genres with distinctive audiences. Yet more than a few of the performers grew restless and impatient with the regimen of a consistent commercial sound. With some injury to their careers, they ventured afield by blending the influences that had lured them to take up an instrument or sing out in the first place.

Sister Rosetta Tharpe and Louis Jordan never failed to turn up the heat. They delivered an ebullient but unsanctified propulsive rhythm that vibrated in the nerve endings of later rock and roll. Conway Twitty followed the Browns (Jim Ed, Maxine, and Bonnie) in sanding down the edges of country music to open the door for Nashville musicians to find a second home on the pop charts. Glen Campbell topped both charts, though discomforting CBS network executives with his frequent invitations to country performers to play on his national television show that aired from 1969 to 1972. Johnnie Taylor was the "philosopher of soul" at Stax Records in Memphis but became an uneasy disco star before making searing blues records that erased for his fans his previous incarnations. Al Green entwined his toughened rural origins with knowing sophistication in a string of 1970s soul hits. The Reverend Green, a righteous man who understood the world's possibilities, built a church in Memphis but annulled his renunciation of popular music to reunite with his old record producer at the advent of the new millennium.

Johnny Cash and Charlie Rich ran afoul of the country music establishment. Rich was never rehabilitated, even as a renegade forefather, and remained an underrated talent whose late work revealed the jazzy underpinnings of rockabilly and country. Cash lived to become an icon but on his own terms. His final six albums for the American Recordings label were stark renderings of the national songbook past and present. Cash, backed by no more musicians than would fill out a Delta house band, excavated the temporal passions from hymns and the redemptive temptations from rock in an archaic voice that at times faltered but always came around in the end.

While listeners could be forgiven for believing music born in Arkansas emerged from a generic American rural frontier, other works of art introduced freshly their creators' native state by bringing to the surface the ordinary and overlooked elements of familiar landscapes.

Newton County, the site of the rise and fall of Dogpatch, gained a parallel fictional existence as the home of Stay More, a familiar locale to readers of Donald Harington. The author began his task of platting his literary hamlet in the Ozarks of his maternal grandparents while teaching art history in New England. After publishing four novels, he returned to Arkansas and soon gained a posting at the University of Arkansas. Beginning with *Lightning Bug* (1970) and continuing through his final novel *Enduring* (2009), Harington wove the rich narrative of Stay More's history through recurring characters rather than the plumb line of chronology. He linked familiar modernist techniques of shifting perspective, multiple narrators, and inverted reality to the older oral folk conventions of direct address to the listener, unapologetic treatment of sexuality, and alteration of the facts on retelling.

The fulcrum of Harington's universe was his widely acknowledged masterpiece *The Architecture of the Arkansas Ozarks* (1975). In this lavish chronicle, Stay More's development is explicated through successive houses representing the cloistered dreams of the builders. Walking in and out of *Architecture* are characters who figure more prominently in both earlier and subsequent Harington novels. As with William Faulkner's Yoknapatawpha and Gabriel García Márquez's Macondo, Harington's village is more than the sum of the books, because its creator honestly reveals that any single description is only one of countless ways to recount the story. Harington insists that it is the task of his readers to complete his narrative and decide the fate of the characters.

Born in Union County on the opposite side of the state from Harington's universe, Charles Portis poised his strike against regional literary traditions from a different direction. Although as firmly outside the mainstream as Ozark uplanders, the characters in Portis's novels do not stay put, always pursuing something last seen falling off the horizon. More than any other major twentieth-century novelist, Portis resembled Mark Twain in portraying drifters, con artists, and cranks as foils and reproaches to established opinion. While the genteel tradition excoriated by Twain had withered long before Portis's emergence, the Arkansas author continued to find the comic form the finest instrument to uncover modern society's secret obsessions, fears, and failed hopes. In 1964 Portis abruptly ended a promising career with the *New York Herald Tribune* to return to Arkansas and write his first novel. In both *Norwood* (1966) and *The Dog of the South* (1979), the protagonists are uprooted innocents partly through their ignorance of the surrounding conditions but primarily because they do not scrutinize the internal dissatisfactions driving them to hit the road.

The flow of Portis's literary reputation would be a fit subject for one of his novels. On the one hand, he was a cult novelist or, as described in a 1998 appraisal in *Esquire*, "perhaps the most original, indescribable sui generis talent overlooked by literary culture in America." Yet he also was able to subsist as writer on the revenue from his tremendously popular *True Grit* (1968). A work of astounding craftsmanship, the novel is the purported first-person account of Mattie Ross from Dardanelle, Arkansas, who hires Marshal Rooster Cogburn to help her hunt down her father's killer after he flees into the Indian Territory. The fourteen-year-old Mattie is already imbued with bourgeois values of piety and thrift, but her demand for vengeance attracts her to the dubious Cogburn, whose taste for violence and contempt for rules make him little different from the outlaws he pursues. Her experiences on the bloody trek confirm Mattie in her independence without deflating her commonplace convictions. The serious child grows to become a somber banker and rigorous Presbyterian. Yet her recollections unintentionally reveal that riding with Marshal Cogburn saved her from an altogether ordinary life.

Even though most of Portis's characters end up back where they started, their travels become memories of a restless time when they stop doing the same thing for awhile. Ray Midge muses toward the end of *The Dog of the South*, "A lot of people leave Arkansas and most of them come back sooner or later. They can't quite achieve escape velocity."

As with many rural states without a metropolis, the literary center of Arkansas resided at the major public university in Fayetteville. The well-regarded creative writing program, established by James Whitehead and William Harrison, drew as students young poets and novelists from throughout the nation. A number, such as Ellen Gilchrist, Barry Hannah, Lee Abbott, and Lewis Nordan, earned notable literary reputations.

Teaching in the program, the poet Miller Williams shared the aesthetic of the other Arkansas writers by displaying a mastery of form without falling into sterile imitation. Williams's poetry is deceptively straightforward in both its depiction of ordinary lives and its accessible language and imagery. Yet he often displays a dexterity of technique that few can match and a high democratic purpose by making his characters intellectually curious. In 1997 Williams, a native of Hoxie, delivered the presidential inaugural poem, a commission awarded to Maya Angelou four years earlier at the first inauguration of Bill Clinton. Lucinda Williams, among the most celebrated of those turning over new ground in American music, entitled an album shortly before her father's death in 2013 after a line in one of his poems: *Down Where the Spirits Meets the Bone.* When asked when looking back whether he reflected on his individual poems or his whole body of work, Miller Williams replied, "My brain holds both visions gladly."

In 2005 Donald Harington published excerpts from a fictional autobiography of Carroll Cloar in the *Oxford American*, a literary and arts journal that would be based in Little Rock after stays in Oxford, Mississippi, and Conway. Cloar, Harington explained by way of introduction, was "Arkansas's only notable painter." Born in Crittenden County, Cloar studied in New York and secured fellowships to travel and paint in Mexico and Central America before returning in 1955 to set up his studio in Memphis. A source of Harington's affection for Cloar is their common practice of juxtaposing familiar and commonplace elements so that landscapes and communities become unfamiliar while remaining recognizable. Cloar also wields the magic realism haunting the works of Faulkner and García Márquez to transform his memories and old photographs of his native Delta into intense and bold dream environments. His paintings do not contort reality but thicken it by altering the perspectives of figures and objects. Cloar defies modern abstraction through incorporating techniques from many schools. While Cloar's deceptive vernacular style gives credence to his own candid self-assessment that his work is simply what he "saw," it also reminds the viewer that perception has multiple lenses, trained inward as well as outward. Even some of his large, sun-filled canvases of rural socials and children at play undercut the tempting romantic nostalgia with an ominous current that is more than a trick of light.

Harington suggested in the imagined Cloar "memoir" that the painter continued through remembrance and reflection to traipse the circuit of his life, always ending up where he started but with new knowledge and greater regret:

> There is a joy, and a sadness, in coming back from abroad, and in coming back to our childhood from a grown-up perspective. There is a delight in the sense of belonging, of possessing and being possessed, by the land where you were born. There is the mixed emotion of remembering places altered, people long passed: your father, whom you promised yourself you would measure against the oak tree to see which was biggest, but never did.

Born in Fayetteville, Edward Durrell Stone left and did not come back except when he took on commissions that included the design of the fine arts center at the University of Arkansas and the medical school campus in Little

Rock. His early work, such as the collaboration on New York's Museum of Modern Art, were in the International Style, but the forging of his signature blending of classical and modern characteristics became evident in his design of the Kennedy Center for the Performing Arts in Washington.

Remaining in his native Arkansas throughout his career, E. Fay Jones designed structures no less distinctive than those of Stone, though sharply contrasting in style and materials. Born in Pine Bluff, Jones grew up in El Dorado, where his first building project was an elaborate tree house with a brick fireplace. Shortly before his high school graduation, he saw at the Rialto Theatre a short film on the newly erected Johnson Wax headquarters in Racine, Wisconsin. Designed by the modernist titan Frank Lloyd Wright, the curving, light-filled structure proved to Jones that one could be both artist and builder through architecture. In 1953 Jones worked under Wright at his Taliesin workshop in Wisconsin, and the two maintained a life-long friendship. Wright was the prime exponent of the organic style, emphasizing both the internal cohesion of a building and its integration with the natural environment.

Jones did not confuse organic architecture with the preservationist impulse to restore nature to its original state. He knew the end of his craft was artifice. An architect enabled individuals to live more completely within the environment by redeeming nature's promise through thought and art. Jones insisted a well-designed building held meaning that amplified wonder: "We have the power and responsibility to shape new forms in the landscape—physical and spatial forms that will nourish and express that all-important intangible of the human condition at its spiritual best. As architects, as transformers of the landscape, we *must*."

Jones's appreciation for the sacred in everyday life led him to design primarily two types of structures: residences and places of worship. Following Jones's stint at Taliesin, John Williams recruited him for the newly established architecture program at the University of Arkansas. If Wright cared little for the expense of his projects, Jones early learned restraint by designing houses for professors whose desire for originality was checked by modest bank accounts. In 1964 Orval Faubus turned to Jones to build a large retreat on a mountainside overlooking Huntsville.

In 1978 James Reed asked Jones to design a small chapel in a wooded glade off a busy highway two miles from Eureka Springs. A self-described "frustrated cathedral builder," the architect braced the glass walls with an elaborate interior lattice that both framed the natural light and directed the vision up through ascending planes. Thorncrown Chapel brought international recognition to its creator. A series of impressive awards culminated in 1990 as Jones became one of only fifty individuals to earn the American Institute of Architects Gold Medal for lifetime achievement.

Throughout his career, Jones worked with materials at hand, learned from others but did not imitate them, and understood history without being in thrall to it. The accomplishments of the other artists coming of age in modern Arkansas emerged from what Jones called the "countenance of principles at work."

VI. Changing the Guard in a One-Party State

In August 2005 Governor Mike Huckabee rebuked U.S. Immigration and Customs Enforcement (ICE) officials for swarming into a poultry-processing plant south of Arkadelphia and rounding up 119 people suspected of residing in the country illegally. Among those arrested and facing deportation to Mexico were the parents of thirty to thirty-five children left without caretakers. "Very little thought was given to what would happen to the children, who are by the way American citizens. I hope next time the feds will operate with a little more common sense," Huckabee explained. Pronouncing the accused employees "lawbreakers," the spokesman for the ICE office in charge of the raid dismissed the Arkansas governor's criticism and emphasized that providing the accused a few days to make arrangements for the care of their children before incarceration was appropriate.

Huckabee also questioned whether working while undocumented was a crime that required the same punitive actions taken against those nabbed for violent incidents: "I resent the implication that people are making that they are illegal and they ought to be dragged out like common thugs and hauled off to sit in jails. Is a chicken plucker a greater threat than a meth dealer or a terrorist or an armed robber? I don't think so."

During that year's spring session of the General Assembly, Huckabee had endorsed a bill authored by Rep. Joyce Elliott, one of the handful of liberals in the legislature, to permit all graduates of Arkansas high schools, regardless of immigration status, to pay the lower in-state tuition rate. Elliot's measure fell short after attorney general Mike Beebe issued an opinion that the measure was at odds with federal legislation denying undocumented residents services unavailable to all other American residents. Beebe concluded the proposed bill permitted undocumented residents of the state to enjoy an advantage over students from other states who were subject to a higher rate when they enrolled in an Arkansas college. The two Republican legislators from northwest Arkansas who had requested the attorney general's opinion had earlier introduced in the session a bill to deny state services to those unable to provide proof of citizenship.

Huckabee denounced this measure filed by members of his own party as "inflammatory . . . race-baiting and demagoguery." The governor, who was also a Baptist minister, observed pointedly that the Senate sponsor often professed adherence to Christian beliefs: "I drink a different kind of Jesus juice. My faith says don't make false accusations against somebody. In the Bible, it's called 'Don't bear false witness.'" The bill died in a Senate committee.

During his presidential campaigns in 2008 and 2016, Huckabee puzzled both friends and adversaries from his Arkansas days when he laced his socially conservative views with incendiary language, particularly in the latter race. Huckabee, however, remained solicitous during these campaigns of the plight of immigrant children even as other aspirants for the GOP nomination jostled to outdo one another with hardline reprisals.

The most serious headwinds buffeting Huckabee during his two failed bids for the White House were stirred by conservative think tanks that counted on donations from an expanding circle of ideological tycoons. These institutes awarded the former Arkansas governor low grades for the steady rise in taxes and size of government during his nearly ten years in office. More often than not the increases in revenue and public services that earned Huckabee's blessings were initiated by legislators or organized interests rather than by his office.

Following the resignation of Governor Jim Guy Tucker, Huckabee had not been in office long before he beat the drums in support for a tax proposal with a checkered history and dim prospects. The state Game and Fish Commission (G&FC) had suffered a sharp setback in 1984 when voters backhanded its proposed constitutional amendment to capture the revenue from an increase of one-eighth of a cent in the general state sales tax. Counties with the busiest hunting seasons were particularly adverse to the proposal. More than a few hunters were suspicious that the agency would use the additional money to toughen enforcement and heap on regulations. Campaigns in 1986 and 1994 were aborted after legal complications kept the matter from getting to the voters. For its 1996 effort, the Commission announced it would spend the new moneys on educational programs and improving access to public lands. To improve chances for a good outcome, the G&FC estimated it could broaden support by agreeing to split the proceeds from the proposed tax with Arkansas State Parks (45 percent) as well as the Department of Arkansas Heritage (9 percent) and the Keep Arkansas Beautiful Commission (1 percent). The G&FC could not spend public money to campaign for the amendment and relied on its private foundation to raise funds. Witt Stephens Jr., son of the founder of the bond firm, chaired the foundation during the drive and encouraged the governor to get on board.

Huckabee, an avid hunter who loved to fish, had signaled his support for the tax while still lieutenant governor. His florid endorsement was both romantic and pecuniary: "Our future might be in starry skies and the views off the top of Mount Magazine, being able to sit down along the banks of the Buffalo River and put one's feet in and be run over by a tourist canoe spending lots of money." In August 1996 the new governor and first lady, Janet Huckabee, motored in a bass boat down the Arkansas River along with a barge and other vessels on occasion, making twenty-two stops along the way to tout the conservation sales-tax amendment. Opposition rose as callers to talk-radio programs, which had become the new barber shop and morning coffee group political forums, insisted the amendment would lead to property seizures and federal secret encampments. However, the Huckabees' flotilla was decisive in the approval of the tax. Although rural voters spurned the proposal, urban counties provided the narrow margin for approval.

The G&FC stuck to funding its promised list of projects, including four nature education centers, two of which were named after the First Couple. For most Arkansans the immense makeover of the state parks, including long-deferred rehabilitation of deteriorating structures as well the new conveniences that smoothed out rustic edges, was the most apparent return on their investment. Since its origins as a New Deal program, the parks system had gained incremental funding during the administrations of Faubus and Bumpers, but the 1996 tax kept the "Natural State" motto from becoming an empty marketing slogan. This development was a rare example in Arkansas of public services being upgraded without an injection of federal dollars.

Huckabee deserved and took full credit for the state's first major expansion of Medicaid services to low-income Arkansans. Shortly after assuming office following the resignation of Jim Guy Tucker, Huckabee announced that a shortfall in Medicaid funding required reducing benefits. He soon reversed course. As would often prove the case throughout his governorship, Huckabee was moved to go against the conservative grain upon hearing a personal appeal supported by evidence and poignant stories.

U.S. Representative Wilbur Mills, from his post as chair of the House Ways and Means Committee, was chiefly responsible in 1965 for incorporating Medicaid into the measure that also authorized Medicare. The authors of these amendments to the original Social Security Act intended to expand the health-care safety net to include the elderly and certain classes of indigent persons.

Mills's own state of Arkansas benefited from one of the nation's most generous cost-sharing ratios. The federal government bore 70 percent of the cost of the state's Medicaid program. Still, Arkansas prior to the Huckabee administration had not emulated other states outside the South by extending coverage significantly beyond the primary recipients: low-income elderly in nursing homes, the disabled poor, and children in households below the poverty line.

In 1996 Amy Rossi explained to Huckabee that the state would realize greater savings by expanding Medicaid instead of cutting it back. Rossi, the executive director of Arkansas Advocates for Children and Families, whose founders included Hillary Rodham Clinton, Betty Bumpers, and Dr. Betty Lowe, had exhaustive research at hand from years of buttonholing lawmakers to do something about the large proportion of uninsured children in the state. The bottom line on avoiding expensive chronic health ailments in untreated children made sense to Huckabee, as did Rossi's descriptions of distraught parents. Huckabee included Rossi's proposal to insure children in households with incomes up to 200 percent of the poverty level as part of his 1997 legislative package. The passage of what became known as ARKids First largely accounted for the decline within six years in the number of uninsured Arkansas children from 19 to 10 percent. The unlikely emergence of this pioneering bipartisan agreement within an enduring one-party political system did not allay festering mutual suspicions and recriminations between Democratic lawmakers and the Republican governor.

In 1997 Democratic legislators, fearing that Huckabee would deploy public moneys to subvert their reelections, transferred to the General Assembly nearly all of the surplus budget funds that had been reserved for governors to fund capital spending requests by state agencies and institutions. Signaling something of a détente, Democratic lawmakers in the following regular session restored half of the General Improvement Fund (GIF) to the governor while the Senate and House divvied up the balance among all of their members. In the wake of reforms that had closed off opportunities for pork barrel projects, legislators seized upon their GIF allotment to help out folks back home.

Beginning in 2001 hundreds of local organizations and projects absorbed GIF funds that were distributed through no process or formal assessment other than the assurances of the representatives and senators that the money was well spent. Lawmakers often won favors from colleagues by handing over portions of their own GIF shares to underwrite a project they knew little about. A June 2003 *Arkansas Democrat-Gazette* article identified examples of the destinations for these subsidies: "local fire departments, bicycle trails, sidewalks, community centers, American Legion posts, camps for at-risk kids, ball fields and libraries."

Private nonprofit groups that commanded local support and endeared themselves to legislators also procured these public funds while evading the oversight imposed on public agencies. Government leaders knew the means by which GIF cash seeped throughout the state was indefensible, but neither elected officials nor constituents proved able to spurn the largesse. In October 2017 the state Supreme Court ruled the practice violated the constitution but not before news reports and court indictments revealed the extent of payoffs and fraud revolving around the dispersal of GIF funds by General Assembly members.

During the recession that swept the nation following the 9/11 terrorist attack in 2001 on New York City, state programs were pared as balances dwindled. Medicaid faced particularly onerous cuts even as unemployment rose. Huckabee initially ridiculed a strategy by Mike Beebe, the Senate Democratic leader, to shift funds from the so-called rainy-day fund and other accounts that would be replenished from a nationwide settlement with tobacco companies. In 2000 the voters had approved an initiated act authorizing a commission to award grants to advance healthcare goals and activities from the $62 million that was the state's share of the settlement. The governor relented on Beebe's fix, and a special session of the General Assembly approved the proposed solution by near consensus margins. In contrast to many other states that used tobacco settlement funds to shore up shaky budgets, Arkansas steadfastly funneled the dollars for health-related purposes until 2017, when the General Assembly shaved off a portion to create a long-term reserve account to ride out future recessions.

The hard-hit national economy continued to wobble. In 2003 the governor warned that tens of thousands would be hoisted off the Medicaid rolls unless taxes were increased. Legislative Democrats were cool to his proposed one-cent increase in the sales tax and mustered majorities in a special session to raise the excise on tobacco products and levy an income tax surcharge. While the surcharge was slated to sunset when revenues improved, it was the first income-tax boost since the General Assembly approved Dale Bumpers's 1971 proposal. Huckabee signed the revenue bills: "While I'm not happy we were forced to raise taxes, it was the responsible thing to do to protect those Arkansans who are the most vulnerable but the least connected politically."

Throughout his tenure, Huckabee endorsed measures crafted by experienced hands in the opposition-dominated General Assembly. These laws and reforms underpinned a legacy rivaling that of the "Big Three" Democratic governors. The growth of government employees and budgets predictably discomfited the ideological wing of the Republican Party perched in the northwest region. Hutchinson-Hendren family members conspicuously held the ramparts in the GOP hilltop bailiwicks. Their influence showed that personality and kin connections still mattered in a political culture that had largely shed coarse granules of a rural order.

The twin sons of U.S. Senator Tim Hutchinson both came to serve in the General Assembly, as did his brother-in-law Kim Hendren and nephew Jim Hendren. Brother Asa succeeded Tim Hutchinson in the U.S. House of Representatives for the Third District following his move to the upper chamber in 1997. This dynastic network did not control party politics in the hills but was sufficiently potent to rival Huckabee's standing among Republicans. In 2001 Huckabee supported John Boozman, a Rogers school board member, over Jim Hendren in the party primary contest for the congressional seat that Hendren's uncle Asa had vacated to lead the federal Drug Enforcement Administration. Boozman, whose brother was Huckabee's state health department director, won the nomination and bested the Democratic candidate. In 2010 Kim Hendren launched a primary campaign for the U.S. Senate but finished deep in the pack behind Boozman, who went on to unseat the Democratic incumbent. Steve Womack, the Rogers mayor who contended undocumented immigrants threatened the community, overcame an opponent endorsed by the Hutchinson and Hendren clan to succeed Boozman as the Third District representative.

Boozman swept to victory in the 2010 Republican tsunami that washed the deep blue from the Arkansas electoral map but that disruption was unforeseen in 2006 when term limits kept Huckabee from standing for reelection. In addition, neither of the Arkansas Democratic senators was slated to face the voters that year. Like Bill Clinton, Huckabee's next bid was for the presidency. And like Clinton, Huckabee had been tested by a school equalization lawsuit in his last term. The outcome provided the Republican ex-governor fewer bragging points for national audiences although he had staked out a position that Clinton had avoided owing to the undeniable political risk.

IN 1994 A CHANCERY JUDGE ruled in a suit filed by the rural Lake View school district (Phillips County) that the state had permitted the gaps in resources between wealthy and poor districts such as Lake View to widen since the enactment of the 1980s education reforms. In 1937 the Farm Security Administration had organized Lake View as one of three cooperative resettlement communities in the state reserved for African American families. The federal agency had also overseen the building and opening of schools.

Governor Jim Guy Tucker and the General Assembly shied away from achieving equalization by consolidating school districts and instead referred to the voters a constitutional amendment requiring all districts to impose a minimum rate of twenty-five mills. The state, following the approval of the amendment in 1996, collected the revenue raised by the first twenty-five mills in each district and redistributed the proceeds to narrow the disparities in wealth among the districts. The legislature also boosted state taxes to supplement those districts that still had too little money to meet minimum educational standards after local levies were raised. Nevertheless, Tucker knew the state had not escaped constitutional jeopardy. He reflected, "I wish we could have done a great deal more."

In 2001 Circuit Judge Collins Kilgore agreed in an amended suit by the Lake View district that indeed the state needed to do more. His decision went beyond previous rulings in holding that not only were districts hampered by unbalanced funding but the legislature had failed to meet the constitutional standard of providing an "adequate" education for all students. Kilgore echoed the conclusions of blue ribbon commissions, committee studies, and consultants stretching back to the 1920s: Arkansas youth were immeasurably harmed by attending Arkansas schools. "Too many of our children are leaving school for a life of deprivation, burdening our culture with the corrosive effects of citizens who lack the education to contribute to their community's welfare but who will be unable to live their own lives except, in many cases, on the outermost fringe of human existence."

After the state Supreme Court upheld Kilgore, Governor Huckabee presented to the 2003 legislative session a sweeping plan that permitted no district, with a handful of exceptions, to continue with fewer than 1,500 students and that extended state authority over local school boards. Governors in the past had gone no further than offering incentives for consolidation and none approached the Huckabee program that would have likely sliced the 310 existing districts to around 100. Yet it was not to be. The governor defended his initiative as a fiscally responsible alternative to the over $800 million additional spending under consideration by a legislative committee. The administration, however, was unable to provide potential urban allies with solid figures on the savings gained under his proposal. Lawmakers from both parties were skeptical of an ambitious proposal that had been announced with scant warning and minimal ground work.

A livid Huckabee withdrew from the field but agreed to call a special session to allow legislative leaders to attempt a solution amenable to the courts. Lawmakers had become accustomed to the governor's aversion to walking up to the third floor of the capitol to sell his agenda to them. Before adjourning the education session, the General assembly raised $360 million by increasing the sales tax seven-eighths of a cent and requiring the merger or dissolution of school districts falling below 350 students. By the 2016–17 school year, the state's students attended classes in 238 districts. The Lake View district, having been combined with another, was not one of those surviving districts. School districts remained largely autonomous even as they became more dependent upon state funding. Measures were enacted, however, that gave the state the means to take over and merge districts judged to be in financial distress and, later, academic distress.

Huckabee excoriated the General Assembly for merely tinkering with a broken system, and the tax and consolidation bills became law without his signature. The state's strongest defense of the reform package in subsequent court hearings was its adoption of a statutory mandate that appropriations for the school funding formula be approved ahead of other state programs. The Supreme Court agreed that the results of the 2003 special session had met constitutional requirements but revived the case when it found that the 2005 legislature failed to uphold its financial commitments to the schools. In 2007 two special masters appointed by the Court concluded that the additional revenue and reconfiguration of the funding formula approved by the legislature in 2006 justified closing the books on Lake View. The justices agreed and pronounced the school system constitutional.

———————————

BUSINESS INTERESTS IN ARKANSAS throughout the twentieth century generally backed gubernatorial school reform programs. Corporate leaders, however, in the course of the debate over the Huckabee proposals edged away from expanding revenue to insisting schools verify what students were learning with the resources already available to teachers and administrators. The school accountability drive, emphasizing that student progress could be measured through standardized examinations, was prominent in the domestic program of the first twenty-first-century president, George W. Bush. Increasingly the mantle of reform was claimed by those who charged that ineffective teachers and outmoded methods were greater obstacles to student achievement than inadequate funds. Huckabee did not recant his support for higher taxes but favored expanding the number of charter schools in the state.

In 2005 the governor invited scholars associated with the conservative Hoover Institution to present recommendations on improving education in the state. In December the chair of the state Chamber of Commerce applauded the proposals to boost the salaries of only those teachers whose students did better than expected on quantitative measures and to expand the number of charter schools in the state. During its regular session earlier in the year, the legislature had doubled to twenty-four the maximum permitted open-enrollment charter schools, entities that received the same public funds per student as did public schools. When students migrated from public to charter schools, state revenue traveled with them. Proposals to set up charters came before the state board of education for review and authorization. Some local school boards had already converted schools in their districts into charters, which the state education department described as freed from "regulations created for traditional public schools" but still "accountable for academic and financial results." The open-enrollment charters, operated by nonprofit organizations rather than school districts, enjoyed the same autonomy but were more controversial.

The Arkansas Education Association, the teachers' union, and school leaders in urban districts were apprehensive over losing to the open-enrollment charters both funding and students who scored well on assessment tests. In 2017 only two of the twenty-four open-enrollment charters had schools outside a metropolitan statistical area. The majority of charters were located in central Arkansas where their effect on the racial composition of public schools ignited new debates.

In the post–Lake View era, voluminous accountability reports and evaluations by policy groups generated ample data on the performance of the state's school districts. In general, progress was undeniable, although the state continued to languish in the bottom tier across a range of comparative performance measures. Students steadily improved in reading and math exams, scored higher on the ACT college admission exam, and were more likely to attend college free of remediation requirements. Teacher salaries rose to place Arkansas among the leaders in the region, while the financing and other policy reforms earned the state strong marks in the annual *Education Week* ranking on the status of schools throughout the nation. But the gap between white and black students on performance outcomes remained distressingly wide, while funding for early childhood programs stagnated after 2008. Although Arkansas had made students' educations much less dependent upon where they lived, poorer and rural districts were often unable to pay the salaries needed to secure hard-to-find science and math teachers.

Huckabee had left office before the final pieces of the school funding puzzle related to buildings and facilities were affixed to meet the Lake View obligations. From his new roost as governor, Mike Beebe deftly shepherded the $456 million appropriation through a legislative process he had mastered and shaped through twenty years in the state Senate. In that 2007 session he achieved a long-standing objective by persuading the General Assembly to halve the sales tax on groceries and to set in motion its incremental elimination.

A 2010 study tabbed the state as maintaining the third-highest income tax burden on poor families, but the following year Beebe endorsed a bill approved by large margins in the General Assembly that finally brought relief to low-income households with children. During his tenure Beebe pushed the legislature to increase both the tobacco tax to address rising healthcare expenses and the natural gas severance levy to fix roads damaged by trucks crisscrossing the Fayetteville Shale region.

The governor's fiscal caution coupled with the continuing expansion of public services, particularly to those citizens with fewer resources and options, piqued the curiosity of the national media just as the Great Recession razed state budgets throughout the nation. A January 2011 story in the *New York Times* surveyed Arkansas's bond default in 1933 as a cautionary historical background to contemporary communities and states facing mounting debts. The piece concluded by noting the state's comparative financial health: "For the record, Arkansas 2011 is not facing the level of economic misery of some other places. State officials are predicting a slight rise in revenue. Some leaders are talking of cutting the sales tax rate on groceries. And the state owes 2.6 percent of its spending—among the lowest in the country—to debt interest." In that same year, *Governing* magazine honored Beebe as an exceptional public official for leading one of only four states that evaded a budget shortfall during the economic crisis (the publication had also tabbed Mike Huckabee for a similar recognition in 2005).

Beebe was no less zealous than his Democratic and Republican predecessors in leveraging state resources to woo new industries and companies to settle in Arkansas. He early coaxed the legislature to furnish him with a sizable reserve fund to deploy at his discretion if a large employer gazed toward the state. He also instinctively understood that the amplification through social media of the national Democratic Party's liberal stands on social issues inspired the mistrust of the religiously faithful toward local Party candidates. Yet even the most astute of politicians could not always find neutral ground on the battlefields in the culture wars.

During his 2006 contest with Asa Hutchinson to become governor, Beebe initially opposed and then concurred with Hutchinson's demand for legislation to circumvent the state Supreme Court's ruling that voided the statutory ban on adoption and foster parenting care by gay and lesbian applicants. But in 2008 Beebe publicly opposed an initiated act designed to prevent gays or lesbians from adopting or fostering children. He would go on to praise the Court for striking down the measure after it was approved by 56 percent of the voters: "By expanding the pool of potential applicants, today's Supreme Court decision will create more opportunities to match children with loving and supportive homes."

No Democratic political figure in the modern era proved more adept than Beebe in melding pragmatism, a progressive regard for government's capability to aid people, a managerial discipline toward budgets, and sensitivity toward communities at cross-purposes over values. He won reelection by 30 percentage points in 2010, and polls showed him no less popular at the end of his allotted two terms in office.

From the perspective of Arkansas Republicans, the 2008 election appeared to produce the usual melancholy results. Neither Senator Mark Pryor nor the three Democratic congressmen were troubled with Republican opponents in the general election. Democrats maintained their monopoly on the constitutional offices and boasted solid majorities of 70 percent in both chambers of the General Assembly. Yet the party's dominance was already in its final stages.

Arkansans in election cycles since the 1970s had split their votes between Republican presidential candidates and conservative or moderate Democratic state office seekers except when Jimmy Carter and Bill Clinton, white Southern governors, headed the national ticket for the party (although the state failed to back Carter's reelection bid in 1980). John McCain's twenty-point advantage over Barack Obama in 2008 placed Arkansas among the four states that awarded the largest margins to the losing GOP nominee. No state had a more pronounced swing from the previous election toward the Republican presidential candidate than did deep-blue Arkansas. John Kerry, the 2004 Democratic nominee, carried twenty-one counties (including Bill Clinton's native Hempstead County) as he lost the state to George W. Bush; Obama eked out majorities in only nine counties (Hempstead County was not among them). McCain's vote totals in the rural swing counties, the anchors of Democratic supremacy, were immense.

Obama had also been overwhelmed in the 2008 state primary by Hillary Rodham Clinton, the state's former First Lady, who would have been more competitive in the general election contest for the state's Electoral College votes if she had secured the Democratic nomination. Obama's liberalism weighed down his chances as it had Kerry and other past Democratic nominees, including Michael Dukakis and Walter Mondale. Obama understandably conceded Arkansas to McCain and his short-staffed Little Rock headquarters concentrated on landing votes in surrounding states.

The Arkansas Poll, conducted in October, discerned uneasiness among whites over the election of "the first black president." The same survey found that 47 percent of all those polled (81 percent identified as white, 9 percent African American) agreed with the statement "if blacks would only try harder they could be just as well off as whites" while 35 percent disagreed. In response to whether or not black leaders had pushed "too fast, not fast enough, moving at about the right speed," 49 percent believed the pace was "about right," 13 percent "too fast," and 20 percent "not fast enough."

Two political scientists, Andrew Dowdle and Joseph Giammo, writing before the 2010 elections observed that statewide and congressional Democratic officeholders continued to distance themselves from the national party by heightening their support for conservative economic and social positions. The scholars concluded that as long as Arkansas Democrats kept their distance from party liberals, the voters would continue to accept that bargain as they had for decades: "[The] pattern of being reliably red at the presidential level and reliably blue below that seems unlikely to change."

––––––––––––

BEFORE 2010 THE REPUBLICAN PARTY had not shed the institutional infirmities that historians and political scientists cited as factors in keeping Arkansas from being a two-party state. The party remained largely a top-down operation without a deep pool of experienced candidates to run at each level of government; rank-and-file members were concentrated in two regions, with the central Arkansas suburban dwellers more attuned to the business establishment than the northwest residents who were more likely to demand restrictive immigration policies; and party leaders struggled to define a set of issues that contrasted with those supported by Arkansas Democrats and that resonated with the voters.

The 2010 results, however, left little doubt Arkansas had shaken off its outlier status to the solid-red South. Blanche Lincoln, whose Senate seat would have been invulnerable in past years after she became the first Arkansan to head the Senate Agriculture Committee, was soundly defeated by U.S. Rep. John Boozman in her bid for a third term. Republicans Rick Crawford and Tim Griffin easily captured congressional seats that opened when the Democratic incumbents retired. Aside from the governor's race, the Republican Party did not mount challenges to sitting Democratic state constitutional officers, but its candidates triumphed over better-known and more experienced Democrats contesting for the three offices without incumbents. Republican membership in the state Senate nearly doubled and grew by two-thirds in the House. The slim Democratic majority in the General Assembly would not endure past

2012, and Mike Beebe became the first Democratic governor to share power with a Republican-dominated legislature. But divided government would not last long.

Political parties in Arkansas, with the briefest of transitions, had changed places. Hal Bass, a political scientist and long-time observer of the state, concluded in 2016 that "for whatever reason, there seems to be something in Arkansas' political culture or political heritage to be a one-party government. We don't seem to have an affinity for two-party competitive politics."

In the initial phase of its ascendancy the Republican Party was organizationally no more strapping than was the Democratic operation in full flower, although the ideological debates among Republicans appeared more vigorous. Governing required compromise, but voices grew louder over whether partial victories were enough to justify diluting principles. Nevertheless, electoral success and antagonism toward liberal policies preserved the united front against the Democrats. As a practical matter, Republicans grew stronger as a Democratic president with dismal approval ratings statewide became an anathema in the rural communities.

The Obama administration's mortgage relief plan during the national financial crisis ignited the Tea Party movement in 2009, and the passage of the Affordable Care Act (ACA), or Obamacare, the following year stoked the anti-government backlash. The movement, appealing generally to older white males who had solid incomes and better-than-average educations, had a tenuous relationship to the Republican Party even while its adherents supported GOP candidates over Democrats. The 2011 Blair-Rockefeller poll discovered that Tea Party followers in Arkansas were more likely than other white Republicans to disapprove of government programs assisting minority citizens to move up the ladder through better jobs and education. Almost two-thirds of Tea Party members agreed that "we have gone too far in pushing equal rights in this country."

Whites in rural swing counties for a time identified themselves out of habit and tradition as Democrats, but they no longer split their tickets in elections. Republicans had long been frustrated with conservatives voting for local Democrats, but the party's role in altering that behavior was minor. Rather, many Arkansans judged that Obama was "not one of us," a verdict that had once upon a time crippled Republican candidates.

During the Obama era, even local candidates in Arkansas faced demands that they announce their positions on national policies unrelated to the responsibilities of the offices they sought. Retail politics had long endured in Arkansas, but the voters no longer expected every candidate to look them in the eye when asking for support. After the U.S. Supreme Court in 2010 lifted the restrictions on the entities allowed to throw money at campaigns, national organizations with national agendas inundated carefully selected households with direct mail and targeted social-media consumers. Candidates were hard put through personal, face-to-face campaigning to dispel harsh attacks thrown up on screens by distant political action committees.

In 2014 Tom Cotton, a Republican who had served one term in the U.S. House, unseated two-term U.S. senator Mark Pryor. Senator David Pryor had remained popular in the state since leaving office, but that esteem was unable to sustain his son in the new political environment. After graduating from Dardanelle High School, Cotton earned undergraduate and law degrees from Harvard and was deployed to Iraq and Afghanistan following his enlistment in the U.S. Army. In 2012 he returned to his hometown, which had been just attached to the Fourth Congressional District, to run for the seat given up by Mike Ross. Cotton, unknown in the state and awkward on the hustings, was still able to defeat in the Republican primary a former Miss Arkansas who had the endorsement of Mike Huckabee and who had run a valiant but doomed campaign against Ross two years earlier. In an earlier era, she would have been the prohibitive favorite. Cotton benefited from contributions from wealthy conservatives outside of Arkansas and affluent counterparts from within as well as from rapturous editorials in the statewide newspaper. Cotton's victory over Pryor was not unexpected in a year in which Republicans maintained their hold on all four U.S. House districts in the state. Asa Hutchinson, who had endured losses to Dale Bumpers and Mike Beebe, easily overcame former congressman Ross to reach the governorship.

During the 2014 campaign Hutchinson avoided a firm commitment to preserve a component of the Affordable Care Act that had at that point extended health insurance coverage to 200,000 Arkansans. Obamacare remained toxic for Republican stalwarts and Tea Party crusaders. They protested that Arkansas's participation in the program covering low-income residents was voluntary and out of step with the rest of the South. Nevertheless, this second and larger expansion of Medicare was a bipartisan innovation crafted in 2013 by GOP legislative leaders and the Democratic administration.

The ACA set up regulated healthcare exchanges that offered insurance to individuals who could count on federal subsidies, depending upon their income, to meet the premium costs. The federal government also fully funded for three years the expansion of Medicaid to those whose income fell below 138 percent of the federal poverty line (states after this grace period were required to begin making contributions that would rise eventually to 10 percent of the federal outlay).

A U.S. Supreme Court ruling left it up to the states to decide whether to accept the federal revenue to extend Medicaid coverage to their newly eligible residents. Before 2013 the restrictions by Arkansas on who could receive Medicaid ranked it among those states with the highest rate of adult uninsured citizens. At the beginning of the 2013 session the Republican majority in the Arkansas General Assembly was largely unmoved by arguments from Governor Mike Beebe and agency heads that the state would realize large savings by signing up additional Medicaid recipients and that rural hospitals, staggering under uncompensated medical expenses, would have a better chance to survive.

Three of the conservative lawmakers—Jonathan Dismang, John Burris, and David Sanders—sharply asserted in negotiations they would prefer to rein in Medicaid rather than expand a program they believed ineffective and an illegitimate exercise of government power. Out of their disdain sprouted a plan to privatize Medicaid with public funding.

Under this strategy the state would move most of those eligible through existing Medicaid rules as well those low-income individuals qualifying under the new federal rules into the market exchanges. Billions of federal dollars would pour into the state's economy as ACA grants paid the premiums for the Medicaid recipients enrolled in the private plans on the exchanges. The three Republican policy virtuosos forged the complex bill through intensive sessions with the Medicaid director and leaders from the departments of human services and health. No less intensive were the subsequent lobbying efforts to persuade doubtful Republican legislators that Medicaid expansion, an Obamacare creation, had been supplanted by the "private option" (paid for by Obamacare dollars). Needing a three-fourths majority in each chamber, the measure survived close votes.

What one reporter described as a "circuitous and maddening" journey led to an "improbable" outcome: arguably the most thorough expansion of a federally subsidized social welfare program since the Great Society era of the Lyndon Johnson presidency. By the end of 2014, Arkansas boasted the second-largest drop in uninsured residents among all states. Three years after the approval of the private option, the uninsured percentage of Arkansans was reduced by half. While 8 percent of the overall population in 2016 was still without health coverage, only 4 percent of children were. ARKids First, the first Medicaid expansion under Huckabee, continued to insure over half of the children in the state. By 2017 over 300,000 Arkansans had enrolled in the private option, although that figure would begin dropping in the following year.

Latter-day Arkansas conservatives, much like the 1930s politicians grappling with the woes of the Great Depression, regretfully accepted federal assistance but only after negotiating the terms. Arkansas was the first state granted a waiver by the Obama administration to launch the private option but others followed its lead. The Arkansas model was singled out in 2015 by the Kaiser Family Foundation, a recognized authority in healthcare policy, for accomplishing its purposes in a manner that won broad acceptance: "The Arkansas experience highlights the considerable flexibility available to design an extension of coverage to newly eligible adults consistent with a state's delivery system, political culture, and larger health care goals."

Governor Asa Hutchinson soon after taking office requested and secured additional waivers from federal authorities. Hutchinson wanted to reduce income taxes but foresaw an acute budget squeeze if the state threw over the private option. The administration, alongside influential legislators, took the lead in the annual nail-biting exercise of rounding up the necessary legislative supermajority to fund Medicaid expansion. Many Republican lawmakers disagreed with the Republican governor's assertion that the private option was separate and apart from Obamacare. Hutchinson countered in 2016, "It is perfectly consistent, it is perfectly conservative and logical to oppose Obamacare as a federal policy and yet to accept federal dollars under the Medicaid program in Arkansas. It is a logical position. It is an Arkansas-oriented position, and it does not embrace the federal policy that is the framework of Obamacare."

The federal Health and Human Services secretary approved Hutchinson's request for waivers to move forward in January 2017 with a slightly modified alternative of the private option the governor dubbed "Arkansas Works." The next year the governor solicited permission from federal officials to phase in a requirement for adults to work or be enrolled in a training program to continue to be eligible for Medicaid benefits. In June Arkansas became the first state in the history of the Medicaid program to impose a work requirement on recipients. Although defenders of the policy pointed to exemptions that kept some classes of unemployed on the insurance rolls, health policy researchers examining the Arkansas experiment observed that recipients needing to document employment or file a waiver faced a complex process that contributed to individuals losing benefits. By January 2019, over 18,000 became ineligible for Medicaid coverage.

Arkansas officials also requested that federal authorities permit them to limit Medicaid to those at or below the poverty line, but the Donald Trump administration balked on this application. Hutchinson had insisted that the sixty thousand likely to be dismissed from the rolls on those grounds could secure "the same level of financial support" by purchasing federally subsidized plans on the health market exchanges if their employers did not step up to provide insurance. This shift of financial responsibility from the state, which was on the hook for an increasing share of matching costs for Medicaid expenses, to the federal treasury was a long-standing Arkansas policy tradition. In the short run, these cost-cutting expedients persuaded a number of Republican legislators to reverse their earlier opposition to the private option benefit.

From its earliest days, the Trump administration grew frustrated with failed attempts in the Republican-dominated congressional chambers to repeal Obamacare outright and resorted to executive directives to weaken the program. Hutchinson, in contrast to the members of the Arkansas congressional delegation, was hesitant to scrap an entitlement benefit that buoyed the state budget. Just as would have been the position of his predecessors, the governor signaled support for repealing ACA if it was replaced by generous block grants shorn of nearly all federal regulations.

The creation and survival of the Medicaid expansion program was the most prominent example that the bipartisan compromises that defined the Huckabee and Beebe years were not extinguished at the dawn of Republican supremacy. Hutchinson relied upon Democratic votes to counterbalance those legislators from his own party who remained ill-disposed toward what they judged to be illegitimate government benefits and government outlays.

THE HUTCHINSON-HENDREN political circle had been a mainstay of northwest Arkansas ideological rigor during the Republican Party's envelopment of the region. Asa Hutchinson, along with his brother Tim, had earned superior ratings from conservative organizations for a steadfast voting record during his congressional stint. Asa Hutchinson earned the admiration of Republican leaders and persistent enmity of Arkansas Democrats by serving as one of the House of Representatives managers charged with making the case for the removal of Bill Clinton during the Senate impeachment trial.

As governor, Asa Hutchinson usually sided with the corporate and economic development organizations if they feared proposed social legislation jeopardized the state's business-friendly reputation. He deflected measures that would have permitted businesses to refuse services to LGBT customers on religious grounds and restricted transgendered individuals from entering public restrooms based upon their gender identity. The governor was lukewarm toward the successful bill permitting adults to bring concealed weapons onto college campuses but backed a waiver for football venues after Southeastern Conference officials suggested teams might not be allowed to visit Razorback Stadium.

Governor Hutchinson along with Senators Jeremy Hutchinson and Jim Hendren, two nephews who often carried water for him in the General Assembly, increasingly took unfriendly fire from the Party's clamorous right flank. A conservative website in late 2017 suggested that Senator Hendren was preparing to "write his own version of the 'Republican Platform' to match his big government, pro-Obamacare, and tax and spend philosophy." Hutchinson's unsuccessful challenger in the 2018 party primary charged that the governor, who had headed a National Rifle Association task force on the mass shootings in schools, was wobbly on upholding the Second Amendment.

The governor surmounted intra-party factionalism, an Arkansas tradition, to secure the bulk of his legislative package throughout the sessions in his first term. Hutchinson initially abolished several state boards and commissions and appointed an advisory commission to develop plans for a broader reorganization and consolidation of government agencies in order to lower budget outlays. The commission's report formed the basis of the governor's legislative proposals in the 2019 session to merge forty-two executive agencies into fifteen. Governors in the modern era, both Democratic and Republican, had attempted similar restructuring with sundry outcomes. Hutchinson's program to reduce state personal income taxes from top to bottom was customarily welcomed by the Republican legislative majority, which had already sliced taxes on capital gains and granted numerous sales tax waivers in the final years of the Beebe administration. The residual Democratic caucus in the Hutchinson years outlined the services compromised by lost revenue and made little headway when introducing bills to concentrate tax relief on lower income residents. The opposing party coalesced to enact measures touted by their sponsors as paring the size and expense of state government. Those same goals, before the 1970s, had predominated among the dominant Democratic party lawmakers.

Hutchinson did, however, face unprecedented challenges by the General Assembly to the independence and authority of executive branch departments. Voters in 2014 endorsed a constitutional amendment proposed by the General Assembly that entitled the legislature to approve rules and regulations promulgated by state agencies before they went into effect. Before 2014 the Legislative Council had long reviewed agency decisions, but state courts consistently held that any legislative veto of executive actions violated the separation of powers set forth in the constitution. With the constitutional objection removed by the adoption of Amendment 92, the Legislative Council—to the displeasure of the governor—questioned and moved to revoke service contracts negotiated by the agencies.

The question over the constitutional limits of the legislature's extending jurisdiction was revived in September 2017 when the Council demanded that the Game and Fish Commission submit its rules for review and approval. G&FC and the Highway Commission were constitutionally independent bodies based upon Amendment 35 (1944) and Amendment 42 (1952) respectively. The adoption of these amendments had represented the initial stage of the modernization of Arkansas government by replacing the brokering of divergent factional and personal interests with a system of structured policies and procedures. The Legislative Council subsequently backed off the requirement for review and approval when the G&FC agreed to include the legislature's staff in the customary distribution of its proposed rules for public comment.

Republicans followed the Democratic example of aggressively pushing job development campaigns, but the outreach and recruitment expanded from enticing U.S. firms to an emphasis on wooing foreign-based employers, particularly those in China. Prospective manufacturing openings announced with great fanfare early in the Hutchinson administration fit well within familiar Arkansas industrial sectors—a massive paper mill in Clark County to be operated by Shandong Sun Industries and a $20 million Suzhou Tianyuan factory slated to employ 400 in Little Rock to oversee 330 robots stitching T-shirts. Shandong Ruyi Technology Group accepted generous incentives to hire 800 to spin Arkansas cotton into yarn on the site of the shuttered Sanyo plant in Forrest City, once viewed by successive governors as a harbinger of the state's advance toward high-end manufacturing.

State officials could do little to wall off publicly traded Arkansas companies during the consolidation surge that roiled the millennial digital economy much as the merger movement had birthed industrial behemoths a century earlier. The acquisitions after 2005 of Alltel, Beverly Enterprises, and Acxiom winnowed down the list of native enterprises that state leaders had cited as proof that Arkansas was an entrepreneurial seedbed.

Professionalization in government operations, term limits, and the downfall of the entrenched Democratic Party had not cleansed the General Assembly of corrupt practices. Given a free hand to distribute state General Improvement Funds to non-public entities, individual legislators were able to exact favors in return for public subsidies. In 2017 a state representative pled guilty to accepting kickbacks to direct GIF funds to a small religious college, and in the following year a federal jury convicted a state senator representing Springdale of snaring for his personal use a portion of the GIF funds he had bestowed upon the same college. The two had persuaded eight of their legislative colleagues, who were unaware of the payoff schemes, to channel shares of their GIF allotments to the private institution. In 2018 a state senator from Fort Smith acquiesced to charges that he had fraudulently channeled GIF money through his own construction firm into his personal accounts.

U.S. attorneys and multiple federal agencies brought these charges as part of an investigation that ranged across several states. In Arkansas the inquiry produced an admission in 2018 by a former state representative from Pine Bluff that he took bribes while in office to steer GIF dollars to nonprofit companies that provided behavioral and substance-abuse treatment services for youth. The federal probe branched beyond the misuse of GIF funds to examine steps taken by lawmakers to insure a continuing stream of Medicaid reimbursements to certain health care companies.

The executive director of the state ethics commission acknowledged, as the barrage of stories on legislative graft mounted, that state statutes left compliance by lobbyists to report expenses and by officials to disclose financial interests largely voluntary. A 2015 study by the D.C.-based Center for Public Integrity ranked Arkansas forty-sixth among the fifty states in "legislative accountability." David Ramsey, the author of the Arkansas profile in the report, explained that while legislators were barred from serving as lobbyists within two years of leaving office, firms and agencies could hire them as consultants or government relations officers to perform lobbying duties during the so-called "cooling off period." Ethics rules did not prevent entities with business before the General Assembly from adding sitting legislators to their payrolls. Such endemic conflicts of interest were not confined to Arkansas. Part-time state legislators casting about for paid employment that gave them the time and flexibility to hold office triggered scandals elsewhere. The director for the Center for Public Integrity noted, "Lawmakers having ties to nonprofits that receive government funds, and not disclosing those ties, is a serious problem nationwide."

Just as political corruption endured in the midst of the state's continuing political transformation, echoes of old battles resonated in contemporary arguments. The long reform of state government since World War II had tracked the unfolding of a diverse and complex economy in which companies demanded the public services and stable operations taken for granted in other states. The rise of early twenty-first-century anti-government disciples within the dominant Republican Party revived debates from the early twentieth century, when traditional conservatives within the then dominant Democratic Party resisted the expansion of government by the original business and social progressives.

ON SEPTEMBER 25, 2017, Bill Clinton spoke from the stage of the Little Rock Central High School auditorium. Melba Pattillo Beals, Elizabeth Eckford, Ernest Green, Gloria Ray Karlmark, Carlotta Walls LaNier, Minnijean Brown Trickey, Thelma Mothershed Wair, and Terrance Roberts were seated nearby along with an empty chair in memory of Jefferson Thomas, who died in 2010. The former president recalled sharing the platform with Hillary Rodham Clinton and Mike Huckabee at the fortieth commemoration of the Little Rock Nine's entrance into the school under the protection of the 101st Airborne.

In remembering the earlier event, Clinton admitted, "The most important thing I had to do that day was to hold the door open so the world could see the reality of what its symbolic message was." The sight of the Arkansas governor and the American president stepping aside for the nine to walk into the building was indeed a moving symbol of a state and nation following the arc of justice toward democracy and inclusiveness. Twenty years later in Little Rock, contending voices were raised over whether the pace of advancement toward equality had slowed, while others disputed if the grim shadows of 1957 had ever lifted.

The city and the National Park Service organized the official sixtieth commemoration of the school crisis around the uplifting theme "Reflections of Progress." In an essay published in the *Arkansas Democrat-Gazette* the day before the speeches were given from the Central High stage, Terrance Roberts questioned whether the emphasis upon forward steps acknowledged the persistence of unequal treatment: "Yes, it has been 60 years, perhaps better stated as one year repeated 60 times. . . . A review of the social and economic statistics for a majority of the 99 percent of us tells a story at odds with the progress narrative." During a symposium at the Clinton Presidential Center that weekend, Judge Wiley Branton Jr., the son of the civil rights attorney and participant in *Aaron v. Cooper*, reflected on the Court decision that declared segregation unconstitutional: "If as *Brown* tells us that segregation harms black students, are our students now being harmed by a re-segregated school system, which has been caused in some measure by white flight and some governmental policies? . . . We are at another major crossroads in our history, with issues that challenge the very core of our democracy and freedom."

In 2007, fifty years after the crisis, federal judge Bill R. Wilson declared the Little Rock school district unitary. For the first time since 1957 the district was not subject to court order or oversight. Wilson's ruling concluded, "LRSD's Board can now operate the district as it sees fit; answerable to no one except LRSD's students and patrons and the voters who elected them to office. While the road has been long and at times frustrating—for LRSD and for me—I want to express my heartfelt best wishes as LRSD begins to operate, as our Founders intended, under control of the citizens of the City of Little Rock." Local control lasted eight years.

In the decade between the fiftieth anniversary and the sixtieth, the Little Rock school district lost around 10 percent of its enrollment. Although a smaller percentage of African American students were now in the district, that decline was far below the proportion of white students who left. Whites were 16 percent of the enrollment in the district, which did not encompass the full city. White residents made up half the population of Little Rock but only 36 percent of those living within the LRSD boundaries. The diversity of the Central High student body—58 percent black, 30 percent white, 7 percent Asian, and 5 percent Latino—was unusual for an urban American high school. One explanation rested with Central's broad attendance zone, which reached into the western suburbs. An arts and science magnet high school, employing a lottery to select from those who applied for admission, served a student population that was 21 percent white. The combined white enrollment of the other three district high schools stood at 4 percent.

In 2015 those three schools, along with three others serving lower grades, were designated by the state department of education to be in academic distress. The findings on these six, out of the forty-eight schools in the Little Rock district, led the state board of education to set aside the local board and turn management of LRSD over to the director of the state Department of Education.

In 2017 a number of opponents to the state takeover of the district organized an alternative observance to the official "Reflections of Progress" entitled "Sixty Years: Still Fighting." In raising the call to "save our schools," the group self-consciously evoked the 1959 Women's Emergency Committee campaign to reopen the high schools in the city. The activists also contended that "the expansion of privately owned charter schools" fostered resegregation by draining students and dollars from public schools. Pulaski County was home to a significantly disproportionate number of the Arkansas students enrolled in charter schools.

A formidable proponent of the national charter school movement had an Arkansas address. The Walton Family Foundation in Bentonville was among the most prominent of a phalanx of organizations that bankrolled the expansion of charter schools. The foundation's website noted that it had supplied funding to support "a quarter of the 6,700 charter schools in the United States." In Arkansas the foundation awarded grants to charter schools as well as to the Arkansas Public School Resource Center that advocated on behalf of and offered support services to charter schools.

Champions of the open-access charters asserted, not infrequently on the opinion pages of the sympathetic *Arkansas Democrat-Gazette*, that whites had long fled the Little Rock public schools to enter private academies rather than to enroll in the charters. The backers praised charters for offering children who could not afford steep tuition costs the chance to escape a public school that consistently fell short on measures of reading, writing, and math achievement levels. Supporters of public schools, on the other hand, highlighted insufficient empirical evidence that the charters employed more effective educational techniques and strategies or that they out-performed Little Rock schools serving students with similar demographics.

Johnny Key, the state education department director, had promoted charter school expansion during his earlier service in the General Assembly. Those in Little Rock who wanted the reinstatement of the elected local board feared state oversight under his supervision would lead to the creation of an alternative charter school system in the city.

Not unexpectedly, many LRSD patrons were wary when Key appointed Baker Kurrus in May 2015 to serve as superintendent. Kurrus, however, won over foes the following year when he published an analysis that offered columns of data detailing that the charters served a lower proportion of disadvantaged students than the public schools: "The students who exit are more likely to be higher achievers. This compounds LRSD's academic distress problems. The characterization of LRSD as distressed causes additional direct costs for school improvement specialists, and fuels a downward spiral in enrollment that further reduces revenue." The greater confidence in Kurrus by those pressing to restore the local school board heightened their disappointment when Key replaced him with Michael Poore, the Bentonville superintendent.

Yet Poore also disappointed charter school advocates when he appeared in September 2017 before the state board of education to oppose the establishment of three additional charter schools in Little Rock. He cited the recent improvement on state assessment tests among the district's schools as well as the relentless outmigration of students: "We need a pause right now to let things settle." The board praised Poore's accomplishments but approved the charter applications.

The following day Sen. Joyce Elliott, a leader of the movement to restore local control in Little Rock, and Sen. Jim Hendren, whose conservative record was under fire from movement conservatives, presented the Legislative Council with a resolution to create a race relations subcommittee that would offer "recommendations on ways to address historic and current divisions within the state." Elliott, an African American Democrat, explained in an interview that her collaboration with her white Republican colleague represented a model for breakthroughs to address "this scar on our history." In describing why she enlisted Hendren, Elliott explained, "We grew up in very different environments, but we're friends. And sometimes we would talk about these things honestly with one another." Hendren, for his part, was troubled by inequities that persisted in the state: "There are great disparities that we need to figure out how to fix, why those disparities are there and how can we not bring others down but bring everybody up." The Council, however, rejected the proposal.

Over a week later, a reporter asked Jay Barth which of the speeches from the stage of the Central High Auditorium left the greatest impression on him. The foremost scholar of Arkansas politics and government, Barth as a member of the state board of education in 2015 had voted against the motion for the state to take over the Little Rock school district. He responded by singling out as "powerful and lovely" the remarks of Gloria Ray Karlmark.

Karlmark had mused that, while she was often asked about the day she entered Central High School under troop escort, few inquired about the final day of that tumultuous year. It was the day yearbooks were distributed.

"I had a book, and I knew people signed each other's books. But here I was, now a 15-year-old girl, and who was going to sign my book? Who would I dare go up and ask to sign my book?"

Karlmark had secretly exchanged notes throughout the year with a white girl named Becky, who approached and signed the book. Then another girl came up and wrote a line in her book.

"In a different age, we could have been friends."

Selected Sources

No study of recent and contemporary history can only rely upon secondary works. This is particularly true of Arkansas, which attracted the attention of few historians of Southern history and did not support an academic press until 1980. Nevertheless, scholars have made notable strides in examining and interpreting recent developments in the state.

At Special Collections, University of Arkansas, Fayetteville, I consulted the manuscript collections of the Arkansas Centennial Celebration, Arkansas Council on Human Relations, Daisy Bates, Virgil Blossom, Robert Leflar, Hamilton Moses, Sara Alderman Murphy, National Organization of Women Arkansas Chapter, Herbert Thomas, University of Arkansas Cooperative Extension Service, Work Projects Administration—Arkansas Administration.

At the Butler Center for Arkansas Studies, I consulted the manuscript collections of the Couch-Remmel Family, Fred K. Darragh Jr., Quapaw Quarter Association. At the University of Arkansas at Little Rock Archives and Special Collections I consulted the Metroplan records.

I conducted interviews with Dale Bumpers, Marcus Halbrook, Brownie Ledbetter, Sydney S. McMath, Emon Mahony, Sheffield Nelson, David Pryor, and Henry Woods.

Arkansas appears in numerous overviews of recent Southern history but this essay will include only those sources that concentrate on the state.

In-depth and invaluable one-volume general histories of the state are Jeannie Whayne, Thomas DeBlack, George Sabo, and Morris S. Arnold, *Arkansas: A Narrative History*, 2nd ed. (Fayetteville: University of Arkansas Press, 2013); and Michael Dougan, *Arkansas Odyssey: The Saga of Arkansas from Prehistoric Times to Present* (Little Rock: Rose Publishing, 1994). More concise surveys are Harry S. Ashmore, *Arkansas: A History* (New York: Norton, 1978); David M. Tucker, *Arkansas: A People and their Reputation* (Memphis: Memphis State University Press, 1985); and C. Fred Williams, *Arkansas, Independent and Proud: An Illustrated History* (American Historical Press, 1986). Indispensable guides to political developments are Diane D. Blair and Jay Barth, *Arkansas Politics and Government: Do the People Rule?*, 2nd Ed. (Lincoln: University of Nebraska Press, 2005); and Timothy P. Donovan, Willard B. Gatewood, and Jeannie M. Whayne, eds., *The Governors of Arkansas: Essays in Political Biography*, 2nd ed. (Fayetteville: University of Arkansas

318 | SELECTED SOURCES

Press, 1995). The evolution of governmental institutions and policy can be followed in Kay Collett Goss, *The Arkansas State Constitution: A Reference Guide* (Westport, CT: Greenwood Press, 1993). Identity and image have been as much a concern of historians as it has the state's citizens, and Brooks Blevins astutely considers the topic in *Arkansas/Arkansaw: How Bear Hunters, Hillbillies, and Good Ol' Boys Defined a State* (Fayetteville: University of Arkansas Press, 2009). David Ware, *It's Official: The Real Stories Behind Arkansas's State Symbols* (Little Rock: Butler Center, 2015) uncovers how the designation of state symbols revealed the state's changing aspirations and perception of its role in the nation. Arkansas's core historical topic is undertaken passionately and forthrightly by Grif Stockley in his *Ruled By Race: Black/White Relations in Arkansas from Slavery to the Present* (Fayetteville: University of Arkansas Press, 2009).

Michael B. Dougan, Tom W. Dillard, and Timothy G. Nutt, comps., *Arkansas History: An Annotated Bibliography* (Westport, CT: Greenwood Press, 1995) can be supplemented with the Cumulative Index to the *Arkansas Historical Quarterly, 1942– 2000*, hosted online by the University of Arkansas, Fayetteville, Libraries, which also maintains the invaluable *Index of Arkansas*.

Researchers and those interested in the state's history are indebted to the Butler Center for Arkansas Studies at the Central Arkansas Library System for developing and overseeing *The Encyclopedia of Arkansas History & Culture* that came online in 2006. The David and Barbara Pryor Center for Arkansas Oral and Visual History, the University of Arkansas, Fayetteville, has made available since 1999 a rich and abundant range of interviews

The state's residents are well-served in an era of diminishing sources for news by the availability in print and online of superior and conscientious statewide publications. These outlets include the *Arkansas Democrat-Gazette, Arkansas Times, Arkansas Business*, and *Talk Business & Politics*. They have been thoroughly exploited for this study.

One

Carl H. Moneyhon, *Arkansas and the New South, 1874–1929* (Fayetteville: University of Arkansas Press, 1997) acutely established that social and economic developments in the era before 1930 show that the state was less distant from the rest of the nation as commonly assumed. A good introduction to the most studied region in the state is Jeannie Whayne and Willard B. Gatewood, eds., *The Arkansas Delta: Land of Paradox* (Fayetteville: University of Arkansas Press, 1993), although helpful is a recent collection of essays examining the broader region is Janelle Collins, ed., *Defining the Delta* (Fayetteville: University of Arkansas, 2015). Those looking to the hills can start with Milton D. Rafferty *The Ozarks: Land and Life* (Norman: University of Oklahoma Press, 1980). Brooks Blevins has explored comprehensively the scope of Ozark culture, society, and economy through numerous publications; readers can begin with the noteworthy *Hill Folks: A History of Arkansas Ozarkers and Their Image* (Chapel Hill: University of North Carolina Press, 2002).

Early twentieth-century exploitation of timber is addressed in Kenneth Smith, *Sawmill: The Story of Cutting the Last Great Virgin Forest East of the Rockies* (Fayetteville: University of Arkansas Press, 1986); and George. W Balogh, *Entrepreneurs in the Lumber Industry: Arkansas, 1881–1963* (New York: Garland Publishing, 1995). Stephen Strausberg, *A Century of Research: Centennial History of the Arkansas Agricultural Experiment Station, 1888–1988* (Fayetteville: Arkansas Agricultural Experiment Station, 1989) outlines often futile attempts to boost agricultural production. The consequences of the 1930 drought are described in Nan E. Woodruff, "The Failure of Relief During the Arkansas Drought of 1930–31," *Arkansas Historical Quarterly* 39 (Winter 1980): 301–313, and in her *Rare As Rain: Federal Relief in the Great Southern Drought of 1930–31* (Champaign: University of Illinois Press, 1985); Roger Lambert, "Hoover and the Red Cross in the Arkansas Drought of 1930," *Arkansas Historical Quarterly* 29 (Spring 1970): 3–19; and John I. Smith, "Reminiscences of Farming and Business in the Depression, 1929–1933," *Arkansas Historical Quarterly* 45 (Winter 1986): 321–29.

A solid brief overview of the Great Depression is Donald Holley, "Arkansas and the Great Depression," in *Historical Report of the Secretary of State*, vol. 3 (Little Rock: Secretary of State, 1978), while a more comprehensive treatment is David Rison, "Arkansas During the Great Depression," (PhD diss., University of California, Los Angeles, 1974). A number of works describe everyday life during the Depression, but a readers can find value in *The WPA Guide to 1930s Arkansas* (1941, repr. with new introduction by Elliott West. Lawrence: University Press of Kansas, 1987). Williams D. Downs Jr. conducted extensive interviews with survivors of the Depression, and informative excerpts are found in *Stories of Survival: Arkansas Farmers During the Great Depression* (Fayetteville: Phoenix International, 2011). Personal memoirs from the era include John G. Ragsdale, *As We Were in South Arkansas* (Little Rock: August House, 1995); William H. Bowen, *The Boy from Altheimer: From the Depression to the Boardroom* (Fayetteville: University of Arkansas Press, 2006); and Dee Brown, *When the Century Was Young* (Little Rock: August House, 1993).

The Parnell highway scandal is put in legislative context by Lee Reaves, "Highway Bond Refunding," *Arkansas Historical Quarterly* 2 (Dec. 1943): 316–30. Works on the major political figures of the decade include Carl Edward Weller Jr., *Joe T. Robinson: Always a Loyal Democrat* (Fayetteville: University of Arkansas Press, 1998); Brooks Hays, *Politics is My Parish* (Baton Rouge: Louisiana State University Press, 1981); Calvin R. Ledbetter, "Carl Bailey: A Pragmatic Reformer," *Arkansas Historical Quarterly* 57 (Summer 1998): 134–62; Donald Holley, "Carl E. Bailey, the Merit System, and Arkansas Politics, 1936–1939," *Arkansas Historical Quarterly* 45 (Winter 1986): 291–320; and Calvin Ledbetter Jr., "The Special Senatorial Election of 1937 and Its Legacy for Arkansas Politics," *Arkansas Historical Quarterly* 63 (Spring 2004):

1–23. The election of Hattie Caraway is described in David Malone, *Hattie and Huey: An Arkansas Tour* (Fayetteville: University of Arkansas Press, 1989); and Nancy Hendricks, *Senator Hattie Caraway* (Charleston, SC: History Press, 2013).

The struggle of state and federal authorities over relief programs is told well in Floyd W. Hicks and C. Roger Lambert, "Food for the Hungry: Federal Food Programs in Arkansas, 1933–1942," *Arkansas Historical Quarterly* 38 (Spring 1978): 23–43. The advent of black political reform is introduced in John Kirk, "Dr. J.M. Robinson, the Arkansas Negro Democratic Association and Black Politics in Little Rock, Arkansas, 1928–1952," *Pulaski County Historical Review* 41 (Spring 1993): 2–16, Part II (Summer 1993): 39–47.

David Moyers, "Trouble in a Company Town: The Crossett Strike of 1940," *Arkansas Historical Quarterly* 48 (Spring 1989): 34–56, is one of the few accounts of an industrial strike since 1930. By contrast, much has been published on the rise and fall of the Southern Tenant Farmers' Union, including worthwhile examinations with contrasting interpretations by Donald H. Grubbs, *Cry from the Cotton: The Southern Tenant Farmers' Union and the New Deal* (Chapel Hill: University of North Carolina Press, 1971); Jeannie Whayne, *A New Plantation South. Land, Labor, and Federal Favor in Twentieth Century Arkansas* (Charlottesville: University Press of Virginia, 1996); Nan Elizabeth Woodruff, *American Congo: The African American Freedom Struggle in the Delta* (Cambridge: Harvard University Press, 2003); Erick S. Gellman and Jarod Roll, *The Gospel of the Working Class: Labor's Southern Prophets in New Deal America* (Urbana: University of Illinois Press, 2011); and James D. Ross, *The Rise and Fall of the Southern Tenant Farmers Union in Arkansas* (Knoxville: University of Tennessee Press, 2018). Memoirs by organizational leaders include H. L. Mitchell, *Mean Things Happening in This Land: The Life and Times of H. L. Mitchell* (Montclair, NJ: Allanheld, Osmum, 1979); and Howard Kester, *Revolt Among The Sharecroppers* (New York: Covici, Friede, 1936). A rigorous study of the resettlement communities is Donald Holley, *Uncle Sam's Farmers: The New Deal Communities in the Lower Mississippi Valley* (Urbana: University of Illinois Press, 1975). The saga of Arkansas's labor college is splendidly related in William H. Cobb, *Radical Education in the Rural South: Commonwealth College, 1923–1940* (Detroit: Wayne State University Press, 2000).

Wendy Richter, "Celebrating Fifty Years of the Arkansas Historical Association," *Arkansas Historical Quarterly* 55 (Summer 1996): 167–72, reports the founding of the organization. The importance of the Home Demonstration Agents and the pressures of segregation are confirmed in Cherisee Jones-Branch, "Empowering Families and Communities: African-American Home Demonstration Agents in Arkansas, 1913–1965 in *Race and Ethnicity in Arkansas: New Perspectives*, edited by John A. Kirk (Fayetteville: University of Arkansas Press, 2014). Examples of community life during the Depression are conveyed in Raymond L. Muncy, *Searcy, Arkansas: A Frontier Town Grows Up with America* (Searcy: Harding Press, 1976); Nancy Apple and Suzy Keasler, *History of Lee County, Arkansas* (Marianna: Lee County Sesquicentennial

Committee, 1987); and Stephen H. Dew "The New Deal and Fayetteville, Arkansas, 1933–1941," (MA thesis, University of Arkansas, 1987). The Depression-era search for cultural authenticity is noted in Pamela Webb, "By the Sweat of the Brow: The Back-to-the Land Movement in Depression Arkansas," *Arkansas Historical Quarterly* 42 (Winter 1983): 332–43; Ben F. Johnson III, *Fierce Solitude: A Life of John Gould Fletcher* (Fayetteville: University of Arkansas Press, 1994); and Robert B. Cochran, "'All the Songs in the World': The Story of Emma Dusenbury," *Arkansas Historical Quarterly* 44 (Spring 1985): 3–15.

The discovery and celebration of Ozark folklore is cogently observed in Robert Cochran, Vance *Randolph: An Ozark Life* (Urbana: University of Illinois Press, 1985); Ethel Simpson, "Arkansas Lives: The Ozark Quest of Otto Ernest Rayburn," *Arkansas Libraries* 39 (March 1982): 12–19; Ellen Shipley, "'But a Smile Looks Better in Print': The Literary Enterprises of Otto Ernest Rayburn," *Arkansas Libraries* 39 (March 1982): 20–23.

Interest in the state's image is not confined to civic boosters, as indicated by the literature on the topic. A catalogue of Arkansas references in national publications is found in William Foy Lisenby, "A Survey of Arkansas's Image Problems," *Arkansas Historical Quarterly* 30 (Spring 1971): 60–71; while Bob Lancaster, "Ill Fame," Chap. 8 in *The Jungles of Arkansas: A Personal History of the Wonder State* (Fayetteville: University of Arkansas Press, 1989) is a shrewd commentary by the finest writer of Arkansas popular history.

The influence of federal jobs programs on the state's cultural and community development is revealed in Joey McCarty "Civilian Conservation Corps in Arkansas" (MA thesis, University of Arkansas, 1977); Sandra Taylor Smith, *The Civilian Conservation Corps in Arkansas, 1933–1942* (Little Rock: Historic Preservation Program, 1991); Fred H. Lang, "Two Decades of State Forestry in Arkansas," *Arkansas Historical Quarterly* 24 (Winter 1965): 208–19; Lynda B. Langford, "The Works Projects Administration in Pulaski County District," *Pulaski County Historical Review* 35 (Spring 1987): 2–15; and William B. Worthen, "Louise Loughborough and Her Campaign for 'Courage and Fineness,'" *Pulaski County Historical Review* 40 (Summer 1992): 26–33. An overlooked but excellent account is Holly Hope, *An Ambition to Be Preferred: New Deal Recovery Efforts and Architecture in Arkansas, 1933–1943* (Little Rock: Arkansas Historic Preservation Program, 2006).

The movement to preserve African American history is brought to light in Bob Lancaster, "Early Hurt," Chap. 7 in *The Jungles of Arkansas*; Thomas E. Jordan, "The Collection of Ex-Slave Narratives in Little Rock by the Federal Writers' Project," *Pulaski County Historical Review* 40 (Spring 1992): 2–14, Part II (Summer 1992): 42–47; and Fon Gordon, "Black Women in Arkansas," *Pulaski County Historical Review* 35 (Summer 1987): 26–37. Students interested in two native African American composers can consult Barbara Jackson, "Florence Price, Composer," *Black Perspective in Music* 5 (Spring 1977): 30–43; Linda Rae Brown, "Florence B. Price, 1887–1953," in *Women Composers: Music through the Ages*, edited by Sylvia Glickman and Martha

Furman Schleifer (New Haven, CT: G.K. Hall, 2003); and Catherine Parsons Smith, *William Grant Still* (Urbana: University of Illinois Press, 2008).

The conflicts surrounding the electrification of Arkansas are detailed in Stephen Wilson, *Harvey Couch: An Entrepreneur Brings Electricity to Arkansas* (Little Rock: August House, 1986); D. Clayton Brown, "Hen Eggs to Kilowatts: Arkansas Rural Electrification," *Red River Valley Historical Review* 3 (Winter 1978): 119–126; D. Clayton Brown, *Electricity for Rural America: The Fight for the REA* (Westport, CT: Greenwood Press, 1980); E. F. Chesnutt, "Rural Electrification in Arkansas, 1935–1940: The Formative Years," *Arkansas Historical Quarterly* 46 (Autumn 1987): 215–60; Clyde Ellis, *A Giant Step* (New York: Random House, 1966); Sherry Laymon, "Arkansas's Dark Ages: The Struggle to Electrify the State," *Arkansas Historical Quarterly* 71 (Autumn 2012): 283–300.

John Kirk reintroduced scholars to William Harold Flowers through various articles, including "The Legacy of William Harold Flowers," *Arkansas Times*, February 1, 2018. Persistent racial violence deep into the twentieth century is documented through the essays in Guy Lancaster, ed., *Bullets and Fire: Lynching and Authority in Arkansas, 1840–1950* (Fayetteville: University of Arkansas Press, 2017).

Two

Robert Palmer, *Deep Blues* (New York: Viking Press, 1981), is a wonderful history by a Little Rock native of Delta blues music. Both Robert Cochran, *Our Own Sweet Sounds: A Celebration of Popular Music in Arkansas*, 2nd ed. (Fayetteville: University of Arkansas Press, 2005); and Ali Welky and Mike Keckhaver, eds., *Encyclopedia of Arkansas Music* (Little Rock: Butler Center Books, 2013) are necessary guides to the state's contributions to popular music. The club scene in West Memphis is invoked in Simon Hosken, "Policing the Blues: Remembering the Desegregation of Law Enforcement in West Memphis, Arkansas," *Arkansas Historical Quarterly* 72 (Summer 2013): 120–38.

The starting point for understanding 1940s Arkansas is C. Calvin Smith, *War and Wartime Changes: The Transformation of Arkansas, 1940–1945* (Fayetteville: University of Arkansas Press, 1986). A serviceable introduction to the period is Boyce Drummond, "Arkansas 1940–1954," in *Historical Report of the Secretary of State*, vol. 3 (Little Rock: Secretary of State, 1978), but more thorough coverage is found in Holly Hope, *We've Gotta Get Tough: History of World War II Home Front Efforts in Arkansas, 1941–1946* (Little Rock: Historic Preservation Program, 2008). A full history of an Arkansas military unit is Donald M. Goldstein and Katherine V. Dillon, *The Williwaw War: The Arkansas National Guard in the Aleutians in World War II* (Fayetteville: University of Arkansas Press, 1992).

A number of strong essays examine the operations of government internment camps in the state. On the conscientious objectors, see Cynthia Morris, "Arkansas's Reaction to the Men Who Said 'No' to World War II," *Arkansas Historical Quarterly* 43 (Summer 1984): 153–177; as well as a memoir by the notable poet William Stafford, who was assigned to the Columbia County camp, *Down in My Hear: Peace Witness in War Time* (Corvallis: Oregon State Press, 1998). The internment camps in Arkansas that held Japanese Americans have attracted a growing body of literature. Among the earliest treatments were Russell Bearden, "Life Inside Arkansas's Japanese-American Relocation Centers," *Arkansas Historical Quarterly* 48 (Summer 1989): 169–96; C. Calvin Smith, "The Response of Arkansans to Prisoners of War and Japanese Americans in Arkansas, 1942–1945," *Arkansas Historical Quarterly* 53 (Autumn 1994): 340–66; a more recent consideration is Jason Morgan Ward, "'No Jap Crow': Japanese Americans Encounter the World War II South," *Journal of Southern History* 73 (February 2007): 75–104; a poignant and unvarnished portrait is found in Vivienne Schiffer, *Camp Nine: A Novel* (Fayetteville: University of Arkansas Press, 2011). Prisoners of war conditions are addressed in Merrill Pritchett and William L. Shea, "The Afrika Korps in Arkansas, 1943–1946," *Arkansas Historical Quarterly* 37 (Spring 1978): 3–22, and in the few references to Arkansas in Arnold Krammer, *Nazi Prisoners of War in America* (Chelsea, MI: Scarborough House, 1996). The STFU's unequal fight with landowners is documented in Nan Elizabeth Woodruff, "Pick or Fight: The Emergency Farm Labor Program in the Arkansas and Mississippi Delta During World War II," *Agricultural History* 64 (Spring 1990): 74–85. The operation of the Mexican Farm Labor Agreement in Arkansas is examined in Julie M. Weise, "The Bracero Program: Mexican Workers in the Arkansas Delta, 1948–1964," in *Race and Ethnicity in Arkansas*, 125–140; and J. Justin Castro, "Mexican Braceros and Arkansas Cotton: Agricultural Labor and Civil Rights in the Post-World War II South," *Arkansas Historical Quarterly* 75 (Spring 2016): 27–46.

In addition to the local histories cited above, the effect of World War II on town life is also covered in Odie B. Faulk and Billy Mac Jones, *Fort Smith: An Illustrated History* (Fort Smith: Old Fort Smith Museum, 1983); John Fergus Ryan, "An Argenta Memoir," *Arkansan*, Aug. 1979, 12–21; B. C. Hall, "When Mississippi County was the Land of the Pharaohs and Sunset Carson was King," *Arkansas Times,* June 1983, 48–56; James W. Bell *Little Rock Handbook* (Little Rock: Publishers Bookshop, 1980); and Jim Lester and Judy Lester, *Greater Little Rock: A Pictorial History* (Norfolk, VA: Donning, 1986).

Histories of the largest church organizations in the state include C. Fred Williams, S. Ray Granade, and Kenneth M. Startup, *A System & Plan: Arkansas Baptist State Convention, 1848–1998* (Franklin, TN: Providence House, 1998); E. Glenn Hinson, *A History of Baptists in Arkansas, 1818–1978* (Little Rock: Arkansas State Convention, 1979); Nancy Britton, *Two Centuries of Methodism in Arkansas, 1800–2000* (Little Rock: August House, 2000); Walter N. Vernon, *Methodism in Arkansas, 1816–1976* (Little Rock: Joint Committee for the History of Arkansas Methodism, 1976); and James M. Woods, *Mission and Memory: A History of the Catholic Church in Arkansas* (Little Rock: Diocese of Little Rock, 1993). Carolyn Gray LeMaster, *A Corner of the Tapestry: A History of the Jewish Experience in Arkansas, 1820s-1990s* (Fayetteville: University of Arkansas Press, 1994) is a comprehensive narrative of a small but influential community. An influential and significant figure in that community is profiled in James L. Moses, *Just and Righteous Causes: Rabbi Ira Sanders and the Fight for Racial and Social Justice in Arkansas, 1926–1963* (Fayetteville: University of Arkansas Press, 2018).

Early general surveys on the experience of women in the post-1930 era provided the groundwork for later overdue gender studies: Janet Allured, "The Women of Arkansas: A Historical Overview," in *Behold Our Works Were Good*, edited by Elizabeth Jacoway (Little Rock: August House, 1988); Carol T. Gaddy, "Women of Arkansas," in *Historical Report of the Secretary of State*, vol. 3 (Little Rock: Secretary of State, 1978); Kitty Sloan, ed., *Horizons: 100 Arkansas Women of Achievement* (Little Rock: Rose Publishing, 1980); and Shirley Abbott, *Womenfolks: Growing Up Down South* (New York: Ticknor & Fields, 1983). Recently published overviews are Nancy Hendricks, *Notable Women of Arkansas: From Hattie to Hillary, 100 Names to Know* (Little Rock: Butler Center Books, 2016); and Cherisse Jones-Branch and Gary T. Edwards, eds., *Arkansas Women: Their Lives and Times* (Athens: University of Georgia Press, 2018).

Federal investment in wartime Arkansas is surveyed in S. Charles Bolton's *Airfields, Camps, and Plants: Little Rock District U. S. Army Corps of Engineers Military Construction in World War II* (Little Rock: U.S. Army Corps of Engineers, 2000); and his "Turning Point: World War II and the Economic Development of Arkansas," *Arkansas Historical Quarterly* 61 (Summer 2002): 124–49. Carolyn Yancey Kent has examined two ordnance plants in "Uncle Sam Needs Your Resources: A History of the Ozark Ordnance Works," *South Arkansas Historical Journal* 5 (Fall 2005): 4–20; and "Last Hired: African American Hiring in North Pulaski County's Citadel for Defense," *Pulaski County Historical Quarterly* 62 (Fall 2014): 77–84. The vitality of the African American business district in Little Rock is portrayed in Berna J. Love, *End of the Line: A History of Little Rock's West Ninth Street* (Little Rock: Center for Arkansas Studies, University of Arkansas at Little Rock, 2003).

An evolving twentieth-century industry is covered in Ray Poindexter, *Arkansas Airwaves* (North Little Rock, 1974). The beginnings of industrial recruitment are disclosed in C. Hamilton Moses, "The Arkansas Plan," *Arkansas Economist* 3 (Spring 1961): 1–7. A sympathetic but not uncritical examination of the developing poultry industry is Stephen Strausberg, *From Hills and Hollers: Rise of the Poultry Industry in Arkansas* (Fayetteville: Arkansas Agricultural Experiment Station, 1995). The impact of mechanization on cotton agriculture is perceptively explored in Donald Holley, *The Second Great Emancipation: The Mechanical Cotton Picker, Black Migration, and How They Shaped the Modern South* (Fayetteville: University of Arkansas Press, 2000). The post-WWII anti-union campaign can be followed in F. Ray Marshall, *Labor in the South* (Cambridge: Harvard University Press, 1967); Edward Chess, "Agrarian and Labor Unions in Arkansas from 1870 to the Union Control Legislation of the 1940s" (MA thesis, University of Arkansas at Little Rock, 1996);

and Michael Pierce, "The Origins of Right-to-Work: Vance Muse, Anti-Semitism, and the Maintenance of Jim Crow Labor Relations," Labor Online, Labor and Working Class History Association, https://www.lawcha.org/2017/01/12/origins -right-work-vance-muse-anti-semitism-maintenance-jim-crow-labor-relations/.

Guerdon D. Nichols, "Breaking the Color Barrier at The University of Arkansas," *Arkansas Historical Quarterly* 27 (Spring 1968): 3–21, describes the state's initial public desegregation, though a more recent consideration is Judith Kilpatrick, "Desegregating the University of Arkansas School of Law: L. Clifford Davis and the Six Pioneers," *Arkansas Historical Quarterly* 68 (Summer 2009): 123–156. C. Calvin Smith, "From 'Separate but Equal to Desegregation': The Changing Philosophy of L. C. Bates," *Arkansas Historical Quarterly* 42 (Autumn 1983): 254–70 outlines the early career of the important civil rights leader.

Three

Hot Springs National Park is chronicled in Dee Brown, *The American Spa: Hot Springs, Arkansas* (Little Rock: Rose Publishing, 1982); and Ray Hanley, *A Place Apart: A Pictorial History of Hot Springs, Arkansas* (Fayetteville: University of Arkansas Press, 2011); the rise and fall of a political boss is described in Nancy Russ, "The Life and Times of Leo P. McLaughlin," *The Record* 24 (1983): 65–71; and Orval E. Allbritton, *Leo and Verne: The Spa's Heyday* (Hot Springs: Garland County Historical Society, 2003). A vanished era in the city's history is retold in the graceful Shirley Abbott, *The Bookmaker's Daughter* (New York: Ticknor & Fields, 1991).

The effect of reforms on public institutions is evident in Jerry E. Hinshaw, *Call the Roll: The First One Hundred Years of the Arkansas Legislature* (Little Rock: Rose Publishing, 1986); Keith Sutton, ed., *Arkansas Wildlife: A History* (Fayetteville: University of Arkansas Press, 1998); Robert A. Leflar, *The First 100 Years: Centennial History of the University of Arkansas* (Fayetteville: University of Arkansas Foundation, 1972); T. M. Stinnett and Clara B. Kennan, *All This and Tomorrow Too: The Evolving and Continuing History of the Arkansas Education Association* (Little Rock: Arkansas Education Association, 1969); and Xavier Zinzeindolph Wynn, "The Development of African American Schools in Arkansas, 1863–1963: A Historical Comparison of Black and White Schools with Regards to Funding and the Quality of Education," (EdD diss., University of Mississippi, 1995); C. Calvin Smith and Linda W. Joshua, eds., *Educating the Masses: The Unfolding History of Black School Administrators in Arkansas, 1900–2000* (Fayetteville: University of Arkansas Press, 2000); Linda Pine, "A Minimum Degree of Opportunity: A History of the Minimum Foundation Program Aid in Arkansas, 1951–1983" (MA thesis, University of Arkansas at Little Rock, 1986); and Calvin R. Ledbetter, "The Fight for School Consolidation in Arkansas, 1946–1948," *Arkansas Historical Quarterly* 65 (Spring 2006): 45–57; Grif Stockley, *Black Boys Burning: The 1959 Fire at the Arkansas Negro Boys Industrial School* (Jackson: University Press of Mississippi, 2017).

Electoral politics in the postwar era is deciphered in Boyce Drummond, "Arkansas Politics: A Study of a One-Party System," (PhD diss., University of Chicago, 1957). An accomplished, underrated study is James E. Lester, *A Man for Arkansas: Sid McMath and the Southern Reform Tradition* (Little Rock: Rose Publishing, 1976), which is complemented by McMath's memoir, *Promises Kept* (Fayetteville: University of Arkansas Press, 2003). Randall Bennett Woods, *Fulbright: A Biography* (New York: Cambridge University Press, 1995) is a well-regarded portrait, although a dissenting perspective is found in Lee Riley Powell, *J. William Fulbright and His Time: A Political Biography* (Memphis: Guild Bindery Press, 1996). Ben Laney's Dixiecrat career is skillfully parsed in Numan V. Bartley, *The New South 1945–1980* (Baton Rouge: Louisiana State Press, 1985), and also treated in Kari Frederickson, *Dixiecrat Revolt and the End of the Solid South, 1932–1968* (Chapel Hill: University of North Carolina Press, 2001).

Roy Reed, *Faubus: An American Prodigal* (Fayetteville: University of Arkansas Press, 1997) remains essential to understanding the pivotal figure and his era. Faubus had his say in the two *Down from the Hills* volumes (Little Rock: Pioneer, 1980, 1985). An important social welfare reform in the Faubus years is described in Elizabeth F. Shores, "The Arkansas Children's Colony at Conway: A Springboard for Federal Policy on Special Education," *Arkansas Historical Quarterly* 57 (Winter 1998): 408–34. Studies of the powerful chairman of the U.S. House Ways and Means Committee are Kay Collett Goss, *Mr. Chairman: The Life and Legacy of Wilbur D. Mills* (Little Rock: Parkhurst Brothers, 2012); and Julian E. Zelizer, *Taxing America: Wilbur D. Mills, Congress, and the State, 1945–1975* (New York: Cambridge University Press, 2000). An admiring portrait of the influential U.S. senator is found in Sherry Laymon, *Fearless: John L. McClellan, United States Senator* (Mustang, OK: Tate Publishing, 2011), while less approving is Michael Pierce, "John McClellan, the Teamsters, and Biracial Labor Politics in Arkansas, 1947–1959" in *Life and Labor in the New South*, edited by Robert H. Zeiger (Gainesville: University Press of Florida, 2012). The segregationist leader is adeptly studied in, Elizabeth Jacoway, "Jim Johnson of Arkansas," in *The Role of Ideas in the Civil Rights South*, edited by Ted Ownby, 137–56 (Jackson: University Press of Mississippi, 2002).

The progress of postwar industrial recruitment winds its way through Becky Thompson, "The Evolution of the Arkansas Industrial Development Commission From 1955 to the Present," (MA thesis, Economic Development Institute, University of Oklahoma, 1996); James E. P. Griner, "The Growth of Manufactures in Arkansas, 1900–1950" (PhD diss., George Peabody, 1957); and Kornelis Walraven, "Financing New Industry," *Arkansas Economist* 3 (Winter 1961): 1–7. The career of Witt Stephens is detailed in an incisive series of articles by Ernest Dumas for the *Arkansas Gazette*, June 27–29, 1977. The beginnings of what would become the major crop in Arkansas are unearthed in D. Brooks Green, "Irrigation Expansion in Arkansas: A Preliminary Investigation," *Arkansas Historical Quarterly* 45 (Autumn 1986): 261–268; and

John Gates, "Groundwater Irrigation in the Development of the Grand Prairie Rice Industry, 1896–1950," *Arkansas Historical Quarterly* 64 (Winter 2005): 394–413.

The gains made by those who left Arkansas is clarified in Donald Holley, "Leaving the Land of Opportunity: Arkansas and the Great Migration," *Arkansas Historical Quarterly* 64 (Autumn 2005): 245–261. Brooks Blevins in "Life on the Margins: The Diaries of Minnie Atteberry," *Arkansas Historical Quarterly* 75 (Winter 2016): 289–318, reveals how isolated Ozark residents acquired and adapted consumer goods as way of edging into modern circumstances.

A firsthand account of the revival of deer hunting is Herbert H. Lunday, "Memories of Buckeye Deer Camp," *Rivers & Roads & Points In Between* 13 (Summer 1985): 2–8. The definitive history of the university football team is Orville Henry and Jim Bailey, *The Razorbacks: A Story of Arkansas Football* (rev. 1973 ed. Fayetteville: University of Arkansas Press, 1996). A rockabilly pioneer tells his story in Jeannie Whayne, "Interview with Billy Lee Riley," *Arkansas Historical Quarterly* 55 (Autumn 1996): 297–318; while another major figure is highlighted in Marvin Schwartz, *We Wanna Boogie: The Rockabilly Roots of Sonny Burgess and the Pacers* (Little Rock: Butler Center Books, 2014).

The desegregation of the Fayetteville schools is carefully and clearly explained in Willard Gatewood's introduction to *Civil Obedience: An Oral History of School Desegregation in Fayetteville, Arkansas, 1954–1965*, edited by Julianne Lewis Adams and Thomas A. DeBlack (Fayetteville: University of Arkansas Press, 1994), while another fine examination of early moderation is Jerry J. Vervak, "The Hoxie Imbroglio," *Arkansas Historical Quarterly* 48 (Spring 1989): 17–33; an exceptional online exploration of the Hoxie confrontation that includes interviews with contemporaries is "Hill Foundation Hoxie 21 Collection," at the *Crossroads to Freedom*, http://www.crossroadstofreedom.org/detail.collection?oid=15. The racial cleansing in Sheridan is recounted in James W. Loewen, *Sundown Towns: A Hidden Dimension of American Racism* (New York: New Press, 2005). The attempt to integrate Southern minor league baseball is related in Jay Jennings, "The Black Bathers," *Arkansas Times* 17 (July 1991): 40–43, 52–57.

Four

Shaped by the expansion of civil rights historiography and new research approaches, the narrative of the 1957 Little Rock crisis has shifted from a focus on personalities to a greater recognition of community involvement, economic structure, and political culture.

The range of perspectives is demonstrated in several collections of essays and documents: Elizabeth Jacoway and C. Fred Williams, eds., *Understanding the Little Rock Crisis: An Exercise in Remembrance and Reconciliation* (Fayetteville: University of Arkansas Press, 1999); John A. Kirk, ed., *An Epitaph for Little Rock: A Fiftieth Anniversary Retrospective on the Central High Crisis* (Fayetteville: University of

Arkansas Press, 2008); Catherine M. Lewis and J. Richard Lewis, eds., *Race, Politics, and Memory: A Documentary History of the Little Rock School Crisis* (Fayetteville: University of Arkansas, 2007).

Memoirs of leading participants include Daisy Bates, *The Long Shadow of Little Rock* (1962; repr. Fayetteville: University of Arkansas Press, 1987); Harry Ashmore, *Hearts and Minds: The Anatomy of Racism from Roosevelt to Reagan* (New York: McGraw-Hill, 1982); Virgil T. Blossom, *It Has Happened Here* (New York: Harper, 1959); Brooks Hays, *A Southern Moderate Speaks* (Chapel Hill: University of North Carolina, 1959); Elizabeth Huckaby, *Crisis at Central High: Little Rock, 1957–1958* (Baton Rouge: Louisiana State University Press, 1980); and Dunbar H. Ogden, *My Father Said Yes: A White Pastor in Little Rock School Integration* (Nashville: Vanderbilt University Press, 2008). Several of the students who desegregated Central High have recalled those troubled years: Melba Patillo Beals, *Warriors Don't Cry* (New York: Pocket Books, 1994); Carlotta Walls LaNier with Lisa Frazier Page, *A Mighty Long Way: My Journey to Justice at Little Rock Central High School* (New York: One World/Ballantine, 2009); Terrence Roberts, *Lessons from Little Rock* (Little Rock: Butler Center Books, 2009). Interviews with white former students are the basis for two studies with differing aims: Beth Roy, *Bitters in the Honey: Tales of Hope and Disappointment across Divides of Race and Time* (Fayetteville: University of Arkansas Press, 1999); and Ralph Brodie and Marvin Swartz, *Central in Our Lives: Voices from Little Rock Central High School, 1957–1959* (Little Rock: Butler Center for Arkansas Studies, 2007).

The development and strategy behind the Congressional opposition to the *Brown* decision is expertly analyzed in John Kyle Day, *The Southern Manifesto: Massive Resistance and the Fight to Preserve Segregation* (Jackson: University Press of Mississippi, 2014). The unsettled white moderates are highlighted in Tony Badger, "Southerners Who Refused to Sign the Southern Manifesto," *Historical Journal* 42 (1999): 517–534; David L. Chappell, *Inside Agitators: White Southerners in the Civil Rights Movement* (Baltimore: John Hopkins University Press, 1994); and Elizabeth Jacoway, "Taken By Surprise" in *Southern Businessmen and Desegregation*, edited by Elizabeth Jacoway and David Colburn (Baton Rouge: Louisiana State University Press, 1982).

Key overviews have delivered compelling narrative accounts and constructed original interpretations of the desegregation of Central High School beyond the televised clashes: Irving J. Spitzberg, *Racial Politics in Little Rock, 1954–1964* (New York: Garland, 1987); Tony Freyer, *Little Rock on Trial: Cooper v. Aaron and School Desegregation* (Lawrence: University Press of Kansas, 2007); Elizabeth Jacoway, *Turn Away Thy Son: Little Rock, the Crisis That Shocked the Nation* (New York: Free Press, 2007); Karen Anderson, *Little Rock: Race and Resistance at Central High School* (Princeton: Princeton University Press, 2009). John Kirk with clarity and insight places the crisis within the larger civil rights struggle in *Redefining the Color Line: Black Activism in Little Rock, Arkansas, 1940–1970* (Gainesville: University Press of

Florida, 2002). Shawn A. Fisher, "The Battle of Little Rock," (PhD diss., University of Memphis, 2013) offers a fresh perspective through a discerning examination of the U.S. Army mission preparations and experiences of the National Guardsmen. Scholars over the years have benefited from the indispensable essays of Graeme Cope that have uncovered the radical white resistance, and readers unfamiliar with his work may wish to begin with "'A Thorn in the Side'? The Mothers' League of Central High School and the Little Rock Desegregation Crisis of 1957," *Arkansas Historical Quarterly* 57 (Summer 1998): 160–190; and "'Honest White People of the Middle and Lower Classes'? A Profile of the Capital Citizens' Council during the Little Rock Crisis of 1957," *Arkansas Historical Quarterly* 61 (Spring 2002): 37–58.

Contrasting assessments on the decision by the Little Rock school board to request a delay in integration in 1958 are found in Elizabeth Jacoway, "Richard C. Butler and the Little Rock School Board: The Quest to Maintain 'Educational Quality'," *Arkansas Historical Quarterly* 65 (Spring 2006): 23–38; and Judith Kilpatrick, "Wiley Austin Branton and Cooper v. Aaron: American Fulfills Its Promise," *Arkansas Historical Quarterly* 65 (Spring 2006): 7–21.

Based in part on extensive interviews, Sondra Gordy, *Finding the Lost Year: What Happened When Little Rock Closed its Public Schools?* (Fayetteville: University of Arkansas Press, 2009) is an evocative book-length study of the closure of the Little Rock high schools.

Biographies of civil rights leaders remain a work in progress, but readers can begin with Grif Stockley's fine and deeply researched *Daisy Bates: Civil Rights Crusader from Arkansas* (Oxford: University Press of Mississippi, 2005); and Judith Kilpatrick, *There When We Needed Him: Wiley Austin Branton, Civil Rights Warrior* (Fayetteville: University of Arkansas Press, 2007).

The background and activities of the Women's Emergency Committee are related in the essential Sara Alderman Murphy, *Breaking the Silence: Little Rock's Women's Emergency Committee to Open Our Schools, 1958–1963* (Fayetteville: University of Arkansas Press, 1997); as well as valuable contributions in Lorraine Gates, "Power from the Pedestal: The Women's Emergency Committee and the Little Rock Crisis," *Arkansas Historical Quarterly* 55 (Spring 1996): 25–57; and Laura A Miller, "Challenging the Segregationist Power Structure in Little Rock" in *Throwing Off the Cloak of Privilege: White Southern Women Activists in the Civil Rights Era*, edited by Gail S. Murray (Gainesville: University Press of Florida, 2004); Vivion Brewer, *The Embattled Ladies of Little Rock, 1958–1963: The Struggle to Save Public Education at Central High* (Fort Bragg, CA: Lost Coast Press, 1998) is a memoir by one of the organization's founders; and Stephanie Bayless, *Obliged to Help: Adolphine Fletcher Terry and the Progressive South* (Little Rock: Butler Center Books, 2011) is a full biography of the other leader.

Michael Pierce in his closely argued "Historians of the Central High Crisis and Little Rock's Working-Class Whites: A Review Essay," *Arkansas Historical Quarterly* 70 (Winter 2011): 462–83, observes that several of the works noted above have not acknowledged the contributions of organized labor to anti-segregation electioneering. He extends the argument in "Odell Smith, Teamsters Local 878 and Civil Rights Unionism in Little Rock, 1943–1965," *Journal of Southern History* 84 (November 2018): 925–958.

The dearth of scholarship on the 1960s civil rights movement is beginning to be addressed with studies of the Student Nonviolent Coordinating Committee's work in Arkansas. Readers would do well to begin with the impressive set of essays along with documents in Jennifer Jensen Wallach and John A. Kirk, eds., *Arsnick: The Student Nonviolent Coordinating Committee in Arkansas* (Fayetteville: University of Arkansas Press, 2011). The organization is also examined in Brent Riffel,"In the Storm: William Hansen and the Student Nonviolent Coordinating Committee in Arkansas, 1962–1967," *Arkansas Historical Quarterly* 63 (Winter 2004): 380–403; and Randy Finley, "Crossing the White Line: SNCC in Three Delta Towns, 1963–1967,"*Arkansas Historical Quarterly* 65 (Summer 2006): 117–37. Tensions between student activists and university administrators is outlined in Holly Y. McGee, "'It was the Wrong Time, and they Just Weren't Ready': Direct-Action Protest in Pine Bluff, 1963," *Arkansas Historical Quarterly* 66 (Spring 2007): 18–42. The confrontation in a Delta town is traced in Michael R. Deaderick, "Racial Conflict in Forrest City: The Trial and Triumph of Moderation in an Arkansas Delta Town," *Arkansas Historical Quarterly* 69 (Spring 2010): 1–27. A copy of John Kirk's "Facilitating Change: the Arkansas Council on Human Relations, 1954–1964" can be downloaded from http://plaza.ufl.edu/wardb/Kirk.doc.

The desegregation of the Little Rock schools following 1960 is assessed in David Gene Vinzant, "Little Rock's Long Crisis: Schools and Race in Little Rock, Arkansas, 1863–2009 (PhD diss., University of Arkansas, 2010); and Ben F. Johnson III, "After 1957: Resisting Integration in Little Rock," in *An Epitaph for Little Rock*: 115–134.

The little-known but critical court decision surrounding the policies of Lake Nixon is unearthed in Travis Raterman, "Lake Nixon National Register of Historic Places Nomination Form," National Park Service, United States Department of the Interior, Washington, D.C., 2017, accessible at http://www.arkansaspreservation.com /National-Register Listings/PDF/PU10111_nr.pdf. School desegregation cases outside Little Rock are surveyed in John A. Kirk, "Not Quite Black and White: School Desegregation in Arkansas, 1954–1966," *Arkansas Historical Quarterly* 70 (Autumn 2011): 225–57, while the same author examines the growing impatience with the progress of racial justice in An 'Eyeball-to-Eyeball Kind of Organization': Black United Youth and the Black Power Movement in Arkansas," *Arkansas Historical Quarterly* 75 (Autumn 2016): 206–38.

Urban development in Little Rock is followed through Stuart Eurman, "Consolidating Cities: An Urban Fiction," *Pulaski County Historical Review* 42 (Spring 1994): 19–22; Martha Walters, "Little Rock Urban Renewal," *Pulaski County Historical Review* 24 (March 1976): 12–16; Margaret Arnold, "Little Rock's Vanishing Black Communities," *Arkansas Times* (June 1978): 36–43; Raymond Rebsamen,

"Urban Renewal: Progress on a Timetable," *Arkansas Economist* 4 (Fall 1961): 1–8; John A. Kirk and Jess Porter, "The Roots of Little Rock's Segregated Neighborhoods," *Arkansas Times,* July 10, 2014, 12–16. The debates over the construction of the Wilbur Mills expressway in Little Rock are traced cogently in Darcy Atwood Pumphrey, "An Interstate Runs Through It: The Construction of Little Rock's Interstate 630 and The Fight to Stop It." (MA thesis, University of Arkansas at Little Rock, 2013).

Election reform is described in Calvin R. Ledbetter, "Arkansas Amendment for Voter Registration without Poll Tax Payment," *Arkansas Historical Quarterly* 54 (Summer 1995): 134–162; while the fate of one of the casualties of the change is detailed in Robert Thompson, "Barefoot and Pregnant: The Education of Paul Van Dalsem," *Arkansas Historical Quarterly* 57 (Winter 1998): 377–407. The movement for the Equal Rights Amendment in Arkansas is ably observed in Janine A Parry, "'What Women Wanted': Arkansas Women's Commissions and the ERA," *Arkansas Historical Quarterly* 59 (Autumn 2000): 265–98.

The first twentieth-century Republican governor is examined in Cathy K. Urwin, *Agenda for Reform: Winthrop Rockefeller as Governor of Arkansas, 1967–1971* (Fayetteville: University of Arkansas Press, 1991); John Ward, *The Arkansas Rockefeller* (Baton Rouge: Louisiana State University Press, 1978); Ernest Dumas, "Rockefeller: Champion of Change," *UALR Magazine* (Fall 2003): 13–19; Billy B. Hathorn, "Friendly Rivalry: Winthrop Rockefeller Challenges Orval Faubus in 1964," *Arkansas Historical Quarterly* 53 (Winter 1994): 446–73; John A. Kirk, "A Southern Road Less Traveled: The 1966 Arkansas Gubernatorial Election and (Winthrop) Rockefeller Republicanism in Dixie" in *Painting Dixie Red: When, Where, Why, and How the South Became Republican,* edited by Glenn Feldman (Gainesville: University Press of Florida, 2011). Dale Bumpers, *The Best Lawyer in a One-Lawyer Town: A Memoir* (New York: Random House, 2003) is a brief, impressionistic autobiography, while a preeminent veteran journalist with an encyclopedic knowledge of the state's political developments offers an overview on the occasion of Bumpers's death in Ernest Dumas, "The Life and Times of Dale Bumpers," *Arkansas Times,* January 14, 2016, 14–18, 20–23. Jim Ranchino, *Faubus to Bumpers: Arkansas Votes, 1960–1970* (Arkadelphia: Action Research, 1972) reports the findings of the state's first professional political pollster.

Political struggles in Conway County can be followed in Tom Glaze with Ernie Dumas, *Waiting for the Cemetery Vote: A Memoir* (Fayetteville: University of Arkansas Press, 2011); and the entertaining if the less than forthcoming Marlin Hawkins with C. Fred Williams, *How I Stole Elections: The Autobiography of Sheriff Marlin Hawkins* (Morrilton, AR, 1991).

Conditions in Lee County and the conflict over the health clinic are noted in Juanita D. Sandford, *Poverty in the Land of Opportunity* (Little Rock: Rose Publishing, 1978); and Marvin Schwartz, *In Service to America: A History of VISTA in Arkansas, 1965–1985* (Fayetteville: University of Arkansas Press, 1988). A unique examination of the evolution of a rural working-class African American community is found in Charles E. Thomas, *Jelly Roll: A Black Neighborhood in A Southern Mill Town* (1987; repr., Fayetteville: University of Arkansas Press, 2012).

River development is catalogued in S. Charles Bolton, *25 Years Later: A History Of The McClellan-Kerr Arkansas River Navigation System In Arkansas* (Little Rock: U.S. Army Corps of Engineers, Little Rock District, 1995); Mary Y. Rathburn, *Castle on the Rock: The History of the Little Rock District U.S. Army Corps of Engineers, 1881–1985* (Little Rock: U.S. Army Corps of Engineers, Little Rock District, 1990); Gary B. Mills, *Of Men and Rivers: The Story of the Vicksburg District* (Vicksburg, MS : U.S. Army Corps of Engineers, Vicksburg District, 1978); and Sherrel Johnson, "Rolling on the River: Ouachita River Navigation in Arkansas" (BA Thesis, Southern Arkansas University, 1988).

A vivid account by one of the state's pioneer environmentalists is Neil Compton, *The Battle for the Buffalo River: A Twentieth-Century Conservationist Crisis in the Ozarks* (Fayetteville: University of Arkansas Press, 1992). An informative overview of the effects of the environmental movement by the state's pioneering writer of modern environmental journalism is found in Carol Griffee, *Environmental Quality Index* (Little Rock: Arkansas Wildlife Federation, 1994). David Pryor's decision to thwart lake developers eyeing the Strawberry River is recounted in Robert L. Brown, *Defining Moments: Historic Decisions by Arkansas Governors from McMath through Huckabee* (Fayetteville: University of Arkansas Press, 2010); and in David Pryor With Don Harrell, *A Pryor Commitment: The Autobiography of David Pryor* (Little Rock: Butler Center Books, 2008). Several books were quickly published upon the sighting of the ivory-billed woodpecker, but Tim Gallagher relates in *The Grail Bird: The Rediscovery of the Ivory-Billed Woodpecker* (Boston: Houghton-Mifflin, 2006) that he had already been searching tirelessly for the bird when the purported Eureka moment arrived.

Five

Hope, Arkansas, is fondly described in Berton Roueché, *Special Places: In Search of Small Town America* (Boston: Little Brown, 1982).

Essays that survey recent history include Dan Durning, "Arkansas, 1954 to Present," in *Historical Report of the Secretary of State*, vol. 3 (Little Rock: Secretary of State, 1978); and C. Fred Williams, "Modern Arkansas: World War II to the Present," in *Historical Report of the Secretary of State* (Little Rock: Secretary of State, 1998).

Much of the material in this chapter was based on U.S. Census Bureau records and reports, news accounts, and research findings published by a variety of organizations and institutions that are noted in the narrative. When the Arkansas Census State Data Center, Arkansas Economic Development Institute, University of Arkansas, Little Rock ceased publishing the *Arkansas Statistical Almanac* by the University in 2008, researchers were able to turn to the online repository at https://ualr.edu/aedi /census-state-data-center/.

The barriers to African American opportunities are revealed in Lawrence Santi, "Black-White Differences in Household Income in the State of Arkansas, 1989: Results of a Regression Analysis," *Arkansas Business and Economic Review* 31 (Spring 1998): 1–13. A more recent study is Eleanor Wheeler, "Breaking Down the Barriers: The State of Black Men and Boys in Arkansas," Arkansas Advocates for Children and Families, http://www.aradvocates.org/publications/breaking-down-the-barriers-for -arkansass-black-men-and-boys-part-i/. Analysis of the patterns of bank loans in the 1990s is found in John R. Hall and Ralph B. Shull, "Arkansas Small Banks in the Nineties," *Arkansas Business and Economic Review* 31 (Fall/Winter 1999): 1–6.

Early histories of Arkansas corporations are commissioned works, including Marvin Schwartz, *J. B. Hunt: The Long Haul to Success* (Fayetteville: University of Arkansas Press, 1992); Leon J. Rosenberg, *Dillard's: The First Fifty Years* (Fayetteville: University of Arkansas Press, 1988); and Marvin Schwartz, *Tyson: From Farm to Market* (Fayetteville: University of Arkansas Press, 1992). An insightful and balanced study of the poultry industry in Arkansas is Brent E. Riffel, "The Feathered Kingdom: Tyson Foods and the Transformation of American Land, Labor, and Law, 1930–2005" (PhD diss., University of Arkansas, 2001). As has been the case with recent books concerned with poultry processing and Tyson Foods, Steve Striffler, *Chicken: The Dangerous Transformation of America's Favorite Food* (New Haven: Yale University Press, 2005) and Christopher Leonard, *The Meat Racket: The Secret Takeover of America's Food Business* (New York: Simon & Schuster, 2014) are critical treatments. Working conditions are starkly portrayed within the context of the intersection of race and labor in small manufacturing towns in Laguana Gray, *We Just Keep Running the Line: Black Southern Women and the Poultry Processing Industry* (Baton Rouge: Louisiana State Univ. Press, 2014). A complementary examination is Kathleen C. Schwartzman, *The Chicken Trail: Following Workers, Migrants, and Corporations Across the Americas* (Ithaca: Cornell University Press, 2013).

A strong, early review of the growth phase of Walmart is Sandra S. Vance and Roy V. Scott, *Wal-Mart: A History of Sam Walton's Retail Phenomenon* (New York: Twayne, 1994), which marks a useful contrast with Walton's autobiography, *Made in America* (New York: Doubleday, 1992). Although the retailer prompts strong emotions and skepticism, the scholarship on the company is often nuanced and analytical. Readers can profit from Nelson Lichtenstein, *The Retail Revolution: How Wal-Mart Created a Brave New World of Business* (New York: Metropolitan Books, 2009); and Bethany Moreton, *To Serve God and Wal-Mart: The Making of Christian Free Enterprise* (Cambridge: Harvard University Press, 2009). Among the accounts by journalists are Charles Fishman, *The Wal-Mart Effect* (New York: Penguin Books, 2006); and Liza Featherstone, *Selling Women Short: The Landmark Battle for Workers' Rights at Wal-Mart* (New York: Basic Books, 2004).

Paul Theroux's tour of rural Arkansas is recounted in *Deep South: Four Seasons on the Back Roads* (New York: Houghton Mifflin Harcourt, 2015). Incisive and

334 | SELECTED SOURCES

data-filled studies of poverty in the state are tracked in the University of Arkansas Cooperative Extension Service's series, Rural Profile of Arkansas; the 2019 edition (publication number MP551) is available at https://www.uaex.edu/business -communities/economic-development/rural-profile-of-arkansas.aspx. The expansion of rice agriculture is introduced in Jordan Purnell Wimpy, "Turning Loose: How 1970s Agricultural Policy Altered Arkansas's Farming Landscape (MA thesis, University of Arkansas, Fayetteville, 2009). Jeannie Whayne depicts the broad sweep of Delta developments through the evolution of a plantation dominion into the modern era in her indispensable *Delta Empire: Lee Wilson and The Transformation of Agriculture in the New South* (Baton Rouge: Louisiana State Press, 2011).

A number of essays devoted to post-Faubus political topics are reprinted in Richard P. Wang and Michael B. Dougan, eds., *Arkansas Politics: A Reader* (Fayetteville: M&M Press, 1997), as well as an updated edition, Janine Parry and Richard Wang, *Readings in Arkansas Politics and Government* (Fayetteville: University of Arkansas Press, 2009). Essential reading are two milestone essays by Diane Blair: "The Arkansas Plan: Coon Dogs or Community Service?" *Publius* 8 (Winter 1978): 117–34; and "The Big Three of Late Twentieth-Century Arkansas Politics: Dale Bumpers, Bill Clinton, and David Pryor," *Arkansas Historical Quarterly* 54 (Spring 1995): 53–79. A valuable overview of the growth of African American political influence is Janine Parry and William H. Miller, "'The Great Negro State of the Country?' Black Legislators in Arkansas: 1973–2000," *Journal of Black Studies* 36 (July 2006): 833–872.

The declining support by leading Democratic officeholders for policies advanced by the state labor movement is pointedly reviewed in Martin Halpern, "Arkansas and the Defeat of Labor Law Reform in 1978 and 1994," *Arkansas Historical Quarterly* 57 (Summer 1998): 99–133; and Michael Pierce, "How Bill Clinton Remade the Democratic Party by Abandoning Unions: An Arkansas Story," *Labor Online, Labor and Working Class History Association,* https://lawcha.org/wordpress/2016/11/23 /bill-clinton-remade-democratic-party-abandoning-unions-working-class-whites/.

The downfall of the *Arkansas Gazette* and the triumph of the *Arkansas Democrat* is chronicled with clear regrets at the outcome in Donna Lampkin Stephens, *If It Ain't Broke, Break It: How Corporate Journalism Killed the Arkansas Gazette* (Fayetteville: University of Arkansas Press, 2015). Firsthand memories from opposites camps are available in two vital collections of interviews: Roy Reed, ed., *Looking Back at the Arkansas Gazette: An Oral History* (Fayetteville: University of Arkansas Press, 2009); and Jerry McConnell, ed., *The Improbable Life of the Arkansas Democrat: An Oral History* (Fayetteville: University of Arkansas Press, 2016).

The production of works on Bill Clinton continues since he left the White House, although few systematically examine his public career in Arkansas. Among the initial considerations of the gubernatorial phase are Phyllis Finton Johnston, *Bill Clinton's Public Policy for Arkansas: 1979–1980* (Little Rock: August House, 1983); and Charles F. Allen and Jonathan Portis, *The Comeback Kid: The Life and Career of Bill*

Clinton (New York: Carol, 1992). Although devoted to the first year of the Clinton presidency, John Brummett, *Highwire: From the Backwoods to the Beltway—The Education of Bill Clinton* (New York: Hyperion, 1994) also reviews the Arkansas background from the perspective of a veteran state reporter. The most comprehensive personal portrait of the years leading up to the presidency is David Maraniss, *First in His Class: A Biography of Bill Clinton* (New York: Simon & Schuster, 1995). Arkansas is far from overlooked in Clinton's memoir, *My Life* (New York: Alfred A. Knopf, 2004) and also seen from the perspective of Hillary Rodham Clinton in *Living History* (New York: Simon & Schuster, 2003). Carl Bernstein, *A Woman in Charge: The Life of Hillary Rodham Clinton* (New York: Alfred A. Knopf, 2007) is a sympathetic and in-depth narrative that takes into account its subject's complexities. The harsher Jeff Gerth and Don Van Natta, *Her Way: The Hopes and Ambitions of Hillary Rodham Clinton* (New York: Little, Brown, 2007) demonstrates the persistence of the Whitewater wars.

James B. Stewart, *Blood Sport: The President and His Adversaries* (New York: Simon & Schuster, 1996) written in the midst of the Starr investigations finds merit in accusations of financial wrongdoing in Arkansas by the First Couple, but its errors along with those of other reporters covering Whitewater are cited in Joe Conason and Gene Lyons, *The Hunting of the President: The Ten Year Campaign to Destroy Bill and Hillary Clinton* (New York: St. Martin's, 2000). Similar objections to the coverage of the investigation and impeachment are highlighted in Marvin Kalb, *One Scandalous Story: Clinton, Lewinsky, and the 13 Days that Tarnished American Journalism* (New York: Free Press, 2001). Contrasting views of the impeachment and trial of the president are Richard A. Posner, *An Affair of State: The Investigation, Impeachment, and Trial of President Clinton* (Cambridge: Harvard University Press, 1999); and Jeffrey Toobin, *A Vast Conspiracy: The Real Story of the Sex Scandal That Nearly Brought Down a President* (New York: Random House, 2000).

A skeptical assessment of the interstate highway expansion in Little Rock is Alana Semuels, "The Cities Doubling Down on Highways," *The Atlantic*, March 28, 2016. Metroplan, the association of local governments in the Central Arkansas MSA, beginning in 1996 began publishing each year two editions of its *Metrotrends* analysis, one of which is the "Demographic Review and Outlook" and the other the "Economic Review and Outlook." Digital versions of the publications are available at http://www.metroplan.org/content/publications. The giant retailer's effect on the growth of Bentonville is largely celebrated in Marjorie Rosen, *Boom Town: How Wal-Mart Transformed an All-American Town into An International Community* (Chicago: Chicago Review Press, 2009). The Hispanic migration into Arkansas has stimulated a number of solid reports, among the most useful are Randy Capps, Kristen McCabe, Michael Fix, and Ying Huang, *A Profile of Immigrants in Arkansas: Changing Workforce and Family Demographics,* vol. 1 (Little Rock and Washington, DC: Winthrop Rockefeller Foundation and Migration Policy Institute, 2013); and Stephen J. Appold, James H. Johnson Jr., and John D. Kasarda, *A Profile of*

Immigrants in Arkansas: Economic and Fiscal Benefits and Costs, vol. 2 (Little Rock and Chapel Hill: Winthrop Rockefeller Foundation and University of North Carolina, 2013).

A pioneering overview of the evolution of mountain folklore practices and studies is W. K. McNeil, *Ozark Country* (Jackson: University Press of Mississippi, 1995). Readers can look forward to the forthcoming (at the time of this writing) three-volume history of the Ozarks by the exemplary contemporary scholar of the region, Brooks Blevins, *A History of the Ozarks* (University of Illinois Press).

A shaper of modern Eureka Springs is portrayed in Glen Jeansonne, *Gerald L. K. Smith: Minister of Hate* (New Haven: Yale University Press, 1988); while the rejuvenation of the town by a new set of entrepreneurs is recounted in Brock Thompson, *The Un-Natural State: Arkansas and the Queer South* (Fayetteville: University of Arkansas Press, 2010). A well-meaning group of migrants are acknowledged in Jared Phillips, "Hipbillies and Hillbillies: Back-To-The-Landers in the Arkansas Ozarks During the 1970s," *Arkansas Historical Quarterly* 75 (Summer 2016): 89–110.

The annual survey reports and data conducted by the UA Little Rock School of Public Affairs for the Anderson Institute for Race and Ethnicity at UA Little Rock can be downloaded at https://ualr.edu/race-ethnicity/research/about/racial-attitudes/.

The case for investment in preservation as bringing a return in tourism dollars is made in Center for Urban Policy Research at the Edward J. Bloustein School of Planning and Public Policy, Rutgers University, "Economic Benefits of Historic Preservation." (Arkansas Historic Preservation Program, 2006). The report is available at http://www.arkansaspreservation.com/About-Us/economic-benefits-of-historic-preservation.

A suggestive examination of the Helena blues festival is David S. Rotenstein, "The Helena Blues: Cultural Tourism and African-American Music," *Southern Folklore* 49 (1992): 133–46. The formation of the Ozark Folk Center State Park and the influence of Jimmy Driftwood have been addressed in several sources but none more cogently than Brooks Blevins, *Hill Folks.* The same author's *Arkansas/Arkansaw* offers the authoritative account of Dogpatch U.S.A. that necessarily corrects the elegant but imaginative description of the woebegone theme park in Donald Harington, *Let Us Build Us a City* (New York: Harcourt Brace, 1986). Many of the musicians noted here have composed memoirs and been the subjects of biographies, but readers are advised to begin by listening to their records.

Thoughtful appreciations for Donald Harington's productive and singular career is Bob Razer "Donald Harington and His Stay More Novels: A Celebration of Thirty-Five Years" (Fayetteville: Special Collections Department, University of Arkansas Libraries, 2006); and the special issue of the *Southern Quarterly: A Journal of the Arts in the South (Winter 2002).* Ron Rosenbaum, "Our Least-Known Great Novelist," *Esquire* (January 1998) launched the reconsideration of Charles Portis's extraordinary novels, which were reprinted and given the attention they deserved.

Discerning commentary and generous reproductions of the painter's work highlight Stanton Thomas, *The Crossroads of Memory: Carroll Cloar and the American South*, Exhibition catalogue (Little Rock: Arkansas Arts Center, 2014). Cloar's "autobiography" is in Donald Harington, "The Witness of Hummingbirds," *Oxford American* 51 (Fall 2005).

Robert Adams Ivy Jr. *Fay Jones* (Washington, D.C.: American Institute of Architects Press, 1992) is an illustrated examination of a rich legacy. Other overviews are *Outside the Pale: The Architecture of Fay Jones* (Fayetteville: University of Arkansas Press, 1999) and Cheryl Nichols and Helen Barry, *The Arkansas Designs of E. Fay Jones, 1956–1997* (Little Rock: Arkansas Historic Preservation Program, Department of Arkansas Heritage, 1999).

The prolonged campaign to win additional funding for the Game & Fish Commission and eventually for the state parks is adroitly detailed in Carol Griffee, *Odyssey of Survival: A History of the Arkansas Conservation Sales Tax* (Little Rock: Arkansas Game & Fish Foundation, 1999). An indispensable description and analysis of the maturation of state government in the face of continuous challenges is Jay Barth, *Ripe for Reform: Arkansas as a Model for Social Change* (Little Rock: Arkansas Public Policy Panel, 2012).

The recapitulation of Mike Huckabee's record as governor in Adam Nossiter and David Barstow, "The Long Run: Charming and Aloof, Huckabee Changed State," *New York Times*, December 22, 2007, was prompted by his first presidential campaign. An earlier favorable short essay explained why *Governing* magazine recognized him in 2005 as the top governor among its Public Officials of the Year in Alan Greenblatt, "Mike Huckabee: 2005 Honoree," http://www.governing.com/poy /Mike-Huckabee.html.

Earl Black and Merle Black, *The Rise of Southern Republicans* (Cambridge: Harvard University Press, 2002) is the starting point for the overhaul of Southern politics but only glances intermittingly at Arkansas. The state's unique route to shifting political allegiance can be followed by the assessments of political scientists of election outcomes in the early twenty-first century. Unlike other states in the region, Arkansas did not gradually move toward Republican loyalty through steps that were discernible in hindsight. While conditions were favorable in the late twentieth century to tip the state into realignment, this outcome did not appear inevitable. The essays noted below suggest that the extraordinarily rapid triumph of the Republican Party and/or decline of the Democratic Party caught many perceptive observers by surprise.

Jay Barth, Diane D. Blair, and Ernie Dumas, "Arkansas: Characters, Crises, and Change," in *Southern Politics in the 1990s*, edited by Alexander P. Lamis (Baton Rouge: Louisiana State University Press, 1999); Jay Barth, Janine A. Parry, and Todd G. Shields, "Arkansas: He's Not One of (Most Of) Us," in *A Paler Shade of Red: The 2008 Presidential Election in the South*, edited by Branwell DuBose Kapeluck, Laurence W. Moreland, and Robert P. Steed (Fayetteville: University of

338 | SELECTED SOURCES

Arkansas Press, 2009), 119–36; Andrew Dowdle and Joseph D. Giammo, "Arkansas:
Deep Blue and Bright Red at the Same Time?" in *The New Politics of the Old South:
An Introduction to Southern Politics*, 4th ed., edited by Charles S. Bullock, III and
Mark J. Rozell (Lanham, MD: Rowman and Littlefield, 2010), 207–218; Janine A.
Parry and Jay Barth, "Arkansas: Another Anti-Obama Aftershock," in *Second Verse,
Same as the First: The 2012 Presidential Election in the South*, edited by Scott E.
Buchanan and Branwell DuBose Kapeluck (Fayetteville: University of Arkansas
Press, 2014): 123–42; Jay Barth and Janine A. Parry, "Arkansas: Trump is a Natural
for the Natural State," in *The Future Ain't What It Used to Be: The 2016 Presidential
Election in the South*, edited by Scott E. Buchanan and Branwell DuBose Kapeluck
(Fayetteville: University of Arkansas Press, 2018): 127–146.

The complex and multi-layered story of the evolution of the expansion of Medicaid
benefits through what was first known as the "private option" was covered extensively
and proficiently by the state's major news organizations. Nevertheless, the series of
articles on the topic by David Ramsey in the *Arkansas Times* were the most authoritative and probing.

Arkansas-based organizations that favor the expansion of charter schools in urban
centers dominate the debate over the issue within the state and have issued reports
and studies that find the movement beneficial with limited drawbacks. The Office
for Education Policy, University of Arkansas, Fayetteville, whose studies are cited
frequently by charter school advocates, published in 2016 the five-part "Integration
in the Little Rock Area," (http://www.officeforeducationpolicy.org/category/oep
-publications/policy-briefs/) and concluded in the final installment: "Overall, students exiting traditional public schools and/or entering area charters are advancing
racial and economic integration in the Little Rock metro area traditional public
schools." Also in 2016 the Little Rock School District Civic Advisory Committee,
established by the state department of education in the wake of the state takeover to
discern the views of the city's residents and school patrons, issued a report revealing
widespread apprehensions that charter schools threatened the quality and effectiveness of the public schools. The committee recommended that those leading the district "continue to vocally oppose the expansion of charter schools in Pulaski County."
("Little Rock School District Civic Advisory Committee Final Report, May 2016,"
http://www.lrsd.org/content/lrsd-civic-advisory-committee.

Index

Arkansas Polytechnic College (Arkansas
Tech University), 124
Arkansas Post, 37
Arkansas Power and Light (AP&L,
later Entergy Arkansas) 40, 97, 260;
and deregulation, 234–235; economic
development promoted by, 48, 68,
106, 157; and electric cooperatives,
77, 99, 104; and federal hydroelectric
projects,7,103; formation of, 41; and
Grand Gulf controversy, 233; and
Little Rock crisis, 140; declining
political influence of, 91,112; relations
with REA 42; and World War II
plants, 56–57. *See also* Couch, Harvey;
Moses, Hamilton
Arkansas Resources and Development
Commission, 68
Arkansas River, 154, 156, 191, 294; and
hydroelectric projects, 103; and
McClellan-Kerr project, 171–73;
and proposed irrigation project,
231–32
Arkansas State College (Arkansas State
University), 124, 283
Arkansas State Federation of Labor, 21
Arkansas State Teachers College
(University of Central Arkansas),
124
Arkansas Teachers Association, 153
Arkansas Territorial Restoration
(Historic Arkansas Museum), 40
Arkansas Wildlife Federation, 92, 173,
178
Arlington Hotel (Hot Springs), 90
Army Corps of Engineers, United States:
and Arkansas River project, 172; and
Buffalo River project, 174–75; and
Cache River project, 219; and Greers
Ferry Dam project, 127; and ground-
water issues, 231; and hydroelectric
dam issues, 66, 171; Lower Mississippi

River flood control, 103; and Ouachita
River Project, 172–74; and Strawberry
River project, 177; and White River
lakes development, 114
Ashley County, 199
Ashmore, Harry: as *Gazette* editor, 129–
30, 140, 146; and McMath 98–99,
129, 133
AT&T. *See* Southwestern Bell Telephone
Company
Atkins, 194
Atkinson, J. H., 30
Audubon Society, 173
Augusta, 18, 115
Aurora, 64

Babcock, Bernie (*The Soul of Ann
Rutledge*), 38–39
back to land movement: in 1930s, 31–32;
in 1970s, 268
Bailey, Carl, 12, 18, 91, 98 ; gubernatorial
policies of, 19, 42; and World War II,
49, 56
Bald Knob, 69
Bank of the Ozarks (Bank OZK), 203
Banking 12, 111, 203; and agricultural
lending, 204; and 1980s crisis, 201–2
Banks, A. B., 12, 18
Baptist. *See* Southern Baptist Convention,
Missionary Baptist Association
Barling, 243
Barnett Shale (Texas), 221
Barnhill, John, 116–17
Barth, Jay, 257, 315
Barton, T.H., 75, 116
Bass, Hal, 304
Bass, Harry, 62
Bates, Alvin, 115
Bates, Daisy Gatson, 128, 143; and Little
Rock crisis, 137–40; marriage to L. C.,
80, 147–48; as president of NAACP,
131–32, 148

Bates, L. C (Lucious Christopher): commitment to integration by, 128, 131–32; and COCA, 147; publishes Arkansas State Press, 79–80, 140
Bauxite (community), 57, 201
Baxter County, 114
Bayou Meto Water Management Project, 232
Beard, Veda, 64
Bearden, 146
Beaver Lake, 114; and Beaver Water District 119–220. See also Northwest Arkansas Council.
Becker, J. Bill, 153–54; and Bill Clinton, 247; and Jim Guy Tucker, 254
Beebe (community), 69, 71
Beebe, Mike, 305; state senate career of, 238, 296; as governor, 257, 300–302, 304, 306, 308–9; as attorney general, 292
Bell-Tolliver, LaVerne, 263
Bell, Louise, 122
Bell, Richard, 229
Bella Vista, 114, 218
Belvedere Club (Hot Springs), 90
Ben Franklin stores (retail chain), 211
Bennett, Bruce, 140, 145, 163
Bennett, Sam, 26
Benson, Buddy Bob, 117
Benton County, 7, 114, 210, 218, 220, 268
Bentonville, 174, 210, 216, 275, 282, 314; in metropolitan corridor, 202, 218, 220, 264; and Walton family, 211, 213, 265, 313
Bethune, Ed, 180, 240
Bethune, Mary McLeod: Camp Bethune named after, 38
Bismarck (town), 9
Black United Youth, 151
Blair, Diane, 160, 237, 257
Blair, Jim, 206
Blakely Mountain Dam, 114

Blossom, Virgil, 136; and Blossom Plan, 132–34, 139–40, 146; and Orval Faubus, 135
blues music, 39, 47–48, 59, 119–20, 281–82, 287
Blytheville, 55, 59–60
Boas, Franz, 33
Bolton, Charles, 66
Boone County, 218
Boozman, John, 297, 303
bowie knife, 109
bracero labor program, 53–54
Bradford, Jay, 248
Branton, Wiley, 78, 133
Branton, Wiley, Jr., 312
Brewer, Vivion, 143
Bright, Lloyd, 194
Brinkley, 180, 240
Brotherhood of Teamsters, 103–4
Brough, Charles H., 7
Brown v. Board of Education of Topeka (1954), 128, 139, 263, 312; African American response in Little Rock to, 132; and Brown II (1955)107–8; Dwight Eisenhower response to, 138; early compliance in Arkansas with, 121, 123; Harry Ashmore response to, 129–30; and 1954 election, 105; and Southern Manifesto, 134; and Supreme Court ruling (1958), 141
Brown, Darrell, 117–18
Brown, Minnijean (Trickey), 137, 139, 151, 312
Browns, The (Jim Ed, Maxine, Bonnie), 287
Broyles, Frank, 117–19
Brummett, John, 118
Bryant, Louise, 43
Bryant, Louise, 43
Buffalo River Improvement Association (BRIA), 175

Elliott, Joyce, 292, 314–15
Ellis, Clyde, 42, 103, 171
Ellison, James, 268–269
Elohim City, 269
Emerson (community), 194
Engel, K. A., 129
Enron Corporation, 234
environmental movement, 114, 127,
129, 168, 180, 242 ; opposition to
U. S. Corps of Engineers projects by,
127, 171–75, 177–79; and regulations
on livestock waste, 176–77. See also
Buffalo River, Cache River Basin,
Ouachita River, Strawberry River
Environmental Working Group,
226–228
Equal Rights Amendment (ERA), 159
Eureka Springs, 31, 291; and 1930s Ozark
folk movement, 33–34; and Gerald
L. K. Smith projects, 269–270; and
LGBT entrepreneurs, 270–27; and
nondiscrimination ordinance, 272
Evans, Audrey R., 278

Fair Employment Practices Committee
(U.S.), 79
Fair Field Price Law, 112
family: marriage and birth patterns, 59,
276–277
Farm Bureau, Arkansas, 92, 158, 169, 239;
and regulation of animal waste,176;
stands on labor issues by, 52, 72 university extension service alliance with,
42, 68
Farm Security Administration (FSA),
30, 50, 65, 297; resettlement projects,
27–28
Farm Services Agency, 204
Farmers Home Administration, 201
Farrell, Olivia, 278
Faubus, Orval Eugene, 114, 146, 152, 172,
291; and Commonwealth College, 29;

death of, 250; Dogpatch managed by,
285; elections won by 70, 104–6, 109,
162; gubernatorial reform program
of, 90, 106–7, 134, 158, 294; and Little
Rock crisis, 128, 135–38, 140–41, 143;
and 1970 election, 167; and 1974 election, 235; pre-1957 segregationist strategy of, 108, 124, 126, 134 ; and river
development, 172, 175; and scandals
in administration of, 163–64; surveillance of adversaries by, 145; and Witt
Stephens, 112, 249–250
Faulkner County, 222
Fayetteville Shale, 221, 232, 301
Fayetteville, 31, 272, 290; part of new
metropolitan center, 202, 218, 220,
264; school desegregation in, 91, 121–
23, 133; and University of Arkansas,
78, 116–17, 124–25, 289
Federal Aviation Administration (FAA),
218
Federal Bureau of Investigation (FBI),
160
Federal Communications Commission
(FCC), 259–260
Federal Deposit Insurance Corporation
(FDIC), 202–3
Federal Emergency Relief
Administration (FERA), 16–18, 37
Federal Energy Regulatory Commission
(FERC), 233–234
Federal Home Loan Bank, 201
federal spending, 102, 105, 110, 113, 127,
130, 155, 161–62, 167, 197, 224, 247;
and agricultural support with, 73, 198,
204, 209, 226–229, 231–232 ; and anti-
poverty support payments, 74, 169,
225–226; and Depression era, 14–20,
22, 24–25, 30–33, 37–38, 40, 42, 93;
health care expanded with, 294–295,
305–8; integration aims supported
through, 150, 152; folklore revival

233–234; environmental issues considered by, 168, 176–77; and General Improvement Funds, 295–296; health issues considered by, 107, 275, 306–7; and highways, 8, 12, 92, 242–243, 301; influence of special interest lobbying, 112, 238–239; labor issues considered by, 72, 154, 207, 254–255; Laney reforms of, 95–96; limits on appropriations by, 16; and New Deal funding, 17–18, 37; and oversight of state government, 92, 309–10; and prisons, 164–65; and scandals, 238, 310–11; and Republican majority, 303–4; and support for preservation, 281, 283; and tax measures considered by, 17, 99, 134, 167–68, 236, 296, 300, 301; and term limits, 239, 257; women in, 240

General Improvement Fund (GIF), 295–296, 310–11

Geological Survey, United States (USGS), 230

George, Lloyd, 238

GI Revolt (Government Improvement League), 79, 90, 98, 107,

Giammo, Joseph, 303

Gibson Products (retail chain), 211

Gilchrist, Ellen, 289

Gillam Park (Little Rock), 79, 131

Glass, David, 214

Glaze, Tom, 161

Gleason, George, 203

Glenwood, 14

Goff, Norris ("Abner Peabody"), 35

Goldberg, Dorothy, 63

Goldwater, Barry, 162

Gordy, Sondra, 142

Gould (community), 150

Government Accounting Office (GAO/ Government Accountability Office), United States, 218, 227

Grand Gulf Power Plant, 233–234

Grand Ole Opry (radio program, Ryman Auditorium), 43, 286

Grand Prairie (region), 7, 229–232

Grand Prairie Demonstration Project, 232

Gray, LaGuana, 209

Greasy Creek, 106

Green, Al, 287

Green, Ernest, 137, 140, 146; and commemorations of school crisis, 194, 312

Greers Ferry Dam and Lake, 114, 127–28, 172, 175

Grice, Geleve, 78

Griffin, Marvin, 136

Griffin, Tim, 303

Grinage, Benjamin, 151

Griswold, Nat, 123

Guthridge, Amis, 124, 135

Guy (village), 9

Hay, Abner, 80

Hays, Lee, 29

Helm, Levon, 286

Hendren, Kim, 297

Hendren, Jim, 297, 309, 314–15

Holmes, Leon, 107

human development centers (state), 107

Hill, Jane, 137

Historic Preservation Alliance, 281

Hutchinson, Asa: and Buffalo River, 176; campaigns for governor by, 301, 305; congressional career of, 297; economic development actions of, 310; proposals on Medicaid expansion by, 307–8; relations with legislature by, 309; and standoff at CSA compound, 269

Hall, John B.: coauthor, bank solvency study, 202

Hawkins, Ronnie (The Band), 286

Hawkins, Ruth, 283

Heritage Sites Office (Arkansas State University), 283